# The Principles of Building Construction

**Madan Mehta**
University of Texas at Arlington

Prentice Hall

*Upper Saddle River, New Jersey*     *Columbus, Ohio*

*Dedicated to Henry J. Cowan and Krishan L. Datta, my teachers*

**Library of Congress Cataloging-in-Publication Data**

Mehta, Madan
    The principles of building construction / Madan Mehta.
        p.    cm.
    Includes index
    ISBN 0-13-205881-2 (hc)
    1. Building.  I. Title
TH146.M43  1997
690--dc20                96-33105
                                  CIP

Cover art/photo: Tom Carroll/Photo Bank, Inc.
Editor: Ed Francis
Production Editor: Rex Davidson
Design Coordinator: Julia Zonneveld Van Hook
Cover Designer: Russ Maselli
Production Manager: Deidra M. Schwartz
Marketing Manager: Danny Hoyt
Illustrations: Author

This book was printed and bound by Courier/Kendallville. The cover was printed by Phoenix Color Corp.

© 1997 by Prentice Hall, Inc.
A Pearson Education Company
Upper Saddle River, NJ 07458

Photo credits: All photos not otherwise credited are by the author.

Printed in the United States of America

10 9 8 7 6 5 4 3 2 1

ISBN: 0-13-205881-2

Prentice-Hall International (UK) Limited,London
Prentice-Hall of Australia Pty. Limited, Sydney
Prentice-Hall Canada Inc., Toronto
Prentice-Hall Hispanoamericana, S.A., Mexico
Prentice-Hall of India Private Limited, New Delhi
Prentice-Hall of Japan, Inc., Tokyo
Pearson Education Asia Pte. Ltd., Singapore
Editora Prentice-Hall do Brasil, Ltda., Rio de Janeiro

# Foreword

As Madan Mehta notes in the preface to this book, building construction is the largest industry in the United States and probably in the rest of the world. Immense quantities of human effort, financial capital, and natural resources are devoted to building — for business, government, institutions, infrastructure and homes. Building construction is the means by which we adapt our places to our needs. It is a very big and complex enterprise.

In addition to its huge size and scope, the building construction industry is also remarkable for the variety of its parts. Small individual proprietorships work and prosper along with multibillion dollar firms employing many thousands. Local and regional building traditions continue even as transnational construction corporations deploy technology and sophisticated expertise anywhere on earth.

The process of learning building is often as fragmented as the industry itself, relying on anecdotal knowledge growing from the conventions of practice. At its best, this mode of acquiring knowledge is very effective within a circumscribed scope; crafts and trades pass along their lore of skills and ideas in this way. In most modern construction, however, knowing a single or even several crafts is not enough. The ability to understand numerous components, systems, materials and participants becomes vital. In fact, it is the *meshing*, the *coordination*, the *management* of the parts into a working economical whole that characterizes construction today.

The more generalized set of responsibilities in construction requires a more generalized way of learning. *Principles* are logical tools we use to explain the behavior of a large number of circumstances — principles give us leverage on familiar problems and allow us to understand new situations as they emerge.

At their root, most modern constructional principles derive from science, from the studies of matter, energy, chemical behavior, and organic composition that theorists and experimenters over the last several centuries have given us.

Madan Mehta has used this broad legacy as the basis of this book. He develops a constructional idea from the general to the particular; he contextualizes it within our knowledge of how the world works. Such a strategy makes good pedagogical sense. It reflects the conceptual hierarchy from concept to abstract and back again. But this approach also makes common sense by responding to the types of people entering architecture and the construction professions today: people often with prior experience in the sciences, liberal arts and business. These professionals-to-be have not entered through the traditional trade or craft route; they demand broader and more widely operational knowledge.

*The Principles of Building Construction* offers just such an introduction. By relating knowledge and norms to basic principles, the reader can understand more fully and, more important, can continue learning with confidence.

Edward M. Baum, Dean
School of Architecture
University of Texas at Arlington

# Preface

**Objectives of the Book**     Building construction, the largest industry in any national economy, is also highly dynamic. A part of its dynamism is due to the changing socioeconomic framework caused by increasing population and decreasing resources, but most of it results from man's inherent desire to innovate. The impact of this dynamism on building construction is that new building products and construction systems are being continually added to the existing stock in a never ending process. In addition to the new materials, new versions of traditional materials are also proliferating. In fact, the array of competing building materials and systems available for any given application is so large that the modern architect faces unprecedented challenges in their selection.

The information related to building products is provided largely by individuals who are engaged in producing them. Although product testing is generally done by independent agencies, manufacturers' vested interests and aggressive sales strategies often slant the product literature unduly in favor of the specific product.

How do we develop a critical faculty in architecture and construction students so that they can sift facts from exaggerations and relevance from insignificance? How do we prepare them to deal with the immense regional and international diversities of construction? How do we prepare architects and builders to function successfully in an increasingly litigious environment?

This work is in response to these questions and is based on the premise that only a strong foundation in the science of materials and construction can prepare future architects and builders to deal with increasing complexities of building. It attempts to fill the vacuum left by available books, some of which are excellent compendiums of "conventional wisdom" but do not develop the principles of building sufficiently, or provide answers to why a given material or system is used. After all, it is the principles of construction that will remain; conventional practices will become dated all too soon. And the universities' primary commitment is to disseminate principles of a subject, not merely to elucidate the lore of application.

Because this book deals with the principles of construction, several topics covered here interface between construction and technology courses, and are therefore not covered in a typical architecture curriculum. Even if they are covered, the coverage lacks the necessary integration with related construction issues. For instance, insulating materials are dealt with in a construction course but how much and what type of insulation is required is either not covered at all, or if covered, is done summarily in a course on energy. This curricular approach assumes that students are able to successfully integrate the knowledge gained from various disparate courses — a fact that is not always true.

Thirty-five years of teaching has convinced me that the teaching of materials and construction should take an integrated approach. Because after all, construction is the discipline that synthesizes several areas of expertise required in building design, and it is the synthetic skills that are most fundamental to the architect. The development of these skills cannot be left to chance. I hope this book will cut across established course boundaries to present an integrated approach to teaching construction.

There is more to the principles of building construction than is covered in this volume, which is simply the first leg of a long journey. Therefore, only the more important topics have been covered — those that are relevant to every building type regardless of whether the primary material used in the building is wood, masonry, steel or concrete.

*The Principles of Building Construction* begins with a brief treatment of building codes and standards since all building construction must conform to building codes as a minimum requirement. Because most code provisions are based on definite and quantifiable facts, a discussion of codes serves as a useful introduction to the science of construction. The succeeding chapters deal with structural properties, thermal properties, air infiltration, water vapor and (bulk) water penetration, transparency, fire-related properties, and movement control in buildings.

This is not a conventional text on construction. Therefore it discards conventions at a number of places. For instance, a full chapter on structural loads is included because the loads condition all aspects of construction — even the nonstructural aspects, such as the construction of windows, curtain walls, roof membranes, etc. In another instance, acoustical properties, which are usually not covered in a construction text, are also included because sound control has become fundamental to virtually all buildings.

The book may be used as a main text or as a companion to another reading on construction. I use most of the subject matter covered here in the initial nine weeks of the first construction course. I organized the book so that the instructor can cover only certain portions in the classroom, leaving the rest to the student for self study. A few sections or chapters may be omitted to suit the instructor's teaching philosophy or the school's curriculum. On the other hand, an instructor wishing to go into greater depth of the subject may use the entire book as a semester-long text, augmenting it with additional material as needed.

Although primarily intended for use in an architecture curriculum, the text will also be useful to the students of architectural engineering and building construction. Practicing architects, engineers, construction specifiers and building product manufacturers and sales personnel will also find it a valuable resource.

**Acknowledgments**     In preparing this work, many individuals who are experts in their respective fields have helped me by reading one or more chapters of the manuscript and giving their valuable suggestions. I am indebted to them. These include:

Jack Burleson, Southern Building Code Congress International; Jerry Barbera, International Conference of Building Officials, Whittier, California; Carroll Pruitt, International Conference of Building Officials, Austin, Texas; Narinder Tally, California State University, Los Angeles; Ron Shaeffer, Florida A & M University, Tallahassee, Florida; Bill Lingnell, Glass Consultant, Garland, Texas; Bill Bailey, Acme Brick Plant, Denton, Texas; Jim Johnson, Acoustical Consultant, Dallas, Texas; Kumar Kumaran, National Research Council of Canada, Ottawa, Ontario; R. Christopher Mathis, National Fenestration Rating Council, Silver Spring, Maryland; Jens Pohl, California Polytechnic State University, San Luis Obispo, California; and Kenneth L. Carper, Washington State University, Pullman, Washington.

I am grateful to several building product manufacturers who provided me with photographs of their products for inclusion in the book. These manufacturers have been duly credited in the book for their courtesy. Photographs with no underlying credit lines are by the author.

I am also grateful to my students who have picked up several errors in the manuscript while reading it to prepare for tests and quizzes in my course.

An important acknowledgment is due to the Prentice Hall staff, particularly my editor Edward Francis, managing editor JoEllen Gohr and production editor Rex Davidson for providing me with much needed help. Acknowledgment is also due to my copy editor Mary Bucher Fisher, who did a splendid job in bringing this manuscript up to a publishable form.

Finally, I would like to express my sincere appreciation to Edward Baum, Dean of the School of Architecture at the University of Texas at Arlington, who has this wonderful gift of inspiring confidence and encouraging colleagues in their creative efforts.

**Disclaimer**     The information in this book has been derived from a large number of sources, such as reference books, journals, construction sites, manufacturers' literature, building codes and the author's professional experience. It is presented in good faith, and although the author and the publisher have made every reasonable effort to present the information accurately, they do not warrant or assume any liability for its accuracy, its completeness or its fitness for any specific purpose. The book is primarily intended as a learning and teaching aid. It is the responsibility of the user to apply his/her professional knowledge in the use of the information presented here, and to consult original sources for current detailed information as needed.

Madan Mehta

# Contents

# LEGISLATIVE CONSTRAINTS ON CONSTRUCTION

**1.1 INTRODUCTION**

The primary requirement of a building is that it should be safe. Visual appeal and economic viability, though important, are secondary requirements. To deliver a safe building is indeed the responsibility of the design and construction professionals — the architects, engineers and builders. However, as with all public health and safety issues, the design and construction of buildings is regulated by numerous laws. The most important such laws are contained in a document called the *building code*.

A building code is enforced by local jurisdictions such as the cities or municipalities, under police powers granted to them by the state. No building may be constructed unless it meets the requirements of the building code of the jurisdiction[1].

Although a few building code provisions are based on traditional construction practices, most provisions are firmly grounded in scientific and quantifiable data of construction performance. There is, therefore, a strong link between code requirements and the scientific principles of construction. This chapter begins with building code objectives, the difference between prescriptive and performance type codes, and the contents of a typical building code.

The continual technological developments in building industry require

---

[1] Note that there are often unregulated regions in a state or country where buildings may be constructed without conforming to any building code. Rural communities and areas outside urban boundaries are generally unregulated.

that the building codes must be constantly reviewed and revised. This task is usually beyond the resources of most local jurisdictions. It is, therefore, handled by independent agencies whose primary function is to develop, maintain and publish building codes. These codes are then adopted by local jurisdictions with some amendments to suit local conditions. In North America, there are currently four such organizations — three in the United States and one in Canada. These organizations are called the *model code organizations*. Their roles and the differences between them are described. Finally, the chapter deals with zoning ordinances and other important laws that affect building construction.

## 1.2 OBJECTIVES OF A BUILDING CODE

A building code is a document that regulates all aspects of building construction in order to safeguard the property, life, health, safety and welfare of the occupants of buildings, and the general public. A building code regulates not only the design and construction of new buildings but also the repair, alteration and the maintenance of existing buildings so that they continue to remain structurally safe and sanitary. In the case of buildings which have become hazardous and (or) insanitary, the code mandates suitable corrective action.

Note that a building code does not regulate aspects of design that relate to a building's formal and spatial configuration. In other words, aesthetics, color and form-related issues are outside the purview of building codes.

The objectives of a building code are best illustrated with reference to the Uniform Building Code[1.1] which states :

"The purpose of this code is to provide minimum standards to safeguard life or limb, property and public welfare by regulating and controlling the design, construction, quality of materials, use and occupancy, location and maintenance of all buildings and structures within this jurisdiction and certain equipments specifically regulated herein."

Note that a building code specifies only the minimum requirements. The "minimum" here refers to regulations that have been determined to provide safe and sanitary buildings. Although under no obligation to do so, the owner or the architect may choose to exceed the requirements of the code. For the sake of economy, however, most buildings are generally designed to satisfy only the minimum requirements.

Additionally, the code protects not only the welfare of the owner or the developer of the project but also the general public since the interests of the developer, the general public and the building occupants may be at variance with one another. What may be in the best interest of the owner may not be in the best interest of the public or the occupants of the building. It is for this reason that building construction is regulated by an impartial authority, such as the state, county or the city. It is the responsibility of the regulatory authority to ensure that the interests of all concerned are protected.

Although the main preoccupation of a code is with traditional concerns of life safety, fire safety and structural adequacy in buildings, it also deals with such issues as the type of materials used, lighting, ventilation, sanitation, and noise control. Regulations pertaining to energy conservation and accessibility for the physically disabled are relatively more recent additions to building codes.

## 1.3 ENFORCEMENT OF A BUILDING CODE

A building code is a legal document, enforced through the police powers of the state. It is under these powers that a state is authorized to enact legislation for the safety of its citizens. The health, morals and general welfare of the public are also promoted by the state under the same legislation. Since it is generally agreed that the construction of buildings and the development of neighborhoods is best left under the direct control of local citizens, the state usually delegates this power to the local (city or municipal) governments. Thus, it is under the police power delegated to them by the state legislature that local jurisdictions are able to enact, adopt, review or change a provision of the code, subject to any overriding state or federal legislative constraint.

### 1.3.1 Building Official

The local jurisdiction's authority to enforce and administer the code is exercised through the building official (also referred to as the code official) who is an employee of the jurisdiction. Since the building official's authority stems from the police power of the state, he (she) has the powers of a law enforcement officer. As the head of the building department of the city, the building official is usually assisted by several other functionaries to carry out such tasks as plan reviews and field inspections. In a small city or jurisdiction, on the other hand, the building official may be the only person performing these tasks.

Whatever the situation, it is the responsibility of the building official to ensure that buildings constructed in his (her) jurisdiction are safe, and meet with the provisions and the intent of the code. It is the building official's duty to prevent, and take action to correct, any violation of the code. According to one authority[1.2]:

"A building official ... is a highly specialized law enforcement officer whose prime mission is the prevention, correction, or abatement of violations. ... A building official designs nothing, builds nothing, repairs nothing. His responsibility is merely to see that those persons who are engaged in these activities do so within the requirements of the law."

In order to effectively discharge duties, a building official must have a thorough knowledge of the building code, related city regulations and the science of building construction. The law enforcement responsibilities require that a building official's dealings with the public are fair and impartial.

### 1.3.2 Building Permit and Occupancy Certificate

The general procedure followed in administering the code is to require that the design of a proposed building complies with the provisions of the code before an official sanction to commence construction is granted by the city.

Before granting approval for construction in the form of a *building permit*, the city requires the submission of a building permit application along with copies of plans for the proposed building. A typical building permit application form is shown in Figure 1.1. If the plans are in accordance with the building code and other applicable laws, the building permit form, duly approved by the city, is returned to the owner. After receiving the building permit, the owner may commence construction. If the plans do not comply, they must be revised until conformance with the code has been achieved.

Once the construction begins, periodic and progressive inspection by the building official (or his/her representative — the building inspector) ensures that the construction abides by the code. The building is inspected at several stages during construction. Every inspection concludes with a report generated by the inspector to indicate whether or not the construction is progressing as per the code. Some cities color code the inspection result: a "green tag" left on the site indicates that the construction is proceeding in accordance with the code, and a "red tag" indicates that it has "failed" the inspection.

In the case of a failed inspection, the owner is obliged to make immediate corrections and request reinspection until the construction meets the city's approval. If the corrections are not made, or if in the opinion of the inspector, gross violation of the code has been committed, a "stop work order" by the city is generally issued, Figure 1.2. Noncompliance of the stop order results in administrative and (or) legal action against the offender.

**Building Permit Application**

Job Address

Legal Descr. | Lot No. | Blk | Tract

Contractor | Mail Address | Zip | Phone

Permit Applicant (Engineer/Architect/Owner) | Mail Address | Zip | Phone

Use of Building | (Describe fully) | Number of floors

Work Use (Check one)

- New construction ☐
- New construction - shell ☐
- Remodel ☐
- Interior finish ☐
- Addition Conversion ☐
- Rehab ☐
- Repair ☐
- Fire repair ☐
- Demolition ☐
- Move ☐
- Swimming pool ☐
- Spa/hot tub ☐
- Misc. uses ☐

Square feet in area | Square feet in garage | Type of slab ☐ Post tensioned ☐ Rebar

NOTICE

Separate permits are required for electrical, plumbing, air conditioning, and signs.

This permit becomes null and void if work or construction authorized is not commenced within 120 days or if construction or work is suspended or abandoned for a period of 120 days at any time after work is commenced.

Applicant is the owner and/or has the owner's consent to do the requested work.

I hereby certify that that I have read and examined this application and know the same to be true and correct. All provisions of law and ordinances governing this type of work will be complied with whether specified herein or not. The granting of a permit does not presume to give authority to violate or cancel the provisions of any other state or local ordinances regulationg construction or the performance of construction.

Plan check fee | Permit fee

Type of const. | Occupancy group and Division

Size of building (Total sq. ft) | No. of stories

Use zone | Max. occ. load

Fire sprinklers required ☐ Yes ☐ No

Off street parking spaces

Special approvals

Zoning

Health Dept.

Fire Dept

Soil report

Other (specify)

WHEN PROPERLY VALIDATED (IN THIS SPACE) THIS IS YOUR PERMIT

**FIGURE 1.1** A typical building permit application.

**STOP WORK ORDER**

City of __________

ADDRESS ______________________________

You are hereby notified that a Stop Work Order is hereby issued by the Building Official of the City of __________ as of __________ and that no further work shall be performed on this job until such time as it is authorized under the Codes of the City of ________ .

Violations subject to $ 1000.00 Fine

__________________
Inspector

DO NOT REMOVE THIS TAG

**FIGURE 1.2** A typical stop work order notice.

**Certificate of Occupancy**

City of __________

Department of Building Inspection

This certificate issued persuant to the requirements of Section ____ of the Building Code of the City of ________ certifying that at the time of issuance this structure was in compliance with various ordinances of the city regulating building construction or use. For the following:

Use Classification ______________ Building Permit No. ______

Group ________ Type Construction ________ Use Zone ________

Owner of Building ______________ Address ______________

Building Address ______________ Locality __________

By: __________

__________________ Date: __________
Building Official

POST IN A CONSPICUOUS PLACE

**FIGURE 1.3** A typical occupancy certificate.

Once the building is complete in all respects, the owner must request a final inspection and apply for a *certificate of occupancy*. Permission for the occupation of the building is forthcoming only after the city officials have satisfied themselves that all work has been completed in accordance with the code. No building may be occupied, in whole or in part, unless the certificate of occupancy has been granted. Among other details, a certificate of occupancy must specify the occupancy group of the building, the type of construction (see Section 1.7), and any other special stipulation of the code, Figure 1.3.

### 1.3.3 Board of Appeals

Since a building code is a legal document, it is a concise version of regulations as agreed to among the experts. Like most other laws, it does not contain any background material or explanatory facts on the basis of which decisions were made. A building code is, therefore, subject to interpretations which may differ from jurisdiction to jurisdiction. In many cases, a clear-cut interpretation of a code provision may not even exist since its original intent may have been either lost or not recorded. In such a situation, the owner (or the architect working as the owner's representative) may consult with the local building official or the technical staff of the appropriate model code organization (see Section 1.5) for an interpretation. In the event of an unresolved difference between the interpretations of the owner and the building official, it is the building official's interpretation and decision that is binding on the owner unless it is appealed.

Appeals against the building official's interpretation are referred to a board of appeals which is usually a standing body of the city. The board's task is to hear appeals and adjudicate on the validity of the building official's decision. In certain situations, the building official may on his/her own bring the matter before the board to seek its assistance in the interpretation of a code provision. The board of appeals is generally not authorized to waive any provision of the code, nor can it render judgment on the administrative provisions of the code. Its task is simply to render interpretation of the technical aspects of the code taking into account the code's objectives and intent.

The board's decision is binding on the city and in most cases, an appeal against the board's decision can be taken only to a court of law. The board consists of individuals who are qualified by training or experience in building construction, and are not the employees of the city. The building official usually serves as the ex officio secretary of the board but does not have voting rights on the board.

## 1.4 PRESCRIPTIVE AND PERFORMANCE CODES

The older and traditional type of building codes have been *prescriptive codes*. Such codes gave clear prescriptions for construction systems, types of materials and the devices to be used without permitting any alternatives. They have the advantage of definitiveness in interpretation and are therefore easy to use and enforce. Their main drawback is that they cannot remain apace with the developments in building materials, technology and safety concepts.

In a *performance code*, only the performance criteria of a component are specified instead of the material or the construction method. The performance criteria are based on the function that the component is expected to perform. For example, a prescriptive code might require an 8 in. thick brick wall as a party wall between two semi-detached houses. It may further specify the type of bricks and the type of mortar to be used in joints.

A performance code, on the other hand, states the required properties of the wall such as the fire resistance, sound insulation, load carrying capacity, and the durability characteristics of the wall. The choice of material and the thickness of the wall is left to the discretion of the designer. As long as the wall meets the stated performance requirements, it is acceptable to the code regardless of its material or thickness. A performance code is, therefore, more flexible and provides greater freedom for the innovation of new building products or construction systems.

Though the modern building codes have become increasingly more "performance" oriented, there is still a considerable degree of prescriptiveness in them. A part of the prescriptiveness is the legacy of history since the earlier codes were mainly prescriptive. Several prescriptive provisions have not yet been replaced by equivalent performance criteria while several others serve as an alternative to the performance type provisions. Where the alternative provisions exist, the user of the code has the option to follow either the performance provisions or the prescriptive provisions.

The alternative prescriptive provisions are included in the code because of their relative simplicity. For instance, conventional wood frame construction, which accounts for nearly two-thirds of the investment in buildings in North America, is in the hands of small builders who have neither the training nor the resources to effectively use the performance type provisions. Building codes therefore contain prescriptive provisions which are applicable to wood frame construction only. A builder of a wood frame building may comply with either the general performance type provisions of the code or the specific prescriptive provisions of conventional wood frame construction.

**1.5 MODEL CODES**

There are two principal activities relating to building codes: the enforcement of codes, and the formulation and updating of codes. As stated in Section 1.3, the enforcement of a code is mainly an administrative function and is handled by local jurisdictions. The formulation and updating of building codes, which must be based on the latest knowledge in the realm of public safety and welfare, are, however, beyond the resources of most local jurisdictions. It is a complex activity which requires the input of a large number of technical experts such as the architects, structural engineers, building officials, fire safety engineers, building material manufacturers, chemists and chemical engineers — to name just a few.

In most countries, therefore, building codes are developed by an independent agency which not only reduces the cost burden on local governments but also avoids unnecessary duplication of work among them. Such a code, usually referred to as the National Building Code of the country, is then adopted by local governments. For example, the National Building Code of Canada is the only model code in the country. Although voluntary, the code has been adopted by various Canadian cities. The adoption is usually accompanied by local amendments to take into account the uniqueness of the jurisdiction.

Because of the size and diversity of local conditions in the United States, there is no federal (i.e., one consensus) model building code. Instead, there are three such codes, developed by three independent code writing organizations. Their codes are called the *model building codes*. Including the National Building Code of Canada, there are therefore four model codes in North America. The code writing organizations and their respective building codes are given in Table 1.1.

Each model building code is an independent and complete document containing all necessary building code regulations. They are revised annually and a new edition of each code is published every three years. Although the publication of the building code is the most important activity of each model code organization, it publishes several other related documents, some of which are:

- Mechanical code — relating to hvac, incinerators and other equipment in buildings.
- Plumbing code — relating to water supply, waste water and storm water disposal.
- Fire prevention code — to ensure fire safe maintenance of buildings.
- Existing structures code.
- Housing code.

**Table 1.1 Model Code Organizations and Their Building Codes**

| Code organization | Name of building code | Organizational headquarters |
|---|---|---|
| International Conference of Building Officials (ICBO) | Uniform Building Code (UBC) | Whittier, California |
| Southern Building Code Congress International (SBCCI) | Standard Building Code (SBC) | Birmingham, Alabama |
| Building Officials and Code Administrators International (BOCA) | National Building Code (NBC) | Country Club Hills, Illinois |
| National Research Council of Canada (NRCC) | National Building Code of Canada (NBCC) | Ottawa, Ontario |

Note that a model code, by itself, is not a legal document unless adopted by a jurisdiction through appropriate legislation. In the United States, as in most other countries, the power for model code adoption rests with the states. In some states, this power has been delegated to local governments who may adopt any one of the three model codes. As such, it is not uncommon for jurisdictions close to each other to adopt different model codes, and in some cases, the neighboring cities may use different versions of the same model code. For example, a city may be using the 1994 version of a model code, while a neighboring city may using the 1991 or even 1988 version of the same model code.

The adoption of different model codes by jurisdictions which are geographically close to each other causes hardship to architects, designers, product manufacturers, and contractors. To avoid these problems, some states have adopted a state-wide code. For instance, the state of Georgia has adopted the Standard Building Code for the entire state. In Texas and several other states, on the other hand, a local jurisdiction is free to adopt a model code of its choice. Thus, the cities of Dallas and Fort Worth follow the Uniform Building Code while the cities of Richardson and Highland Park, which share their boundaries with Dallas, follow the Standard Building Code. Some areas in Texas are unregulated, and buildings are not required to conform to any code. Additionally, some cities in the United States, particularly the larger ones such as New York and Chicago, do not follow a model code but have their own building codes. A detail listing of building code adoptions by various states in the United States is given in Appendix III.

Each model code organization endeavors to increase the region of its influence by soliciting member cities. While there is some overlapping of influence areas, the country is divided into areas which are dominated by one model code group. The ICBO dominates in the western U.S., BOCA in the northeast and SBCCI in the southeast, Figure 1.4. In other regions, either two or all three model code organizations compete against each other for membership of cities.

Apart from their publications, each model code organization offers a number of other services. The more frequently used services are code interpretation, plan review and product evaluation. Plan reviews may be sought either by the architect, or a local jurisdiction which does not have an adequate staff of its own. Potential code deficiencies and items of non-conformance with the code are identified by the reviewers, and findings submitted to the client. Product evaluation involves determining whether a product complies with the code. This is required for new materials or products not expressly mentioned in the code.

Since the final authority for code enforcement lies with the city, code interpretation, plan review and the product approval by the model code group staff is only advisory and not binding on the city. But in actual practice, a city will seldom refuse to accept its own model code organization's opinion in these matters.

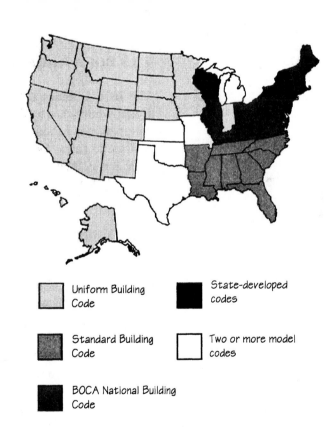

**FIGURE 1.4** Regions of influence of model codes in the United States. Source: Reference 1.3 with permission.

### 1.5.1 Uniform Building Code

This model code, commonly known as the UBC, is published by the International Conference of Building Officials (ICBO) headquartered in Whittier, California with regional offices in Kansas City, Missouri; Bellevue,

Washington; Indianapolis, Indiana; Pleasanton, California; and Austin, Texas. The ICBO was formed in 1922 and the first edition of the UBC was published in 1927.

The Uniform Building Code has been adopted by most cities and states in the western United States. It is best known for its seismic design provisions and forms the basis of the national building codes of Japan, Saudi Arabia, Brazil and several Latin American countries.

### 1.5.2 Standard Building Code

This model code is published by the Southern Building Code Congress International (SBCCI) headquartered in Birmingham, Alabama with regional offices in Austin, Texas; Orlando, Florida; and Greenville, South Carolina. SBCCI was formed in 1940, and the first edition of the code was published in 1945. Best known for its high wind load provisions, the Standard Building Code is primarily used in the southeastern United States, particularly by cities lying on the Atlantic and Gulf coast lines.

### 1.5.3 BOCA National Building Code

The BOCA National Building Code (earlier known as the Basic Building Code) is published by the Building Officials and Code Administrators (BOCA) International headquartered in Country Club Hills, Illinois with regional offices in Tulsa, Oklahoma; Columbus, Ohio; and Trevose, Pennsylvania. BOCA was founded in 1915, and the first edition of this code was published in 1950. It is primarily used in the northeastern United States.

### 1.5.4 National Building Code of Canada

The National Building Code of Canada (NBCC) is published by the National Research Council of Canada headquartered in Ottawa, Ontario. The first edition of NBCC was published in 1941. Prior to the publication of NBCC, there was a multiplicity of building codes in Canada, causing hardship among architects and designers who had projects in different regions of the country. After the publication of the 1995 edition, NBCC is expected to be on a 3-year publication cycle, like the model codes in the United States.

## 1.6 UNIFORMITY IN MODEL CODES

The duplication of work and the lack of uniformity among the U.S. model codes has been a matter of concern for a long time. The architecture profession has been at the forefront of criticism of the unnecessary differences between the codes. Some differences are indeed justifiable because of the large size of the country which creates geographic and climatic differences, and differences due to particular soil conditions or the region's susceptibility to hurricanes, tornadoes or earthquakes. However, most differences cannot be so justified. For instance, each of the three model codes prescribes different methods for determining the permissible built-up area and height of a building. None of these is better than the other two; they are just different.

Demands have frequently been made to replace the three model building codes with a single model building code, similar to a national building code in other countries. The demand can be appreciated when one visualizes an architect developing a uniform design for a national chain store. The uniformity of design may be essential to the marketing and distribution strategy of the chain. However, under the present set-up, three separate versions of the same design would have to be produced to satisfy the requirements of three different codes, in addition to any local requirements.

A national building code of the United States is therefore necessary. However, some believe that a national code, if developed, will simply become the fourth model code, adding to the existing multiplicity and confusion. Others see the positive side of the three codes. With each model code organization competing with the other, there is an incentive for improvement.

### 1.6.1 Council of American Building Officials

In order to address some of the concerns resulting from the duplicity and nonuniformity of codes, and to provide a united representation of building officials' interests at the national level, the Council of American Building Officials (CABO) was formed in 1972. The membership of the CABO board comprises the boards of directors of ICBO, SBCCI and BOCA. CABO is based in Falls Church, Virginia.

The technical and administrative staff of the three model code organizations provides support for CABO activities. One of the recent successes achieved by CABO is that of formulating a common code format. The format has been accepted by all three model code organizations and contains input from the American Institute of Architects and the Society of Fire Protection Engineers.

The common code format means that all three model codes are organized into identical chapter headings, chapter contents and chapter sequence. For instance, if provisions relating to "Means of Egress" are contained in Chapter 10 of the Uniform Building Code, then Chapter 10 of the Standard Building Code and Chapter 10 of the BOCA National Building Code will also deal with the means of egress. The actual provisions relating to the means of egress may be different from code to code but their location in each code document is the same.

This is the first major step forward in achieving uniformity among the model codes[2]. The first version of the BOCA National Building Code under the common code format was published in 1993, and that of the Uniform Building Code and the Standard Building Code in 1994.

---

[2] After successfully achieving the common code format, the three model code organizations in the United States are fast moving towards the goal of one consensus code. It is difficult to predict when this goal might be realized, but serious efforts are under way.

### 1.6.2 National Evaluation Service

All model building codes permit the use of new and innovative products as substitutes for those specified in the code. Theoretically, the authority to approve and accept the new product lies with the building official of the city. This approval must be based on performance data provided by the manufacture or the innovator. The data should substantiate the equivalence of the new product with that specified in the code. However, the evaluation of performance data is often quite involved and beyond the expertise of most building officials. Therefore, each model code organization provides a centralized evaluation service which examines the data and issues an *evaluation report*. Although not bound to accept this report, the building official will generally do so.

As with everything else, the evaluation services of the three code organizations unnecessarily duplicate work. To avoid duplication, CABO developed the National Evaluation Service (NES) whose purpose is to evaluate the new product on behalf of all three model code organizations. A manufacturer has the option to either seek national approval through NES, or from the evaluation service of an individual model code organization — ICBO, SBCCI or BOCA. If the product receives approval from the NES, it automatically stands approved from the individual code organizations. Manufacturers of several products utilize this facility unless the product has limited geographical application, in which case the manufacturer may seek only the relevant model code organization's approval.

The NES board has representation from all three model code groups and one of the model code groups provides the secretariat for NES activities by rotation.

### 1.6.3 One and Two Family Dwelling Code

One of the most important contributions of CABO is the formulation of the One and Two Family Dwelling Code (OTFDC). OTFDC is a model code applicable only to the construction of single family or two family dwellings. It has been recognized by all three model code organizations.

OTFDC must be adopted by the local jurisdiction if it is to have any validity there. Thus, apart from adopting one of the three model codes, a city may also adopt OTFDC. In such a city, the builder of one or two family dwelling units has the option to follow either the provisions of the applicable model building code or OTFDC. Being a specialized code which applies only to one or two family dwellings, OTFDC is easier to use than any of the three model codes because of its greater prescriptiveness.

Another important contribution of CABO is the Model Energy Code. This code is published jointly by all three model code organizations and is maintained by a committee composed of membership from all three code organizations and the National Conference of States on Building Codes and Standards (NCSBCS).

### 1.6.4 National Conference of States on Building Codes and Standards

As the title suggests, the aim of this organization is to advance interstate cooperation in building codes and standards. Among its members are appointees of the governor of each state in the U.S. and U.S. territories. A major contribution of NCSBCS is the publication of the Directory of Building Codes and Regulations which provides information on the codes that have been adopted by various cities in the United States. NCSBCS is headquartered in Herndon, Virginia.

## 1.7 CONTENTS OF A BUILDING CODE

Under the common code format, a model building code is organized into nine parts. Each part consists of two or more chapters.

- *Administration*: deals with the administrative aspects of the code, such as the duties and functions of a building official, plans examination, board of appeals, issuance of a building permit, occupancy certificates, inspections and fees. The definitions of various terms used in the code are also contained in this part.
- *Building Planning*: deals with the classification of buildings according to occupancy and type of construction. The occupancy of the building refers to its use, and the type of construction refers to the fire resistance of various components of the building, see Section 8.5.
- *Fire Protection*: deals with fire-resistive materials and construction, fire-resistive interior finishes, and fire protection systems. Fire protection systems include those installed in the building to detect and suppress fires.
- *Occupant Needs*: deals with the means of egress, accessibility and interior environment. Interior environment provisions relate to lighting, ventilation, sanitation and sound control.
- *Building Envelope*: deals with energy conservation and the exterior envelope of the building. The exterior envelope includes external walls, cladding, windows and the roof.
- *Structural Systems and Materials*: deals with loads on buildings, structural tests and inspections, and foundations. It is the most extensive part of the code, and includes a separate chapter for each structural material — wood, steel, concrete, masonry and lightweight materials.
- *Nonstructural Materials*: deals with the use of nonstructural materials — glass, gypsum board, and plastics.
- *Building Services*: deals with electrical, mechanical and plumbing systems.
- *Special Devices*: deals with miscellaneous concerns such as construction in the public right of way, site work and demolition, and existing structures.

### 1.7.1 Application of Building Code

Every building presents a certain amount of hazard to its occupants. The degree of hazard depends on several factors, such as the occupancy (use) of the building, type of construction, height and number of stories, and whether any fire detection and suppression system has been provided.

The occupancy of a building is one of the major hazard-determining factors. Buildings which accommodate a large number of people such as stadiums, assembly halls, auditoriums, and churches present a greater hazard than buildings with a smaller concentration of occupants such as individual dwellings and apartments. The occupancy classification is also an index of the fuel (combustible content) in the building. Buildings which contain flammable materials such as automobile repair garages, paint and chemical stores, and woodworking mills are more hazardous since they contain more combustibles than other buildings. For the same reason, a library building is more hazardous than an apartment building.

The occupancy of a building is also a determinant of how familiar the occupants are with the building. The greater the occupants' familiarity with the building, the smaller the hazard. This is based on the premise that in the event of a fire, the occupants will be able to egress from a building easily if they are familiar with it. Based on the familiarity criterion, a hotel or office building is more hazardous than an individual dwelling.

Thus, the first step in applying the building code to a proposed building consists of determining its occupancy classification. Building codes classify buildings in several occupancy groups. Although there are differences between the individual model codes, the occupancy groups listed in Table 1.2 may be regarded as being somewhat representative of all the model codes.

Each occupancy group is given a letter designation and is further classified into subgroups, called *divisions*. For example, in the Uniform Building Code, assembly occupancy is divided in 5 divisions which are designated as A-1, A-2, A-2.1, A-3 and A-4. According to this classification, an auditorium consisting of a stage and an audience capacity of more than or equal to 1,000 is an Assembly occupancy — Division I (i.e., A-1). An auditorium with a stage but with less than 1,000 capacity is occupancy A-2.

The second step in the application of building code to a proposed building is to determine its type of construction. The type of construction also creates its own hazard. The more fire-resistive the construction, the smaller the hazard. Building codes classify construction into several types. For instance, the Uniform Building Code divides buildings into five types — I, II, III, IV, and V. This classification is based on the degree of fire resistance of various structural components of the building such as floors, roof, columns, beams, external walls and internal partitions. Type I is the most fire-resistive construction and Type V, the least fire-resistive. (See Section 8.5.1.)

The third step is to determine the location of the building on the site, particularly its clearances from the property lines and any existing buildings. The greater the clearances, the smaller the hazard.

The next two steps involve determining the maximum allowable height and the maximum allowable area of the building. This is related to the degree of hazard present in the building. The fundamental premise is that if the

**Table 1.2 Typical Occupancy Classifications of Buildings**

| Letter designation | Occupancy |
|---|---|
| A | Assembly |
| B | Business |
| E | Educational |
| F | Factory and Industrial |
| H | Hazardous |
| I | Institutional |
| M | Mercantile |
| R | Residential |
| S | Storage |
| U | Utility |

Note: This table represents occupancy classification as prescribed in the Uniform Building Code.

hazard in the building is small, the allowable area can be large, and vice versa. Therefore, allowable area is a function of occupancy classification, construction type and site clearances. The more fire-resistive the construction and (or) greater the site clearances, the greater the area allowed for a particular occupancy. In addition, the provision of automatic fire detection and suppression system affects the allowable area and height.

Other steps in the application of building code to a proposed building include reviewing the conformity of the building with the detailed provisions of its particular occupancy, type of construction, and reviewing requirements for egress and accessibility. Finally, the building must be reviewed for conformity with structural engineering requirements. The various steps involved in the use and application of a building code are summarized in Table 1.3.

**Table 1.3   Steps Involved in Applying Building Code to a Proposed Building**

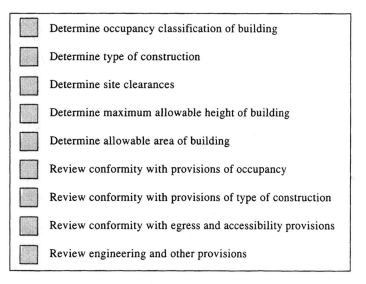

Determine occupancy classification of building

Determine type of construction

Determine site clearances

Determine maximum allowable height of building

Determine allowable area of building

Review conformity with provisions of occupancy

Review conformity with provisions of type of construction

Review conformity with egress and accessibility provisions

Review engineering and other provisions

## 1.8 CONSTRUCTION STANDARDS

Standards are the foundations of modern building codes. They contain technical specifications which address the properties of a building product or a component, test methods to determine properties of materials, and the method of installation or construction.

The word "standard" is used here as an adjective which qualifies words such as the properties, test methods, or the method of installation. Thus, in referring to a standard, one is in fact referring to one of the following:
- Standard specification which deals with quality of materials, products and components.
- Standard method of determining particular performance of a product or system including methods of sampling and quality control.
- Standard method of construction, installation or maintenance.

A standard must not be confused with a building code provision. Although a code specifies the design criteria or the required properties of a component, the standard specifies the procedures and equipment required to verify the criteria or measure the properties. For instance, although a building code will give the required fire resistance (e.g., 2 hours) for a wall or floor, the building standard prescribes the test procedure and equipment required to measure the fire resistance. A fully prescriptive code does not require any standards since it does not refer to any performance criterion or property. On the other hand, a performance type code must rely heavily on the use of standards. As the trend toward performance type codes has grown, the use of standards in building codes has increased accordingly.

### 1.8.1 Standards-Producing Organizations

It is beyond the scope of local jurisdictions or even the model code organizations to develop standards since several standards are referenced by a model code. For example, the BOCA National Building Code references nearly 330 standards produced by 34 organizations. The task of formulating and updating standards is therefore performed by organizations which have the necessary facilities and expertise for obtaining performance data and evaluating it. These organizations may be divided into three types: trade associations, professional societies, and organizations whose primary purpose is to publish standards.

*Trade Associations*: A trade association is an association of manufacturing companies making the same product. For example, the American Wood Preservers' Association (AWPA) is an organization whose membership comprises industries which treat lumber, plywood and other wood products with preservatives and fire-retardant chemicals.

The function of a trade association is to coordinate the task of member companies and to protect their interests. It deals with all matters that affect the specific industry such as collecting statistics, dealing with tariffs and trade regulations, and disseminating information to architects and engineers about the product, particularly emphasizing its benefits over any competing or alternate product. In order to ensure quality and competitiveness, most trade associations publish standards for the products they serve to which all member companies must conform. Several trade associations also have certification programs to grade and stamp the product. AWPA is such an organization and an AWPA grade stamp on wood and wood products is regarded as a mark of quality and standardization.

*Professional Societies*: Another source of standards, although not extensive, is the professional societies such as the American Society of Civil Engineers (ASCE) and American Society of Heating, Refrigeration and Air Conditioning Engineers (ASHRAE). These organizations develop standard specifications and testing procedures as professional obligation. For example, the American Society of Civil Engineers' publication *Minimum Design Loads for Buildings and Other Structures*, ASCE 7 (see Section 2.1), is a publication that is referenced by all model building codes.

*Standards-Producing Organizations*: By far the largest and most referenced standards-producing organizations are those whose main function is to produce standards. In countries other than the United States, this task is normally handled by a single umbrella organization at the national level. In Britain, there is the British Standards Institution (BSI), in Australia, the Standards Association of Australia (SAA) and in Germany, the Deutsches Institute fur Normung (DIN). In the United States, the picture is somewhat less clear because of the large number of organizations involved in the development of standards at the national level. These are the American National Standards Institute (ANSI), American Society for Testing and Materials (ASTM), National Institute of Standards and Technology (NIST), earlier called the National Bureau of Standards, and the Underwriters Laboratories (UL).

In addition to the national standards organizations, there are regional and international standards organizations which harmonize standards at the regional and international levels. These organizations are becoming increasingly important due to stronger regional and international trade agreements. In Western Europe, the European Committee for Standardization (CEN) carries out this task to facilitate free trade and develop mutual cooperation in spheres of scientific, technological and economic activities among the countries of the European Common Market. (CEN is an acronym for the French designation "Comite European de Coordination des Normes"). On the global level, this function is performed by the International Standards Organization (ISO). ISO membership consists of standards organizations, one from each country — each the most representative of standardization activity in that country.

Each model code adopts several ASTM, ANSI and various trade associations' standards. The adoption is accomplished in two ways: (i) by reference, in which case a particular standard is adopted in its entirety without any change, and (ii) by inclusion, in which case the standard is incorporated in the code either entirely or partially. In the case of a partial inclusion, only those parts of the standard are included which are relevant to the given provision of the code. If there is a conflict between a code provision and the standard, the code provision governs.

The BOCA National Building Code and the Standard Building Code adopt standards by reference. The Uniform Building Code publishes its own separate publication on standards every three years along with a new edition of the building code.

A brief description of the three primary standards-writing organizations in the United States, the American National Standards Institute, American Society of Testing and Materials, and Underwriters Laboratories is given below.

### 1.8.2 American National Standards Institute

The American National Standards Institute is a body similar to, but not identical with, the national standards organizations in other countries such as the BSI, DIN, SAA, etc. Unlike these organizations, however, ANSI generally does not develop its own standards. It functions primarily as the approving body and a clearinghouse at the national level for voluntary standards developed by other organizations in the United States. Thus, it provides an official and a nationally recognized status to standards developed by private organizations. However, ANSI ensures that the standards approved by it have been developed in an open and fair manner after due consultations among various interest groups such as the producers, users, professional experts and the general public. In case no standards exist for a product, ANSI will bring together and coordinate the expertise needed to develop the required standards.

ANSI is a nongovernmental and privately financed body. It obtains its funding primarily from membership dues and the sale of its publications. It was founded during World War I (1918) to standardize production of war-related items (bullets and guns) by several different manufacturers. It was initially known as the American Standards Association (ASA) — an acronym well known internationally for its use in designating photographic film speeds. This name was later changed to the United States of America Standards Institute (USASI) and finally to ANSI in 1969. It represents the United States in ISO and distributes within the United States the ISO standards and standards from other countries.

### 1.8.3 American Society for Testing and Materials

Founded in 1898, the American Society for Testing and Materials is a privately funded, nonprofit organization established for "the development of standards on characteristics and performance of materials, products, systems, and services; and the promotion of related knowledge"[1.4]. It is by far the largest single source of standards in the world.

The Society was established in 1898 as the American Section of the International Society for Testing Materials and incorporated in 1902 as the American Society for Testing Materials. In 1961, its name was changed to its present name, the American Society for Testing and Materials, to emphasize its interest in both the materials as well as their testing.

The work of the Society is divided into 135 main technical committees and 2080 subcommittees. The committee composition ensures balanced participation from producers and product users, and the general interest group such as the architects, engineers and other design professionals. With over 32,000 active members, the membership of the society is open to all concerned.

ASTM standards are "voluntary consensus standards". "Voluntary" implies that the standard is not mandatory, unless so required by a code or regulation which references it. In other words, the existence of an ASTM standard for a particular product (or procedure) does not mean that the product (or procedure) cannot be produced (or used) if it does not conform to the standard. "Consensus" implies that the standard is arrived at by a consensus of various members of the committee or subcommittee which produced it.

ASTM standards are designated by a unique serial designation, comprising an uppercase letter followed by a number (one to four digits), a hyphen, and finally the year of issue. The letter refers to the general classification of the material or test procedure, as shown in Table 1.4.

The year of issue refers to the year of original preparation or the year of

**Table 1.4  Letter Designation of ASTM Standards**

| Letter designation | Type of material or test |
| --- | --- |
| A | Ferrous metals |
| B | Nonferrous metals |
| C | Cementitious, ceramic, concrete, and masonry materials |
| D | Miscellaneous materials |
| E | Miscellaneous subjects |
| F | Materials of specific applications |
| G | Corrosion, deterioration, and degradation of materials |
| ES | Emergency standards |
| P | Proposals |

the most recent revision of the standard.  Thus, a standard prepared or revised in 1989 carries as its final number 89.  If a letter follows the year, it implies a rewriting of the standard in the same year.  For instance, 89a implies two revisions, 89b implies three revisions in 1989, and so on.

ASTM standards can be revised at any time by the appropriate technical committee.  At any rate, a standard must be reviewed every five years which may result in its revision, reapproval or withdrawal.  In case a standard has been reapproved without any change, then the year of reapproval is placed within parentheses as part of the designation.  Thus (1989) means that the standard was reapproved in 1989.  A typical ASTM standard is designated as: C 136-95a: Standard Test Method for Sieve Analysis of Fine and Coarse Aggregates.

### 1.8.4  Underwriters Laboratories

A different kind of standards organization is the Underwriters Laboratories (UL).  It was established in 1894 by insurance companies which were paying excessive claims caused by fires generated by the failures of new electrical and mechanical devices in buildings.  Today, the UL is a self-supporting and not-for-profit organization which finances itself through the testing of various building and engineering products, and the sale of its publications.  Currently, the Laboratory tests nearly 80,000 products annually.  It also certifies and labels products. In fact, the UL mark on a product is a certificate of its having successfully undergone some of the world's most rigorous tests for safety evaluation.  In other words, the UL mark indicates that the product is safe and free from any foreseeable risk of hazard.

The Underwriters Laboratories is an independent organization, implying that it has no monetary interest in the product or its success in the marketplace. If a product passes UL's required safety testing, and the manufacturer wants it to carry the UL mark, the Laboratory's field representative visits the manufacturing facilities unannounced several times during a year to ensure continued compliance of the product with the required safety standards. Certified products are listed in the UL Directories which are published annually.

The UL maintains four testing laboratories in the United States. The corporate headquarters is located in Northbrook, Illinois. The other facilities are in Melville, New York; Research Triangle Park, North Carolina; and Santa Clara, California.

The tests must obviously be conducted according to recognized safety standards. Currently, the UL has nearly 560 standards, most of which are approved as ANSI standards. UL standards are used by other independent testing laboratories nationwide and internationally. Additionally, they are recognized by the U.S. federal and state governments, a task facilitated by UL's active participation in various code and standards writing agencies such as ANSI, ASTM, and the National Fire Protection Association.

## 1.9 OTHER LEGAL CONSTRAINTS

In addition to building codes and standards, building construction must also conform to several other legal constraints. The two most important such constraints are:

- Zoning Ordinance
- Americans with Disabilities Act

## 1.10 ZONING ORDINANCE

A zoning ordinance (also called the zoning code) of a city is a document containing city planning laws. Its primary aim is to regulate the use of land under the jurisdiction of the city according to a comprehensive master plan. Thus, a zoning ordinance segregates the land of a city into different use groups and specifies the activity for which each piece of land can be used. Areas of land on which the same type of activity is allowed are called *districts*.

The number of districts and their designation varies from city to city. Usually, a city will divide its territory into four primary district groups: residential districts, commercial districts, industrial districts and special purpose districts.

Each of the above district groups is subdivided into several districts. For instance, the commercial district group may consist of a professional district, office district, local retail district, local business district, and general business district. Similarly, the residential district group may consist of a low density single family dwelling district, medium density single family dwelling district, high density single family dwelling district, duplex dwelling district, and townhouse district.

A zoning ordinance consists of two basic elements: (i) a zoning map, and (ii) a zoning regulation text.

A zoning map shows the district to which a piece of land belongs, and the zoning text specifies the type of building/s that can be built in that district. For instance, in a single family dwelling district, the zoning ordinance will permit the construction of single family residences and several other facilities that may be needed in that district such as fire stations, local churches, community centers, parochial schools, playgrounds and parks. A zoning map is based on a comprehensive master plan of the city which takes into account the present and the future use of land under the city's jurisdiction.

Apart from specifying the land use, a zoning text also gives the development standards for that land. These standards include: the maximum ground coverage, maximum floor area ratio, minimum setbacks, maximum height, and the number of stories that may be built on a piece of land.

Ground coverage refers to the percentage of land area that may be covered by the building. For instance, for an office building in a downtown area, the ground coverage permitted may be as high as 100%, while for a single family dwelling in a suburban location, the maximum ground coverage may be as low as 25%.

Floor area ratio (FAR) refers to the total built-up area (sum of the built-up areas on all floors) divided by the total land area. An FAR of 2.0 means that the total built-up area of the building on all floors is equal to twice the land area. Thus, an FAR of 2.0 is achieved by a 2-story building covering the entire piece of land, or a 4-story building covering 50% of the land area, or a 6-story building covering one-third the land area, and so on.

Ground coverage and FAR are powerful zoning restrictions that control the overall volume (bulk) of buildings in a district without greatly jeopardizing design freedom. Bulk control is an indirect means of aesthetic control of the development. It also controls population density, traffic volume, environmental pollution and open spaces.

Restrictions placed on the height or the number of stories under a zoning ordinance also affect population density and traffic volume in the same way as ground coverage and FAR, but the main purpose of height restriction is that the buildings are within the capabilities of fire fighting equipment of the city. In some cities, height restrictions may be imposed to maintain views of existing buildings, or to preserve the aesthetic character of a district.

Setbacks refer to the distances by which a building must be *set back* from property lines, thereby specifying the minimum sizes of open areas around the building. Historically, the purpose of front setback was to reserve land for any future widening of the street. In modern times, setbacks provide greater privacy and help to insulate buildings from traffic noise, fumes and otherwise enhance the aesthetic appeal of neighborhoods.

In many situations, building code and zoning ordinance provisions (or an applicable state or federal regulation) may conflict with each other. In such a case, it is obvious that the more restrictive provision would hold.

### 1.10.1 Zoning Ordinance Review and Administration

The formulation and enforcement of a zoning ordinance are usually delegated by the state to local authorities under the "zoning enabling act of the state". The zoning enabling acts of most states are derived from the "Standard State Zoning Enabling Act" prepared by the U.S. Department of Commerce in the 1920s[1.5]. Practically all major U.S. cities except Houston, Texas, have a zoning ordinance. Like the building code, the zoning ordinance is enforced under police powers of the state.

Each local authority has several decision-making bodies that contribute to the formulation and review of the zoning ordinance. Theoretically, the legislature of the city, the city council, is the apex zoning ordinance authority. For practical purposes, however, the zoning ordinance is under the charge of the *zoning and planning commission* of the city, which is a body consisting of several local citizens. The responsibilities of the zoning commission include the formulation, development and review of the zoning plan.

The zoning commission is composed of individuals who have distinguished themselves by demonstrating outstanding and unselfish interest in civic affairs. They are appointed by the city council to serve for a fixed term, and receive no remuneration for their work. The zoning commission is aided in its task by city planners and urban designers who are usually full-time employees of the city.

The initial formulation and the subsequent reviews of the city's zoning plan by the zoning commission must go through a public hearing. Public hearings are an important component of land use control at the local level. It is through public hearings that citizens are able to participate in city planning and zoning process.

Although the zoning commission and the city council are the bodies responsible for zonal plan review, the day-to-day work related to zoning administration is carried out by the zoning administrator. In most cities, the building official functions as the zoning administrator. Thus, the owner of a piece of land who desires to rezone the property would submit his/her request to the zoning administrator, who would then forward it to the zoning commission for decision.

If the zoning commission agrees with rezoning, a public hearing is arranged. After the public hearing, the zoning commission makes its decision, which is usually a recommendation to city council, since the city council is the final decision-making authority on zoning. The city council may hold its own public hearing on the matter after receiving the zoning commission's recommendations.

### 1.10.2 Board of Zoning Appeals

The implementation of land use control involves more than a mere formulation or review of the zoning plan. It also involves the enforcement of zoning ordinances which give rise to problems of application and interpretation. These problems are referred to the board of zoning appeals, also called the *board of adjustment*. This board consists of several members, usually appointed by the mayor or the city council.

The primary responsibility of the board of adjustment is to hear appeals on actions taken by city officials who administer zoning regulations and to make special exceptions to zoning regulations. Special exceptions generally refer to granting variances to setbacks, ground coverage, FAR, etc., whose literal enforcement may cause unnecessary and undue hardship to the owner. Variances granted by the board must not be contrary to public interest and must not act to relieve the owner of self-created hardship. The meetings of the board are open to the public.

## 1.11 AMERICANS WITH DISABILITIES ACT

The Americans with Disabilities Act (ADA) is a 1990 federal law which came into effect in January 1992. The objective of the act is to ensure equal opportunity to the physically disabled in all of life's activities. A part of the act is devoted to regulating access to buildings so that they are usable by the physically disabled. It requires that all new construction and alterations to existing constructions provide barrier-free access routes on the site, into and within all spaces of buildings. Single family dwellings, multifamily dwellings, private clubs and facilities controlled by religious organizations, such as day care centers and nursing homes operated by a church are exempt from ADA's accessibility provisions.

The concept of barrier-free access existed for nearly two decades before the promulgation of the ADA. The ANSI 117.1 standard entitled "American National Specifications for Making Buildings and Facilities Accessible to and Usable by the Physically Handicapped" had been adopted by several states and local jurisdictions. (ANSI 117.1 is now known as CABO/ANSI 117.1 since CABO is now the secretariat for this standard).

In 1969, the U.S. federal government passed the Architectural Barriers Act (ABA) which required that if federal funds are spent in the construction of a facility, that facility must be designed to be accessible to the physically handicapped according to the Uniform Federal Accessibility Standard (UFAS). In 1980, UFAS provisions were absorbed into ANSI 117.1. The difference between ABA and ADA is that ADA is much wider in scope than ABA. Additionally, ADA is mandated for application to all buildings except those mentioned earlier, regardless of the source of funds used in constructing them.

ADA is a comprehensive legislation that addresses four major concerns. Title I addresses concerns pertaining to employment discrimination of handicapped people. Title II refers to the accessibility of public transportation lines such as railroads and buses. Title III deals with accessibility in buildings and Title IV with accessible telecommunication facilities, such as telephones for the hearing impaired or individuals with other handicaps, and automatic teller machines.

Only Title III and Title IV of the ADA are of concern to architects and designers. The provisions of Title III are detailed in ADA Accessibility Guidelines (ADAAG). ADAAG is similar to CABO/ANSI 117.1 and it is expected that in due course, the differences between ADAAG and CABO/ANSI 117.1 will be abridged. In that situation, if a building meets with the building code requirements, it would in most respects meet the accessibility requirements of ADA. However, it must be recognized that a building code and ADA are two different legislative provisions. A building code is a local juridiction's law, while ADA is a federal law. The owner of the building is required to meet with the provisions of both laws. Additionally, the provisions of Title IV of ADA are not covered in building codes, but must be satisfied.

ADA's accessibility requirements relate primarily to the design of entrances, doors, stairways, ramps, changes of level, sidewalks, elevators, drinking fountains, toilet facilities, door width, door knobs, etc.

**REVIEW QUESTIONS**

1.1    What is the purpose of a building code? Explain.

1.2    What is the difference between a prescriptive and a performance code? Explain with the help of an example. To which category do modern building codes belong?

1.3    What is the difference between a building code and a model building code?

1.4    Write at least a 100-word paragraph on the enforcement of building codes.

1.5    List the model code organizations in North America and the building codes published by them.

1.6    What is meant by the "common code format"? Explain with the help of examples.

1.7    Describe the relationship between a building code and construction standards. List three important standards organizations in the United States.

1.8    What information can you derive from a given designation of an ASTM standard such as E 119-95a?

1.9    How does a building code allow the use of materials or construction systems which are not specifically mentioned in the code? Explain.

1.10   List the steps you will follow in ascertaining that a building conforms to the provisions of the building code.

1.11   What is the difference between a building code and a zoning ordinance? Explain.

1.12   Explain the terms ground coverage and FAR.

1.13   Write a brief note on the Americans with Disabilities Act.

1.14   What do the following acronyms stand for: (i) CABO, (ii) ICBO, (iii) BOCA, (iv) SBCCI, (v) ASTM, (vi) ANSI, (vii) UL, (viii) ASHRAE, and (ix) ADA.

**REFERENCES**

1.1    International Conference of Building Officials, Whittier, California: *Uniform Building Code*, 1994, Vol. 1, p. 1.

1.2    Sanderson, R: "Code and Code Administration", Building Officials and Code Administrators, Country Club Hills, Illinois, 1969, p. 102.

1.3    National Conference of States on Building Codes and Standards, Herndon, Virginia: *Introduction to Building Codes*, 1994, p. 3.

1.4    American Society for Testing and Materials, Philadelphia, Pennsylvania: *1995 Annual Book of Standards*, p. xii.

1.5    Moss, E: *Land Use Control in the United States*, The Dial Press/James Wade, Washington, D.C., 1977, p. 321.

**SUGGESTIONS FOR FURTHER READING**

American Institute of Architects, Washington D.C: *An Architect's Guide to Building Codes and Standards*, 1991.

Terry, E: *Americans with Disabilities Act Facilities Compliance*, John Wiley and Sons, New York, 1993.

# 2
# LOADS ON BUILDINGS

**2.1 INTRODUCTION**     There are several types of loads to which buildings are subjected. However, these loads are usually classified under two primary categories: (i) gravity loads, and (ii) lateral loads, Figure 2.1. Gravity loads are caused by the gravitational pull of the earth and act in a vertical direction. Therefore, they are also referred to as vertical loads. The materials and components of which the buildings are constructed, people, rain water, snow, furniture, equipment, and all that is contained within the building are some of the sources of gravity loads. Gravity loads are further classified as *dead loads* and *live loads* as explained in subsequent sections.

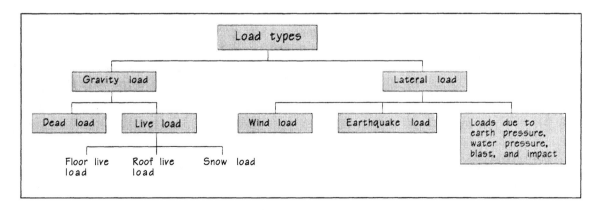

**FIGURE 2.1**  Types of loads on buildings.

The two primary sources of lateral loads on buildings are wind and earthquakes. The effect of both, the wind and the earthquake, is to create loads in the lateral (other than vertically downward) direction. For example, wind creates vertically upward forces (suction) on a flat roof, and horizontal forces on a wall. The main effect of earthquake ground motion is to create horizontal forces in buildings, although a small amount of vertical forces is also created. Some other examples of lateral loads are earth pressure on basement walls, water pressure on tank walls, and loads caused by blasts and moving vehicles or equipment.

An architect is usually not interested in a detailed investigation of loads on a building, since this task is a part of the realm of structural engineering. However, a general understanding of loads and the ability to determine their approximate magnitudes is required in several tasks routinely performed by the architect. For instance, an architect may decide to choose the sizes of simple structural members, such as floor joists and rafters, from a given table in which the values of loads acting on the member are required. In selecting the thickness of glass and sizing the members of the frame of a simple curtain wall, or in deciding the weight of ballast on a roof, the value of loads is required. For such tasks, an architect will usually not seek a structural engineer's help.

In this chapter, we shall examine the nature of different types of loads on buildings, and discuss the methods of determining their values. The treatment given here is brief and simplified. For a more rigorous treatment, reference should be made to a structural engineering text.

In the United States, the most authoritative source for recommendations concerning loads is the applicable building code, which as stated in Chapter 1, is based on one of the three model codes. Under the common code format, Chapter 16 of each model code deals with loads on buildings. (See Section 1.8). Another frequently referenced source is the American Society of Civil Engineers' publication *Minimum Design Loads for Buildings and Other Structures*[2.1].

In the U.S. customary system of units, a load is expressed in pounds (lbs) or kilo-pounds (kips). 1 kip is equal to 1,000 lbs. Thus, 2.5 kips = 2,500 lb. The corresponding units of load in the SI system of units are the newton (N) and kilo-newton (kN). Note that 1 lb = 4.448 N, and 1 kN = 224.8 lb = 0.2248 kip. (See Appendix I).

When a load is distributed over a surface, such as on a floor slab, it is expressed in pounds per square foot (psf). In the SI system, the distributed load is expressed in newtons per square meter ($N/m^2$). Newton per square meter is abbreviated as pascal (Pa), and $kN/m^2$ is abbreviated as kPa. Thus, $1.0 \ N/m^2$ is synonymous with 1.0 Pa, and $1.0 \ kN/m^2$ with 1.0 kPa. Note that 1 psf = 47.88 Pa.

## 2.2 DEAD LOADS

Dead loads are always present in a building and generally do not vary with time. They include the weights of materials and components of which the structure is built. The dead load of a component is computed by multiplying its volume or surface area by its density. Since both the densities and the dimensions of the components are known with reasonable accuracy, dead loads in a building can be estimated with greater certainty than other load types. Volume and surface densities of some of the commonly used materials are given in Tables IV.1 and IV.2 respectively of Appendix IV.

The dead load on a structure also includes the weights of fixtures and equipment that are permanently installed such as plumbing, electrical or HVAC equipment. The weight of nonloadbearing space-dividing partitions (demountable or otherwise) is also included in the dead loads. The rationale is that although these partitions may be rearranged, their load is always present on the structure. Building codes recommend a minimum of 20 psf (0.96 kPa) dead load due to partitions in office buildings[2.2].

The dead load for which a building component is designed includes the self weight of the component plus the dead loads of all other components that it supports. For example, the dead load on a column includes the weight of the column itself plus all the dead load that is imposed on it. In Figure 2.2, the dead load on a column is the weight of the column plus the dead load from the beams and slab resting on it. Similarly, the dead load on a beam is the weight of the beam itself plus the dead load from the slab that it supports. The dead load on the slab is only the self weight of the slab. However, if the slab supports a floor finish, ceiling, light fixtures, or plumbing and electrical pipes, their weights must be included in the dead load acting on the slab.

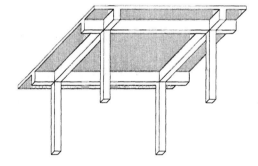

**FIGURE 2.2** The dead load on a column of a building includes the weight of all components that it supports, such as the beams and floor slab, plus the self weight of the column.

Historically, the dead loads on buildings have progressively decreased. Modern buildings are much lighter than comparable structures built decades or centuries ago. The application of scientific principles to the design of buildings has resulted in a better understanding of how and why buildings stand up (or fall down). This and the development of stronger materials have resulted in smaller size walls, columns, beams and slabs, and hence in smaller dead loads in modern buildings.

### 2.2.1 Tributary Area

In computing the dead loads and other loads on a component, the concept of tributary area is useful. Tributary area for a component is the area (or areas) of the building which "contributes" load on that component. For example, in a floor system which consists of wood planks supported by parallel beams, the tributary area for a beam is the area of the floor that lies halfway to the adjacent beam on the left and halfway to the adjacent beam on the right. In Figure 2.3, the tributary area for beam A has been shown by the shaded area. All of the load that is placed on this shaded area must be carried by beam A.

The tributary area for a column in a building is similarly obtained. In the framing plan of the building shown in Figure 2.4, the tributary areas of an interior column X, exterior column Y, and a corner column Z, have been shown by shaded areas. Thus, column X receives all the load placed on the shaded area of the floor surrounding it. This is a rectangular area whose dimensions are: $0.5(L_1 + L_2)$ by $0.5(W_1 + W_2)$. Thus, if $L_1$ and $L_2$ are 12 ft and 18 ft respectively, and $W_1$ and $W_2$ are each 13 ft, the tributary area for column X is 15 ft x 13 ft in dimensions.

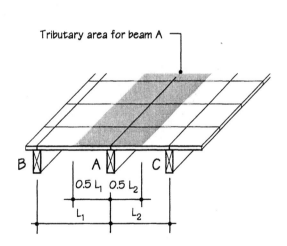

**FIGURE 2.3** The tributary area for beam A is the shaded area. The width of this area is $0.5(L_1 + L_2)$, where $L_1$ and $L_2$ are the center-to-center distances between beams.

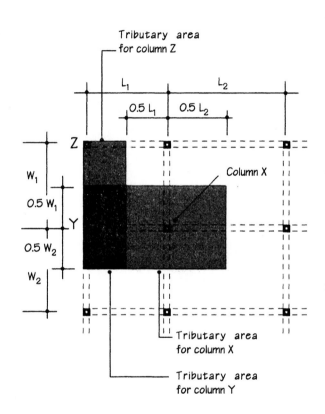

**FIGURE 2.4** Tributary areas for columns X, Y, and Z.

**Example 2.1**

Determine the dead load on an interior beam (designated as A) of the floor deck of Figure 2.5. Assume that the beams are of 4 x 10 southern pine, spaced 6 ft (1.83 m) on center. The deck consists of $1^{1}/_{2}$ in. (38 mm) thick southern pine wood planks.

Note: A planed and dressed 4 x 10 wood beam has actual dimensions of $3^{1}/_{2}$ in. x $9^{1}/_{4}$ in. (90 mm x 235 mm).

*Solution:* The load on a linear element such as a beam is expressed in terms of the load on its unit length. Therefore, we will calculate the dead load on 1 ft length of the beam. (In the SI system, a length of 1 m of beam is considered in place of 1 ft).

The tributary area for a 1 ft length of beam = 6 ft$^2$, shown by shaded area in Figure 2.5. All of the gravity load acting on this area of the floor will be supported by the 1 ft length of the beam.

From Appendix IV, the density of southern pine = 37 lb/ft$^3$. Hence, self weight of (1 ft length of) the beam = [1 x (3.5/12) x (9.25/12)] 37 = 8.3 lb.

Thickness of the deck = 1.5/12 = 0.125 ft. Hence, weight of the deck = (0.125 x 6)37 = 27.8 lb.

The total dead load on the beam = self weight of the beam + weight of the deck = 8.3 + 27.8 = 36.1 lb.

Since the above load is carried by a 1 ft length of the beam, it is expressed as 36.1 lb/ft (or 36.1 per running foot or 36.1 lb per lineal ft).

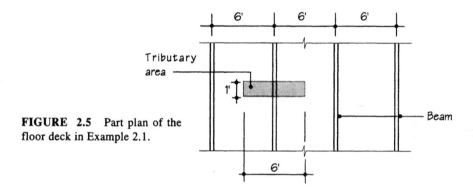

**FIGURE 2.5** Part plan of the floor deck in Example 2.1.

**Example 2.2***

Determine the dead load of a typical residential floor constructed of 2 x 12 nominal Douglas fir floor joists spaced 16 in. (405 mm) on center. The subfloor consists of $^{5}/_{8}$ in. (16 mm) thick plywood and a $^{1}/_{4}$ in. (6 mm) thick hardboard underlayment. Vinyl tiles are used as floor finish and the ceiling consists of $^{1}/_{2}$ in. (13 mm) thick gypsum wallboard, Figure 2.6.

Note: A (nominal) 2 x 12 floor joist has actual dimensions of $1^{1}/_{2}$ in. x $11^{1}/_{4}$ in. (38 mm x 285 mm).

*Solution:* The load on a two dimensional element such as a floor deck (or slab) is expressed in terms of the load on its unit area. Thus, we will calculate

---

* May be omitted on first reading.

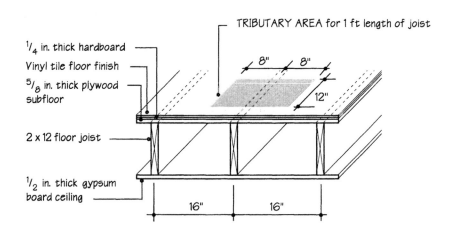

**FIGURE 2.6** Section through a floor in a wood frame building. Refers to Example 2.2.

the load of 1 ft$^2$ of the floor. The simplest way to do this is to consider the tributary area of 1 ft length of a joist and calculate all the loads acting on this area.

The tributary area of 1 ft length of a joist = 1 x 16/12 = 1.33 ft$^2$.

Density of Douglas fir = 34 lb/ ft$^3$ (Table IV.1, Appendix IV). Hence, the weight of floor joist = [1.5/12 x 11.25/12 x 1] 34 = 4.0 lb.

With the densities of plywood, hardboard and vinyl tile floor obtained from Table IV.2, Appendix IV:

Weight of (1.33 ft$^2$ ) plywood subfloor, $^5/_8$ in. thick  = (5 x 0.4)(1.33) = 2.7 lb.

Weight of (1.33 ft$^2$ ) hardboard underlayment, $^1/_4$ in. thick = (2 x 0.4)(1.33) = 1.1 lb.

Weight of (1.33 ft$^2$) vinyl floor tiles = 1.0 x (1.33) = 1.3 lb.

Weight of (1.33 ft$^2$) gypsum board, $^1/_2$ in. thick  = (4 x 0.55)(1.33) = 2.9 lb.

Total dead load of floor = 4.0 + 2.7 + 1.1 + 1.3 + 2.9 = 12.0 lb.

The above load refers to 1.33 ft$^2$ of floor area. Hence, the dead load of 1 ft$^2$ of floor = 12.0/1.33 = 9.0 lb. Since it is the load of 1 ft$^2$ of floor area, it is expressed as 9.0 psf.

This is an important result since the dead load of a floor in a conventional wood frame building is generally assumed as 10 psf (500 Pa).

*Alternative solution*: A simpler method to solve this problem is to add the weights of 1 ft$^2$ of all sheet materials of the floor system: plywood, hardboard underlayment, vinyl tiles and gypsum board. These weights are:

|                 |              |         |
|-----------------|--------------|---------|
| Vinyl tiles     |              | 1.0 lb  |
| Hardboard       | 2 x 0.4 =    | 0.8 lb  |
| Plywood         | 5 x 0.4 =    | 2.0 lb  |
| Gypsum board    | 5 x 0.55 =   | 2.2 lb  |
| Total           |              | 6.0 lb  |

To the above total weight we add the weight of the floor joist. The weight of 1 ft length of floor joist has already been determined as 4.0 lb. Since a 1 ft length of floor joist carries 1.33 ft$^2$ of floor, the weight of the floor joist that contributes to 1 ft$^2$ of the floor = 4.0/1.33 = 3.0 lb.

Hence, the dead load of 1 ft$^2$ of floor = 6.0 + 3.0 = 9.0 lb.

## 2.3 FLOOR LIVE LOAD

Although the dead load is a permanent load on the structure, live load is defined as the load whose magnitude and placement changes with time. Such loads are due to the weights of people (animals, if the building houses animals), furniture, movable equipment and stored materials. Live loads are further divided into *floor live load* and *roof live load*. Floor live load depends on the occupancy and the use of the building and is therefore also called the *occupancy load*. Evidently, floor live load is different for different occupancies. For instance, the floor live load for a library stack room must be higher than the floor live load for a library reading room, which in turn is higher than the floor live load for an apartment building.

Floor live loads are determined by aggregating the loads of all people, furniture and movable equipment that may possibly result from the particular occupancy. Safety considerations require that the worst expected situation must be considered so that the structure is designed for the maximum possible live load that may be placed on it. In other words, the probability that the live load actually placed on the structure during its lifetime will exceed that for which the building has been designed should be negligibly small.

Based on a large number of surveys, floor live loads for various commonly encountered occupancies such as individual dwellings, hotels, apartment buildings, libraries, office buildings, industrial structures, etc., have been determined, and are contained in building code tables. Table 2.1 is one such table. For instance, the floor live load for a library stack room is given as 125 psf, for a library reading room, 60 psf and for an apartment building, 40 psf. Note that these are the minimum floor live loads for which the building must be designed. Even if the actual live load on the floor is smaller, it must be designed for the minimum live load specified by the building code.

Floor live load values of Table 2.1 are conservative and in most situations, the actual loads are smaller than those given. However, the architect or the engineer must recognize unusual situations which may lead to a greater actual load than the one specified in the code. In such a situation, the higher anticipated load should be used. Additionally, if the live load for an occupancy not included in building code tables is to be obtained, the architect or the structural engineer must determine it from first principles, taking into account all the loads that may be expected on the structure. Most building codes require such live load values to be approved by the building official.

Floor live loads are usually assumed to be uniformly distributed over the entire floor area. However, an absolutely uniform distribution is seldom obtained in practice. Building codes therefore recommend that the effects of live load concentration must be investigated in those occupancies where live load concentration may be critical to design. These occupancies are parking garages (where loads are concentrated on vehicle tires), libraries, offices,

**Table 2.1  Minimum Floor Live Loads — Uniform Load and Concentrated Load**

| Category | Description | Uniform load (psf) | Concentrated load[1] (lbs) |
|---|---|---|---|
| Access floor system | Office use | 50 | 2,000 |
| | Computer use | 100 | 2,000 |
| Armories | | 150 | 0 |
| Assembly areas and auditoriums | Fixed seating areas | 50 | 0 |
| | Movable seating areas | 100 | 0 |
| | Stage areas and enclosed platforms | 125 | 0 |
| Cornices, marquees and residential balconies | | 60 | 0 |
| Exit facilities | | 100 | 0 |
| Garages | General storage and/or repair | 100 | |
| Private or pleasure type motor vehicle storage | | 50 | |
| Hospitals | Wards and rooms | 40 | 1,000 |
| Libraries | Reading rooms | 60 | 1,000 |
| | Stack rooms | 125 | 1,500 |
| Manufacturing | Light | 75 | 2,000 |
| | Heavy | 125 | 3,000 |
| Offices | | 50 | 2,000 |
| Printing plants | Press rooms | 150 | 2,000 |
| | Composing and linotype rooms | 100 | 2,000 |
| Residential dwellings, apartments and hotel guest rooms | | 40 | 1,000 |
| Restrooms | Same as the occupancy but not to exceed 50 psf | | |
| Reviewing stands, grandstands, bleachers and folding and telescoping seats | | 100 | 0 |
| Roof decks | Same as the area or type of occupancy accomodated | | |
| Schools | Classrooms | 40 | 1,000 |
| Sidewalks and driveways | Public access | 250 | |
| Storage | Light | 125 | |
| | Heavy | 250 | |
| Stores | Retail or wholesale | 100 | 3,000 |
| Pedestrian bridges and walkways | | 100 | |

Source: Reference 2.2 with permission.  Multiply values in lbs by 0.0045 to obtain values in kN.  Multiply values in psf by 0.048 to obtain values in kPa.

[1] For blank spaces in this column see original table.

schools and hospitals.  Apartments, hotels, individual residences, assembly buildings (auditoriums, concert halls, grandstands) and exit areas of all buildings do not require investigation for concentrated loads, Table 2.1.

In situations where the effect of live load concentration is to be investigated, it is done by assuming that a concentrated load of a specified magnitude can be placed on any 2.5 feet (0.75 m) square of floor area.  The building must be designed for the concentrated load or uniform load distribution, whichever creates worse effect (greater stresses).  It is to be assumed that both the concentrated load and uniform load act separately, not together.

**Example 2.3**
Determine the total gravity load (dead load + live load) on the floor of Example 2.2. The floor is part of an apartment building.

*Solution*: The dead load of the floor = 10 psf, Example 2.2.
　　　Live load on a residential floor = 40 psf, Table 2.1.
　　　Hence, the total gravity load (dead load + live load) = 50 psf.

## 2.4 ROOF LIVE LOAD

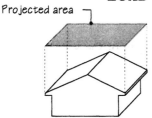

Projected area

**FIGURE 2.7** Horizontal projected area of roof.

The live load on a roof is due to repair personnel and other incidental loads caused by temporary storage of construction or repair materials and equipment on the roof. The maximum roof live load is generally given as 20 psf (0.96 kPa) acting on the horizontal projected area of the roof, Figure 2.7. This applies to a roof which will not be used as a floor in the future. If a flat roof is provided and the building is expected to be extended vertically in the future, the roof live load must be the floor live load for the anticipated future occupancy. Additionally, if the roof is to be landscaped, the load due to landscaping must be considered as a dead load on the floor.

## 2.5 SNOW LOAD

The roof is designed for either the roof live load or the snow load, whichever is greater. The reason is that in the event of full snow load on a roof, the roof is not likely to be accessed by repair or construction crew to impose live load on it. Like the roof live load, snow load is also expressed in terms of the horizontal projected area of the roof.

For a given location, the snow load on a flat roof must obviously be related to the snow load on the ground. In fact, the flat roof snow load should theoretically be equal to the ground snow load. However, records of measurements of snow deposits on roofs have shown that less snow is present on flat roofs than on the ground because wind blows the snow off the roofs and some snow slides down. Snow load on flat roofs in open areas (i.e., areas which are not obstructed by wind-shielding elements such as higher structures, terrain and trees) can be as low as half that on the nearby ground.

In this text, we shall adopt a conservative approach and assume that the flat roof snow load is equal to the ground snow load. This approach has been assumed by (the main provisions of) the Uniform Building Code.

### 2.5.1 Design Snow Load on a Sloping Roof

Since the snow will slide off a sloping roof, the snow load on a sloping roof must be less than the flat roof snow load. Building codes permit the reduction of snow load on sloping roofs according to the following relationship provided that the flat roof snow load (i.e., the ground snow load) is greater than 20 psf and the slope of the roof is greater than 20 degrees.

$$R_s = \left[ \frac{S}{40} - 0.5 \right] (\theta - 20^\circ) \tag{2.1}$$

For S > 20 psf and $\theta$ > 20°
where   $R_s$ = reduction in roof snow load (in psf)
            S   = ground snow load (in psf )
            $\theta$   = roof pitch (in degrees)

Note that for the reduction to apply, both conditions must be satisfied: (i) ground snow load must be in excess of 20 psf and (ii) the pitch of the roof must be greater than 20 degrees. If either of these two conditions is not met, no reduction is permitted and the roof is designed for the same snow load as the ground snow load.

Since the design snow load on a roof is a function of the ground snow load, the latter must represent the worst condition for the location. In other words, the ground snow load value used in calculating roof snow load must be the maximum expected value for the location. The most reliable and accurate source for obtaining this information is the building department of the city. However, reasonably precise values for most locations (except the Rocky Mountains and some areas to the west of them) can be obtained from a ground snow load map of the country which is included in building codes.

The ground snow load values obtained from building codes represent a 2% annual probability of being exceeded, i.e., these values are expected to recur every 50 years. Ground snow loads for a few locations in the United States, based on a 50-year recurrence interval, are given in Table 2.2.

Snow load is usually considered as uniformly distributed on roofs. However, a nonuniform distribution may result from snow drifts which can cause the accumulation of snow in valleys, at the base of parapet walls and in roofs with offsets, Figure 2.8. Accumulation may also result from snow sliding on a roof from adjacent taller buildings. Building codes require investigation of such concentrations since they may result in larger member sizes than those obtained by considering uniform snow load distribution.

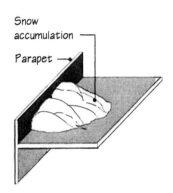

Snow accumulation ——

Parapet ——•

**FIGURE 2.8** Snow accumulation near the parapet of a flat roof.

---

**Example 2.4**

Determine the design snow load on the roof of a building in Buffalo, New York. The pitch of the roof is 7:12, Figure 2.9.

*Solution*: Since roof pitch = 7:12, roof slope ($\theta$) = $\tan^{-1}$ [7/12] = 30.3°.
        Ground snow load (S) = 39 psf, Table 2.2.
        Snow load reduction ($R_s$) = [S/40 - 0.5][$\theta$ - 20°] = [39/40 - 0.5][30.3° - 20° ] = 4.9 psf.
        Hence, the design snow load on the roof = 39 - 4.9 = 34.1 psf.

**Table 2.2   Ground Snow Loads at Selected Locations**

| Location | Snow load (psf) | Location | Snow load (psf) |
|---|---|---|---|
| Huntsville, Alabama | 5 | Jackson, Mississippi | 3 |
| Flagstaff, Arizona | 48 | Kansas City, Missouri | 18 |
| Little Rock, Arkansas | 6 | Concord, New Hampshire | 63 |
| Mt. Shasta, California | 62 | Newark, New Jersey | 15 |
| Denver, Colorado | 18 | Albuquerque, New Mexico | 4 |
| | | | |
| Hartford, Connecticut | 33 | Buffalo, New York | 39 |
| Wilmington, Delaware | 16 | New York City | 16 |
| Atlanta, Georgia | 3 | Charlotte, North Carolina | 11 |
| Boise, Idaho | 9 | Fargo, North Dakota | 41 |
| Chicago, Illinois | 22 | Columbus, Ohio | 11 |
| | | | |
| Indianapolis, Indiana | 22 | Oklahoma City, Oklahoma | 8 |
| Des Moines, Iowa | 22 | Portland, Oregon | 8 |
| Wichita, Kansas | 14 | Philadelphia, Pennsylvania | 14 |
| Jackson, Kentucky | 18 | Providence, Rhode Island | 23 |
| Shreveport, Louisiana | 3 | Memphis, Tennessee | 6 |
| | | | |
| Portland, Maine | 60 | Dallas, Texas | 3 |
| Baltimore, Maryland | 22 | Salt Lake City, Utah | 11 |
| Boston, Massachusetts | 34 | Seattle, Washington | 18 |
| Detroit, Michigan | 18 | Charleston, West Virginia | 18 |
| Minneapolis, Minnesota | 51 | Madison, Wisconsin | 35 |

Source:  Reference 2.1 with permission.  Multiply values in psf by 0.048 to obtain values in kPa.

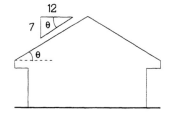

**FIGURE 2.9**   Refers to Example 2.4.

### Example 2.5

Determine the design snow load on the roof of a building in Denver, Colorado. Roof slope = 6:12.

*Solution*:  Ground snow load for Denver, Colorado = 18 psf, Table 2.2.  Since this is less than 20 psf, no reduction is permissible.  Hence, the design snow load = 18 psf.

**2.6  OTHER ROOF LOADS**

Although roofs are designed to have adequate drainage so that no ponding of water occurs, load resulting from accidental ponding from melted snow or rain water must be considered as a possibility.  The blocking of drains may occur due to wind-blown debris aggregating on the roof or the formation of ice dams near the drains.

Long-span flat roofs are particularly vulnerable to ponding since, being flexible, they deflect under the weight of water.  This deflection leads to ponding which leads to additional water on the roof, and that leads to additional deflection which increases the ponding further.  If adequate stiffness is not provided in the roof, the progressive increase of deflection can cause excessive load on the roof. Water ponding has been the cause of complete collapse of several long-span roofs.

Generally, roofs with slope greater than $1/4$ in. to one foot (nearly 1:50 slope) are not subjected to ponding unless roof drains get blocked. Building codes mandate $1/4$ in. to one foot as the minimum slope required for roofs, which, apart from providing positive drainage, also helps to increase the life and improve the performance of roof membranes. Additionally, building codes require that in addition to primary drains, buildings must be provided with secondary (overflow) drains. The secondary drains must be 2 in. above the primary drains so that if the primary drainage system gets blocked, the secondary system will be able to drain the water off the roof. The load of water collected on the roof deck due to the blocked primary drainage system must be taken into account in the design of a flat or low-slope roof.

## 2.7 STATIC vs DYNAMIC LOADS

As described earlier, live loads vary with time but their variation is gradual and relatively small in magnitude. Consequently, they do not create any vibrations in structures. A load which does not create vibrations in a structure is called a *static load*. Gravity loads (dead loads and live loads) are static loads because: (i) they vary slowly in magnitude and (ii) buildings have a great deal of rigidity in the vertical direction — the direction in which the gravity loads act. Gravity loads therefore do not create any significant vibrational effects in buildings.

A load which may induce vibrations in buildings is called a *dynamic load*. For a load to create vibrations in buildings, two conditions must exist: (i) its magnitude must change somewhat abruptly, i.e., it must cause impact loads on the structure and (ii) the structure must be flexible. Because of gusts, wind creates abrupt changes in wind pressure, and earthquake excitation is virtually instantaneous. Thus, wind and earthquake loads behave as dynamic loads. Additionally, a building (particularly a tall and slender building) is quite flexible in the horizontal direction. To wind and earthquake loads which are primarily horizontal loads, a building behaves as a flag pole cantilevered off the ground. When subjected to a rapidly changing load, the building vibrates like a pendulum.

Another important difference between a static and a dynamic load is that while the effect of a certain static load is the same on all structures, the effect of a dynamic load generally varies from structure to structure. This is due to the complex interaction between the magnitude and the variational characteristics of the load on one hand, and the dynamic characteristics of the structure on the other, such as its weight, relative stiffness and the frequency of vibration. Thus, a dynamic load is more difficult to quantify than a static load. However, in order to simplify load determination, building codes permit the replacement of a dynamic load by an *equivalent static load*.

An equivalent static load is a load whose effect on the structure is approximately the same as that of a dynamic load. Although the dynamic load is defined by its magnitude and its variational characteristics, the equivalent static load is defined by its magnitude only.

## 2.8 WIND LOADS

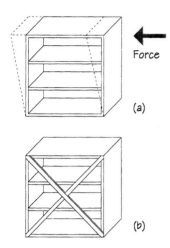

Force

(a)

(b)

**FIGURE 2.10** (a) A book rack constructed of several horizontal shelves supported on two vertical supports will move sideways ("rack") when pushed by a force, as shown by dotted lines. (b) The racking of the shelves can be prevented by diagonal braces as shown, or by sheet bracing.

Although wind loads are primarily horizontal, they also exert upward force on horizontal elements such as flat and low-slope roofs. Resistance against upward wind force is provided by anchoring the building to its foundations. Resistance against horizontal loads requires the use of stiffening elements. These stiffening elements are commonly referred to as *wind bracing elements*.

Wind bracing requirement for a building is precisely the same as the requirement for either diagonal bracing or sheet bracing on a book rack. If a book rack is constructed of several shelves mounted on two side supports, it will be found quite adequate to carry the gravity load from the books but such an assembly will be unstable. When acted upon by a horizontal force from either direction, it will move sideways (or "rack") as shown by dotted lines in Figure 2.10(a). The sideway motion of the rack can be prevented by diagonally bracing one of its faces, Figure 2.10(b). An alternative method of stiffening the book rack is to apply a sheet material instead of diagonal braces. This method is more commonly used since it provides greater lateral stiffening than diagonal braces and also prevents books from falling off the back of the shelves.

For buildings, several methods of wind bracing are used depending on the functional and aesthetic constraints of the building and the magnitude of wind loads. Since wind loads increase with the height of a building, stiffening of the building against wind loads becomes increasingly important as the height of the building increases. In fact, the design of tall buildings is heavily dominated by wind bracing requirements.

Architects have sometimes used this structural requirement as a forceful aesthetic expression. Two successful examples of this are the John Hancock Tower and the Sears Tower, both in Chicago. The John Hancock Building uses diagonal braces on all its four facades, Figure 2.11(a). The Sears Tower uses the concept of "bundled tubes" to provide lateral stiffening. The number of tubes bundled together reduces from nine at the base of the tower to two at the top, Figure 2.11(b).

### 2.8.1 Mathematical Procedure vs Wind Tunnel Testing

Two methods are available for determining wind loads on buildings: (i) the mathematical procedure, and (ii) the wind tunnel test. The mathematical procedure is most commonly used, and is the one described here. This procedure may be used for all buildings except those that are sensitive to aerodynamic effects, for which wind tunnel testing is mandated. According to the Uniform Building Code[1], wind loads on following building types must be obtained from wind tunnel tests :

- A building with height greater than 400 ft.
- A flexible building. A flexible building is one which has significant dynamic amplification in its response to wind forces. It is defined as a building in which the height-to-width ratio is greater than 5.
- A building with an (aerodynamically) unusual form.

---

[1] The mathematical procedure for determining wind loads described in this chapter is as per the Uniform Building Code. It is a simplified version of the wind load provisions of ASCE 7 document (Reference 2.1).

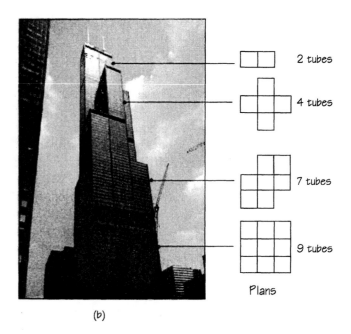

(a)                                                    (b)

**FIGURE 2.11** (a) John Hancock Tower in Chicago. (b) Sears Tower in Chicago.

### 2.8.2 Wind Direction

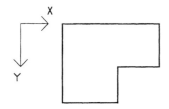

**FIGURE 2.12** Wind loads on a building with a rectilinear plan are determined assuming that the wind may blow from either of the two main directions: the X or the Y direction.

The wind may blow horizontally from any direction. It may also move up or down or along an inclined path. However, being a fluid, wind exerts pressure on building surfaces so that wind loads are assumed to act perpendicular to building surfaces.

In the case of a building with a rectilinear profile, the load effects are examined only for the wind blowing along the two main directions of the building, although in reality the wind may blow along any direction. For example, with respect to the building of Figure 2.12, the wind loads are determined assuming that the wind will blow either along the X or the Y direction. If the building, as a whole, has adequate strength to resist wind loads from both the X and the Y directions, it will be adequate against wind loads from any other direction.

Additionally, no reduction in wind loads due to the shielding effect of adjacent structures is permitted. For example, in the building of Figure 2.12, the outstanding leg of the L-shape building will tend to shield the part of the structure behind it, causing some reduction in wind loads on the shielded portion. Similar reductions may be caused by adjacent structures. Such reductions are difficult to estimate and are consequently ignored.

### 2.8.3 Induced Pressure and Suction

Wind movement causes inward force (positive pressure) on the windward wall and outward force (suction or negative pressure) on the other walls (leeward wall and side walls) of a building. The largest pressures act on the windward and leeward walls; on the side walls, the pressures are usually smaller[2], Figure 2.13(a). Since a wall must be designed to withstand both the maximum positive pressure and maximum negative pressure, we usually consider the windward and leeward walls only in determining wind loads on buildings.

Wind tunnel tests have shown that on the windward wall, wind pressure varies with height, increasing as the height increases. On the leeward wall, there is no appreciable change in pressure with respect to height. Hence, uniform pressure is assumed to act on the leeward wall, Figure 2.13(b).

A roof may be subjected to positive pressure or negative pressure (suction) depending on its slope. If the wind blows parallel to the ridge, the roof is entirely under suction, Figure 2.14(a). For wind blowing perpendicular to the ridge, the leeward slope is always subjected to suction. The windward slope, on the other hand, comes under suction for a low-slope roof, which turns to pressure as the slope increases, Figure 2.14(b). A flat roof is always subjected to suction.

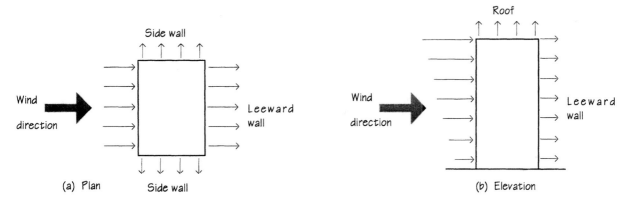

**FIGURE 2.13**   Wind pressures exerted on the walls of a rectilinear building: (a) in plan, and (b) in elevation. Note that on the windward wall, wind pressure increases with increasing height. On a leeward wall, the pressure is approximately constant over the entire height of the wall.

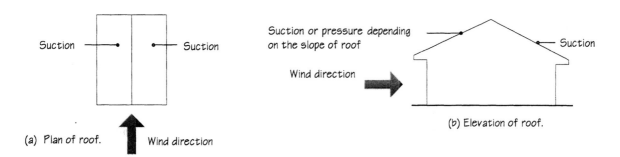

**FIGURE 2.14**   Wind pressures on a sloping roof.

---

[2] The wind load on the side walls of a partially enclosed building may be higher than on its windward or leeward walls.

### 2.8.4  Components and Primary Structural Frame

We have already mentioned the dynamic nature of wind loads, i.e., their variation with respect to time (temporal variation). In addition to temporal variation, wind loads exhibit a great deal of spatial variation. In other words, the actual wind loads on a building's facade vary from point to point. For example, significantly larger pressures are obtained at the edges and corners of a building facade than in the central part. The spatial variation implies that the components of buildings which have small tributary areas must be designed for greater load than those with large tributary areas. This is because there is more averaging of pressure on larger areas than on smaller ones. In recognition of this fact, wind loads on buildings are considered under two separate headings:
- Elements and components of structures, and
- Primary structural frame.

The elements and components of a structure refer to those parts of the building which help to transfer wind loads to the primary structural frame. They include all of the cladding elements of the building such as the enclosing walls, roof, and external doors and windows.

Primary structural frame refers to the entire structural assemblage that helps to resist wind loads. That is why it is also called the *lateral load resisting system* (LLRS). In a frame structure, the LLRS consists of columns and beams, together with floors and the roof. (The floors and the roof are generally referred to as *diaphragms*.) In a load-bearing masonry or wood structure, walls and the floor and roof diaphragms perform this function.

The design wind load on LLRS is based on the average pressure ignoring the effects of spatial pressure variations. There is also an additional difference between the LLRS and the components. A component is designed to withstand positive pressure or negative pressure (suction) acting on it separately because a component will be subjected to one or the other at a time, depending on whether it is the windward wall or a nonwindward wall. The LLRS, on the other hand, must be designed to withstand the effects of pressure and suction acting simultaneously — pressure on the windward face and suction on the leeward face.

Architects are usually not involved in the design of LLRS. Therefore, the following discussion will be restricted to determining the approximate wind loads on building components only, such as windows, curtain walls, roofing membranes etc.

### 2.8.5  Enclosed, Unenclosed and Partially Enclosed Structures

Building envelopes are not perfectly airtight. They are subject to air infiltration and exfiltration. Additionally, they have windows and doors which may be partially open, left open or broken by flying debris. Because of openings, the interior of a building may also be subjected to forces created by wind. The interior of a building may be subjected to pressure or suction depending on whether the openings are primarily on the windward or the leeward wall, Figure 2.15.

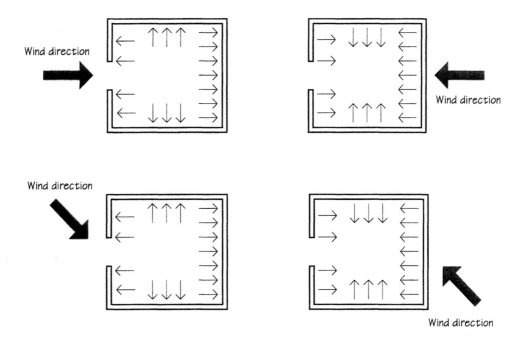

**FIGURE 2.15** Openings on one face of a building tend to "cup" the wind, creating pressure or suction on interior surfaces. This internal pressure is in addition to the pressure or suction created by wind on external surfaces.

Internal forces are particularly critical in buildings which have large openings on one side, or two adjacent sides, as these tend to "cup" the wind. Buildings such as these are called *partially enclosed structures* and include aircraft hangars and garages. The distinction between a partially enclosed and an *enclosed structure* is only applicable in determining wind loads on components of structure, not on LLRS.

In a partially enclosed structure, the outward pressure (suction) is substantially greater than in an enclosed structure. A partially enclosed structure is defined as one in which: (i) more than 15% of wall area is open on any windward side and (ii) the area of openings on all other walls is less than half the area of openings on the windward side. An unenclosed structure is one which has 85% or more openings on all sides. For the record, an enclosed structure is one that does not meet the definition of an unenclosed structure or partially enclosed structure. As we shall see in Table 2.4, enclosed and unenclosed structures are lumped together in one category. Thus, in practice, a building is classified as either partially enclosed or not.

**2.9 WIND SPEED**    Fundamental to determining wind loads on buildings is the wind speed. Obviously, buildings must be designed for the maximum probable wind speed at that location. The highest wind speeds are usually contained in tornadoes. A tornado is a rotating, funnel-shaped column of air which produces strong suction, Figure 2.16.

The suction produced in a tornado funnel lifts objects into the air like a giant suction pump. If a tornado hits a water body such as a lake or a sea, a waterspout is formed. Nearly 60% of all tornadoes are weak in intensity; 38% are strong — capable of toppling walls and blowing roofs off the buildings. Nearly 2% of tornadoes are so violent that they destroy virtually everything in their wake.

Actual measurements of wind speeds in a tornado are not available. The diameter of a tornado funnel near the ground is quite narrow, seldom exceeding 1500 ft (460 m) end-to-end, and its life span seldom exceeds a few minutes. Thus, the probability of a tornado hitting a particular building or intercepting a permanently located wind speed measuring instrumentation, such as that installed at an airport, is very small. Additionally, the destructive power of a tornado is so large that whenever a tornado has hit such measuring instruments, it has completely destroyed them. However, photogrammetric analyses of tornado movies reveal that the actual wind speeds in the center of a violent tornado may be of the order of 275 mph (440 km/h), while 85% of all tornadoes have wind speeds less than 150 mph (240 km/h)[2.3].

Tornadoes occur mainly between the latitudes of 20° and 45° and are relatively frequent in New Zealand, parts of Australia, South Africa, Argentina, India (Assam-Bangladesh region), Japan, Europe, the former Soviet Union and the United States. In the United States, the region east of the Rocky Mountains is tornado-prone, Figure 2.17. The region formed by North Texas, Oklahoma, Kansas, Iowa, Nebraska, and Missouri is particularly prone to tornadoes.

Because of the extremely small probability that a violent tornado will hit a particular building, design wind speeds adopted by building codes for various locations do not reflect the wind speeds obtained in tornadoes. Tornadoes have a 0.02% probability of occurring at a given location in a year, i.e., a recurrence interval of 500 years. Design wind speeds, as stated earlier, are based on a 50-year recurrence interval. In spite of the fact that design wind

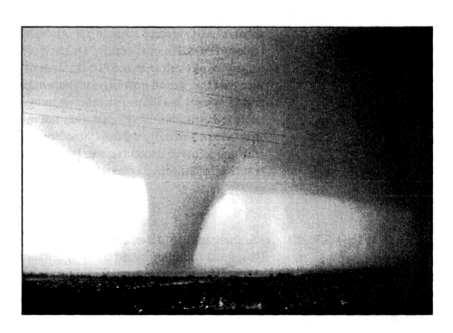

**FIGURE 2.16** Tornado in Seymour, Texas, on April 1979. Photo by: National Severe Storms Laboratory, National Oceanic and Atmospheric Administration, Norman, Oklahoma.

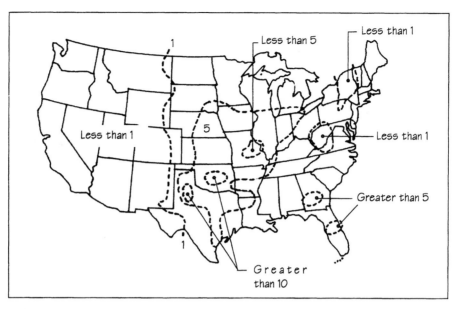

**FIGURE 2.17** Map showing average number of annual tornado occurences per 10,000 sq miles (26,000 sq km). Toward the west of "1" contour line, tornado occurence is less than 1 per year per 10,000 sq miles. Reference 2.3, page 465 with permission.

speeds do not account for tornadoes, buildings have to be designed to resist tornadoes in tornado-prone locations. For this purpose, sufficient empirical information is available to design and construct tornado-resistant buildings

After tornadoes, hurricanes represent the next most severe wind storms. Known as typhoons or tropical cyclones in Asia, hurricanes pose greater life safety and economic hazards to buildings and urban infrastructure than tornadoes. A hurricane covers a much larger area than a tornado, up to 600 miles (950 km) in diameter, and may have a lifespan of one week or more. Most damage from hurricanes occurs in coastal areas, and is caused primarily by the uplifting of roofs, windborne debris and uprooted trees or branches of trees. Tidal surges caused by hurricanes can be more devastating than wind-created damage.

As a hurricane travels inland, it loses energy and degenerates into a tropical rain storm. In the United States, hurricanes develop over warm areas in the Atlantic Ocean, Caribbean Sea, Gulf of Mexico and the northeastern Pacific Ocean. Although hurricane-induced property damage has increased over the years in the United States due to the migration of population toward coastal areas, the loss of life has decreased due to improvements in forecasting and warning systems.

Peak wind speeds in a hurricane can be as high as 190 mph (300 km/h). However, since the peak wind speed occurs for a short duration, usually only a few seconds, engineers use the concept of fastest mile wind speed instead of the peak wind speed for design purposes. Fastest mile wind speed is defined as the average speed of one mile of air passing a point. Thus, a fastest mile wind speed of 60 mph at a point means that a mile of wind passed that point in one minute. Similarly, a fastest mile wind speed of 120 mph implies that a mile of wind passed a point in 30 seconds.

### 2.9.1 Design Wind Speed

Wind speeds for several selected locations are continuously being recorded in the United States. The fastest-mile wind speed at a location which has not been exceeded in the past 50 years is defined as the *basic wind speed* for that location. It is this wind speed[3] that is used in determining the design wind loads on buildings. Like the ground snow load, basic wind speed has 2% annual probability of being exceeded, i.e., a 50-year recurrence value.

A contour map giving basic wind speed values for the United States is shown in Figure 2.18. Map values are to be used as a general guide. Local building codes may specify a higher value, in which case this higher value must be used as the basic wind speed. For example, some cities along the coastal belt of Florida specify the 100-year recurrence wind speed as the basic wind speed for the location.

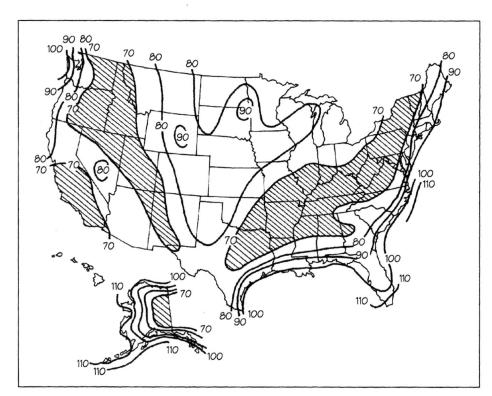

**FIGURE 2.18** Basic wind speed map of the United States showing wind speeds in miles per hour. Inside hatched areas, wind speed is approximately 70 mph. Multiply values in mph by 1.61 to obtain values in km/h. Source: Reference 2.2 with permission. For greater detail, see the original map.

---

[3] The United States National Weather Service no longer keeps a record of the fastest mile wind speeds. Instead, records are now maintained for 3-second gust speeds. Therefore, building codes and standards are changing to defining the basic wind speed as the 3-second gust speed at a location. The 1997 version of the Uniform Building Code is expected to change accordingly, which will change code provisions, but the overall wind loads on a building will not change significantly. The difference between 3-second gust speeds and the fastest mile wind speeds is given on the following page.

## FASTEST MILE WIND SPEED vs 3-SECOND GUST SPEED

One of the important characteristics of wind is its turbulence, implying that wind speed varies continuously. Because of this variation, one must deal with some sort of average wind speed. The question now arises as to what time interval should be used for the average speed. A time interval that is commonly used to assess wind energy utilization potential of a location is one year. For instance, the average annual wind speed for Dallas, Texas, is nearly 10 miles per hour.

Although the average annual wind speed may be a good index of wind energy utilization potential, it cannot be used for the structural design of buildings. For structural design, one must obviously use the peak wind speed averaged over a short time interval. The shorter the time interval, the greater the average peak wind speed.

The longest averaging time interval used for structural design purposes is 1 hour. The Canadian wind load design provisions use 1-hour average peak speeds. The fastest mile wind speed concept used in the United States, however, does not have a constant averaging time interval. By its very definition, the averaging time interval for the fastest mile wind speed varies with wind speed itself, and is equal to (3600/V) seconds, where V is the fastest mile wind speed. Thus, if the fastest mile wind speed is 60 mph, the averaging interval is 60 seconds. If the fastest mile wind speed is 120 mph, the averaging interval is 30 seconds.

In fact, one of the major weaknesses of the fastest mile concept is its variable averaging time interval. Another weakness of the concept is that the structural behavior of most buildings is sensitive to peak gust speed of nearly 1 second duration, while in the fastest mile concept, the averaging interval varies form nearly 60 seconds to 30 seconds. In response to the above criticism, wind load design provisions in the United States are changing to defining the basic wind speed as the peak wind speed averaged over 3 seconds. Thus, the basic wind speed in the 1997 version of the Uniform Building Code will no longer be the fastest mile speed, but the 3-second gust speed. Due to this change, the provisions to determine design wind loads will change somewhat, but the overall design wind loads will be approximately the same.

There is an empirical relationship between the fastest mile wind speed and 3-second gust speed. Approximately, the 3-second gust speed is 15 to 18 mph higher than the fastest mile speed, as shown in the following table[2.8]. The 3-second gust speed map of the United States is given below. Observe the simplicity of the map below. Research has indicated that only the hurricane prone areas of the United States have defined contours.

| Fastest mile speed | 3-second gust speed |
|---|---|
| 70 | 85 |
| 80 | 96 |
| 90 | 106 |
| 100 | 117 |
| 110 | 127 |
| 120 | 138 |
| 130 | 148 |

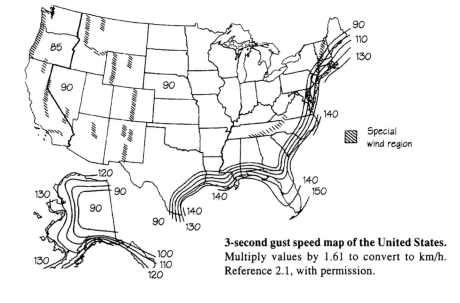

**3-second gust speed map of the United States.** Multiply values by 1.61 to convert to km/h. Reference 2.1, with permission.

### 2.9.2 Wind Stagnation Pressure

Like all other fluids, air has mass (a 10 ft x 10 ft x 10 ft volume of air weighs nearly 76.5 lb). Thus, moving air possesses kinetic energy which is converted to pressure when it meets an obstruction. The pressure exerted by moving air can be obtained from Bernoulli's equation for fluid flow. A simple mathematical manipulation of Bernoulli's equation gives the pressure exerted by wind. Thus:

$$q_s = 0.00256 \, V^2 \qquad\qquad (2.2)$$

In the above equation, V is wind speed in miles per hour (mph) and $q_s$ is the wind stagnation pressure in psf. Wind stagnation pressure is the pressure exerted by air on an obstruction which brings it to stagnation — zero speed. Theoretically, such an obstruction must be of infinite dimensions because in the case of a finite obstruction, such as a building, the air will not come to complete stagnation but will flow around it. The point where the flow divides itself in two or more parts on a finite obstruction is the stagnation point because at this point the wind speed is zero. Wind pressure at the stagnation point (or on an infinitely large obstruction) is the wind stagnation pressure.

In the SI system of units, wind speed is expressed in km/h and pressure in kPa. In that case, the constant in Equation (2.2) becomes 0.000047 in place of 0.00256.

By international agreement, wind speeds are measured at a height of nearly 33 ft (10 m) above the ground. Thus, V refers to the basic wind speed at 33 ft height, and hence $q_s$ gives wind stagnation pressure at this height. The primary reason for choosing 33 ft height is that below this height, and particularly below 15 ft, the turbulence is so chaotic that the measured wind speeds are too random to provide us with any useful information.

---

### Example 2.6

Calculate the wind stagnation pressure ($q_s$) for a basic wind speed of 80 mph.

*Solution*: From Equation (2.2), $q_s = 0.00256 \, V^2$
$q_s = 0.00256 \, (80)^2 = 16.4$ psf.

---

### 2.9.3 Design Wind Load

Note that $q_s$ is not the design wind load, since the design wind load is also affected by several other factors. One of these factors is the height of the building surface above the ground. (Note that $q_s$ refers to the pressure at a height of 33 ft above the ground). Other factors are: gustiness of wind, the type of terrain, and the size and type of building component. To account for these factors, the following equation is used to obtain the design wind pressure (p) as a function of $q_s$.

$$p = (C_e \, C_q \, I) \, q_s \qquad\qquad (2.3)$$

where $C_e$, $C_q$ and $I$ are coefficients which modify the value of $q_s$.

Coefficient $C_e$ is called the *combined height, exposure and gust factor coefficient*. Exposure refers to the extent of irregularities in the terrain such as those due to trees, buildings and other obstructions. The greater the extent of terrain irregularities, the smaller the wind load. In other words, a building built in a location which has ground obstructions such as forest cover, buildings and other large size irregularities is subjected to a smaller wind load than a building located in an open terrain. Exposure is classified under three categories: exposure categories B, C and D.

Exposure B refers to a (built-up) terrain. This terrain has buildings, a forest, or other irregularities 20 ft or more in height, covering at least 20% of the area extending one mile or more from the site. Most buildings are sited in exposure category B. Exposure category C defines a (clear) terrain which is flat and generally open (openness extending for at least one-half mile in any full quadrant). Exposure D is the severest exposure, commonly found near a coastline of a sea or a large lake. It is defined as a flat and unobstructed terrain facing a large water body one mile or more in width in any full quadrant.

As shown in Figure 2.13(b), the wind load on a windward wall varies with height above the ground but is constant on the leeward wall. The value of $C_e$ reflects this fact, i.e., $C_e$ varies with height for the windward wall but is assumed constant (equal to that evaluated at mean roof height of the building) for the leeward wall and the roof. Table 2.3 gives the values of $C_e$ for various heights above the ground. Note that this table extends to a height of only 400 ft since the static procedure (being described here) can be used only for buildings up to a maximum of 400 ft in height. Above this height, most buildings are subjected to dynamic effects of wind, requiring wind tunnel investigation.

Coefficient $C_q$ is called the *building pressure coefficient*. It takes into account the fact that the magnitude of wind loads on individual components of a structure (walls, roofs, eaves, parapet walls, etc.) are different. Values of $C_q$ for a few building components are given in Table 2.4.

Coefficient I, called the *importance factor*, represents an additional safety factor. For essential and hazardous facilities, the value of I is 1.15 and for all other (nonessential) facilities, I = 1.0. The purpose of the 15% enhancement in wind loads for essential facilities is that they should remain safe and usable for emergency purposes after a windstorm. Essential buildings consist of hospitals and other medical facilities, fire stations, police stations, local government disaster centers, standby power generating centers, and emergency vehicle shelters and garages.

Hazardous facilities include structures which house sufficient quantities of certain toxic or explosive substances that are dangerous to the safety of general public. For a detailed list of essential and hazardous facilities, the interested reader may refer to Reference 2.2.

The 15% enhancement of wind loads on "important" buildings through the use of the value of I effectively changes the annual probability of calculated wind load being exceeded from 2% to 1%. In other words, if we multiply the basic wind speed by 1.15, the resulting value represents a 100-year recurrence wind speed.

**Table 2.3  Combined Height, Exposure and Gust Coefficient, $C_e$**

| Height above ground (ft) | Exposure D | Exposure C | Exposure B |
|---|---|---|---|
| 0 - 15 | 1.39 | 1.06 | 0.62 |
| 20 | 1.45 | 1.13 | 0.67 |
| 25 | 1.50 | 1.19 | 0.72 |
| 30 | 1.54 | 1.23 | 0.76 |
| 40 | 1.62 | 1.31 | 0.84 |
| 60 | 1.73 | 1.43 | 0.95 |
| 80 | 1.81 | 1.53 | 1.04 |
| 100 | 1.88 | 1.61 | 1.13 |
| 120 | 1.93 | 1.67 | 1.20 |
| 160 | 2.02 | 1.79 | 1.31 |
| 200 | 2.10 | 1.87 | 1.42 |
| 300 | 2.23 | 2.05 | 1.63 |
| 400 | 2.34 | 2.19 | 1.80 |

Source:  Reference 2.2 with permission.

**Table 2.4  Pressure Coefficient, $C_q$**

| Element | Pressure coefficient, $C_q$ |
|---|---|
| Wall elements | |
| All structures | 1.2 inward |
| Enclosed/unenclosed structures | 1.2 outward |
| Partially enclosed structures | 1.6 outward |
| Parapet walls | 1.3 inward or outward |
| Wall corners | 1.5 outward, 1.2 inward |
| Roof elements | |
| Enclosed/unenclosed structure | |
| Slope < 7:12 | 1.3 outward |
| Slope 7:12 to 12:12 | 1.3 outward or inward |
| Slope >12:12 | Same as for a wall |

Source: Reference 2.2 with permission. For complete table, see the original table.

**Example  2.7**

Determine the design wind load on a curtain wall located at a height of 70 ft above the ground.  The building is located in exposure category B, basic wind speed = 80 mph, I = 1.0.  Assume that the structure is not partially enclosed.  Roof height = 150 ft.

*Solution*:  From Equation (2.3), p = $(C_e C_q I)q_s$
   $q_s$ = 16.4 psf (Example 2.6).
   $C_e$ = 1.00 at a height of 70 ft, obtained by interpolation from Table 2.3 [to be used for inward (positive) pressure on the component].
   $C_e$ = 1.28 at roof height of 150 ft, obtained by interpolation from Table 2.3 [to be used for outward (negative) pressure on the component].
   $C_q$ = 1.2 inward, and 1.2 outward, Table 2.4.
   Hence, inward pressure, $p_+$ = (1.0 x 1.2 x 1.0)16.4  =  19.7 psf.

Outward pressure, $p_ = (1.28 \times 1.2 \times 1.0)16.4 = 25.2$ psf.

Thus, the above curtain wall will be designed for an inward pressure of 19.7 psf and an outward pressure of 25.2 psf. In actual practice, it is more convenient to design the wall for the same inward and outward pressures, which in this example is 25.2 psf. In other words, in determining the wind load on a component of a building, it is more convenient to use the same value of $C_e$ (evaluated at mean roof height) for both inward and outward pressures.

**Example 2.8**

An architect is considering the use of a loose-laid, single-ply roof membrane covered with a ballast on the (flat) roof of a concert hall building located in downtown Dallas (exposure category B). Basic wind speed = 70 mph. The ballast weighs 16 psf. Is the weight of the ballast adequate to resist wind uplift on roof membrane? Assume roof height = 60 ft, I = 1.0.

*Solution*: $p = (C_e\ C_q\ I)\ q_s$
Basic wind speed for Dallas is 70 mph. Hence, $q_s = 12.5$ psf (Equation 2.2).
$C_e = 0.95$.
$C_q = 1.3$ (Table 2.4). Hence,
$p = (0.95)(1.3)(1.0)12.5 = 15.6$ psf (uplift) < weight of ballast (16.0 psf).
Hence, the weight of the ballast provided is adequate.

Calculations of Examples 2.7 and 2.8 give wind load values in the field of the curtain wall or the roof. At edges and corners of the wall or the roof, the wind loads are higher, which must be accounted for. Thus, a flat roof needs a greater weight of ballast along edge strips and corners.

**2.10 EARTHQUAKE LOADS**

A severe earthquake is one of mankind's most terrifying experiences. Regardless of where it occurs, it makes instant news headlines all over the world. In the past, earthquakes killed a large number of people. The worst recorded earthquake disaster in history occurred in China in 1976, killing more than half a million people. Today, earthquakes pose a smaller threat to life than in the past (at least in developed nations) because of our improved knowledge of constructing earthquake-resistant structures.

Statistics indicate that the current annual loss of life resulting from earthquakes is much smaller than those due to hurricanes, building fires, floods or even automobile accidents. In spite of this, an earthquake has the most adverse psychological impact on humans. Ground shaking, the most commonly associated phenomenon with earthquake, causes damages to buildings and other infrastructural facilities, Figure 2.19. Records show that the earthquakes of 1811 and 1812 in Missouri shifted the course of the Mississippi River considerably[2.4]. In addition to ground shaking, a major

**FIGURE 2.19** A railroad deformed by an earthquake. Courtesy of: Author's student.

earthquake can produce several related disasters such as landslides, surface fractures, soil liquefaction, tsunamis and fires.

Soil liquefaction usually occurs in water-saturated, sandy soils in which the particle sizes of sand are of relatively uniform size. When such soils are shaken, the water rises to the surface, resulting in loss of foundation support to buildings constructed on them. The most notable example of soil liquefaction occurred in Nigata, Japan, during the 1964 earthquake[2.5]. In this earthquake several high-rise buildings simply tipped over and fell on their facades while otherwise remaining intact.

A tsunami is caused by the physical displacement of the seabed during an earthquake which creates waves of up to 50 ft in height. So far most tsunamis have occurred in the Pacific Ocean, with Japan witnessing the largest number of them, hence its Japanese name.

Although we have made some progress toward forecasting earthquakes, we are still far from perfecting a methodology to accurately predict the location and time of the next earthquake. However, the cause of earthquakes (as to why they occur) is fairly well established.

Geologists believe that the earth's crust is divided into several individual segments called *crustal* or *tectonic plates*, Figure 2.20. These plates, floating on a molten mantle below, are constantly in motion relative to each other[2.6]. The motion is so slow that it is significant only in geological time. The relative motion in the earth's crust causes compressive, tensile or shear forces to develop, depending on whether the plates press against each other, pull apart or slip laterally under one another. When these stresses exceed the maximum capacity of the crust to absorb them, a fracture at the crust occurs. It is this fracturing or slippage, which is always sudden, that produces a shock wave known as an earthquake motion.

The plane where the fracture occurs is called a *fault*. The location where the fault originates is called the *focus*, which is generally inside the earth's

**FIGURE 2.20** Map of the earth showing major tectonic plates.

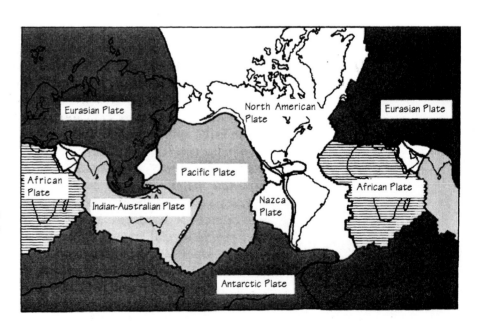

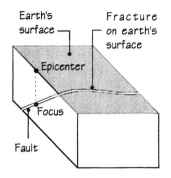

Earth's surface

Fracture on earth's surface

Epicenter

Focus

Fault

**FIGURE 2.21** Fault, focus and epicenter of an earthquake.

crust. The point directly above the focus on the earth's surface is called the *epicenter*, Figure 2.21.

The fracture on the surface of the earth may or may not be noticeable. The 1906 San Francisco (California) earthquake, however, left a deep ground rupture extending over hundreds of miles. Known as the San Andreas Fault, it stands as a distinct landmark created by the earthquake.

An earthquake may occur at any location. In fact, mild earthquakes occur quite frequently, several thousand a day, in various regions of the earth. They go unnoticed because their magnitude is below the threshold of human perception but show up on recording instruments. The regions of the earth in proximity to plate boundaries are, however, susceptible to more frequent and severe earthquakes. This is because the plate boundaries represent lines of greater weakness in the earth's crust. Ninety percent of all earthquakes occur in the vicinity of plate boundaries.

Observe in Figure 2.20 that the Pacific Plate and the North American Plate meet along the West Coast of the United States — a region known for its high seismic activity. The remaining ten percent of earthquakes occur because of faults within the plates. Called the *intraplate earthquakes*, they occur far away from plate boundaries. Earthquakes that have occurred in the eastern and midwestern United States are intraplate earthquakes. Intraplate earthquakes are infrequent but may not be less severe than plate boundary earthquakes.

Since seismicity is a geographical activity, it is possible to delineate areas which are seismically more active than others. This has been done by dividing the earth's surface into zones, called the *seismic risk zones*. The United States has been divided into 6 such zones: seismic risk zones 0, 1, 2A, 2B, 3 and 4, Figure 2.22. Zone 0 has no seismic risk; zone 1 has little risk. The risk increases as the zone number increases. The maximum risk is in zone 4. Note that most of the United States lies in seismic zone 0 or 1 where the

**FIGURE 2.22** Seismic risk zone map of the United States. Source: Reference 2.2 with permission. For greater details see the original map.

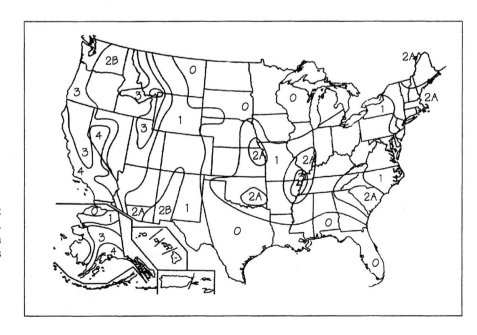

seismic risk is either zero or negligible. Fortunately, regions of high seismic risk in the United States are regions of low wind hazard with the exception of locations such as Alaska and the Virgin Islands.

### 2.10.1 Earthquake Intensity

Two scales are commonly used to describe the intensity of an earthquake: the Modified Mercalli scale and the Richter scale. The latter is more commonly used, particularly in the media. Devised in 1935 by Professor Charles Richter of the California Institute of Technology, the Richter scale begins at zero but has no upper limit. However, the severest earthquake recorded to date on this scale is 8.6.

The Richter scale is a logarithmic scale (to base ten). According to this scale, the total energy released by an earthquake (E) is given by:

$$\log_{10} E = 11.4 + 1.5\,R$$

where E is the energy output of the earthquake in ergs, and R is the number on the Richter scale. Thus, if $R = 6.0$, $E = 10^{20.4}$ ($= 2.5 \times 10^{20}$) ergs, and if $R = 7.0$, $E = 10^{21.9}$ ($= 79.4 \times 10^{20}$) ergs. The ratio of two intensities is $79.4/2.5 = 31.8$ (approximately 32). In other words, an increase of 1 on the Richter scale represents a 32 times increase in the energy output of the earthquake. Thus, an earthquake measuring 8.0 on the scale is nearly 32-fold more powerful than one measuring 7.0, and nearly 1000 times more powerful than one measuring 6.0.

An earthquake of up to 2 on the Richter scale goes unnoticed by humans; 4 to 5 may cause slight damage to poorly designed buildings. At 7, the damage is usually extensive in poorly designed buildings. A magnitude of 6.5 and above is considered a significant earthquake. Table 2.5 gives some of the major earthquakes (Richter intensity 8.0 or greater) that have occurred in various parts of the world in this century.

The ground motion caused by an earthquake consists of random vibrations. Like any other vibration, this motion is also characterized by an amplitude and frequency of vibration. Although the Richter scale gives the total energy released, it provides no information about the vibrational characteristics or the duration of the earthquake, both of which are important in determining the extent of damage to structures. Therefore, the Richter scale cannot be used in determining earthquake loads on buildings. It is, however, the best available measure of the qualitative effect of an earthquake, particularly at or near the epicenter.

### 2.10.2 Total Earthquake Load

In determining earthquake loads on a building, it is important to consider the dynamic aspects of vibration. There are three component vibrations to be taken into account: (i) vibration of the ground, (ii) vibration of the structure and (iii) vibration of the soil. These three vibrations are interactive.

**Table 2.5 Major Earthquakes of the Twentieth Century** (8.0 or greater on the Richter scale)

| Year | Country | Richter magnitude | Loss of life | Year | Country | Richter magnitude | Loss of life |
|------|---------|-------------------|--------------|------|---------|-------------------|--------------|
| 1905 | Kangra, India | 8.6 | 19,000 | 1945 | Iran and Pakistan | 8.2 | 4,000 |
| 1906 | Columbia and Ecuador | 8.9 | 1,000 | 1950 | India and China | 8.6 | 1,500 |
| 1906 | San Francisco, USA | 8.3 | 700 | 1952 | Hokkaido, Japan | 8.6 | 600 |
| 1906 | South Central Chile | 8.6 | 1,500 | 1960 | Alerce, Chile | 8.5 | 2,000 |
| 1907 | Karatag, Tajikistan | 8.0 | 12,000 | 1964 | Alaska, USA | 8.5 | 115 |
| 1920 | Gansu, China | 8.6 | 200,000 | 1976 | Moro, Phillippines | 8.0 | 6,500 |
| 1923 | Tokyo, Japan | 8.2 | 143,000 | 1976 | Tangshan, China | 8.0 | 655,000 |
| 1927 | Qinghai, China | 8.3 | 200,000 | 1977 | Sunda, Indonesia | 8.0 | 200 |
| 1933 | Honshu, Japan | 8.9 | 3,000 | 1985 | Mexico | 8.1 | 5,000 |
| 1939 | Erzincan, Turkey | 8.0 | 33,000 | | | | |

Source: Reference 2.7 with permission.

Consequently, the determination of seismic loads on a building is highly complex. However, building codes provide an equivalent static procedure which gives the magnitude of static earthquake loads whose effect on buildings is equivalent to those of the actual dynamic loads. Although the static procedure is simpler than the dynamic procedure, it is too complicated to be covered in this text. We shall, therefore, cover earthquake loads[4] in general terms, unlike our coverage of other load types.

The fundamental principle on which seismic loads are based is that the acceleration of the ground due to an earthquake produces an inertial force in the building. This force, which tends to oppose the ground motion, is referred to as the *total earthquake load* on the building. The total earthquake load can be obtained from Newton's Second Law of Motion. According to this law, when a body is accelerated, the inertial force (F) acting on it is equal to the product of the acceleration and the mass of the body. Thus:

$$F = ma$$

where m is the mass of the body and a is the acceleration imparted to it. If the weight of the body is W, then $m = W/g$, where g is the acceleration due to gravity whose value is approximately 32 ft/sec$^2$ (9.8 m/sec$^2$). Substituting the value of m, the above equation becomes:

$$F = \frac{a}{g} W \tag{2.4}$$

---

[4] The discussion of earthquake loads presented here is as per the 1994 edition of the Uniform Building Code.

Equation (2.4) may be extended to building structures. Here, W would represent the total dead load of the building; a, the acceleration of the building caused by ground motion, and F would give the total earthquake load on the building.

If the acceleration is small, the earthquake load is small. This is obvious because if the ground moves very slowly (with a negligible acceleration), the building will simply go along with this motion as one unit, and the opposing inertial force (the earthquake load) will be small. In the case of a sudden and swift motion (large acceleration), the lower part of the building translates horizontally, while the upper part remains in its original position. In an effort to maintain a status quo, a large opposing (inertial) force is produced in the building, i.e., the total earthquake load on the building is large.

The acceleration of the building is generally not the same as the ground acceleration. If the building and the soil on which the building rests are both absolutely rigid, the acceleration of the building and the ground will be identical. However, both the building and the soil possess some flexibility and their independent vibrational properties. Hence, the acceleration of the building is generally different from that of the ground but related to it by a factor which depends on the properties of the soil and the structure. In other words, building acceleration (a) is a function of ground acceleration ($a_g$) and a factor (K) which depends on the interaction of the soil and the structural properties of the building. Thus:

Building acceleration, $a = a_g K$.

Hence, Equation (2.4) becomes:

$$F = \frac{a_g}{g} K W$$

If we replace the term ($a_g/g$) by Z in the above equation, we obtain:

$$F = (Z K) W \qquad (2.5)$$

**Table 2.6  Seismic Zone Factors**

| Seismic risk zone | Zone factor |
|---|---|
| 0 | 0.0 |
| 1 | 0.075 |
| 2A | 0.15 |
| 2B | 0.20 |
| 3 | 0.30 |
| 4 | 0.40 |

Source: Reference 2.2 with permission.

The quantity Z is called the *seismic zone factor*. It represents ground acceleration expected at a location as a function of g. Thus, if Z = 0.1, it means that the ground acceleration for which the building should be designed is $0.1 g = 3.2 \text{ ft/sec}^2$.

In determining earthquake loads, ground acceleration must obviously represent its maximum value for the location. The values of expected peak ground acceleration for various locations in the United States have been determined. In fact, the distinction between various seismic risk zones is based on these expected peak values of ground acceleration for those zones, and is given in terms of Z. The values of Z for various seismic risk zones in the United States are given in Table 2.6.

As already stated, K is a factor that depends on the vibrational properties of the soil and the structure. Building codes give the maximum value of K as 0.688. This value applies to unreinforced masonry buildings built on soft clay soil. Such buildings are highly vulnerable to earthquake damage. The value of K (hence the total earthquake force exerted on the structure) is small for buildings that have the ability to absorb earthquake energy by deforming plastically, such as the specially designed steel or reinforced concrete buildings. (For an explanation of plastic deformation, see Section 3.5).

Building codes require that W should include the dead load on the building and the weight of all permanent equipment installed therein. Note that lighter buildings attract a smaller seismic load than buildings constructed of heavy materials. Thus, concrete and masonry structures attract a greater earthquake load than wood structures. Indeed, the earthquake load on a gypsy tent or an Arab Bedouin tent is negligible even under a severe earthquake because of the light weight of the structure and its ability to absorb deformations, Figure 2.23.

Similarly, light engineered steel (moment resisting) structures with lightweight cladding have good earthquake resistance. In fact, the design of such structures even in seismic zones 3 and 4 is usually governed by wind considerations. However, if such structures support heavy walls, floors, or large snow loads, earthquake design considerations may prevail over wind considerations.

Building codes also require enhancement of earthquake loads for essential and hazardous facilities in a similar manner as for wind loads, although in the case of earthquakes, the use of the importance factor does not change the recurrence interval.

**FIGURE 2.23** A gypsy tent or Arab Bedouin tent resists earthquake forces admirably due to the light weight of the structure and its ability to absorb deformations.

## 2.11 EARTHQUAKE vs WIND LOAD RESISTANCE

Buildings are generally designed to resist either the earthquake loads or the wind loads, whichever causes worse effect (greater stresses). This is based on the assumption that there is a negligible probability of maximum wind speeds occurring at the same time as an intense earthquake. Since wind loads are usually greater than earthquake loads in seismic zones 0 and 1, buildings are designed to resist wind loads in these zones.

In zones 3 and 4, earthquake loads usually govern the design of buildings to withstand lateral loads[5]. However, the design of lightweight envelope components, such as glass curtain walls and roof membranes, are governed by wind loads even in seismic zones 3 and 4, since the earthquake loads on lightweight components is smaller than the wind loads on them. (Remember that earthquake loads are influenced by the weight of the component). In zone 2, either the earthquake load or the wind load will govern depending on the basic wind speed and the type of structure.

Since earthquake loads are mainly horizontal loads, the lateral bracing required in a building to resist earthquake loads is, in general, similar to that required to resist wind loads. Nevertheless, there are several differences in details. First, an earthquake shakes not only the entire building but also its contents. Thus, all building components, equipment and fixtures in a building must be adequately anchored to remain intact during an earthquake.

Wind, on the other hand, acts on the building envelope. It is through the envelope that wind loads are transmitted to building structure. If the envelope remains intact, the building will generally retain its overall structural integrity under a storm. Thus, the wind damage in a building usually begins with the damage to envelope components, such as doors, windows, curtain walls and other cladding elements, Figure 2.24. Once the building changes from fully "enclosed" to "partially enclosed", the wind loads on the building increase due to the cupping effect (see Section 2.8.5), which may result in additional damage, or a collapse of the structure.

Second, in determining wind loads on a building we calculate the maximum expected wind load. The structure is designed so that under the action of maximum wind loads, it remains elastic, i.e., the structure is designed to suffer no permanent deformation under the worst expected storm. The

**FIGURE 2.24** Hurricane damage to glass curtain wall of NCNB Bank building, Kendall, Florida. Courtesy of: Federal Emergency Management Agency, Emmitsburg, Maryland.

---

[5] In regions such as Alaska, the structures have to be designed to resist both the earthquake loads and the wind loads, though not simultaneously.

design approach is different for earthquake loads. The loads on a building produced by the worst expected earthquake for the location are so large that if the building was designed to remain elastic after the earthquake, it would be prohibitive in cost.

Therefore, the earthquake loads for which a building is designed are smaller than the actual earthquake loads expected on it. The underlying design philosophy is that the building should remain elastic when resisting minor earthquakes. In the event of an intense earthquake, a part of the earthquake's energy may be dissipated in permanently deforming the building but the building must otherwise remain intact to provide complete safety to its occupants.

Permanent deformations in a structure are possible only if the structure has the ability to sustain such deformations. As we will see in Chapter 3, materials which can sustain permanent deformation prior to failure are called plastic materials. Plastic deformation is an essential property for buildings located in seismic zones but is not a requirement for resisting wind loads. A building must not deform permanently even under the severest storm. Additionally, it must be rigid enough to reduce the deflections caused by strong winds. The swaying of the upper floor of tall buildings under wind loads must be controlled to remain within acceptable limits of human tolerance.

The reverse is true for earthquake loads. Buildings must be able to deform, even permanently, to absorb the energy delivered to them by the earthquake. If brittle materials (materials which remain elastic up to failure) are used, they will fail under earthquake forces. Several concrete frame buildings with brittle masonry infill walls between frames have collapsed or suffered serious damage under earthquake forces, Figure 2.25. Such buildings would have been unharmed by violent storms.

FIGURE 2.25 Earthquake damage to unreinforced masonry wall panels in buildings with reinforced concrete structural frames (1985 Mexico City earthquake). Courtesy of: Author's student.

**REVIEW QUESTIONS**

**2.1**  List the various types of loads that act on buildings.

**2.2**  What is the difference between dead load and live load? Explain with the help of examples.

**2.3**  What is the design floor live load for the following occupancies: (a) guest rooms in an apartment building, (b) corridor in an apartment building, (c) general office building, (d) library stack room, and (e) retail store?

**2.4**  Determine the dead load on a (normal weight) reinforced concrete floor slab. The slab is 8 in. thick and is finished with $1\frac{1}{2}$ in. thick terrazzo floor.

**2.5**  In a wood frame building, the floor-ceiling assembly consists of the following members: 2 x 10 Douglas fir floor joists at 24 in. on center, $1\frac{1}{4}$ in. thick sturdi-floor, carpet, and $\frac{1}{2}$ in. thick gypsum board ceiling. Determine the dead load of the floor-ceiling assembly.

**2.6**  What is wind stagnation pressure? What is the difference between wind stagnation pressure and the design wind load? Explain.

**2.7**  Determine the wind stagnation pressure if the wind speed is: (a) 80 mph, and (b) 90 mph.

**2.8**  Determine the design snow load on: (a) a flat roof in Albany, New York, and (b) a sloping roof in Madison, Wisconsin; roof slope = 6:12.

**2.9**  Determine the design wind load on the windows of a two-story building. Roof height = 25 ft; basic wind speed = 110 mph. The building faces a large water body.

**2.10**  Determine the wind load on the windows of a 200 ft high apartment building in a built-up urban area: (a) window height = 80 ft, and (b) window height = 180 ft; basic wind speed = 80 mph.

**2.11**  Determine the wind uplift on the flat roof of a building, 100 ft high. Basic wind speed = 80 mph; exposure category B.

**2.12**  What is the approximate wind speed in a tornado? Explain why tornado wind speeds are not considered in determining the design wind speed for a location.

**2.13**  Sketch in three dimensions three buildings in which diagonal bracing has been used on exterior facades.

**2.14**  What is the Richter scale? What is the difference between the amounts of energy released by two earthquakes: Richter scale 8.0 and Richter scale 6.0?

**2.15**  List the seismic risk zones in which the United States has been divided. In which seismic zone does your city lie?

**2.16**  What types of construction are (a) suitable and (b) unsuitable in an earthquake prone region?

**REFERENCES**

**2.1**  American Society of Civil Engineers, New York, New York: *Minimum Design Loads for Buildings and Other Structures*, ASCE 7-95.

**2.2**  International Conference of Building Officials, Whittier, California: *Uniform Building Code*, Whittier, California, 1994, Chapter 16. Reproduced from the 1994 edition of the *Uniform Building Code*[TM], copyright© 1994, with the permission of the publisher, the International Conference of Building Officials.

**2.3**  Church, C, et al: *The Tornado: Its Structure, Dynamics, Prediction, and Hazards*, American Geophysical Union, Washington D.C., 1993, p. 328.

**2.4**  Walker, B: *Earthquake*, Time-Life Books, Alexandria, Virginia, 1982, p.7

**2.5**  Botsai, E, et al: *Architects and Earthquakes*, AIA Research Corporation, Washington D.C.,1975, p. 19.

**2.6**  Dowrick, D.J: *Earthquake Resistant Design*, John Wiley and Sons, New York, 1987, p. 34.

**2.7**  Dunbar, Paula K, et al: *Catalog of Significant Earthquakes (2150 B.C. - 1991 A.D.)*, National Geophysical Data Center, Boulder, Colorado, U.S.A., 1992.

**2.8**  Barbera, Jerry: Private communication with the author.

# 3

# LOAD EFFECTS – The Structural Properties of Materials

## 3.1 INTRODUCTION

Building materials have always had a strong influence on architectural form. The history of the development of architectural form coincides with man's understanding of the structural properties of materials and their application to the design of buildings. Every civilization found it necessary to know the strength and limitations of materials in order to design safe and durable structures. The small spans of beams used in Greek temples, for example, were due mainly to their designers' instinctive understanding that stone is a brittle material — weak in tension and bending. Stone's high strength in compression was exploited in columns and walls but the column spacings and the sizes of openings in walls had to be small. Although the main reason for providing capitals at the tops of columns in Greek temples was non-structural[1], the capitals provided greater structural safety by reducing beam spans even further, Figure 3.1.

The discovery of the arch permitted the use of long spans because the material in an arch is primarily under compression. Although the Egyptians built mud brick vaults without centering in the thirteenth century BC, the real use of the vault followed the arch's discovery. The progression from vault to dome was easy since the dome is simply a rotational version of the arch. In both the vault and dome, the material is in compression.

---

[1] The historians claim that the reason for providing column capitals was more to do with visual considerations than the structural advantages of capitals, and that the Greeks had borrowed the tradition from the Egyptians.

**FIGURE 3.1** Parthenon, Acropolis, Greece. Note the relatively small distances between columns, in response to the weakness of stone in bending. Courtesy of: Dr. Jay C. Henry, University of Texas at Arlington.

The arch, the vault and the dome dominated for centuries as the primary form-giving elements in buildings because the major construction materials available at the time, such as stone and brick masonry, were brittle materials. The use of wood, which is less brittle than stone, was limited to either minor buildings or minor components of buildings because of its lack of durability. Sooner or later, wood structures were either consumed by fire or destroyed by termites. Masonry buildings, on the other hand, are extremely durable and some have survived thousands of years. Therefore, the formal, intellectual and the technological use of brittle materials became highly perfected over time. Gothic cathedrals are excellent examples of how the limitations in the tensile strength of brittle materials were overcome to produce magnificent and technically daring structures, Figure 3.2.

The industrial revolution brought in many new developments in architectural form. The availability of wrought iron, and later cast iron, had

**FIGURE 3.2** Bourges Cathedral, Bourges, France. Buttresses and flying arches in Gothic buildings were some of the structural innovations of the time in understanding of the inherent weakness of stone in tension. Courtesy of: Dr. Jay C. Henry, University of Texas at Arlington.

already revived the beam as the horizontal spanning element because of iron's high tensile strength. Large size openings became possible without recourse to arches, and the progression from masonry buildings to the skeleton frame did not require much imagination. The invention of the Bessemer process during the mid-nineteenth century for the commercial production of steel, and the discovery of reinforced concrete made skeleton frame the major structural medium for the design of buildings.

The discovery of new materials — prestressed concrete, high strength steels, reinforced concrete, and masonry — led to the development of new structural forms. In fact, the modern movement in architecture, and presently post-modernism, owes a great deal to the exploitation of the structural properties of materials. In this chapter, we shall discuss some of the important properties that have a bearing on the strength of materials. Emphasis is placed on properties that relate directly to basic structural materials such as steel, concrete, brick, stone and wood. However, the principles discussed have general application.

Structural properties of materials and the behavior of structures under loads cannot be divorced from each other. They are so interrelated that often the distinction between the two is vague at best. Ductility and brittleness, elasticity and plasticity which are properties of materials are also used to describe the behavior of an entire structure or components of a structure. Therefore, structural behavior is discussed in this chapter where necessary to describe the structural properties of materials.

## 3.2 TYPES OF STRESSES

When a force acts on a member (such as a building component), the member develops internal forces to resist the applied force. The intensity of resistance to applied forces is called the *stress*. Quantitatively, stress is defined as the force acting on a unit area of the member. Thus, stress represents the intensity of resistive forces produced inside the member in response to the applied force. If the applied force is large, the stress developed is large, and vice versa.

There are only two basic states of stress in a structure: (i) *normal stress* and (ii) *tangential stress*, also called *shear stress*, Figure 3.3. When the resistive forces are perpendicular (normal) to the cross-sectional area of the member, they are called normal stresses. In the case of shear stress, the resistive forces are tangential to the cross-sectional area of the member.

**FIGURE 3.3** Types of stresses in a structure.

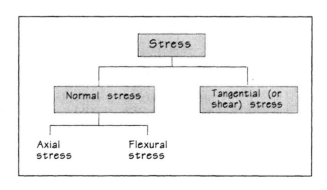

Normal stress can be subdivided into several categories. The two most commonly encountered types of normal stress are (i) *axial stress* and (ii) *flexural stress*. They are distinguished from each other by the orientation of the applied force with respect to the axis of the member. Axial stress is produced by an axial force. An axial force is defined as a force which is parallel to the axis of the member and passes through the centroid of the cross-sectional area of the member.

Flexural stresses (also called bending stresses) are produced when the applied force is perpendicular to the axis of the member. A force which is parallel to the axis of the member but does not pass through the centroid of its cross-sectional area is called an *eccentric force*. An eccentric force produces axial as well as flexural stresses in the member, see Section 3.8.2.

**3.3 AXIAL STRESS AND AXIAL STRAIN**

If an axial force[2], P, acts at the center of a bar as shown in Figure 3.4, the (axial) stress produced in the bar (f) is given by:

$$f = \frac{P}{A} \tag{3.1}$$

where A is the cross-sectional area of the body.

Axial stress may either be a tensile stress[3] (tension) or a compressive stress (compression) depending on whether the applied force pulls on or compresses the member. In Figure 3.4, the stress produced in the bar is a tensile stress since force P is a tensile force tending to stretch the bar. A compressive force, on the other hand, will tend to shorten the bar.

From Equation (3.1), it is obvious that the unit of stress in the U.S. customary system is pounds per square inch (psi) or kips per square inch (ksi) depending on whether the force is expressed in pounds or kips. In the

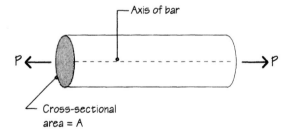

**FIGURE 3.4** A force acting along the axis of a member produces axial stress in it.

---

[2] Forces always occur in equal and opposite pairs to maintain equilibrium but the pair is treated as a single force in all calculations. If a person weighing 150 pounds stands on a floor, the force of his weight is 150 lbs and acts downward. To maintain equilibrium, the floor must exert an equal force in the upward direction. The effect of this force pair on the floor (or on the person's feet), however, is that of one 150 pound force which tends to compress the floor (or the person's feet).

[3] The terms "tensile stress" and "tension" are used synonymously. Similarly, "compressive stress" and "compression" are identical terms.

SI system, the unit of stress is pascal or kilopascal.

Stress is nearly always accompanied by deformation of the member. The exception to this rule is a *rigid body*. A rigid body is defined as one which does not deform at all under the action of loads. A rigid body will not stretch, shorten, bend or change shape regardless of the magnitude of load placed on it. Obviously, such a body does not exist in the real world since all materials deform when loaded. Actual bodies, such as building components, will deform under loads although the deformations in them are usually too small to be visible to the human eye. When measurements of these deformations are required, complex instrumentation is necessary. Because of the small magnitude of deformations, building components are assumed to be rigid bodies for preliminary structural analysis. Thus, the rigid body concept is not a mere abstraction — it has practical significance in the structural design of buildings.

The deformation caused by axial stresses (axial compression or axial tension) is simply the change in the length of the member. Tensile stresses cause the member to elongate and compressive stresses cause it to shorten. We are usually not interested in the absolute value of the change in length of the member but in its relative value. The relative change in length, defined as the change in length divided by the original length, is called the *strain*. Thus in Figure 3.5, if the original length of the bar is L which, under the action of a tensile force, becomes L + δ, then the strain in the bar, denoted by the Greek letter ε (epsilon), is given by:

$$\varepsilon = \frac{\text{Change in length}}{\text{Original length}} = \frac{\delta}{L} \qquad (3.2)$$

The strain caused by a tensile force is called *tensile strain*; that caused by a compressive force is called *compressive strain*. Since strain is the ratio of two lengths, it is simply a number with no units. Since the deformation of building components under loads is usually small, the value of strain obtained in actual practice is an extremely small number. It is therefore more convenient at times to express strain as a percentage. For example, a strain of 0.05 is equal to 5% strain. Sometimes the strain may also be expressed in such units as in./ft (or mm/m) if this yields a more reasonable number, see Example 3.2.

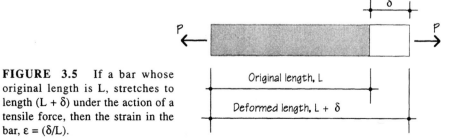

**FIGURE 3.5**  If a bar whose original length is L, stretches to length (L + δ) under the action of a tensile force, then the strain in the bar, ε = (δ/L).

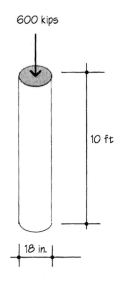

600 kips

10 ft

18 in.

**FIGURE 3.6** Refers to Example 3.1.

## Example 3.1

An axial load of 600 kips acts on the ground floor column of a building, Figure 3.6. The column measures 18 in. in diameter. Determine the type and magnitude of stress in the column.

*Solution*: P = 600 kips. $A = \pi r^2 = \pi(9)^2 = 254.4$ in.$^2$
From Equation (3.1), f = P/A = 600/254.4 = 2.36 ksi (compression).

## Example 3.2

If the column of Example 3.1 is 10 ft high and shortens 0.2 in. under the load, determine the strain in the column.

*Solution*: $\delta = 0.2$ in. L = 10 x 12 = 120 in.
From Equation (3.2), $\varepsilon = \delta/L = 0.2/120 = 0.0017 = 0.17\%$
The strain may also be expressed as 0.2/10 = 0.02 in./ft.

## Example 3.3

A 2 in. x 1 in. rectangular steel plate has a 0.5 in. diameter hole as shown in Figure 3.7(a). The plate is subjected to a tensile force of 60 kips. Determine the stress on the solid cross-section of the bar (the cross-section not containing the hole).

*Solution*: The solid cross-section of the plate is shown in Figure 3.7(b).
P = 60 kips. Area of section (shown shaded) = A = 2 x 1 = 2.0 in.$^2$

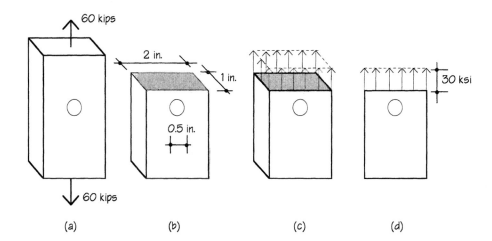

(a)                    (b)                    (c)                    (d)

**FIGURE 3.7** Refers to Example 3.3. (a) Plate subjected to a tensile force of 60 k. (b) Solid cross-section of the plate shown shaded. (c) Stress distribution on the cross-section in three dimensions. (d) Two-dimensional representation of the same stress distribution.

From Equation (3.1), $f = P/A = 60/2.0 = 30.0$ ksi.

The stress distribution on the cross-section is shown in three dimensions in Figure 3.7(c), and in two dimensions in Figure 3.7(d).

### Example 3.4

Determine the stress on the cross-section containing the hole for the plate of Example 3.3.

*Solution*: The cross-section of the member, taken through the center of the hole, is shown in Figure 3.8(a).

$P = 60$ kips. Net area of cross-section (shown shaded) = A = area AA'C'C + area BB'D'D $= (0.75 \times 1) + (0.75 \times 1) = 1.50$ in$^2$.

$f = P/A = 60/1.50 = 40.0$ ksi. The stress distribution is shown in Figure 3.8(b).

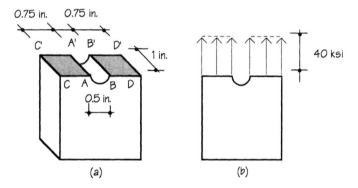

(a)  (b)

**FIGURE 3.8** Refers to Example 3.4. (a) Cross-section of plate containing the hole. (b) Stress distribution on the section.

In Example 3.4, the stress on the cross-section of the member containing a hole was determined assuming that it is uniform across the entire cross-section. As we shall see in Section 3.7, this is not true. The actual stress distribution on the section of a member containing a discontinuity, such as a hole or a crack, is not uniform. Maximum stresses occur near the hole, at edges AA' and BB', and decrease progressively away from the hole. Minimum stresses occur at edges CC' and DD'. In fact, the value of 40 ksi in Example 3.4 represents the average stress on the cross-section.

## 3.4 STRESS-STRAIN RELATIONSHIP

Since a load causes deformation, stress and strain occur simultaneously in a member. Generally, the strain increases as the stress increases. However, there are situations where stress may exist without any strain, and the strain without the stress. For example, a beam resting on two end supports will be subjected to a change in its length as the temperature of the beam increases or decreases. In this case, the strain occurs without any stress. But if the same beam is clamped between the two end supports so that it cannot change its length, the beam will be subjected to stresses as its temperature changes — a case in which the stresses occur without the strain. The beam will be subjected to compressive stresses when its temperature rises, and to tensile stresses when the temperature falls.

The relationship between stress and strain conveys a great deal of information about the structural properties of the material, and is unique for each material. This relationship is usually given in a graphical form, called the *stress-strain diagram*. In the stress-strain diagram, the stress is generally represented on the vertical axis and the strain on the horizontal axis.

We shall now examine the stress-strain relationship for low-carbon steel. It is one of the most important construction materials and is commonly used in such structural shapes as I-sections, C-sections, L-sections, pipes and round bars — the latter mainly as reinforcement in concrete, Figure 3.9.

The stress-strain diagram of steel is obtained by subjecting a round steel bar of standard length and diameter to a tension test in which the ends of the bar are gripped between clamps and the bar subjected to a gradually increasing axial load which produces axial tension in the bar. The ends of the bar where it is gripped are larger in cross-section, Figure 3.10(a), so that the failure of the bar does not occur at the ends but in its main body where the stresses are uniform. A modern tensile test machine such as the one shown in Figure 3.10(b) is fully automated and gives the stress-strain diagram directly without the need to calculate stresses and strains, and to plot them manually.

The stress-strain diagram for low-carbon steel is shown in Figure 3.11. The diagram begins at the origin since the strain must obviously be zero

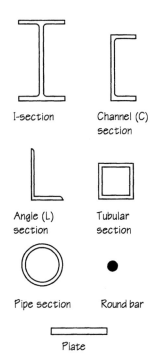

I-section    Channel (C) section

Angle (L) section    Tubular section

Pipe section    Round bar

Plate

**FIGURE 3.9** Commonly used structural steel sections.

(a)

Test specimen

(b)

**FIGURE 3.10** (a) Steel test specimen. (b) Tensile testing machine. Courtesy of: Instron Corporation, Boston, Massachusetts.

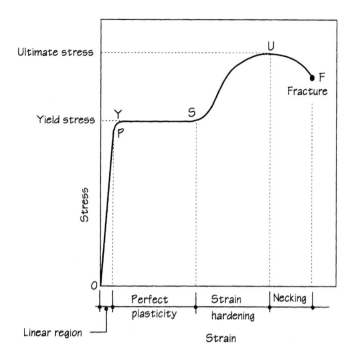

**FIGURE 3.11**   Idealized stress-strain diagram for low-carbon steel under tension (not to scale).

when the stress is zero — a no load condition. It consists of 5 distinct regions: O to P, P to Y, Y to S, S to U and U to F. In region OP, the relationship between stress and strain is a straight line, and stress is proportional to strain. Therefore, it is called a *linearly proportional relationship*[4].

### 3.4.1 Yield Strength and Ultimate Strength

Beyond point P, there is no proportionality. Hence, the stress at P is called the *proportional limit*. With an increase in the load on the bar, the slope of the diagram beyond P decreases until it reaches point Y. Point Y is called the *yield point,* and the stress corresponding to this point is called the *yield stress* or the *yield strength*. Points P and Y are fairly close to each other. Therefore, the stress-strain diagram for steel is usually considered to be a straight line up to its yield stress.

---

[4] A straight line between two variables which passes through the origin implies that the two variables are proportional to each other. In a proportional relationship, the ratio of the two variables is constant. If one variable doubles in value, the other also doubles. For a proportional relationship, the diagram must (i) be linear and (ii) pass through the origin. If either of the two conditions is not satisfied, the relationship is not proportional. Thus, a non-linear relationship, even though it may pass through the origin, is not a proportional relationship. Additionally, a linear relationship not passing through the origin is also not a proportional relationship. In region OP of Figure 3.11, the relationship between stress and strain is a proportional relationship, i.e., the stress is proportional to strain in this region.

Yield stress is an important property of steel. Various types of steel are distinguished from each other by their yield stress values. For instance, low-carbon steel is designated as A-36 steel because its yield stress is 36 ksi (the letter "A"in A-36 symbolizes a ferrous metal as per ASTM classification, see Table 1.4). Steel used as reinforcing bars in concrete is called "grade 40" or "grade 60" steel depending on whether its yield stress is 40 ksi or 60 ksi.

Beyond point Y, the deformation in the bar increases substantially with little or no increase in the load, and the stress-strain diagram becomes (almost) horizontal. In other words, the steel "yields" after reaching point Y like a plastic material (such as the modeling clay). The region between Y and S is therefore called the region of *perfect plasticity*. Since points P and Y are fairly close to each other, the region of perfect plasticity is conventionally assumed to extend from points P to S.

The region of perfect plasticity ends at point S. The yielding of steel produces major rearrangement of the atoms in its crystalline structure which makes steel stronger and harder and the bar is able to sustain a greater load. Consequently, the deformation in the bar beyond point S increases at a smaller rate as compared to that in the region of perfect plasticity. Further increases in the load takes the diagram to point U, the point of maximum stress. The maximum stress is called the *ultimate stress,* or the *ultimate strength* of the material.

The region from S to U is called the region of *strain hardening* (or work hardening) because the material has become harder and stronger through excessive strain. The same effect is obtained by mechanical working on steel such as cold rolling or hammering. We experience this phenomenon when we take a piece of steel wire and bend it between our fingers. The wire becomes harder and stronger after bending, and it is more difficult to bend again at the original bend point.

Beyond point U, the test bar undergoes further deformation until point F is reached where the bar breaks or "fractures". Notice that the stress-strain diagram drops down between points U and F, indicating a loss of strength near failure. This is due to the manner in which the materials are tested and indicates the inability of testing equipment to keep the load on a rapidly disintegrating material.

If we assume that strain hardening did not occur in steel, the stress-strain diagram would have continued to be horizontal after the yield point. The bar would have stretched further and further under a constant load and the failure would have finally occurred in this hypothetical material as shown in Figure 3.12.

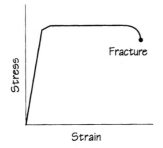

**FIGURE 3.12** The stress-strain diagram of a material in which strain hardening does not occur.

## 3.5 ELASTIC AND PLASTIC MATERIALS

A material is called *elastic* if its deformation is fully recoverable after the load is removed. If measurements of stress and strain are recorded for both the increasing and decreasing loads for an elastic material, it will be observed that the stress-strain diagram for unloading is the same as the stress-strain diagram for loading. For example, let the stress-strain diagram obtained as the load is gradually increased on a material be OA, Figure 3.13(a). Now if the load is gradually removed and the material is an elastic material, then its stress-strain diagram on unloading will follow the same path, from A to O, i.e., the stress-strain diagram for unloading will be AO.

The property responsible for the elastic behavior of the material is called *elasticity*. The converse of elasticity is called *plasticity*. Thus, a material which does not recover its deformation after the removal of the load is called an *inelastic* or a *plastic material*. Materials are generally elastic only up to a small strain value — nearly 0.5%. The maximum strain (strain at failure) in brittle materials such as concrete, brick, stone and glass is of this order (0.5%). Therefore, brittle materials are generally elastic up to failure.

Metals, on the other hand, can sustain large deformations, usually greater than 10%. They are elastic up to a certain stress level, called the *elastic limit*. If loaded beyond the elastic limit, they are plastic, i.e., their deformation beyond the elastic limit is permanent. Materials which have elastic as well as plastic regions in their stress-strain diagrams are called *elastic-plastic materials*. The elastic limit of an elastic-plastic material may, therefore, be defined as the maximum stress to which it may be subjected without becoming permanently deformed.

A material whose stress-strain diagram is represented by Figure 3.13(b) is an elastic-plastic material. It is elastic up to point E (the elastic limit) and plastic thereafter. If loaded to the stress level of point E, it will return to point O on unloading, retracing the loading stress-strain curve OE. If loaded beyond E, say to point B, its unloading stress-strain diagram will not be BEO but will be given by straight line BQ. Thus, after all the load has been removed, the stress-strain diagram will not return to O but to point Q. OQ represents the plastic strain, also called permanent or *inelastic strain*.

Generally, if a material is stressed into the plastic region, the unloading stress-strain diagram is a straight line whose slope is the same as the slope of the initial part of the loading stress-strain diagram. In other words, line BQ

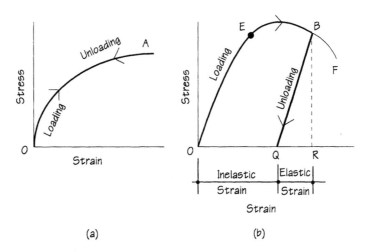

(a)                                   (b)

**FIGURE 3.13** (a) Stress-strain diagram for the loading and unloading of an elastic material. (b) Stress-strain diagram for the loading and unloading of an elastic-plastic material.

is parallel to the tangent to the stress-strain diagram at point O. The total strain in the material when loaded to B is given by OR out of which OQ is the inelastic strain, and QR the elastic strain.

Low-carbon steel is elastic only up to the proportional limit. In other words, the elastic limit and the proportional limit are coincident in the case of low-carbon steel. These two limits may not coincide for other materials. Since the stress-strain diagram for low-carbon steel is linear up to the elastic limit, steel is known as *linearly elastic* up to point P, see Figure 3.11. Beyond P, the strain in steel is inelastic.

Note that the stress-strain diagram for an elastic material need not be linear. Materials such as brick, stone and concrete do not have a linear stress-strain diagram but are elastic almost to failure. Soft rubbers have an S-shaped stress-strain diagram, Figure 3.14, and are also elastic up to failure, as one would expect of rubbers[3.1]. As mentioned previously, metals are elastic up to the elastic limit and have a large plastic region thereafter.

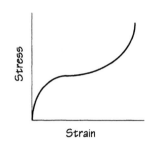

**FIGURE 3.14** Stress-strain diagram for a soft rubber.

### 3.5.1 The Importance of Materials' Elasticity

Building structures are designed so that the stresses in materials remain within the elastic limit and that no inelastic deformations occur under design loads. Being permanent, inelastic deformations affect the appearance of structures. The exception to this general philosophy is made in the design of structures located in highly seismic areas. The maximum intensity of earthquake loads in such areas is so high that if structures were designed to remain elastic, member sizes (columns, beams and floor slabs) would have to be so large as to make the structure highly uneconomical.

Thus, as stated in Section 2.10, the structural design philosophy for buildings located in seismic zones is that the building components should deform elastically under low to moderately intense earthquakes so that after the earthquake event, the building regains its original shape and size. However, under severe earthquake loads the structure is designed to deform inelastically (plastically) but without compromising its safety or integrity[3.2]. The structure may become unusable and unserviceable because of plastic deformations but it must remain integral to provide life safety. The design philosophy is based on the probability of the structure being subjected to the maximum intensity of earthquake loads only once in 50 years, which is typically viewed as the useful life span of most buildings.

## 3.6 MODULUS OF ELASTICITY

Materials which are linearly elastic are called *Hookean materials* because they obey Hooke's Law, named after the British architect-physicist Robert Hooke. Hooke's Law states that in an elastic material, stress is proportional to strain. In other words, according to Hooke's Law the ratio of stress to strain is a constant. Thus:

$$\frac{Stress}{Strain} = Constant = E \tag{3.3}$$

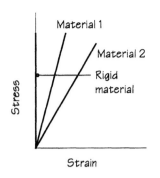

**FIGURE 3.15** The slope of the stress-strain diagram gives the magnitude of the modulus of elasticity, E. The greater the slope, the greater the value of E.

where E denotes the modulus of elasticity.

Equation (3.3) implies that for a Hookean material, stress and strain bear a constant ratio. This ratio, called the *modulus of elasticity* (E), is a property of the material[5]. Since strain has no units, the units of the modulus of elasticity are the same as those of stress, psi or ksi (Pascal in the SI system).

The modulus of elasticity is an important material property since it is a measure of the stiffness of the material. The larger the value of E, the stiffer the material. A material with a larger value of E will deform less under a given load than a material with a lower value of E.

On the stress-strain diagram, the value of E is represented by the slope of the diagram. The greater the slope, the larger the value of E, hence the stiffer the material. Thus, in Figure 3.15, the value of E is larger for material 1 than for material 2. For a "rigid" material, the value of E is infinite. This is obvious from Equation 3.3, because for a rigid material, the strain is zero regardless of the value of stress. Therefore, the stress-strain diagram for a rigid material is a vertical line since on a vertical line, the strain is zero.

The concept of the modulus of elasticity as a constant for a material assumes a linear stress-strain diagram. In other words, the stress-strain diagram for a Hookean material is a straight line. If the stress-strain diagram is a curve, the modulus of elasticity is not constant but varies with the stress level. Most construction materials fall in this category, i.e., they do not obey Hooke's Law. They typically do not have a linear stress-strain diagram (with the exception of steel). The modulus of elasticity of such a material is obtained from the straight line whose slope is approximately equal to the slope of the initial part of its stress-strain diagram. This approximation is justified on the basis that in actual buildings, the materials are usually loaded to low or moderate stress levels so that the slope of the initial part of the diagram is a good approximation to the modulus of elasticity of the material.

Figure 3.16 shows the stress-strain diagram for concrete obtained by loading 6 in. diameter by 12 in. high concrete cylinders under axial compression. Since the diagram is nonlinear, the modulus of elasticity is given by the slope of straight line OA where A represents 40% of the ultimate strength of concrete [3.3]. Thus, if the strength of concrete is 4,000 psi, point A represents a stress level of 1,600 psi.

The modulus of elasticity of materials is usually a large number — in millions of pounds per square inch. (Gigapascals in the SI system, where 1 Gigapascal = $10^9$ Pa). From Equation (3.3), it may be observed that E is equal to stress if strain is equal to one (i.e., 100% strain). Thus, in theory, E is that value of stress which will produce 100% elongation or shortening of a material. Obviously, it requires a large value of stress to double (or halve) the length of a material, and therefore, the value of E is a large number. In practice, construction materials fail well below a strain of 100%. For a soft rubber, the value of E is a relatively small number since it does not require a great deal of stress to double or halve the length of a rubber element.

---

[5] Modulus of elasticity is also called Young's Modulus after another British physicist Thomas Young (1773-1829), who was also a physician. He contributed much to the study of strength of materials and became well known after his successful publication in 1807 on the accommodating power of human eye.

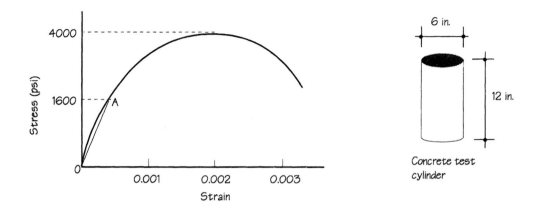

**FIGURE 3.16** Stress-strain diagram in compression for a 4000 psi concrete. The modulus of elasticity of concrete is given by the slope of the secant line OA where A corresponds to 40% of the ultimate strength of concrete.

Of commonly used materials, diamond has the highest value of E (greatest stiffness). That is why diamond-tipped tools are used to cut window glass. Table 3.1 gives the modulus of elasticity values of a few selected materials.

For most materials, the modulus of elasticity increases with the strength of the material. Higher strength species of wood, for example, have higher moduli of elasticity than lower strength species. The same is true of ceramic materials such as concrete, brick and stone. The greater the concrete strength, the greater its modulus of elasticity. However, steel has the same modulus of elasticity regardless of its strength. In other words, high strength steels have the same modulus of elasticity as low-carbon steel.

Steel is the stiffest of all construction materials, i.e., it has the highest value of E — 29 x $10^6$ psi (200 x $10^9$ Pa). Its modulus of elasticity is based on the straight line portion of the stress-strain diagram, points O to P in Figure 3.11. Since, unlike other materials, the modulus of elasticity of steel does not increase with strength, high strength steel is not as commonly used in structural steel sections as low-carbon (A-36) steel.

The use of high strength steel reduces beam and column sizes, resulting

**Table 3.1 Modulus of Elasticity of Selected Materials**

| Material | Modulus of elasticity ( x $10^6$ psi) |
|---|---|
| Wood | 1.0 to 2.0 |
| Brick masonry | 1.0 to 3.0 |
| Concrete | 3.0 to 8.0 |
| Steel | 29.0 |
| | |
| Aluminum alloys | 10.5 |
| Window glass | 10.0 |
| Diamond | 170 |
| Rubber | 0.001 |

Note: To obtain values in kPa, multiply the above values by 6.895 (see Appendix I).

in spatial economy and perhaps some cost advantage. Smaller column sizes provide greater usable floor area, and smaller beam sizes reduce the overall building height. In addition, smaller beam and column sizes reduce the dead loads on buildings. However, since the E-value of steel does not increase with strength, the use of smaller beams and columns increases the deformations of these components. Beams deflect more under gravity loads and columns bend more under lateral loads. Since the deformations of various members in a building must be controlled, the use of high strength steel is used only in those components of buildings whose deformation is not critical.

## 3.7 DUCTILE AND BRITTLE MATERIALS

The stress-strain diagram of low-carbon steel shown in Figure 3.11 was not drawn to scale in order to show details which would have been obscured in a scaled diagram. Figure 3.17 shows the same diagram drawn to scale[3.4]. Also included in the diagram are the stress-strain diagrams of high strength steel, wood and concrete. Note that low-carbon steel deforms substantially before failure. Its ultimate strain (strain at failure) of nearly 35% implies that low-carbon steel will stretch by 35% before failing. Thus, a 10 ft long member will increase to a length of 13.5 ft before breaking. This is a substantial deformation. By contrast, the ultimate strain of concrete is approximately 0.003 (0.3%), see Figure 3.16. In other words, low-carbon steel will deform nearly 110 times more than concrete before failure.

Materials which produce large deformations before failure are called *ductile* materials. Conversely, materials that do not deform much before failure are called *brittle* materials. The corresponding properties are called *ductility* and *brittleness*. There is no general agreement as to the value of

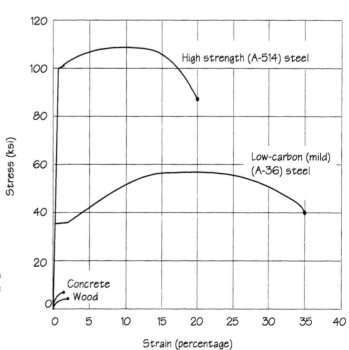

**FIGURE 3.17** Stress-strain diagrams for low-carbon steel, high strength steel, wood (in tension) and concrete (in compression).

ultimate strain that distinguishes a ductile material from a brittle material but we may regard a material as brittle if its ultimate strain is less than or equal to 0.5%. Ceramic materials such as brick, stone, concrete and glass have an ultimate strain of less than 0.5% and are therefore classified as brittle materials. As stated earlier, brittle materials are also elastic up to failure.

Most metals are ductile. Their ductility is primarily due to their large plastic deformations. Therefore, ductility is sometimes considered as being synonymous with plasticity, although theoretically they describe two different properties of a material. A material may be ductile because it has a large deformation at failure but may not be plastic, such as rubber.

Pure metals are more ductile than their alloys. Those who are familiar with jewelry know that pure gold is seldom used in jewelry because it is very ductile, hence prone to damage by deformation. The same is true of pure iron. It is too ductile and weak to be a useful construction material compared with steel, which is an alloy of iron and other compounds. Another disadvantage to using pure iron is that it is more expensive to produce than steel.

The manufacturing process of ferrous metals (cast iron and various types of steels) is such that a certain amount of carbon is inherently alloyed with iron. Cast iron and various steels differ from each other primarily in the amount of carbon present in the iron-carbon alloy. Cast iron contains the maximum amount of carbon — greater than 1.7%, usually between 2.5% to 4%. Steel contains between 0.12% to 1.7% carbon. Low-carbon steel contains nearly 0.25% carbon.

Wrought iron, the earliest ferrous metal used in construction, contains the least amount of carbon — less than 0.1%, usually 0.02%. It is a ductile material and was used extensively in buildings and bridges before the discovery of the Bessemer process in 1855 for the manufacture of steel on a commercial scale. The most significant example of the use of wrought iron is the Eiffel Tower in Paris, completed in 1889. Wrought iron was gradually replaced by steel, which is a stronger material, and today wrought iron is no longer produced. The name of wrought iron continues to be used in decorative furniture and railings, though the material actually used is steel.

Among various types of steel, low-carbon steel (also referred to as mild steel[6]) has the least tensile strength but the greatest ductility. High strength steels have a greater percentage of carbon than mild steel, but are less ductile. For instance, a steel with a yield strength of 100 ksi has an ultimate strain of nearly 20% as compared with 35% for mild steel, Figure 3.17. Furthermore, high strength steels do not have a well-defined yield point as compared with mild steel. However, as stated earlier, the modulus of elasticity of all types of steel is the same ($29 \times 10^6$ psi) and is not affected by the variation in the strength of steel. This is evident in Figure 3.17 where the slopes of the (linear portions of) stress-strain diagrams for both mild steel and high strength steel are the same.

---

[6] Low-carbon steel is known as mild steel because of its higher ductility and the consequent ease with which it can be bent to shape and rolled into various cross-sectional shapes. High strength steels are comparatively more brittle. Therefore, they cannot be bent to shape or rolled into cross-sectional shapes with the same ease.

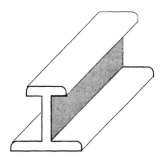

**FIGURE 3.18** Cast iron beams used in the Victorian period consisted of asymmetrical I-sections with wider flanges at the bottom to compensate for the lower tensile strength of the material.

### 3.7.1 Brittleness and Tensile Strength

One of the characteristics of brittle materials is that they are stronger in compression than in tension. For example, the tensile strength of concrete is approximately 7% to 10% of its compressive strength. Concrete with a compressive strength of 4,000 psi has a tensile strength of nearly 400 psi. Brick, stone and glass also behave similarly. Cast iron which contains the maximum amount of carbon is the most brittle of ferrous metals. With 4% carbon, cast iron's tensile strength is 20 ksi but its compressive strength is 90 ksi. As we shall note in Section 3.8, the bending of a member produces simultaneous compressive and tensile stresses. Since a brittle material is weak in tension, it is weak in bending also, and fails at a relatively small load when bent.

Before steel became available commercially, cast iron beams were used in buildings. To compensate for their relative weakness in tension, architects of the Victorian period (1837 - 1901) used asymmetrical I-sections with wider flanges on the tension side[3.5], Figure 3.18. A ductile material such as steel has equal strength in compression and tension. Therefore, when steel became commercially available, the use of cast iron in buildings was discontinued and there was no need to use asymmetrical I-sections.

### 3.7.2 Ductility and Failure Warning

Because its deformation at failure is small, a brittle material does not give any visual warning of its impending failure. Its failure is sudden. Failure of a ductile material, on the other hand, is gentle and is preceded by excessive deformation and ample warning. Structural safety concerns mandate a ductile failure in building structures. Brittle failure is not permitted. Since concrete is a brittle material and steel a ductile material, the use of steel reinforcement helps to impart moderate amount of ductility to reinforced concrete members. The concrete design codes, e.g. the American Concrete Institute's *Building Code Requirements for Reinforced Concrete, ACI 318* include a number of provisions to ensure ductile failure of reinforced concrete members.

### 3.7.3 Ductility and Stress Redistribution

The most significant difference between a ductile and a brittle material is in their abilities to cope with stress concentrations caused by discontinuities. These discontinuities which are represented by holes, notches, cracks and surface indentations produce nonuniform stresses so that greater stress (stress concentration) occurs at edges and discontinuities. Ductile materials have the ability to spread the stresses over the entire area, thereby evening the stresses out. Brittle materials do not have this ability. This is explained below.

Consider once again the rectangular steel plate with a hole of Example 3.4 which is subjected to a tensile force. We determined the stress on the section containing the hole as 40 ksi by assuming that the stresses are uniform on the entire section. In fact, the actual stresses on the section are not uniform. They maximize at edges AA' and BB' in Figure 3.19(a) — and decrease progressively away from the hole. Least stresses occur at edges CC' and DD'. The general stress distribution on the section is shown in Figure 3.19(b). Since the average stress on the section is 40 ksi, the actual stresses are greater than 40 ksi on edges AA' and BB' and less than 40 ksi on edges CC' and DD'.

Now assume that the load on the plate is gradually increased. This will increase the average stress on the section but the general distribution of stresses will remain as shown in Figure 3.19(b) until the maximum stress on the section reaches the yield stress. From Figure 3.11, we note that after the yield stress of steel is reached, the strain in steel increases but not the stresses. Thus, once the stresses on edges AA' and BB' reach the yield stress, there will be no further increase in stresses there. But since the load on the plate is increasing, additional stresses must be developed on the section to balance the load. Hence, the material adjacent to edges AA' and BB' comes under greater stresses until the stresses there also reach the yield stress. The stress distribution at this stage is shown in Figure 3.19(c).

Additional load on the bar will produce stress distribution as shown in Figure 3.19(d) and finally the entire section will come under uniform stresses equal to the yield stress of steel, Figure 3.19(e). Thus, we see that stress concentration has been eliminated by the ability of the material to redistribute stresses. This has been possible because of the yielding of the material.

If the material was brittle, the stress redistribution would not take place. Edges AA' and BB' would reach the ultimate strength of the material, causing failure there. This would increase the size of the hole and reduce the area of the section available to resist the force. Consequently, the stresses on the section would increase, which would cause failure on adjacent edges, further increasing the size of the hole. Finally, the entire plate would fracture, all this happening almost instantaneously.

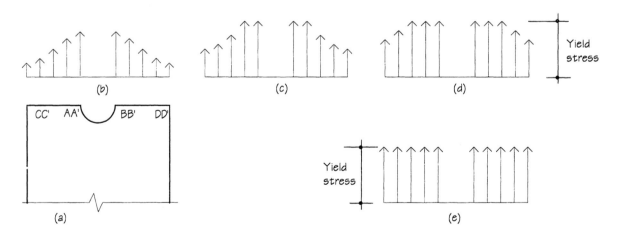

**FIGURE 3.19** (a) Steel plate with a hole acted upon by a tensile force, redrawn in elevation from Figure 3.8(a). (b) Actual stress distribution on the cross-section containing the hole. (c) Stress distribution after the material near edges AA' and BB' begins to yield. (d) Stress distribution as the load increases and the material further away from the hole yields. (e) Stress distribution when the material of the entire cross-section has reached yield stress.

**3.8 BENDING STRESSES**

When a force acts perpendicular to the axis of a member, the member bends. A force acting in a downward direction on a beam which is supported at the ends bends it with a concave (*water-holding*, like the inside of a saucer) curvature. An upward acting force will cause it to have a convex (*water-shedding*, like the outside of a sphere) curvature. Bending (also called flexure) is a predominant action in building structures. Vertical loads produce bending in beams and slabs and lateral loads cause bending in walls and columns.

Bending produces compression in one side of the member and tension in the other side. This can be demonstrated by bending a member made of a soft material such as rubber or sponge. If we mark two vertical lines, PQ and RS, on one of the longitudinal faces of a sponge beam and bend it to produce a concave curvature, as shown in Figure 3.20, we see that the lines have become closer at the top and farther apart at the bottom. Fibers of the beam represented by line PR have become shorter in length, and fibers on line QS have become longer.

Further examination of the deformed shape of rectangle PQSR shows that maximum contraction takes place along line PR, the extreme top fibers of the beam. The maximum elongation is produced along line QS, the extreme bottom fibers of the beam. In other words, compressive stresses are maximum at the top, and tensile stresses are maximum at the bottom of the beam.

The change from compressive to tensile stresses occurs on fibers which neither contract nor stretch, i.e., these fibers maintain their original dimension, and are therefore unstressed. In a beam with a symmetrical cross-section such as a rectangle, circle or a symmetrical I-section, the unstressed fibers lie in the longitudinal surface passing through the center of the beam. This surface intersects the cross-section of the beam in a straight line. This line is called the *neutral axis*[7] of the beam, Figure 3.21. Thus, the neutral axis is a line on the beam's cross-section where the stresses are zero.

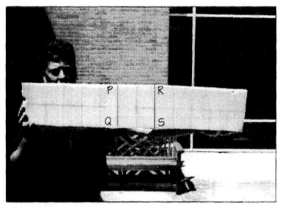

(a) Beam before bending

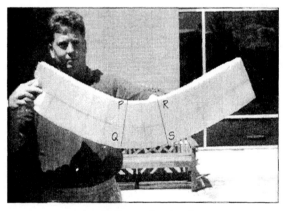

(b) Beam after bending

**FIGURE 3.20** The bending of a beam produces compressive as well as tensile stresses in the beam. In a beam bent with concave curvature, as shown in (b), the extreme top fibers are under maximum compressive stress and the extreme bottom fibers are under maximum tensile stress.

---

[7] The neutral axis is really a plane. Therefore "neutral plane" is a more correct description of the reality. However, the term neutral axis is well established in the literature.

If the beam is made of a linearly elastic material (remember, most construction materials are almost linearly elastic under design loads), the variation of stresses on a beam's cross-section is also linear. The stresses change from maximum compressive stresses at the top, to zero at the neutral axis, to maximum tensile stresses at the bottom of the beam. If we isolate a small length of the beam such as length PQSR of Figure 3.20 and examine the distribution of stresses on cross-sections represented by lines PQ and RS, we see that the distribution is as shown in Figure 3.22. The term *bending stresses* (or *flexural stresses*) is used to describe this distribution of stresses — compressive stresses on one side of the neutral axis and tensile stresses on the other side. These are also referred to as *flexural compression* and *flexural tension*, respectively. Note that flexural stresses are also normal stresses since they act normal to the cross-section of the element.

The stress distribution shown in Figure 3.22 represents stresses in the beam when it bends with a water-holding curvature. If the beam bends with a water-shedding curvature, the stresses will simply be reversed, i.e., tensile stresses will be created in the upper half of the beam and compressive stresses in the lower half of the beam.

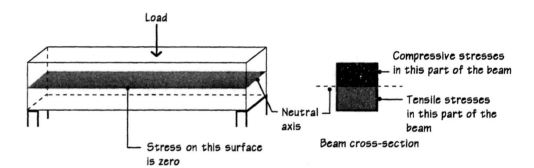

**FIGURE 3.21** In a beam supported at two ends and loaded with a vertically downward load, the upper half of the beam is under compressive stresses and the lower half under tensile stresses. At the neutral axis, the beam is unstressed, i.e. the stress on the neutral axis is zero.

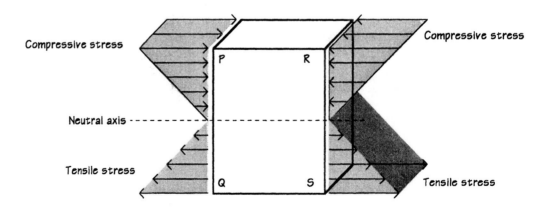

**FIGURE 3.22** Stress distribution on a small length, PQSR, of the beam of Figure 3.20.

### 3.8.1 Bending — an Inefficient Structural Action

The unequal distribution of stresses on a beam cross-section in bending implies that the material of the beam is not being fully utilized. Stresses are concentrated at the top and bottom of the cross-section but the central part of the cross-section is relatively stress free — an inefficient use of material.

One of the ways in which the structural inefficiency in bending is overcome is by using an I-shape in which the material is concentrated at the the top and bottom of the member. It is at the top and bottom of the member where most material is required due to the concentration of stresses at these locations. Thus, an I-section is a more efficient structural form than a rectangular or circular section if the member is in bending. Steel I-sections have been in use for a long time as beams, and recently wood I-sections have been introduced, Figure 3.23.

In fact, the structural inefficiency in bending of an element such as a beam is worse than that described above. The stresses are not only non-uniform on a beam's cross-section but are also nonuniform along the length of the beam. From the laws of statics, it can be shown that the stress distribution on various sections along the length of a beam supported on two ends is as shown in Figure 3.24. The central cross-section is most highly stressed, while the stresses on sections away from the center of the beam are progressively smaller.

It is obvious that when either the maximum tensile or maximum compressive stress on the central cross-section equals the ultimate strength of the material, the beam will fail. Thus, the failure of the beam is caused through the failure of just one (extreme) fiber — the top or the bottom fiber at the center of the beam. The rest of the beam has much lower stresses at failure.

**FIGURE 3.23** Wood I-beams.

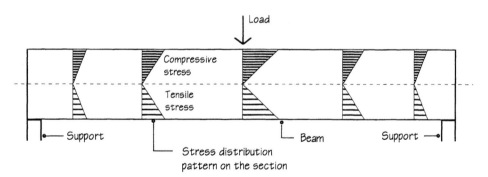

**FIGURE 3.24** Bending stress distribution on various sections along the length of a beam.

By comparison with bending, axial compression or axial tension is a far more efficient structural action because every cross-sectional surface of the member is under equal and uniform stress distribution (disregarding any stress concentration due to voids), see Figure 3.7. That is why if we take a thin bar or rod (of any material) and try to break it by pulling or compressing it, we will most probably not be able to break it. But if we bend the same rod, it will break more easily. The reason is that the maximum resistance to the load in bending is being provided by only a few fibers, thereby causing the rod to break. Therefore, a relatively small load is required to break the rod in bending. By contrast, the entire member participates in resisting an axial load.

Despite their structural inefficiency, beams, joists, decks and slabs are commonly used because of the need for horizontal spanning members in buildings.

Since bending creates tensile as well as compressive stresses, brittle materials, being weak in tension, are also weak in bending. Ductile materials, such as steel, which have equal strengths in tension and compression, work well in applications where bending occurs. Reinforced concrete is a composite material which exploits the moderately high compressive strength of concrete and the high tensile strength of steel. Steel is placed in those locations of a reinforced concrete member where tensile stresses are present. For instance, in a beam supported at two ends, tensile stresses occur in the lower half of the beam cross-section. Therefore, steel reinforcing bars are placed near the bottom of the beam, Figure 3.25.

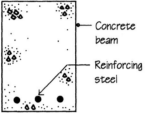

**FIGURE 3.25** Section through a typical reinforced concrete beam.

### 3.8.2 Bending Under an Eccentric Axial Load

When an axial load does not pass through the centroid of the member's cross-section, it is called an eccentric load. An eccentric load produces bending in the member in addition to axial compression or tension. The stresses created are flexural stresses as well as axial stresses. Thus, if a member is loaded with an eccentric compressive load, it will shorten due to compressive stresses, and also bend due to bending stresses, Figure 3.26.

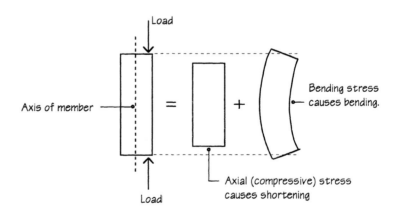

**FIGURE 3.26** An eccentric load creates axial stresses as well as bending stresses in the member. Thus, if a member is loaded with an eccentric compressive force, it shortens as well as bends.

**3.9 SHEAR STRESSES**

So far we have discussed normal stresses which act perpendicular to the cross-section of the member. Another simple state of stress is caused by a force which is tangential to the cross-sectional area of the member. Such a force is called a *shear force*, and the resulting stress and strain are called *shear stress* and *shear strain* respectively.

Because it is tangential, a shear force tends to produce a sliding effect on the body. Shear stress is therefore associated with a body's resistance to sliding. Like the normal stress, shear stress is also defined as the shear force divided by area, and has the same units as the normal stress. Thus:

$$\text{Shear stress} \; = \; \frac{\text{Shear force}}{\text{Area of section on which shear force acts}} \qquad (3.4)$$

Consider an assembly of two wood members glued together at the interface, as shown in Figure 3.27(a). If a force pulls on the assembly, axial tension is developed in each member. In addition to the axial stress, the assembly also develops shear stresses to resist sliding at the interface. The area of the assembly which resists shear is shown by the shaded area. If this area is A, and if the force acting on the assembly is P, then the shear stress developed at the interface is simply P/A.

If the members are joined together with bolts as shown in Figure 3.27(b) instead of being glued together, the shear force will be resisted by the cross-sectional area of the bolts. The following example will help in further understanding the concept of shear stress.

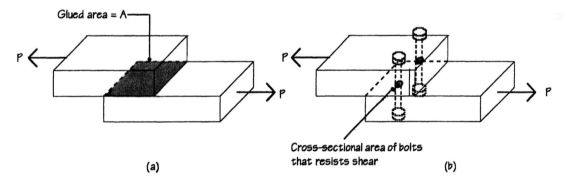

**FIGURE 3.27** (a) Shear resistance in the assembly of two wood members which are glued together is provided by the glued area shown shaded. (b) In the bolted connection, shear resistance is provided by the bolts. The area which resists shear is the cross-sectional area of the bolts.

**Example 3.5**

Determine the shear stress in the assembly of Figure 3.27(b), given that the force acting on the assembly is 4.0 k and the blocks are joined together with two 0.5 in. diameter bolts.

*Solution*:  P = 4.0 kips.  Radius of one bolt = 0.25 in.

Area that resists shear force (cross-sectional area of the two bolts) = A = $2(\pi r^2) = 2\pi (0.25)^2 = 0.393$ in$^2$.

From Equation (3.4), shear stress = 4.0/0.393  = 10.2 ksi.

Although axial stresses produce axial deformation (elongation or shortening), shear stresses produce angular deformation.  Under the action of shear stresses, a rectangular element changes to an oblique element.  This is shown in Figure 3.28 where the rectangular solid ABCDEF suffers an angular change to shape AB'C'D'E'F, indicating the presence of tension along one diagonal and compression along the other diagonal of the element.  Because of the tension created by shear, brittle materials which are weak in tension are also weak in shear.  Thus, concrete beams need steel stirrups to increase their resistance in shear, Figure 3.29.

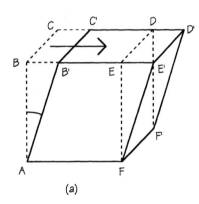
(a)

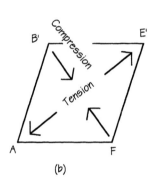
(b)

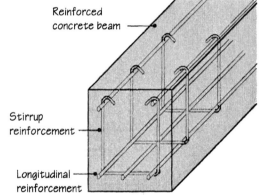

**FIGURE  3.28**  (a) A rectangular parallelepiped ABCDEF deformed to an oblique parallelepiped, AB'C'D'E'F, under the action of shear stresses.  (b) The deformed shape of the parralelepiped shows that shear stresses produce tensile stresses along one diagonal and compressive stresses along the other diagonal.

**FIGURE  3.29**  Steel stirrups in a reinforced concrete beam increase the beam's shear strength.

### 3.9.1  Shear Stresses in Bending

Shear stresses considered in Figure 3.27 are examples of direct shear.  Direct shear stress occurs in connections such as welds, bolts, rivets, screws, nails, and glued joints.  Shear stress also occurs indirectly when members are subjected to bending. In fact, bending is usually accompanied by shear.

Consider once again a beam which is loaded with a vertical load at its center.  If we imagine this beam to be composed of vertical strips bonded together, we will see that these strips have a tendency to slide against each other. Although a real beam is not made of strips, the tendency to shear on vertical planes exists in a beam as shown in Figure 3.30(a). In other words, shear stresses are present on the vertical planes of a beam when it bends.

Shear stresses on vertical planes of a beam (called *vertical shear*) are always accompanied by shear stresses on horizontal planes of a beam, called *horizontal shear*. The presence of horizontal shear in a beam is easily demonstrated if we take several thin strips of a soft material such as cork to make a beam. Note that the strips are not bonded together so that the assembly of strips resembles a deck of cards. If we place two vertical lines on one face of this assembly, lines AB and CD in Figure 3.30(b), and then bend the assembly, we see that the strips slide over each other. The rectangle ABCD goes through an angular deformation due to the bending of the beam and changes into an oblique parallelogram, demonstrating the presence of shear (see Figure 3.28b). In an actual beam, we do not see this deformation because its shear resistance does not allow such deformations to be so large as to be visible.

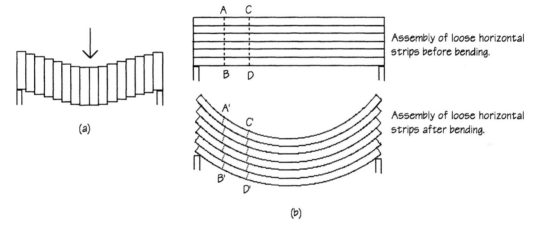

(a)

A  C

Assembly of loose horizontal strips before bending.

B  D

A'

C'

Assembly of loose horizontal strips after bending.

B'

D'

(b)

**FIGURE 3.30** The tendency to shear is produced on both the horizontal and vertical planes of the beam when it bends: (a) tendency to shear along vertical planes of a beam; (b) tendency to shear along horizontal planes.

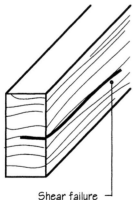

Shear failure

**FIGURE 3.31** Shear failure in a wood beam usually occurs due to the sliding of wood fibers.

It can be shown (from elementary statics) that horizontal shear at a point in the beam is always equal to the vertical shear at that point. Thus, if a beam is to fail in shear, it will either fail by shearing along a horizontal plane or a vertical plane. However, shear failure in wood beams occurs only on horizontal planes. This is due to the fibrous structure of wood. In a wood beam, the fibers are oriented in the horizontal direction, Figure 3.31. Since the bond between the fibers is relatively weak, wood is weaker in horizontal shear than in vertical shear. If a wood beam is to fail in shear, the failure will occur in a horizontal plane, not on a vertical plane. Therefore, for wood beams, only the horizontal shear strength values are quoted since it is the horizontal shear strength that is critical in wood, not its vertical shear strength. Shear failure in a homogeneous material such as steel, on the other hand, may occur either in horizontal or vertical shear.

### 3.10 MECHANISM OF FAILURE OF MATERIALS*

Shear stresses are not only produced when a member is in bending but also when a member is under axial tension or compression. Consider a member which is subjected to an axial tensile force equal to P, Figure 3.32. In Section 3.3, we stated that the stress on a cross-section (normal to the axis) of a member is P/A. In fact, tensile stresses not only occur on planes normal to the axis of the member but also on planes which are obliquely inclined to the axis. It can be shown by statics that both the tensile stresses and shear stresses are present on all planes of the member.

On a plane normal to the axis of a member, the shear stress is zero but the tensile stress is maximum, and equal to P/A. Because of its larger area, the stress on an inclined plane is less than P/A but this plane is subjected to shear stresses also. The shear stress on an inclined plane increases as the angle of inclination of the plane with the axis deviates from the 90° angle. Shear stress is maximum on a plane inclined at 45° to the axis. On a 45° plane, both shear stress and tensile stress are equal to 0.5 P/A. In other words, the maximum shear stress in the member is half the maximum tensile stress.

If the member of Figure 3.32 was subjected to a compressive force, the normal planes would be subjected to compressive stress only while all other planes would be subjected to compressive as well as shear stress. The maximum shear stress would once again occur on 45° planes, and its value would be half the maximum compressive stress.

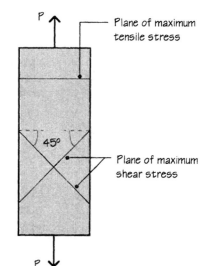

**FIGURE 3.32** Planes of maximum stress and maximum shear stress in a member subjected to a tensile force.

---

* May be omitted on first reading.

### 3.10.1  Failure of a Ductile Material in Axial Tension

Let us now assume that the load P on the member in Figure 3.32 is gradually increased until the member fails. There are two modes in which the member can fail: either in tension or shear, whichever is the weaker mode for the material. For example, if the ultimate tensile strength of the material is 60 ksi and its ultimate shear strength 40 ksi, the member will fail in tension. This is because when the tensile stress in the member is 60 ksi, the maximum shear stress in it is 0.5(60) = 30 ksi, which is less than the material's strength in shear. On the other hand, if the material's ultimate tensile strength is 60 ksi and shear strength 25 ksi, the failure will be controlled by shear because when the tensile stress in the material is only 50 ksi, the shear stress will reach its failure stress of 25 ksi on a 45° plane.

Ductile materials, such as metals, are much weaker in shear than in tension. Therefore, the failure of ductile materials is governed by shear. When tested in a tensile testing machine, a ductile material will not fail in tension but in shear. Failure takes place along the 45° planes where the shear stress is maximum. This is precisely what happens when a mild steel bar specimen (Figure 3.10) is tested in tension. The bar behaves as if it is composed of two parts with one part sliding over the other on a 45° plane, Figure 3.33(a). Usually the sliding takes place on several inclined planes simultaneously so that the bar undergoes local contraction, referred to as "necking".

It is because of the relative weakness in shear that metals yield. The yielding is caused by 45° oblique planes sliding over each other. If the material was strong in shear so that sliding did not take place, the bar would have failed on a plane perpendicular to the applied force where the tension is maximum. As explained later, the failure of brittle materials in tension (which are much stronger in shear than in tension) occurs in this manner, i.e., the failure surface is perpendicular to the force. The final fracture of a ductile material, on the other hand, occurs along a cone-and-cup shaped surface. The sides of the cup (or the cone) make an angle of approximately 45° to the applied force, Figure 3.33(b).

### 3.10.2  Failure of a Ductile Material in Axial Compression

The stresses in a member loaded in compression are similar to that loaded in tension. Both shear stress and compressive stress are present on an inclined plane. For a ductile material, the failure is once again caused by shearing along the 45° plane. This time the effect of shearing, however, is to cause an outward bulge into a barrel-like shape instead of necking, Figure 3.34. The member does not break into two pieces but its shape changes substantially, which is considered as failure.

### 3.10.3  Failure of a Brittle Material in Axial Tension

In Section 3.7.3, we saw that a brittle material does not have the ability to redistribute stresses — to even out stress concentrations caused by holes or

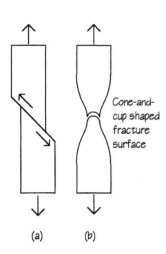

Cone-and-cup shaped fracture surface

(a)        (b)

**FIGURE 3.33** (a) Failure of a ductile material in tension is caused by sliding on 45° planes. (b) The final fracture of a ductile material creates a cone-and-cup surface.

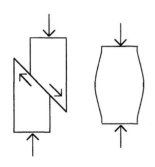

**FIGURE 3.34** Shearing along 45° planes in a member under compression deforms the member into a barrel-like shape.

voids. As the tensile force on the member increases, stress concentration leads to local failure at the edge of the void, which enlarges the void. Consequently, the area of cross-section available to resist the force is reduced. This reduction in cross-sectional area increases the stresses even further, which causes further enlargement of the void. This process continues until the void has extended to the full thickness of the member and the member breaks in two pieces.

The primary factor that determines the degree of stress concentration is the shape of the void. A void with a narrow tip leads to a highly stressed location as compared to a broad tipped void. That is why abrupt changes in cross-sectional profiles of components which produce sharp interior angles should be avoided in structural elements. Thus, from a structural view point, a circular hole or a hole with rounded ends is preferable to a rectangular hole since the latter produces sharp angles.

When the stress at the tip of a critical void in a member reaches the ultimate tensile strength of the material, say at point A or B in Figure 3.35, the material will begin to tear apart under the applied tensile force. As the member tears, the void becomes larger and the area of the member available to resist the force becomes smaller, leading to greater stresses. This action tears the member further and the process continues until the member breaks into two pieces. That is why brittle materials are weak in tension and fail at relatively low stresses. Although the average stress in the material as obtained by dividing the force on the member by its net cross-sectional area (area of cross-section minus the area of void) is low, the actual stress in the member near a void may be several times greater than the average stress because of stress concentration.

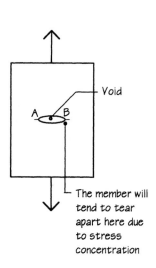

**FIGURE 3.35** Mechanism by which a brittle material with a void tears apart under tension.

This is precisely what a glazier does in cutting a sheet of glass. The glazier does not need to make a deep cut into the glass sheet but simply makes a groove on its surface. After the groove is made, the sheet is bent. The bending produces tensile stresses in the sheet which creates stress concentration at the tip of the groove, and the sheet breaks in two pieces. The breakage is almost instantaneous although the stress concentration has progressed from the top surface to the bottom of the sheet. The glazier's groove must be sharp because the sharper the groove, the greater the stress concentration and hence, the cleaner the cut.

Most brittle materials, such as brick, stone and concrete, have numerous voids. Being composed of granular ingredients (such as clay, sand, stone aggregate, etc.), voids are an unavoidable characteristic of these materials. If the ingredients are densely packed, the voids are smaller and less numerous, but they cannot be eliminated altogether. Additionally, bricks and concrete have voids generated from the evaporation of water. In the case of bricks, evaporation of water occurs when the bricks are dried and fired. In concrete, nearly half the water added in the making of concrete becomes chemically combined with portland cement while the other half evaporates. In fact, the secret of producing high strength concrete lies mainly in reducing the volume of voids.

Although the cause of stress concentration in brick, concrete and stone is the presence of voids and pores, in glass it is the presence of extremely fine cracks (micro-fissures) that are responsible for stress concentration. The cracks are so fine that they can be seen only under powerful magnification. The cracks in glass are of two types — internal cracks and surface cracks. Internal cracks are caused as the molten glass shrinks upon cooling. Surface cracks, on the other hand, are caused by abrasion. Even light contact with other materials or human touch during manufacture and handling can cause surface cracking, which in the case of window glass worsens under normal use, rain and wind storms. In fact, a crack-free glass does not exist. Additionally, the cracks in a glass sheet are randomly distributed over the sheet, Figure 3.36. Surface cracks are responsible for severely weakening the glass (see also Section 7.8).

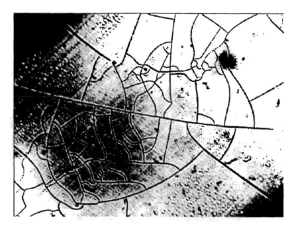

**FIGURE 3.36** Surface cracks in a glass sheet. Reference 3.6 with permission.

### 3.10.4 Failure of a Brittle Material in Axial Compression

The mechanism of failure of a brittle material in compression is different from its failure in tension. Although stress concentration would lead to local crushing, the member will not tear and hence the failure does not propagate. How then does a brittle material fail in axial compression?

Testing to failure in compression is the method employed to determine the compressive strength of brittle materials such as concrete and masonry. In the case of concrete, 6 in. diameter by 12 in. high concrete cylinders are used in the United States and 6 in. cubes are used in Britain and Europe. In the case of masonry, masonry prisms are used. A masonry prism consists of a few masonry units joined together with horizontal mortar joints, Figure 3.37(a).

Compression tests on concrete cylinders and cubes show that they fail by shearing along 45° planes. The failure is initiated by shear stress concentration at the voids. Since the voids are distributed in all directions, a fair number lie along the 45° planes where the shear is maximum. Once the shear stress at the critical void lying in a 45° plane exceeds the shear strength of the material, sliding occurs along the 45° plane. The actual fracture of a concrete cylinder (or cube) takes place by the spalling away of wedge-shaped pieces from the sides, as shown in Figure 3.37(b).

In addition to shear failure, vertical cracking of concrete cylinders takes

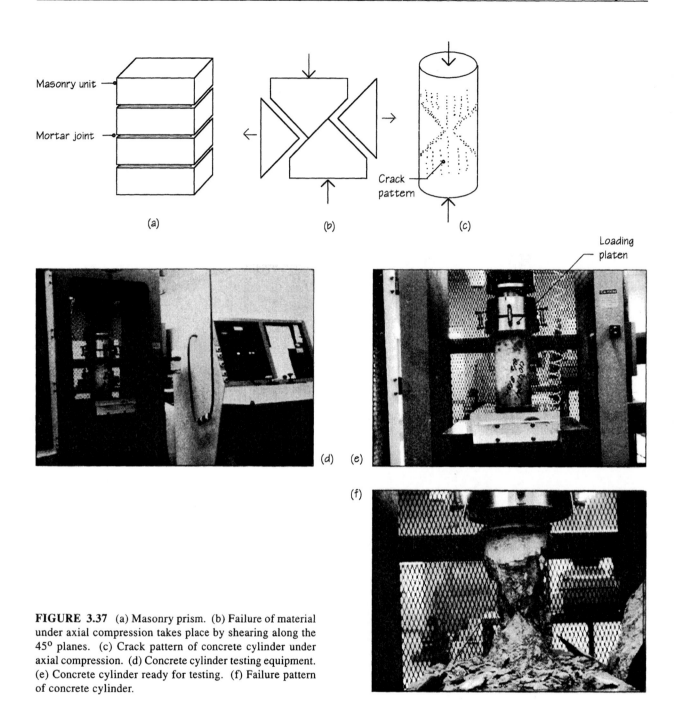

**FIGURE 3.37** (a) Masonry prism. (b) Failure of material under axial compression takes place by shearing along the 45° planes. (c) Crack pattern of concrete cylinder under axial compression. (d) Concrete cylinder testing equipment. (e) Concrete cylinder ready for testing. (f) Failure pattern of concrete cylinder.

place as shown in Figure 3.37(c). This is caused by tensile stresses created in a direction normal to axial compression. However, because of friction between the loading platens of the testing machine and the ends of the test cylinder (or cube), this tension is counteracted by lateral compressive stresses. In other words, when loaded in a compression testing machine, the cylinder (or cube) is in a state of longitudinal as well as lateral compression. The longitudinal compression occurs because of the load, and the lateral compression occurs due to the confining action of the platens of the testing machine. As a result of this state of stress, tension failure of the cylinder is suppressed, particularly at its ends.

Because there is no redistribution of stresses, the compression failure of a brittle material is abrupt. The failure can be mildly explosive, as the energy stored in the member in compression is suddenly released upon its fracture. Therefore concrete and masonry testing equipment is provided with a protective steel mesh, Figure 3.37(f).

## 3.11 CONFINEMENT, STRENGTH AND DUCTILITY

The confining action of loading platens at the top and bottom of a cylinder in the testing machine produces a state of stress in the cylinder that is called *triaxial compression* because the cylinder is stressed in three dimensions. In the vertical direction, the cylinder is compressed by the load. In the two dimensions of the horizontal plane (the lateral direction), the cylinder is compressed by the confining action of the loading platens. The lateral compressive stresses are produced because of the friction between the platens and the ends of the cylinder. If there were no friction between the platens and the end surfaces of the cylinder, the cylinder would tend to expand in the horizontal direction under a vertical load.

Lateral compression increases the axial load-carrying capacity of concrete. If lateral compression were absent, the test cylinder would fail at a smaller load.

Lateral compressive stresses are maximum at the ends of the cylinder where the confining effect of the platens is maximum. They reduce progressively to a minimum at mid-height, Figure 3.38. In the case of a cube which is half the height of the concrete test cylinder, the lateral stresses are practically uniform over its entire height. That is the main reason why cubes made from the same concrete fail at nearly 25% greater stress than concrete cylinders.

Concrete cylinders tested in triaxial compression (using special testing equipment) show that concrete under triaxial compression is not only stronger than concrete loaded in uniaxial compression but also more ductile. Figure 3.39 shows the stress-strain relationships for a concrete with a uniaxial

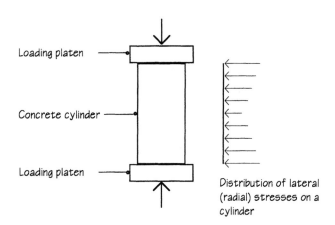

**FIGURE 3.38** Distribution of lateral (radial) stresses on concrete cylinder caused by the confining effect of loading platens.

(unconfined) compressive strength of nearly 3.5 ksi but with different lateral compressive stresses.

Thus, when the lateral compressive stress on the cylinder was 1.0 ksi, its strength under vertical load increased from 3.5 ksi to nearly 9.0 ksi. When the lateral compression was raised to 2.0 ksi, the strength of the cylinder, made from the same concrete, increased to nearly 13 ksi; with 4.0 ksi lateral compression, the strength jumped up to 19.0 ksi. Note that the curve with $f_r$ = 0 in Figure 3.39 refers to the cylinder's uniaxial compressive strength of 3.5 ksi.

The increase in concrete's ductility under lateral compression is more dramatic than the increase in its strength. Thus, although the ultimate strain of concrete in uniaxial compression is nearly 0.3%, it increases to nearly 6% (20 times greater) when the lateral compression increases to 4.0 ksi[3.7]. This implies that a 3.5 ksi concrete is 20 times more ductile when acted upon by lateral compression of 4.0 ksi than the same concrete with no lateral compression.

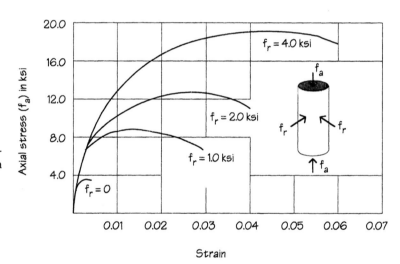

**FIGURE 3.39** Stress-strain relationship under various magnitudes of triaxial compression of a 3.5 ksi concrete.

**FIGURE 3.40** Spiral column for a bridge in Los Angeles, California.

Triaxial compression is the state of stress that occurs in deep and thick concrete columns and walls since the concrete in the interior of these elements is not free to expand laterally. This is also the state of stress in the soils surrounding building foundations.

The increased ductility and strength of concrete obtained through triaxial compression is used in detailing the reinforced concrete columns recommended for use in seismic locations. (Remember that ductility of structural members is an important requirement in seismic locations). These columns are provided with a steel spiral wound around the vertical reinforcing bars, Figure 3.40. As the column is loaded, the spiral creates a confining compressive stress in the lateral direction on the core of the column, thereby increasing the column's strength and ductility.

**3.12 BUCKLING**

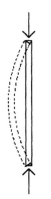

**FIGURE 3.41** Buckling of a long and slender member under axial compression.

In Section 3.10, the failure mechanisms of ductile and brittle members were described. We observed that the failure of a brittle member in axial compression occurs by shearing along 45° planes. This failure mechanism applies only to members which are short in length as compared to their cross-sectional dimensions. If the member is long and slender (i.e., the length of the member is much greater than its cross-sectional dimension), it will not fail as described but will simply tend to bend under the load, Figure 3.41. Bending of a member under axial compression is called *buckling*. For example, if we take a thin plastic ruler and hold it so that it stands on one of its ends and then press it down from the other end, we see that it buckles as we press it hard.

The difference between bending and buckling is that bending is produced by loads which are perpendicular to the axis of the member and buckling is caused by axial loads. A more significant difference between the two, however, is that the bending of a member takes place under all magnitudes of loads, however small. Buckling occurs when the load increases to a certain critical value, called the *critical load* or the *Euler Buckling Load* after the Swiss mathematician Leonard Euler (1707-83). If the load is less than the critical load, buckling will not occur.

Buckling is recognized as one of the failure mechanisms in compression although it usually does not lead to a collapse of the structure. By buckling under the load, the member becomes unstable but will not fracture. In some situations, however, the instability caused by buckling in one member may lead to excessive stresses in other members, thereby causing a progressive collapse of the structure.

Thus, there are two modes in which a member loaded in axial compression may fail. First, if a member is short and squatty, it will fail by crushing under the load as described in Section 3.10.4. Second, if the member is long and slender, it will fail by buckling.

If we take several different heights of bars of the same cross-sectional dimensions and material and test them under axial compression, we will observe that up to a certain height the bars will fail by fracturing. Beyond this height, the bars will fail by buckling. We will also observe that the fracture load is independent of the height of the bars. The buckling load, on the other hand, decreases as the height increases since it is a function of the slenderness of the member, Figure 3.42.

Buckling is an important consideration in the design of columns and loadbearing walls. Steel columns are more prone to buckling than concrete

**FIGURE 3.42** Idealized relationship between the height of a member and its failure load under compression.

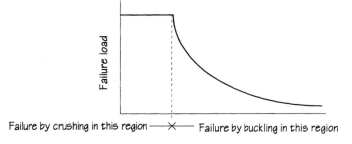

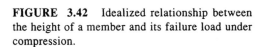

Failure by crushing in this region ——✕—— Failure by buckling in this region

Height of member

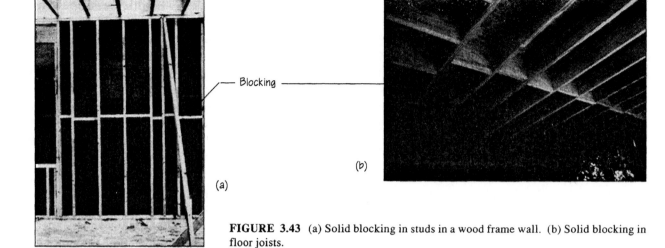

FIGURE 3.43  (a) Solid blocking in studs in a wood frame wall.  (b) Solid blocking in floor joists.

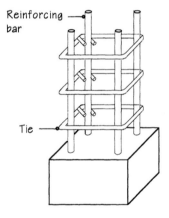

FIGURE 3.44  Horizontal ties in a reinforced concrete column.

columns, since the former are more slender.  Even slender beams and floor joists are prone to buckling because of the presence of flexural compression in them.

To strengthen a member against buckling failure, we can either reduce its slenderness, i.e., increase its cross-sectional dimension or brace it at intermediate point(s) along its length or height.  Usually, the latter approach (bracing the member) is used since increasing the cross-sectional dimension is uneconomical.  For instance, studs in a wood light frame wall need to be solidly blocked if it is determined that they may buckle under loads, Figure 3.43(a).  Slender beams and joists require similar bracing, Figure 3.43(b), because compression is produced in their top fibers as they bend.  This compression may cause the slender beams and joists to buckle sideways, a phenomenon known as *lateral buckling*.

Buckling failure is not just a consideration for the entire structural member but also for its parts.  Because of their slenderness, the vertical reinforcing bars in a concrete column have a tendency to buckle and break through the concrete cover under an axial load on the column.  Horizontal ties are therefore provided along the height of the column to prevent this failure mode, Figure 3.44.

## 3.13 STRUCTURAL SAFETY

The most fundamental requirement of a structure is that it should be safe.  A structure is safe if its strength is greater than the strength required to carry the loads imposed on it.  The excess of the actual strength of the structure over the required strength is a measure of safety provided in the structure and is given by the ratio of the actual strength of the structure to the required strength.  This ratio is referred to as the *factor of safety*.  Thus:

$$\text{Factor of Safety} = \frac{\text{Actual strength}}{\text{Required strength}} \tag{3.5}$$

If we could ascertain the loads that a structure is required to support with perfect certainty, if we were absolutely certain of the strength of the material, if all materials gave the same amount of warning before failure, if the strength of materials did not deteriorate with time, and if the structural design procedures used were without any ambiguity, then a factor of safety, marginally greater than 1.0, is all that would be needed.

The fact, however, is that none of the above "ifs" is obtained in practice. There are uncertainties in the values of design loads used and there is usually a great deal of variation in the strength of materials. For example, if several concrete cylinders were prepared from the same mix of concrete under identical conditions and were tested to failure using the same procedures and testing equipment, the results could vary by as much as 100%. Additionally, materials deteriorate with time and their deterioration is not the same under all conditions. Our design procedures are not exact and involve considerable approximation and generalization. Considering these uncertainties, it is necessary that the factor of safety in structures be much greater than 1.0.

The greater the uncertainty (in many situations the uncertainty is due to our ignorance), the greater the factor of safety needed. In a material such as steel which is manufactured under relatively controlled conditions, a lower factor of safety is used as compared to concrete. Concrete is virtually a site-manufactured material. It is not possible to have the same degree of quality control in the production of concrete as in steel. The strength of concrete is not only dependent on the mix proportions but also on placing, compaction and curing. Similarly, since wood is a naturally grown material, there is considerable variation (uncertainty) in its strength for the same specie and grade. The factor of safety required in designing with wood is even higher than that required for concrete. However, a large factor of safety leads to uneconomical design. A judicious compromise is therefore needed between adequate safety and economic considerations.

### 3.13.1 Allowable Stresses

One of the ways in which the factor of safety is incorporated in structural design is to limit the actual stress in members caused by loads to a value which is less than its failure stress. This limiting stress is called the *allowable stress*. Thus:

$$\text{Allowable stress} = \frac{\text{Maximum stress that the material can sustain}}{\text{Factor of safety}} \qquad (3.6)$$

The actual stress in the material must be less than or equal to the allowable stress.

The maximum stress that the material can sustain is not necessarily the ultimate (fracture) strength of the material since the structural design criteria does not merely require the safety of the structure. An additional requirement is that the structure should remain elastic; that is, no permanent deformations should occur in the structure under loads. Therefore, in the case of steel, the numerator in Equation (3.6) is the yield stress of steel since steel is elastic only up to its yield point. In the case of concrete and masonry, the allowable stresses are based on the ultimate strength of materials since these materials remain virtually elastic up to failure.

**REVIEW QUESTIONS**

**3.1** What is the difference between normal stress and shear stress? Explain with the help of sketches.

**3.2** What are the units of stress and strain in the U.S. customary system and the SI system of units?

**3.3** A 1 in. diameter steel bar is subjected to a tensile force of 30 kips. Determine the stress in the bar.

**3.4** If the bar in Problem 3.3 is 10 ft long, determine the elongation of the bar. The modulus of elasticity of steel is $29 \times 10^6$ psi.

**3.5** Sketch the structural steel sections commonly used in buildings.

**3.6** Draw the stress-strain diagram of low-carbon steel showing all its important parts.

**3.7** What does "grade 60" steel mean?

**3.8** What is "modulus of elasticity"? Which property of material does it represent? What are the values of modulus of elasticity for steel, concrete and wood?

**3.9** Two beams, A and B, are identical in dimensions but of different materials. Both beams are loaded with the same load. Beam A deflects more than beam B. Which beam, A or B, has the higher modulus of elasticity?

**3.10** Briefly describe the properties of: (a) brittle materials and (b) ductile materials. Name three brittle and three ductile materials.

**3.11** With the help of sketches and notes, explain why bending is an inefficient structural action.

**3.12** Explain why a brittle material is weak in shear.

**3.13** With the help of sketches and notes, explain the mechanism of failure of a brittle material in tension.

**3.14** With the help of sketches and notes, explain the mechanism of failure of a ductile material in tension.

**3.15** Explain buckling failure. What measures are commonly used to strengthen building components against buckling failure? Explain with the help of sketches.

**3.16** If the ultimate strength of a material is 6,000 psi and the factor of safety used is 2.5, determine the allowable stress of the material.

**REFERENCES**

3.1     Patton, W.J: *Materials in Industry*, Prentice Hall, New York, 1986, p. 26.

3.2     Structural Engineers Association of California, San Francisco: *Recommended Lateral Force Requirements and Tentative Commentary*, 1988, p. 18-C.

3.3     Nawy, E.G: *Reinforced Concrete*, Prentice Hall, New York, 1990, p. 46.

3.4     McCormac, J.C: *Structural Steel Design*, Harper Collins, New York, 1992, p. 20.

3.5.    Gordon, J.E: *Structures Or Why Things Don't Fall Down*, Plenum Press, 1978, p. 278.

3.6.    Gordon J.E: *The Science of Structures and Materials*, Scientific American Library, New York, 1988, p. 83.

3.7.    MacGregor, J.G: *Reinforced Concrete Design*, Prentice Hall, New York, 1992, p. 51.

# THERMAL PROPERTIES OF MATERIALS

**4.1 INTRODUCTION**     The provision of thermal comfort in buildings has been an important design objective from the earliest times. The considerations of climate and the manipulation of available resources to produce a comfortable building have always exercised a major influence on the design of shelters. The Eskimos' igloo and the adobe houses of the Middle East are some of the early examples of comfort-conscious designs in two extremes of climate. Figures 4.1(a) and 4.1(b) show diurnal variations of temperatures inside a typical igloo and an

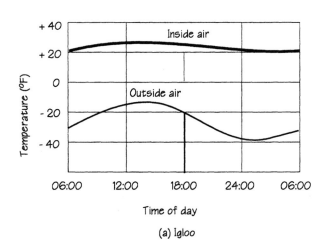

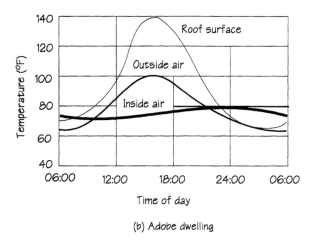

**FIGURE 4.1**  Diurnal variations of temperature in (a) an igloo, and (b) an adobe dwelling.

95

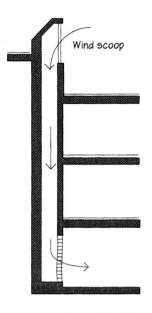

**FIGURE 4.2** Section through a wind scoop showing the penetration of breeze from a vertical shaft into house interior. Wind scoops were used extensively as design elements in the middle east.

adobe dwelling along with the respective outdoor temperatures[4.1]. The relative stability of the indoor air temperature and the large difference between the indoor and outdoor temperatures in both the igloo and the adobe dwelling attest to the success of these designs in providing thermal comfort.

The inclusion of water bodies in open courtyards of the hot dry region of northern India, wind scoops used on the roofs of buildings in the hot humid climates of the Middle East, Figure 4.2, and Le Corbusier's "bris-soleil" (shading devices) are among several more recent examples of building design in context of the local climate — solar radiation, breeze, vegetation, water and other natural resources.

The advances of the twentieth century in electric heating and air conditioning equipment shifted design emphasis from climate-conscious design to the use of fuel-based energy to achieve comfort conditions. Climate and natural resources became largely irrelevant since they posed no constraints in achieving a comfortable building. With the help of mechanical equipment, thermal comfort could be provided in any building and in any climatic region.

The new design freedom was fully exploited by architects to the extent that an all-glass exterior became a recognized facade formula, particularly for commercial buildings. Since energy prices were low, the energy bills of buildings were relatively small. However, the situation changed dramatically in 1973 when the oil-producing countries of the Middle East placed an embargo on the sale of oil and quadrupled its prices.

With the increase in energy prices, energy bills of buildings were no longer insignificant but became the single most important recurring liability. In addition to this came the realization that the earth's fossil fuel reserves are depletable. Consequently, energy conservation became an important design objective which led to a substantial reorientation of architectural thinking. The consideration of thermal properties and thermal behavior of buildings assumed greater importance. The building industry reacted by producing materials and equipment which are thermally more efficient, and the design community responded by using greater amounts of thermal insulation. Today, insulation is one of the most important components of a building envelope.

As shown in Figure 4.3, an energy-conservative building design is a

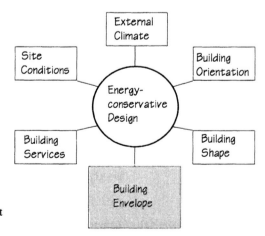

**FIGURE 4.3** Factors that affect energy-conservative building design.

function of several variables. It includes the consideration of the external climate, site conditions, building orientation and shape, building services (air conditioning, water supply, lighting and waste management) and thermal properties of the building envelope. In this chapter, we shall discuss only the thermal properties of the building envelope, as related to its materials and construction.

## 4.2 UNITS OF HEAT, ENERGY AND POWER

Until the middle of the nineteenth century, various forms of energy (such as the electrical energy obtained from electric generating stations, nuclear energy obtained from the splitting of atomic nuclei, and chemical energy obtained from the burning of coal, gasoline and other combustible materials) were considered to be unrelated to each other. Therefore, different types of energy were measured in different units. Today, we know that all energy forms are interrelated by a fundamental property: a natural tendency among all forms of energy to be converted to heat. Thus, all energy forms can be measured by the amount of heat they produce. The unit of heat, the *calorie*, is therefore a convenient unit for the measurement of energy.

One calorie is defined as the amount of heat required to raise the temperature of one gram of water by 1 °C. A useful multiple of calorie is the unit "kilocalorie" (kcal) defined as the amount of heat required to raise the temperature of 1 kilogram of water by 1 °C (1 kcal = 1,000 cal).

The unit "calorie" used by nutritionists and dietitians to specify a particular food's energy or calorie content is in fact the unit kilocalorie. However, it is common practice when referring to a food's calorie content to omit the prefix "kilo" and call it "Calorie" with an upper case "C" and abbreviate it as Cal (1 Cal = 1,000 cal). Thus if a food item is labeled as containing 10 Cal, it means that it is capable of producing 10,000 calories of heat in the body through metabolic action.

In the U.S. system of units, the unit of heat is the British thermal unit (Btu), which is defined as the amount of heat required to raise the temperature of one pound of water by 1 °F. One Btu is approximately equal to 252 calories.

While the units calorie and Btu are used only with reference to heat, the unit that is used for all forms of energy (including heat energy), is the Joule (J). It is the unit Joule that is used in the SI system.

The Joule originated as a unit of work, defined as the amount of work done by a force of one Newton in moving through a distance of one meter in the direction of the force. It was adopted as the unit of energy after the British physicist James P. Joule (1818-1889) established a relationship between work and heat. From that relationship, 1 cal = 4.185 J. Since Joule is a small unit, kilo-Joule (kJ), and Mega-Joule (MJ) are often used; 1 kJ = $10^3$ J and 1 MJ = $10^6$ J.

### 4.2.1 Power

Power is defined as the rate of energy production, energy consumption or energy conversion. Therefore, the unit of power is Joule per second (J/s), also called a watt (W) after the Scottish engineer James Watt (1736-1819). Since 1 J/s = 1 W, a 100 W electric lamp produces 100 Joules of energy per second or 360 x $10^3$ Joules per hour.

Since a watt is an extremely small unit, the unit more commonly used is the kilowatt (kW), where 1 kW = $10^3$ W. The old unit of power, which is still somewhat used, is horsepower (hp). It is the rate at which a healthy horse could do work. In terms of watts, 1 hp = 746 W, or approximately 0.75 kW. In the U.S. system of units, power is expressed as Btu per hour (Btu/h). 1 Btu/h = 0.29 W.

It is clear from the above relationships that power and energy are intimately related concepts and one can switch back and forth between the two quantities as the situation demands. Since power is the rate of energy consumption, the total amount of energy consumed (E) in time (t) by a device whose power is P, is given by:

$$E = P(t) \tag{4.1}$$

**Table 4.1 Joule and Other Energy Units**

| Units of energy | Value in Joules |
|---|---|
| calorie | 4.185 |
| kilocalorie | 4,185 |
| Btu | 1,050 |
| kWh | 3.6 x $10^6$ |

The unit kilowatt-hour (kWh) which we see in our utility bills is derived from Equation (4.1). Thus, 1 kWh is the amount of energy consumed in one hour by a device whose power is 1 kW. A 100 W light bulb which is lit for 24 hours consumes 24(100) = 2,400 Wh, i.e., 2.4 kWh of energy. Electric companies charge their consumers for energy consumption in terms of the kilowatt-hour. For instance, the present price of electrical energy in the United States is nearly 8 cents per kWh. At this rate, the consumer pays the electric company (8 x 2.4), i.e., 19.2 cents for a 100 W lamp kept "on" for 24 hours.

Note that kilowatt-hour and joule are both units of energy and related to each other by the relationship: 1 kWh = 1,000 W (1 hour) = 1,000 (J/second)(3,600 seconds) = 3.6 x $10^6$ J. A list of commonly used energy units and their relationships is given in Table 4.1.

**Example 4.1**

The lighting installation in a room consists of 30 light fixtures each housing four 40 W fluorescent lamps. Calculate the amount of energy consumed by the lamps in one hour in joules, and kWh (disregard the energy consumed by ballasts and starters). Also determine the amount of heat produced by the fixtures in Btu.

*Solution:* Power (wattage) of one fixture = 4 x 40 = 160 W.
   Total wattage in the room = 30 x 160 = 4,800 W.
   Energy consumed in one hour = 4800 W x 1 hour = 4.8 kWh
   From Table 4.1, the above energy is equal to 4.8 x 3.6 x $10^6$ = 17.28 x $10^6$ J = 17.28 MJ.
   Thus, the amount of heat produced by these light fixtures is 17.28 MJ per hour. Since 1 Btu = 1,050 J, the amount of heat produced in Btu = (17.28 x $10^6$)/1,050 = 16,457 Btu/h.

**4.3 MODES OF HEAT TRANSFER**

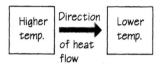

FIGURE 4.4 Heat flows from an object at a higher temperature to that of a lower temperature.

From our daily experience, we know that if two objects which are at different temperatures are placed in contact with each other, the temperature of the warmer object decreases while that of the cooler object increases. The above phenomenon occurs because heat flows from an object at a higher temperature to that at a lower temperature, Figure 4.4. The heat flow will continue until the temperature of two objects becomes equal.

There are three modes by which heat transfer can take place: conduction, convection and radiation.

*Conduction* is the phenomenon of heat transfer between the molecules of a substance which are in contact with each other. It is the only mode of heat transfer within solids and is characterized by the absence of bulk displacement of the molecules in the substance. When one end of a solid substance is heated, the molecules in the neighborhood of the heated end begin to vibrate about their mean positions with a higher average velocity. Because of the physical contact between the molecules of the substance, the increased vibrational energy in the heated molecules is transmitted to adjacent cooler molecules, which in turn transmit their increased energy to still cooler molecules in their neighborhood, and so on.

*Convection* occurs only in fluids and may be described as energy transfer by actual bulk motion of a gas or liquid. A familiar example of convection is the heating of water on a stove. When water in a container is placed on a stove, the water particles nearest the burner become lighter in density on being heated. Being lighter, these particles rise to the top and are replaced by colder (and hence heavier) particles of water from above. The colder particles are heated again, rise to the top, and the cycle continues as long as the water is being heated.

In addition to the transfer of energy by bulk motion which creates fluid flow, a certain amount of energy is also transferred by conduction in fluids because of the physical contact between fluid particles. Thus, convection involves heat transfer by fluid motion as well as by conduction. However, the dominant mode of heat transfer in convection is by fluid flow, and conduction accounts for a very small part of heat transfer in fluids. Therefore, convection is generally regarded to take place through fluid flow only.

The process of heat transfer described by the heating of water on a stove is called *natural convection*. Natural convection results from density changes in the fluid. Convection may also occur without changes in the density of fluid, in which case it is called *forced convection*. Forced convection is produced by fans, pumps, and wind motion.

*Radiation* is the transfer of energy between two objects in the form of electromagnetic waves. Thus, the heat and light received from the sun, a burning candle, or an electric lamp reach us by electromagnetic radiation. Unlike conduction and convection, radiation does not require a medium to travel. It is by virtue of this property that radiation from the sun is able to reach the earth through the vast reaches of space.

It is important to appreciate that heat radiation is a form of electromagnetic radiation. In fact, all electromagnetic radiation (infrared, light, ultraviolet, X-rays, gamma rays, etc.) is transformed to heat when absorbed by an object. As we will see in Section 4.6, various components of electromagnetic radiation differ from each other only in the wavelength of the radiation. Thus, although the radiation from the sun consists of ultraviolet, visible and infrared radiations, all three components of solar radiation are converted to heat when absorbed by a building surface. Similarly, all radiation from electric lamps is converted into heat when absorbed by the occupants, furniture and room surfaces.

During the process of heat transfer through a building envelope, all three modes usually come into play and contribute to heat transfer. Consider the section through a cavity wall of Figure 4.5. Energy from the sun reaches the wall by radiation and is partly absorbed and partly reflected by the wall's external surface. The absorbed energy then travels by conduction through the wall (from surface A to surface B) until it reaches the cavity space. Inside the cavity, the heat transfer mode changes to radiation across the cavity (from surface B to surface C) and also by convection through the air in the cavity. (The conduction mode of heat transfer through the air in cavity is relatively small). The subsequent mode is that of conduction through the inner wythe of the wall (from surface C to surface D). Finally, the energy is transferred from the inner surface of the wall (surface D) to indoor air, room surfaces, furniture and occupants by convection and radiation.

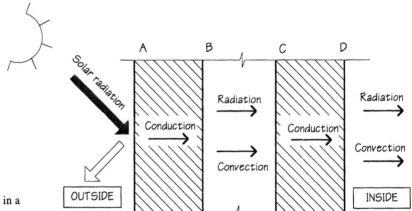

**FIGURE 4.5** Modes of heat transfer in a brick cavity wall.

**4.4 THERMAL RESISTANCE – THE R-VALUE**

Consider a homogeneous rectangular plate of thickness L. Let the surface temperatures of the two faces of the plate be $t_1$ and $t_2$, Figure 4.6. If $t_2$ is greater than $t_1$, heat will travel from face 2 to face 1. The amount of heat conducted through a unit area of the plate in unit time, i.e. the rate of heat transfer by conduction $(q_c)$, can be shown experimentally to be given by:

$$q_c = \frac{k(t_2 - t_1)}{L}$$

(4.2)

where $(t_2 - t_1)$ represents the temperature difference between the two faces of the plate.

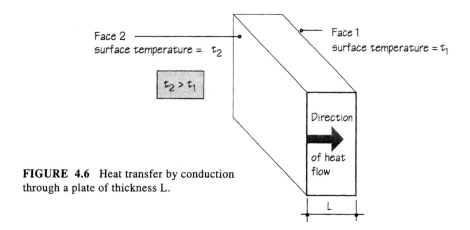

**FIGURE 4.6** Heat transfer by conduction through a plate of thickness L.

Equation (4.2) shows that the rate of heat transfer by conduction through the plate is directly proportional to the difference between the surface temperatures of the two faces of the plate. If there is no difference between the surface temperatures, i.e., if $(t_2 - t_1)$ is zero, no heat transfer will take place. Additionally, the rate of heat conduction is inversely proportional to the thickness of plate L. The greater the thickness of the plate, the smaller the rate of heat conduction.

The term k in Equation (4.2) is called the coefficient of thermal conductivity, or simply the *thermal conductivity*. Thermal conductivity is a property of the material and therefore constant for the material. If the value of k is zero, then $q_c$ is zero, which means that the heat transmitted through the component is zero. However, there is no real material for which the value of k is zero. All materials have a finite value of thermal conductivity. Therefore, they simply retard the flow of heat but cannot stop it altogether.

If the value of k is large, the rate of heat conduction through the plate is large. Such a material is called a *thermal conductor*. Conversely, if the value of k is small, the rate of heat conduction through the plate is small. Such a material is called a *thermal insulator* or an *insulating material*.

If the rate of heat transfer $(q_c)$ is expressed in Btu per hour per square foot, Btu/(h·ft$^2$), L in inches and $(t_2 - t_1)$ in °F, then from Equation (4.2), the units of k are [(Btu·in.)/(ft$^2$·°F·h)].

A property which relates more directly with the insulating value of a material is the reciprocal of thermal conductivity. This is called the *thermal resistivity* of the material and is denoted by r. Hence, r = 1/k. If we replace k by 1/r in Equation (4.2), the following is obtained.

$$q_c = \frac{(t_2 - t_1)}{r L}$$

If we now replace (r L) by R in the above equation, it becomes:

$$q_c = \frac{(t_2 - t_1)}{R} \qquad\qquad (4.3)$$

The term R in Equation (4.3) is called the *thermal resistance*. It is the product of the resistivity of the material and the thickness of the component.

The resistance of a building component is an extremely important thermal property. It is the measure of the component's ability to resist the transfer of heat through its thickness. A component may, therefore, be imagined as some kind of thermal screen in which the value of R represents the solid portion of the screen. A component with a large value of R behaves as a screen with a large solid portion. Therefore, it restricts the passage of heat. A material with a low value of R, on the other hand, behaves as a screen with a greater area of voids, so that it allows an easy passage of heat through it.

### 4.4.1 Units of Resistance and Resistivity

The units of thermal resistance are $(\text{ft}^{2}\cdot{}^{\circ}\text{F}\cdot\text{h})/\text{Btu}$ and that of resistivity, $[(\text{ft}^{2}\cdot{}^{\circ}\text{F}\cdot\text{h})/(\text{Btu}\cdot\text{in.})]$. The reciprocal of thermal resistance is called *thermal conductance*. The units of conductance are $\text{Btu}/(\text{ft}^{2}\cdot{}^{\circ}\text{F}\cdot\text{h})$. The units of resistance and resistivity in both the U.S. system of units and the SI system of units are given in Table 4.2.

It is the value of thermal resistance which is generally quoted in referring to the insulating value of a component. Thus, we speak of the R-value of a component, such as R-10, which implies that the resistance of that component is 10.0 $(\text{ft}^{2}\cdot{}^{\circ}\text{F}\cdot\text{h})/\text{Btu}$. Most insulating products are labeled with their R-value, Figure 4.7. Since the units of resistance and resistivity are rather long and complex, we usually omit the units in practice — a practice that we will follow in this chapter.

When the R-value of a component is given in SI system of units, it is usually referred to as the RSI-value. Thus, if the R-value of a component is R-10, its RSI-value is 1.76, which is referred to as RSI-1.76. Table 4.3 gives the conversion factors for R-values and thermal resistivity.

**Table 4.2 Units of Resistance and Resistivity**

| U.S. system of units | |
|---|---|
| Thermal resistivity (r) | $\dfrac{\text{ft}^{2}\cdot{}^{\circ}\text{F}\cdot\text{h}}{\text{Btu}\cdot\text{in.}}$ |
| Thermal resistance (R) | $\dfrac{\text{ft}^{2}\cdot{}^{\circ}\text{F}\cdot\text{h}}{\text{Btu}}$ |
| SI system of units | |
| Thermal resistivity (r) | $\dfrac{\text{m}\cdot{}^{\circ}\text{C}}{\text{W}}$ |
| Thermal resistance (R) | $\dfrac{\text{m}^{2}\cdot{}^{\circ}\text{C}}{\text{W}}$ |

(a)

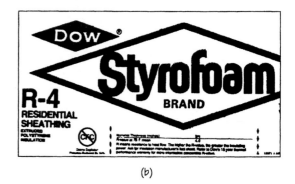

(b)

**FIGURE 4.7** (a) R-11 fiberglass insulation in batt form. (b) R-4 extruded polystyrene insulation in board form.

**Table 4.3 Unit Conversion Factors**

> Multiply resistivity given in U.S. system
> **by 6.93**
> to obtain its value in SI system of units.
>
> Multiply R-value
> **by 0.176**
> to obtain RSI-value.

### 4.4.2 Difference Between Resistance and Resistivity

It is important to note the difference between resistivity (r) and resistance (R). They both are related by the relationship: $R = (r L)$, where L is the thickness of the component. Since the thickness of building components is usually expressed in inches, thermal resistivity is in fact the thermal resistance of a component whose thickness is 1 in. Thus, if we know the resistivity of a material we can determine the resistance of a component of any thickness. For example, if the resistivity of a material is 2.5, then the resistance of a 6 in. thick component made of that material is 2.5 x 6 = 15.0, i.e., the R-value of this component is 15.

Since resistivity refers to resistance of a unit thickness of the material, it is the resistivity that is used to compare the insulating properties of various materials. A material with higher resistivity is a better thermal insulator. The resistivities (resistances of 1 in. thick materials) of some commonly used materials are given in Table 4.4.

---

**Example 4.2**

Determine the R-value of (i) a 3.5 in. thick concrete wall, (ii) a 3.5 in. thick fiberglass blanket, and (iii) a 0.25 in. thick glass sheet.

*Solution*: From Table 4.4, thermal resistivities of concrete, fiberglass and glass sheet are 0.15, 3.2 and 0.14 respectively.
  (i)   For a concrete wall, $R = r L = (3.5)(0.15) = 0.53$
  (ii)  For a fiberglass blanket, $R = r L = (3.5)(3.2) = 11.2$
  (iii) For a glass sheet, $R = r L = (0.25)(0.14) = 0.035$

---

From Example 4.2, note the difference in the R-values of a concrete wall and a fiberglass blanket. Although they both are of the same thickness, the fiberglass blanket has nearly 22 times greater R-value than the concrete wall. Thus, 22 times more heat will be conducted through the concrete wall as compared with that of the fiberglass blanket. Notice also the difference between the R-values of a concrete wall and a glass sheet. The R-value of the concrete wall is 15 times greater than that of the glass sheet, implying that 15 times more heat will be conducted through the glass sheet as compared to the concrete wall.

### 4.4.3 Effect of Density and Moisture Content on Resistivity

In general, metals have a much lower thermal resistivity than nonmetals. The resistivity of a nonmetal is largely dependent on its density. As a general rule, low density materials have a high thermal resistivity. Being fibrous, granular or cellular in its structure, a low density material has air trapped

**Table 4.4  Thermal Resistivity[1] of Commonly Used Materials**

| Material | Resistivity [2]<br>$(ft^{2.\circ}F\cdot h)/(Btu\cdot in.)$ |
|---|---|
| **Metals** | |
|     Steel | $3.2 \times 10^{-3}$ |
|     Copper | $3.2 \times 10^{-4}$ |
|     Aluminum | $3.2 \times 10^{-3}$ |
| **Ceramic materials** | |
|     Clay bricks | 0.20 |
|     Concrete (normal weight) | 0.15 |
|     Concrete (structural lightweight) | 0.25 to 0.35 (depending on density) |
|     Insulating concrete (perlite or vermiculite) | 1.70 |
|     Concrete masonry | Depends on type of concrete and cell insulation |
|     Limestone | 0.15 |
|     Sandstone | 0.18 |
|     Glass | 0.14 |
|     Plaster | 0.35 |
|     Gypsum wallboard | 0.60 |
|     Portland cement plaster | 0.30 |
| **Wood and coal** | |
|     Softwoods (solid lumber or plywood) | 0.9 |
|     Fiberboard | 2.4 |
|     Wood charcoal | 2.2 |
|     Coal | 0.85 |
| **Insulating materials** | |
|     Granulated cork | 3.0 |
|     Vermiculite (loose fill) | 2.1 |
|     Perlite (loose fill, density 5.0 pcf) | 3.0 |
|     Perlite (loose fill, density 10.0 pcf) | 2.4 |
|     Expanded perlite board | 2.8 |
|     Fiberglass (loose fill, assuming all voids are filled) | 3.2 |
|     Fiberglass (batt or blanket) | 3.2 to 3.7 (depending on density) |
|     Mineral wool (rock wool) | 3.2 to 3.7 (depending on density) |
|     Expanded polystyrene (EPS) board (bead board) | 4.0 |
|     Extruded polystyrene (XEPS) board | 5.0 |
|     Polyurethane board (laminations on both sides) | 6.5 |
|     Polyisocyanurate board (laminations on both sides) | 6.5 |
| **Gases** | |
|     Air | 5.6 |
|     Argon | 8.9 |
|     Carbon dioxide | 9.9 |
|     Chlorofluorocarbon (CFC) gas | 16.5 |
|     Hydrochlorofluorocarbon (HCFC) gas | 15.0 |
| **Water** | 0.24 |

[1] Thermal resistivity = Thermal resistance (R-value) of a 1 in. thick material.
[2] To convert resistivity values given above to those in the SI system, multiply values by 6.93.
Values given in this table are representative rather than precise.  Source:  Several sources.

within its voids. Since air has a high thermal resistivity, a low density material is a better insulator than a high density material. In fact, "still" air is one of the best thermal insulators available. Circulating air cannot be a good insulator since it is the circulation of air that causes convection heat transfer.

Thus, for a material to be a good thermal insulator, it must contain air in small packets. In other words, the basic requirement of an insulating material is that the solid constituents of the material must divide its volume into such tiny air spaces that air cannot circulate within them. With tiny air spaces, convection heat transfer is virtually negligible.

For a given material, there is a characteristic relationship between its density and thermal resistivity. In general, there is a value of density which yields maximum thermal resistivity. A high density material has low resistivity because of the small volume of air trapped between the solid constituents of the material. A very low density material also has low resistivity because it contains large air spaces within which convection currents are easily generated. In other words, the thermal resistivity of a material increases with an increase or decrease of density beyond the optimum density, as shown in Figure 4.8.

Another important factor which affects thermal resistivity is the moisture content of the material. Water has a much lower thermal resistivity than air (resistivity of air = 5.6 and resistivity of water = 0.24, a ratio of 23:1, see Table 4.4). Since a moist material has water trapped inside its pores in place of the air, its thermal resistivity is lower than that of a dry sample. It is therefore important to ensure, in the detailing of buildings, that insulating materials remain dry throughout their useful life span. This fact is important since most insulating materials, because of their location, are particularly vulnerable to water absorption from rain. In cold climates where condensation of water vapor within insulating materials is an additional hazard, vapor retarders are installed in roof and external wall assemblies, as discussed in Section 5.7.

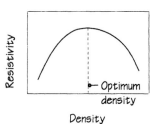

**FIGURE 4.8** Relationship between the resistivity and the density of a material.

### 4.4.4 Entrapment of Low Conductivity Gas

Although most insulating materials contain small volumes of air to provide high thermal resistance, plastic foam insulations such as extruded polystyrene, polyurethane, and polyisocyanurate, have a low conductivity (high resistivity) gas blown into their cell cavities, see Section 4.9.5. At the present time, the gas most commonly used is hydrochlorofluorocarbon (HCFC) gas. Thermal resistivity of HCFC is nearly three times higher than that of air, Table 4.4. Consequently, plastic foam insulations are much better insulators than materials which have air trapped between their fibers or cells. In fact, as shown in Table 4.4, extruded polystyrene, polyurethane and polyisocyanurate foams have the highest thermal resistivity among insulating materials because of the HCFC gas contained in their cells.

Most of the HCFC gas trapped in cell cavities of plastic foams gradually finds its way into the atmosphere. This is due to the fact that the cell walls of foam insulations are not fully impermeable. Therefore, air permeates the foam, driving a part of the HCFC gas out.

The steady migration of HCFC out of plastic foams means that the R-values of plastic foams reduce with time. Therefore, in dealing with R-values of plastic foam insulations which have HCFC gas contained in their cells, such as extruded polystyrene, polyurethane and polyisocyanurate foams, we think in terms of their *stabilized* R-values, also known as *aged* R-values. Most manufacturers of these materials claim that the R-values of their materials stabilize in 6 months, after which the decrease in R-value is negligible.

The use of HCFC as a blowing agent in in the manufacture of plastic foams is a relatively recent phenomenon. Earlier, chlorofluorocarbon (CFC) gas was used which, as we now understand, is responsible for the depletion of the ozone layer in the atmosphere. Although the thermal resistivity of HCFC is slightly lower than that of CFC, its ozone depletion potential is much lower than that of CFC. Consequently, HCFC has replaced CFC in the manufacture of plastic foam insulations.

HEAT TRANSFER MAY
BE IN EITHER DIRECTION

**FIGURE 4.9** The total R-value of a component which consists of several layers of different materials is obtained by adding the R-values of the individual layers.

### 4.4.5  R-value of a Multilayer Component — Series Combination

Usually a wall or roof assembly consists of several layers of different materials, Figure 4.9. For example, an insulated brick cavity wall consists of three layers of materials stacked against each other: a layer of brick, a layer of insulation, and a layer of brick, as shown in Figure 4.10.

In such a multilayer component, the amount of heat which enters the first layer must come out of the second layer, and then out of the third layer, and so on. In other words, the amount of heat passing through each layer must be the same. If this were not so — that is, if less heat left a layer than had entered it, the heat would be stored in that layer, raising its temperature infinitely in due course — an impossibility. Thus, in terms of heat transfer, the multilayer component behaves like an assembly of electrical resistors connected together in series combination, since in such a combination the electrical current flowing through all resistors is the same.

It can be shown mathematically that the total resistance of the multilayer component in Figure 4.9 is obtained by adding the resistances of individual layers. Thus:

$$R_t = R_1 + R_2 + R_3 + ... \tag{4.4}$$

where $R_t$ is the total resistance of the multilayer component, and $R_1$, $R_2$, $R_3$, etc., are the resistances of layer 1, layer 2, layer 3, etc., respectively.

### Example 4.3

Calculate the total resistance of a brick cavity wall which consists of: an 8 in. thick (nominal) internal loadbearing brick wall, a 2 in. thick extruded

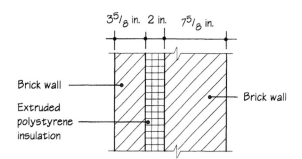

**FIGURE 4.10** Section through an insulated brick wall. Refers to Example 4.3.

polystyrene insulation and a 4 in. thick (nominal) external brick veneer, as shown in Figure 4.10.

*Solution*: From Table 4.4, the resistivities of brick and extruded polystyrene are 0.2 and 5.0 respectively. The actual thicknesses of 4 in. (nominal) and 8 in. (nominal) brick walls are 3.625 in. and 7.625 in., as shown in Figure 4.10. The calculation of the total R-value of the wall assembly is shown below.

| Element | R-value | Reference |
|---|---|---|
| 4 in. thick brick veneer | 3.625(0.2) = 0.725 | Table 4.4 |
| 2 in. thick extruded polystyrene board | 2.0 (5.0) = 10.0 | Table 4.4 |
| 8 in. thick brick wall | 7.625(0.2) = 1.525 | Table 4.4 |

$$R_t = 0.725 + 10.0 + 1.525 = 12.25$$

The total R-value of the wall is 12.25. Thus, the wall is an R-12 wall[1].

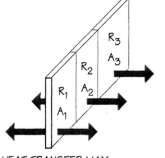

HEAT TRANSFER MAY BE IN EITHER DIRECTION

**FIGURE 4.11** An assembly with components stacked side by side behaves as though various components are joined together in parallel combination.

### 4.4.6 Overall R-value of an Assembly — Parallel Combination

Usually, building assemblies have two or more components of different R-values placed side by side. For instance, a wall may have opaque portions intercepted by glazed areas. The R-values of opaque portions of a wall are usually higher than the R-values of glazing. Similarly, an insulated stud wall has insulation intercepted by studs, in which the R-value of the insulation is much higher than the R-value of the studs. The heat flow paths through various components of such an assembly are parallel to each other, similar to the flow of electrical current through resistors connected in parallel. Hence, such a combination of components is called a parallel combination, Figure 4.11.

The overall R-value of an assembly in parallel combination ($R_o$) is obtained by the area-weighted averaging procedure. Thus, if there are several areas $A_1$, $A_2$, $A_3$, etc., whose R-values are $R_1$, $R_2$, $R_3$, etc., respectively, as shown in Figure 4.11, the overall R-value of such an assembly is given by:

---

[1] Because of the great deal of approximation involved, R-values of assemblies are usually given in whole numbers in the U.S. system of units.

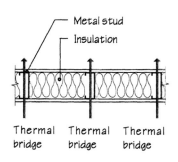

Metal stud
Insulation

Thermal   Thermal   Thermal
bridge    bridge    bridge

**FIGURE 4.12** Metal studs function as thermal bridges in an insulated wall.

$$R_o = \frac{A_1 + A_2 + A_3 + \cdots}{\dfrac{A_1}{R_1} + \dfrac{A_2}{R_2} + \dfrac{A_3}{R_3} + \cdots} \qquad (4.5)$$

If the R-value of a part of an assembly in parallel combination is much smaller than that of other parts, it is called a *thermal bridge* since a relatively large amount of heat will pass through that part. For instance, in an insulated metal stud wall, the studs function as thermal bridges because the R-value of metal studs is much lower than that of the intervening insulation, Figure 4.12. In a wall which consists of opaque and glazed portions, the glazed portions function as thermal bridges since the glazed portions have much lower R-values than the opaque portions.

**Example 4.4**

Calculate the overall R-value of a wall which has 2 x 4 (actual dimensions $1\frac{1}{2}$ in. x $3\frac{1}{2}$ in.) wood studs spaced 16 in. on center. The spaces between the studs are filled with $3\frac{1}{2}$ in. thick fiberglass insulation, Figure 4.13.

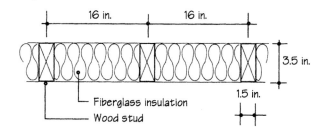

**FIGURE 4.13** Plan of the wall of Example 4.4.

16 in.        16 in.

3.5 in.

Fiberglass insulation
Wood stud

1.5 in.

*Solution*: From Table 4.4,
   R-value of 3.5 in. thick fiberglass insulation, $R_1 = (3.5)(3.2) = 11.2$.
   R-value of 3.5 in. thick wood studs $= R_2 = (3.5)(0.9) = 3.15$.
   The width of the studs = 1.5 in. Hence, the width of the insulation = 14.5 in. From Equation (4.5),

$$R_o = \frac{14.5 + 1.5}{\dfrac{14.5}{11.2} + \dfrac{1.5}{3.15}} = 9.0$$

Thus, the R-value of the assembly is 9.0, which is nearly 20% lower than the R-value of the insulation (= 11.2). In other words, wood studs, being of fairly high R-value, function as weak thermal bridges. Therefore, in the case of an insulated wood stud wall, it is a common practice to ignore the decrease in R-value caused by the studs, and to assume that the entire wall consists of insulation only[2].

### Example 4.5

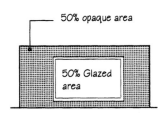

FIGURE 4.14 Wall of Example 4.5.

Determine the overall R-value of a wall which consists of 50% opaque area and 50% glazed area, Figure 4.14. The R-values of the opaque and the glazed areas are 15.0 and 2.0 respectively.

*Solution*: From Equation 4.5, the overall R-value of the wall is:

$$R_o = \frac{0.5 + 0.5}{\dfrac{0.5}{15.0} + \dfrac{0.5}{2.0}} = 3.5$$

Thus, the overall R-value of the wall is 3.5. This is an extremely important result since although the glazed and opaque areas of the wall are equal, the overall R-value of the wall is much smaller than the average of the two R-values (= 8.5). This result underscores the importance of reducing or eliminating thermal bridges from the envelope, since the reduction in the overall R-value of the envelope caused by a thermal bridge is not proportional to its area but far in excess of it.

## 4.5 SURFACE RESISTANCE

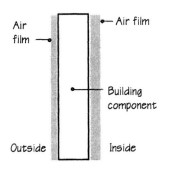

FIGURE 4.15 Thin films of air of nearly zero velocity cling to both sides of a component, adding to the total resistance of the component.

In addition to the layers of materials that comprise a multilayer component, there are two invisible layers that contribute to the total R-value of the component. These layers are thin films of air of nearly zero velocity that cling to the surface of a component on each side, Figure 4.15. In other words, the two air films separate the surfaces of the component from the surrounding air and resist the flow of heat from the surrounding air to the surface of the component.

The thermal resistance of each film of air is called the *surface resistance* or the *film resistance*. Thus, there is an internal surface resistance ($R_{si}$) and an external surface resistance ($R_{so}$) corresponding to the inside and outside air films. These two surface resistances must be taken into account in determining the total resistance of a component. Since the two surface resistances are in series with the component, the total resistance of the assembly is:

$$R_t = R_{si} + [\, R_1 + R_2 + R_3 + \dots \,] + R_{so} \tag{4.6}$$

---

[2] In calculating the overall R-value in this example, we have used the widths of the stud and the insulation instead of their areas, since the areas of stud and insulation are proportional to their respective widths.

**Table 4.5 Surface Resistances**

| Surface | Surface resistance $(ft^2 \cdot h \cdot {}^{\circ}F)/Btu$ |
|---|---|
| Internal surface | 0.7 |
| External surface | 0.2 |

It is the total resistance obtained by including the inside and outside surface resistances, that is used in determining the *air-to-air heat transfer* through a component. Since the inside air velocity is usually smaller than the outside air velocity, the inside air film is thicker than the outside air film. Therefore, the inside surface resistance is greater than the outside surface resistance. In fact, the value of surface resistance does not depend on air velocity alone but also on the texture of the surface of the component and the direction of heat flow through it. For example, an increase in the roughness of the surface tends to increase the value of surface resistance. This is due to the fact that the roughness of the surface reduces the velocity of air in the vicinity of the surface. Thus, in the case of a fluted concrete surface, the surface resistance is higher than that for a smooth concrete surface.

The effect of the direction of heat flow on surface resistance is similar to its effect on the resistance of a cavity space. The effect of the direction of heat flow on the R-value of a cavity space is discussed in Section 4.7.

Although the inside and outside surface resistances vary as previously described, the values given in Table 4.5 may be used as representative approximate values.

Surface resistances generally do not add significantly to the total R-value of most opaque components of a building envelope. Thus in the wall of Example 4.3, the total R-value of the wall when the surface resistances are taken into account is 12.25 + 0.7 + 0.2 = 13.15. In this case, surface resistances contribute less than 7% to the total R-value of the wall.

However, surface resistances contribute greatly to the total R-value of a glazing, particularly a single layer glass window or curtain wall. For instance, we see from Example 4.2 that the R-value of a $1/4$ in. thick glass sheet is only 0.035. When surface resistances are included, the total R-value of glass sheet becomes: 0.035 + 0.7 + 0.2 = 0.935 (or approximately 1.0). In this case, the surface resistances have contributed virtually all the R-value of glazing. In fact, the R-value of a single glass sheet itself is almost negligible.

## 4.6 SURFACE EMISSIVITY AND COLOR

We have so far dealt with two fundamental thermal properties, thermal resistance and surface resistance, which primarily describe the properties of heat transfer by conduction and convection. In this section, we shall discuss the properties of materials that affect radiant heat transfer through a component.

Before doing so, let us review a few facts about radiation. An important fact about radiation is that all objects emit radiant energy and also receive it from the surrounding objects at all times. In other words, there is a continuous exchange of radiant energy between two objects that face each other, Figure 4.16(a). If object A is at a higher temperature than object B, object A will emit a greater amount of radiation towards object B but receive less from it. Object B will emit less radiation towards A but receive more from it. Thus, there will be a net transfer of radiant energy from object A to object B until the temperatures of the two objects become equal. When the temperatures have equalized, the radiant energy received by each object is equal to that emitted by it.

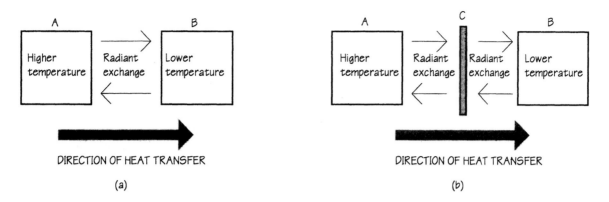

FIGURE 4.16  (a) Radiation exchange between two objects facing each other.  (b) Radiation exchange between two objects with an intervening opaque barrier between them.

For radiant exchange to take place between objects, it is important that there is a direct line of sight between them.  Thus, in Figure 4.16(b), if there is an opaque barrier C between objects A and B, there will be no direct radiant exchange between objects A and B because there is no direct line of sight between them.  In this case, radiant exchange will take place between objects A and C, and between objects C and B.

### 4.6.1  Magnitude and Wavelength of Radiant Emission

The rate at which radiant energy is emitted by a unit area of an object ($q_r$) is given by the following equation.

$$q_r = e \beta T^4 \qquad\qquad (4.7)$$

where T is the absolute temperature of the object in Kelvin (K). Note that T °F = (T+ 492) K.  Thus a temperature of 28 °F = 520 K.  ß is a constant, called the Stefan-Boltzmann constant .  The term e is called the *emissivity* of the object, a dimensionless quantity whose value varies between 0 and 1.

From Equation (4.7), it is clear that the magnitude of radiation is highly dependent on the temperature of the object since it is proportional to the fourth power of the temperature.  Consequently, radiation is an important heat transfer mechanism in combustion chambers and furnaces where the temperatures are high.  In buildings, however, radiation is usually significant if conduction or convection heat transfer mechanisms are relatively small, such as in the cavities of roofs and walls.

The temperature of the object not only affects the magnitude but also the wavelength of radiation emitted by it.  At low temperatures, all the radiation emitted by an object is in long wavelengths, known as *infrared radiation.* Infrared radiation is perceived only as heat.  Our eyes are not sensitive to infrared radiation, i.e., infrared radiation is not visible to the human eye.  As the temperature of the object is raised, it not only radiates an increasingly greater amount of radiation but the wavelength of radiation becomes progressively smaller until at some temperature the object begins to glow red. At this stage, a part of the radiation emitted by the object is visible.

The above fact is indeed common knowledge, derived from our observation of heating an iron rod. At a low temperature, the radiation from the rod is felt as heat. If the rod is heated further, a stage is reached when the radiation from the rod begins to be visible. This happens when the rod becomes red hot. At this temperature, the radiation from the rod is of such small wavelengths that it is not only felt as heat but is also visible to the human eye. With a further increase in temperature, the wavelength of the emitted radiation becomes smaller still. The rod emits more and more visible radiation until it becomes white hot.

Experiments have shown that the progressive decrease in the wavelength of radiation with increasing temperature is a continuous phenomenon. The wavelength region in which the radiation is visible to the human eye is called the *visible region*, or light. The visible region extends from a wavelength of 0.4 micron to 0.7 micron (1 micron = one-millionth of a meter = $10^{-6}$ m). The infrared region extends from a wavelength of 0.7 micron to nearly 1,000 microns (1 mm).

Another important fact about radiation from a heated object is that it is electromagnetic in nature. Thus, infrared radiation and light are parts of the entire spectrum that we call the *electromagnetic spectrum*. The region before the visible region is the *ultraviolet region* which extends from nearly 0.01 micron to 0.4 micron. Gamma rays, X-rays and microwaves are some of the other parts of the electromagnetic spectrum, Figure 4.17.

Radiation to which buildings are subjected is of two types: (i) solar radiation and (ii) terrestrial radiation. Terrestrial radiation is radiation emitted by objects on the surface of the earth, such as the ground, landscape elements, building surfaces and furniture. Although the actual temperature of the interior of the sun is several million degrees Fahrenheit, solar radiation as received on the earth's surface has the same characteristics as the radiation from an object whose temperature is approximately 11,000 °F (6,000 °C). By contrast,

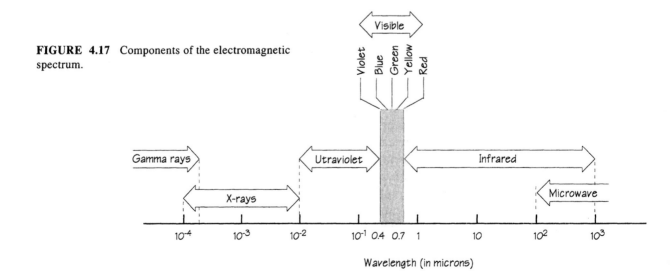

**FIGURE 4.17** Components of the electromagnetic spectrum.

the temperature of terrestrial objects (ground, building surfaces, landscape elements, furniture, etc.) seldom exceeds 150 °F (60 °C).

Thus, the fundamental difference between solar radiation and terrestrial radiation is that solar radiation is a high temperature radiation while terrestrial radiation is a low temperature radiation. Being a high temperature radiation, solar radiation is contained within short wavelengths, hence called *shortwave radiation*. The radiation from terrestrial objects, on the other hand, is called *longwave radiation* because it is contained in longer wavelengths.

The difference between the wavelength composition of solar radiation and radiation from an object at 95 °F is shown in Figure 4.18. Observe that solar radiation extends from a wavelength of 0.3 micron to 2.0 micron. Nearly 3% of solar radiation lies in the ultraviolet region (wavelength less than 0.4 micron), 50% in the visible region (0.4 to 0.7 micron), and the remaining 47% in the infrared region. Radiation from an object at 95 °F extends from a wavelength of nearly 3.5 microns to 50 microns[4.2].

Although building surfaces may receive both the shortwave radiation (from the sun) and longwave radiation (from surrounding surfaces and objects), all building surfaces emit only longwave radiation. For example in the cavity wall of Figure 4.5, the radiation falling on the external surface of the wall, surface A, may be both the shortwave radiation (from the sun) and longwave radiation (from the ground and opposite building surfaces) but the radiation emitted by this surface is only longwave radiation. The radiation falling on surface B is that emitted by surface C which is longwave radiation. Similarly, the radiation falling on surface C comes from surface B, which is also longwave radiation.

From Equation (4.7), it may be seen that the magnitude of radiation is not only proportional to the temperature of the object but also to the emissivity. The larger the emissivity, the greater the radiation emitted. Emissivity is a property of the surface of an object, not its bulk. Thus, a thin surface coating or lamination can alter the emissivity of an object. For most nonmetallic

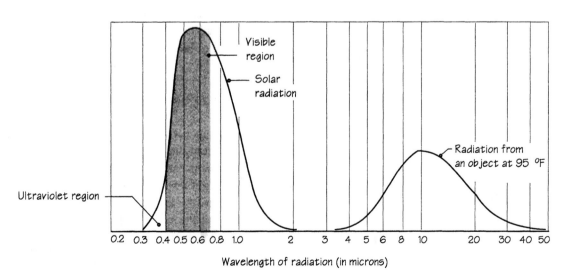

**FIGURE 4.18**    Radiation emitted by the sun and an object at 95 °F.

**Table 4.6  Emissivity, Absorptivity and Reflectivity of Surfaces**

| Material | Longwave radiation | | Shortwave (solar) radiation | |
|---|---|---|---|---|
| | Emissivity or absorptivity | Reflectivity | Absorptivity | Reflectivity |
| **Metals** | | | | |
| Aluminum foil | 0.05 | 0.95 | 0.20 | 0.80 |
| Aluminum (polished) | 0.02 | 0.98 | 0.15 | 0.85 |
| Brass (polished) | 0.05 | 0.95 | 0.30 | 0.70 |
| Cast iron | 0.45 | 0.55 | 0.70 | 0.30 |
| Stainless steel | 0.20 | 0.80 | 0.30 | 0.70 |
| **Nonmetals** | | | | |
| Gypsum board | 0.90 | 0.10 | 0.60 | 0.40 |
| Brick | 0.90 | 0.10 | 0.70 | 0.30 |
| Concrete | 0.90 | 0.10 | 0.60 | 0.40 |
| Marble (white) | 0.90 | 0.10 | 0.30 | 0.70 |
| Wood | 0.90 | 0.10 | 0.60 | 0.40 |
| **Glass sheet** | 0.90 | 0.10 | 0.05 | 0.07 |
| **Paints** | | | | |
| Aluminum | 0.55 | 0.45 | 0.50 | 0.50 |
| White | 0.90 | 0.10 | 0.10 | 0.90 |
| Green | 0.90 | 0.10 | 0.70 | 0.30 |
| Black | 0.90 | 0.10 | 0.90 | 0.10 |

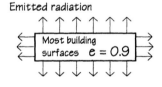

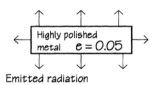

**FIGURE 4.19** Emissivity of commonly used building surfaces and highly polished metals.

building surfaces, the emissivity is high, nearly 0.9. Metals have a low emissivity. That is why a low emissivity glass is made by depositing an extremely thin film of metal or metal oxide on one of its surfaces. Polished metals have an extremely low emissivity, nearly 0.05, Figure 4.19. Emissivity values of various materials are given in Table 4.6.

It is important to note that in practical terms, the concept of emissivity is only applicable to longwave radiation since it is only the longwave radiation that is emitted by (terrestrial) objects.

### 4.6.2  Response of a Surface to Incident Radiation

When radiation falls on a surface, it is partly absorbed, partly reflected and partly transmitted through the component, Figure 4.20. We define absorptivity as the fraction of the total incident radiation which is absorbed by the object. Similarly, reflectivity is the fraction of the total incident radiation which is reflected by the object, and transmissivity is the fraction of the total incident radiation which passes through the object. Since the sum of the absorbed, reflected and transmitted components of radiation must be equal to the incident radiation, the following equation must always be satisfied.

Absorptivity + Reflectivity + Transmissivity  = 1

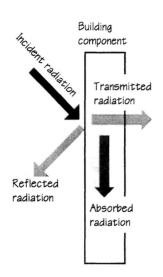

**FIGURE 4.20** Reflection, transmission and absorption of incident radiation.

EMISSIVITY = ABSORPTIVITY

Therefore, a low emissivity surface is a poor absorber, i.e., a good reflector of longwave radiation.

For an opaque surface, transmissivity = 0. Hence, for an opaque material, absorptivity + reflectivity = 1. Thus, if the absorptivity of a surface is 0.2, its reflectivity is 0.8. If 100 Btu of radiation falls on this surface, 20 Btu will be absorbed, and 80 Btu reflected.

Theoretically, the absorptivity and reflectivity of a surface are functions of the wavelength of radiation. The same is true of emissivity, i.e., emissivity also varies with the wavelength. However, the variation of emissivity is usually small within a given wavelength band. The two wavelength bands in which we are interested are: the short wavelength band (solar radiation) and the long wavelength band (low temperature radiation). Within each of these two wavelength bands, the surface properties of materials such as absorptivity, reflectivity and emissivity are virtually constant. Their approximate values are given in Table 4.6.

It can be shown that for a given wavelength band, the absorptivity of a surface is equal to its emissivity. Since the concept of emissivity applies only to longwave radiation, the equality of emissivity and absorptivity is true only for longwave radiation. Thus, if the emissivity of a surface is 0.2, its absorptivity for longwave radiation will also be 0.2 and its reflectivity = 0.8. In other words, a low emissivity surface is a poor absorber and hence, a good reflector of longwave radiation. The lower the emissivity of a surface, the greater its longwave reflectivity.

### 4.6.3 Response of an Opaque Surface to Solar Radiation

In terms of reflection, absorption and transmission characteristics, solar radiation behaves as light. Thus, light-colored and mirrored (or glossy) surfaces have high reflectivity to solar radiation. The lighter the color of the surface, the smaller the solar radiation absorbed by the component. A white surface has the lowest absorptivity value since it absorbs little and reflects most of the incident solar radiation, Figure 4.21(a). If the white surface is glossy, its reflectivity for solar radiation is higher than that of a matt white surface. Thus, if one desires to reduce the admission of solar heat into a building, its external surfaces should be painted white. In fact in tropical regions, it is good practice to use white or light-colored materials on external walls, and to treat the roof with a white roofing material.

### 4.6.4 Response of an Opaque Surface to Longwave Radiation

Since highly polished metals have a low emissivity, they are good reflectors of longwave radiation. Therefore, to reduce radiant heat transfer through a cavity space, one of the cavity surfaces should be lined with a low emissivity material. A low emissivity material will reflect back the longwave radiation. Painting the surfaces of the cavity white will not reduce radiant heat transfer through the cavity since the white color absorbs 90 percent of longwave radiation, see Table 4.6. The reflection characteristics of a white surface and a low emissivity surface with respect to longwave radiation are shown in Figures 4.21(b) and 4.21(c) respectively.

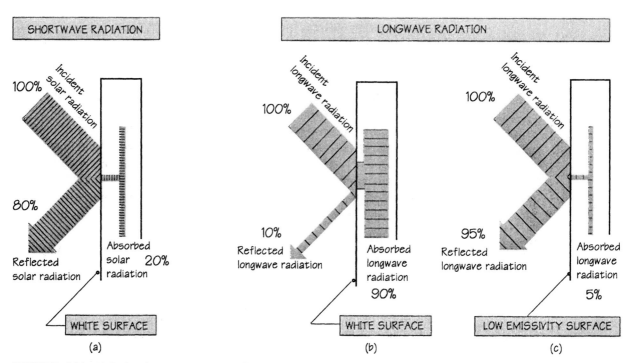

FIGURE 4.21 (a) Reflection and absorption of solar radiation by a white surface. (b) Reflection and absorption of longwave radiation by white surface. (c) Reflection and absorption of longwave radiation by a low emissivity surface such as an aluminum foil.

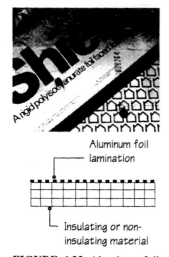

FIGURE 4.22 Aluminum foil laminated material.

A material whose low emissivity is greatly exploited in buildings is aluminum foil (emissivity = 0.05). Since absorptivity is equal to emissivity, aluminum foil is a poor absorber (and hence a good reflector) of longwave radiation. Therefore, aluminum foil is used to line walls or ceiling cavities so that 95% of incident longwave radiation on the foil is reflected. Since emissivity is a surface property, a thin foil of aluminum is all that is required to change the emissivity of a surface.

Aluminum foil is also called a *radiant barrier* or *reflective insulation*, since by reflecting 95% of radiation back, it works as an effective barrier to the transmission of longwave radiation. A large number of proprietary materials are manufactured with aluminum foil as a laminate, Figure 4.22. Usually, these materials are insulating materials, so that the insulating material reduces the conductive heat transfer, while the aluminum foil reduces the radiant heat transfer.

## 4.7 INSULATION PROVIDED BY CAVITY SPACES

Although the concept of R-value is strictly applicable only to solid materials, it can be extended to apply to a cavity space also. Thus, a cavity space is assigned an R-value just like a solid component.

If conduction was the only mode of heat transfer within a cavity space, heat transfer through a cavity would be inversely proportional to the thickness of the cavity, as given by Equation (4.3). In other words, the R-value of the

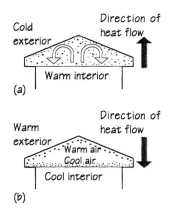

**FIGURE 4.23** The effect of the direction of heat flow in a horizontal cavity: (a) direction of heat flow upward, and (b) direction of heat flow downward.

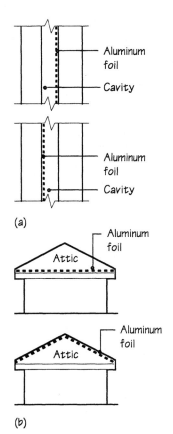

**FIGURE 4.24** Alternative locations of radiant barrier in: (a) a vertical cavity, and (b) an attic.

cavity would increase with an increase in cavity width. However, as noted in Section 4.3, the dominant modes of heat transfer through a cavity space are convection and radiation. Consequently, the R-value of a cavity space is determined by all three modes of heat transfer.

Heat transfer by radiation between the two surfaces of the cavity is independent of cavity width. Convection heat transfer increases with the increase in width of the cavity and, as stated earlier, the conduction heat transfer decreases as the cavity width increases. Consequently, the R-value of a cavity is not a simple function of its width.

Experiments have demonstrated that in a vertical cavity, the combined conductive, convective and radiant heat transfer decreases as the cavity width increases up to nearly 0.75 in., beyond which it increases. Stated differently, the R-value of a vertical cavity is maximum when the cavity width is approximately 0.75 in. A vertical cavity should, therefore, be 0.75 in. wide unless there are other reasons to increase or decrease its width.

In the case of a horizontal cavity, the direction of heat flow affects the amount of heat transferred through it by convection. If the direction of heat flow is upward (this occurs in an attic space when the outside temperature is lower than the inside temperature of a building), air in the cavity will tend to rise after being heated. The heated air will cool at the underside of the roof, become heavier, and therefore return to the bottom of the cavity. This cycle will continue creating convection currents in the cavity. Consequently, the R-value of the cavity in this case is low, Figure 4.23(a).

If the heat flow in a horizontal cavity is downward (as in an attic space during a hot summer afternoon), the convective heat transfer is relatively suppressed since the warm air tends to collect at the top and the cold air at the bottom, preventing or reducing convection currents in the cavity, Figure 4.23(b).

As far as the the radiant heat transfer through a cavity is concerned, it can be reduced by lining one of the surfaces of the cavity with a low emissivity material such as an aluminum foil. It is immaterial which side of the cavity is lined as long as the foil faces an air space, Figure 4.24. Only one side of the cavity need be lined. Lining both sides of the cavity provides such a marginal improvement in thermal performance that it cannot be justified economically.

### 4.7.1 R-value of a Cavity

Although the R-value of an unlined cavity varies somewhat with the width of the cavity, its orientation (horizontal or vertical), and the direction of heat flow, it may be assumed as approximately equal to 1.0 for widths varying from 0.5 in. to 4.0 in. If the cavity is lined with a bright aluminum foil, its R-value increases to nearly 2.5, giving an increase of 1.5 over an unlined cavity, Table 4.7.

The advantage of using an aluminum foil is more pronounced in the attic of a building located in the tropics. Since the roof surface gets quite warm during a summer afternoon, the radiant heat transfer can be substantially reduced by an aluminum foil lining. This is due to the fact that radiant heat

**Table 4.7  Thermal Resistance of Cavity Spaces**

| Type of cavity | Resistance $(ft^2 \cdot °F \cdot h)/Btu$ | |
|---|---|---|
| | Unlined cavity | Cavity lined with bright aluminum foil on one side |
| Vertical or horizontal cavity[1] | 1.0 | 2.5 |
| Attic space (ventilated)[2] | 2.0 | 6.0 |

[1] The R-value of a horizontal cavity varies depending on whether the heat flow is upward or downward. The values given above are average values.

[2] The R-value of an attic space varies with the temperature of the roof. The above values apply to summer conditions in a warm climate.

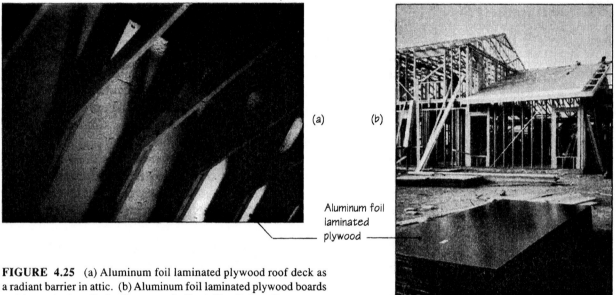

(a)        (b)

Aluminum foil
laminated
plywood

**FIGURE 4.25** (a) Aluminum foil laminated plywood roof deck as a radiant barrier in attic. (b) Aluminum foil laminated plywood boards waiting to be installed. Courtesy of: Kool*Ply, Dallas, Texas.

transfer is highly dependent on the temperature of a surface, see Equation (4.7). Thus during a summer afternoon, a difference of nearly 4.0 in the R-value is obtained between an attic space which is lined with an aluminum foil and the one which is not, Table 4.7.

A better way of providing a radiant barrier in an attic space of a wood frame building is to use a plywood roof deck in which the aluminum foil is laminated to the plywood. In this application, the foil faces towards the cavity space as shown in Figure 4.25.

## 4.8 THERMAL TRANSMITTANCE – THE U-VALUE

Since heat transfer through a building component involves all three modes of heat transfer (conduction, convection and radiation), a composite factor is commonly used to describe its thermal property. This factor is called the *thermal transmittance* or the *U-value* of the component. U-value is the inverse of R-value. Therefore, its unit is the same as that of thermal conductance i.e., Btu/(ft$^2$·°F·h), or W/(m$^2$·°C) in the SI system. In practice, we are concerned with the air-to-air transmittance through a wall or a roof. Hence, the U-value includes internal and external surface resistances, $R_{si}$ and $R_{so}$. Thus, the U-value of a component is given by:

$$U = \frac{1}{R_{si} + (R_1 + R_2 + R_3 + \cdots) + R_{so}}$$  (4.8)

If the total resistance of a component including the internal and external film resistances is 10.0, its U-value is $1/10.0 = 0.10$. Architects and engineers compare the effectiveness of different construction assemblies in terms of their U-values. The real usefulness of the U-value, however, lies in heat transfer calculations, since heat transfer is directly proportional to the U-value. The greater the U-value of a component, the greater the heat transmitted through it. The U-value of an assembly can be calculated as shown in Example 4.6.

## Example 4.6

Determine the U-value of the wall shown in Figure 4.26. The wall consists of 2 x 4 (actual size $1^1/_2$ in. x $3^1/_2$ in.) wood studs spaced 16 in. on center with $3^1/_2$ in. thick fiberglass insulation. A 2 in. wide cavity separates the stud wall from a 4 in. (actual size $3^5/_8$ in.) thick brick veneer.

*Solution*: The resistances of various layers of the wall are tabulated below.

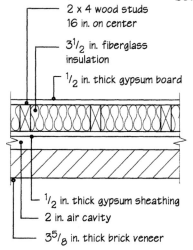

2 x 4 wood studs 16 in. on center

$3^1/_2$ in. fiberglass insulation

$^1/_2$ in. thick gypsum board

$^1/_2$ in. thick gypsum sheathing

2 in. air cavity

$3^5/_8$ in. thick brick veneer

**FIGURE 4.26** Plan of the wall of Example 4.6.

| Element | R-value | Reference |
|---|---|---|
| Inside surface resistance | 0.7 | Table 4.5 |
| 0.5 in. thick gypsum board | 0.5 x 0.60 = 0.30 | Table 4.4 |
| 3.5 in. thick fiberglass | 3.5 x 3.2 = 11.2 | Table 4.4 |
| 0.5 in. thick gypsum sheathing | 0.5 x 0.60 = 0.30 | Table 4.4 |
| 2 in. wide air cavity | 1.0 | Table 4.7 |
| 3.625 in. thick brick veneer | 3.625 x 0.20 = 0.73 | Table 4.4 |
| Outside surface resistance | 0.2 | Table 4.5 |

$$R_t = 0.7 + 0.3 + 11.2 + 0.3 + 1.0 + 0.73 + 0.2 = 14.43$$

Hence, the U-value = $1/R_t = 1/14.43 = 0.069$

### 4.8.1  U-values of Glazing

We saw in Example 4.2 that the R-value of a single glass sheet is almost negligible.  In fact, it is the internal and external surface resistances that provide any resistance to heat flow through a glass sheet.  Since the external and internal surface resistances add to nearly 0.9, the R-value of a single glass sheet is generally assumed as 1.0.  Since U = 1/R, the U-value of a single glass sheet is also 1.0.

The U-value of glazing, however, differs from that of the glass sheet since glazing includes the glass as well as the frame in which the glass is held.  Depending on the material used and the thickness of the frame, the U-value of the frame may be lower or higher than the U-value of glass.  In general, a wood frame has a smaller U-value and a metal frame, a greater U-value than a single glass sheet.  The U-values of glazing are further discussed in Section 7.7.

### 4.8.2  Overall U-value of a Building Envelope

The U-values for various components of an assembly are usually not the same.  For instance, a wall will consist of (one or more types of) opaque portions and fenestration (windows and doors).  The U-value of fenestration is generally higher than the U-value of opaque portions.  Similarly, a roof may consist of opaque portions and skylights where the U-value of the skylight is generally higher than that of the opaque portion of the roof.

The overall U-value of an assembly ($U_o$) can be determined by area-weighting the U-values of various components of the assembly.  Thus, if $U_1$, $U_2$, $U_3$, etc. are the U-values of components whose surface areas are $A_1$, $A_2$, $A_3$, etc. respectively, the overall U-value of the assembly is given by:

$$U_o = \frac{A_1 U_1 + A_2 U_2 + A_3 U_3 + \cdots}{A_1 + A_2 + A_3 + \cdots} \tag{4.9}$$

### Example 4.7

Determine the overall U-value ($U_o$) of the external walls of a single family dwelling given that:
The opaque portion of the wall is as shown in Figure 4.26, i.e. its U-value = 0.069 and its area = 3,000 ft$^2$.  U-value of glazed openings = 0.5; area = 900 ft$^2$.  U-value of doors = 0.3; area = 50 ft$^2$.

*Solution*: Total area of various components of the wall = 3,000 + 900 + 50 = 3,950 ft$^2$.  From Equation (4.9),

$$U_o = \frac{0.069(3,000) + 0.5(900) + 0.3(50)}{3,950} = 0.17$$

### 4.9 INSULATING MATERIALS

Although a large variety of insulating materials are currently used in buildings, they can be classified into the following three categories based on their physical structure.

- Fibrous materials.
- Granular materials, subdivided into: (a) loose-fill granular insulation, (b) insulating concrete, and (c) rigid perlite board.
- Foam insulation, subdivided into: (a) rigid board foam insulation, (b) masonry inserts, and (c) foamed-in-place insulation.

A few of the commonly used materials in each category are shown in Table 4.8.

#### 4.9.1 Fibrous Insulating Materials

These are materials with a fibrous structure. They derive their high thermal resistivity due to the air contained between the fibers. The fibers can be of a mineral base or a cellulosic base. Two types of mineral fibers are generally used: (i) glass fibers, called fiberglass, and (ii) fibers obtained from natural

**Table 4.8  Commonly Used Insulating Materials**

| Physical structure | Formation | Insulating material |
|---|---|---|
| Fibrous materials | Batts, blankets and semi-rigid boards. | Fiberglass, rock wool and slag wool |
| | Loose-fill (blown-in) | Cellulosic fibers, fiberglass, and rock wool |
| | Loose-fill | Expanded perlite and vermiculite granules |
| Granular materials | Insulating concrete | Perlite concrete and vermiculite concrete |
| | Rigid boards | Perlite board<br>Plastic foams: expanded polystyrene (EPS), extruded polystyrene (XEPS), polyurethane (PUR) and polyisocyanurate (PIR)<br>Cellular glass |
| Foamed materials | Masonry inserts | EPS masonry inserts |
| | Foamed-in-place insulation | Polyurethane and aminoplast resin |

**FIGURE 4.27** Fiberglass insulation installed between studs. (a) Unfaced insulation, and (b) kraft paper faced insulation. Courtesy of: CertainTeed Corporation, Valley Forge, Pennsylvania.

rock, called rock wool. Both fiberglass and rock wool are made by converting molten glass or rock into extremely fine fibers. The fibers are then sprayed with a binder and fabricated into the finished product. Fiberglass and rock wool insulations are fire resistant, moisture resistant and vermin resistant.

Included in the cellulosic fibers are recycled newspaper, wood and sugarcane. Cellulosic fibers must be suitably treated for fire resistance, minimization of smoke contribution, fungal growth and decomposition by moisture.

Fiberglass and rock wool are the most commonly used fibrous insulations. They are available as (i) batts, (ii) blankets and (iii) semi-rigid boards. Batts and blankets are normally used as wall insulation. Boards are used in applications where rigidity is required, e.g., on a flat or low-slope roof, in order to withstand foot traffic. Batts and blankets are similar in appearance, composition and density. The only difference between them is that blankets are available in rolls, see Figure 4.7(a), while batts are precut from rolls into standard lengths.

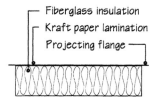

Fiberglass insulation
Kraft paper lamination
Projecting flange

**FIGURE 4.28** Projecting flanges in kraft paper faced fiberglass or rock wool insulation.

Apart from other sizes, both batts and blankets are manufactured in standard widths to fit 16 in. and 24 in. center-to-center spacing between wood or metal studs. They are available either unfaced, Figure 4.27(a), or faced, Figure 4.27(b). Facing is usually of asphalt impregnated paper, called *kraft paper*, which functions as a vapor retarder (see Section 5.7). Kraft paper faced products are also available with projecting flanges for stapling to wood studs, Figure 4.28. Flanges may either be stapled to the faces of studs (face stapled[3]) or to the sides of studs (inset stapled), as shown in Figure 4.27(b).

Unfaced insulation is particularly useful as additional insulation in attic spaces where faced insulation already exists, or in ceiling spaces where rigid ceiling tiles provide support to the insulation. Unfaced batt insulation is also available to pressure fit within stud spaces, which may be used when a cover material has already been placed on one side of the assembly. If a vapor retarder is required in such an assembly, it must be provided separately, Figure 4.29(a).

---

[3] Face stapling is normally avoided since it causes problems in installing the gypsum board.

**FIGURE 4.29** (a) Vapor retarder over unfaced fiberglass insulation. Courtesy of CertainTeed Corporation, Valley Forge, Pennsylvania. (b) and (c) Blown-in insulation in an attic. Courtesy of: Owens Corning, Toledo, Ohio.

Glass wool, mineral wool or cellulosic fiber insulation may also be used as loose-fill insulation. They are usually blown into cavity spaces by pneumatic blowers. Blown-in insulation is popular in retrofit applications where either no insulation or inadequate insulation existed previously, Figure 4.29(b). However, the potential of condensation within the insulation must be examined in a retrofit application, since the addition of insulation may create condensation where none existed earlier, refer to Section 5.8.

Fibrous insulation is also available as rigid boards. They are usually made from wood fibers and are used in situations where structural strength is required, such as in wall sheathing, and as base for built-up or modified bitumen roofs. Thermal resistivity of fiber board is much lower than fiberglass or rock wool insulations, Table 4.4.

### 4.9.2 Loose-fill Granular Insulation

In materials with a granular structure, the air voids are contained inside tiny hollow beads or granules. Two types of granules are in common use: (i) perlite granules, and (ii) vermiculite granules.

Perlite is a glassy volcanic rock which is expanded into granules by heat treatment. The expansion of perlite takes place due to the 2 to 6 percent moisture present in the crude perlite rock. When heated suddenly to a temperature of nearly 1,600 °F, the water in crushed perlite particles converts to steam. The pressure of steam expands perlite particles, creating small air-filled granules, Figure 4.30. The process of expanding perlite is, in fact, similar to making popcorn.

Expanded vermiculite granules are made from mica. The process of making vermiculite granules is similar to that of making perlite granules. Expanded perlite and vermiculite are used as loose-fill insulation in cavities, particularly the cavities of masonry walls, Figure 4.31. Both vermiculite and perlite have good fire resistance but absorb moisture within their pores, which leads to the lowering of insulation values. The freezing of trapped moisture

**FIGURE 4.30** Three stages of perlite production illustrate the great increase in volume that takes place on expansion. Courtesy of: Perlite Institute, Staten Island, New York.

**FIGURE 4.31** Vermiculite loose-fill insulation being poured in masonry walls. Courtesy of: Grace Construction Products, Cambridge, Massachusetts.

may also lead to the deterioration of granules. Manufacturers of vermiculite and perlite loose-fill insulations, therefore, supply these materials with a water repellent treatment.

Expanded perlite is made from a density of nearly 2 pcf to 15 pcf. A 5 pcf expanded perlite is commonly used as loose-fill insulation. The thermal resistivity of 5 pcf perlite granules is nearly 3.0, Table 4.4. When used as loose-fill insulation in the cavities of concrete masonry units, it can substantially improve thermal performance of concrete masonry walls. Expanded perlite manufacturers would provide the R-values and U-values of walls with filled and unfilled cavities.

Expanded polystyrene granules (or beads), which are commonly used as packing material, are not recommended as loose-fill insulation in masonry cavities. Being extremely lightweight, they do not completely fill cavity spaces. Perlite and vermiculite granules, on the other hand, have much better flowability and seek out even small voids. Additionally, being a synthetic polymer, polystyrene granules are combustible, while perlite and vermiculite granules are incombustible.

### 4.9.3 Insulating Concrete

Another application of perlite and vermiculite granules is in (nonstructural) lightweight concrete. Vermiculite or perlite granules combined with portland cement in the ratio of 1 (portland cement): 4 to 8 (perlite or vermiculite) granules by weight, makes a lightweight concrete which has good insulating properties. This concrete is called *insulating concrete*.

Insulating concrete is well suited for insulation on a flat roof since roof slopes can be easily created through wet concrete. The other method of providing slope on a flat roof is to use tapered board insulation, which is far more labor intensive. Because insulating concrete bonds well to most roof substrates, it provides high wind uplift resistance. Additionally, since perlite and vermiculite are inorganic materials, insulating concrete is incombustible and provides high a degree of fire resistance to the roof.

The R-value of insulating concrete is much lower than other insulations such as fiberglass or foamed plastic insulations. However, the advantages of insulating concrete, such as its fire resistance, easy sloping to drains and good bond to substrate, can be combined with the higher R-value of EPS boards to create a hybrid assembly. In this assembly, insulating concrete is poured below and above the EPS boards so that the EPS boards are sandwiched between the concrete. This type of construction[4] is well suited for insulating steel roof decks, Figures 4.32 and 4.33.

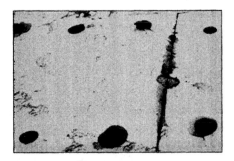

(a) EPS boards

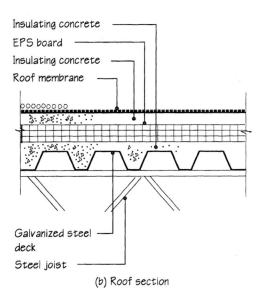

Insulating concrete
EPS board
Insulating concrete
Roof membrane

Galvanized steel deck
Steel joist

(b) Roof section

**FIGURE 4.32** Use of EPS boards. (a) EPS boards are provided with holes to yield a mechanical bond between the layers of concrete and EPS boards. (b) Section through a roof with insulating concrete. Notice the EPS boards sandwiched between two layers of insulating concrete.

### 4.9.4 Rigid Perlite Board

Expanded perlite is also used in rigid board formation. Called *perlite board*, it is made with a combination of expanded perlite and mineral fibers, and widely used as an insulation over flat or low-slope roof decks. The thermal resistivity of perlite board is lower than plastic foams but its advantage lies in its incombustibility.

---

[4] Insulating concrete requires a lot of water in its preparation. Since it is normally not practical to wait several weeks or months required for the concrete to dry before installing the roof membrane, it is recommended that insulating concrete should be used only on slotted roof decks. The slots allow the moisture held in concrete to escape in the form of water vapor from the underside of the deck. (Note that water vapor cannot escape from above the deck due to the impermeability of the roof membrane). If insulating concrete is used on an unslotted deck or on a concrete roof slab, roof ventilation should be provided for water vapor to escape.

(a)

(b)

**FIGURE 4.33** Insulating concrete as roof insulation. (a) EPS boards being laid above a layer of insulating concrete. (b) A layer of insulating concrete being laid above EPS boards. Courtesy of: Grace Construction Products, W.R. Grace & Co., Cambridge, Massachusetts.

### 4.9.5 Rigid Board Plastic Foam Insulations

The most common type of rigid board insulations are made from plastic foams. Plastic foam insulations are cellular in their physical structure. Four types of plastic foam insulations are commonly used in rigid board formation. These are: expanded polystyrene (EPS), extruded polystyrene (XEPS), polyurethane (PUR) and polyisocyanurate (PIR) boards, see Table 4.8. XEPS, PUR and PIR have high thermal resistivity because HCFC gas is used as a blowing agent in producing their foam structure. EPS boards have air trapped in their cells.

EPS boards are made by heating expandable polystyrene pellets in a mold. The heat expands the pellets into beads and fuses the beads together to form "buns" which are simply large rectangular blocks. The manufacturing process of EPS boards is shown diagrammatically in Figure 4.34. The buns are cut into boards of required thickness[4.3]. EPS boards are also called *beaded boards*. Another term used to describe the same product is *molded expanded polystyrene* (MEPS).

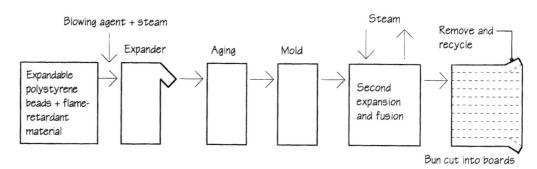

**FIGURE 4.34** Process of manufacturing expanded polystyrene (EPS) boards. Reference 4.4.

The density of the EPS boards depends on the density of pre-expanded beads. The boards are made in densities varying from nearly 1.0 to 3.0 pcf; 1.0 pcf board is the most commonly used. EPS boards are used as wall sheathing and roof insulation. Due to the relatively small capital investment required in their manufacture, there are a large number of manufacturers of EPS boards. By contrast, the manufacture of XEPS boards requires larger capital outlay. Therefore, only a few manufacturers produce XEPS board insulation. Compared to XEPS boards, EPS boards are cheaper but provide a lower insulation value.

XEPS boards are made by mixing a liquid polymer with liquid HCFC and forcing the mixture through a die. The version of HCFC gas used as a blowing agent in the production of XEPS vaporizes at below room temperature so that the polystyrene expands before it is extruded into shape through the die.

By contrast, the version of HCFC gas used as a blowing agent in the production of PUR and PIR vaporizes at room temperature so that the liquid mixture of polymer and blowing agent is spread between the top and bottom facers to give PUR and PIR boards their required shapes. PUR and PIR are, therefore, manufactured with facers on both sides. XEPS boards, on the other hand, do not require facers. The process of manufacturing PUR/PIR boards is shown diagrammatically in Figure 4.35.

XEPS was first manufactured by the Dow Chemical Company in the U.S. during the 1940s under the trade name "Styrofoam". However, today there are several manufacturers of XEPS boards who distinguish their products from each other by using different colors. For instance, Dow Chemical's XEPS board is blue, UC Industries' board is pink, and the Amoco Foam Products' board is green.

The facers used on PUR and PIR boards retard the migration of HCFC gas out of the foam. PUR and PIR foams, therefore, have higher thermal resistivity than XEPS foam. Facers consist of aluminum foil, glass fiber reinforced polyester, plaster boards, wood fiber boards, etc.

The closed cellular structure of XEPS, PUR and PIR implies that they have high resistance to water and water vapor penetration. An EPS board, being a beaded product, is relatively more permeable to water and water vapor than an XEPS, PUR or PIR board.

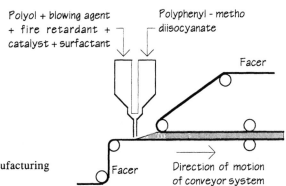

**FIGURE 4.35** Process of manufacturing polyisocyanurate (PIR) boards.

Plastic foams are combustible and require protection from flames and high temperatures. Building codes mandate that if plastic foam is used as interior insulation, it must be covered with a minimum of $^1/_2$ in. thick gypsum board or an equivalent thermal barrier. Plastic foams are resistant to fungal growth and chemical decomposition. Polystyrene is sensitive to daylight and will deteriorate after prolonged exposure.

XEPS, PUR and PIR boards are commonly used as insulation on flat or low-slope roof decks. PIR is relatively more common as roof insulation because it can better withstand the high temperature of hot asphalt than XEPS and PUR boards. Additionally, PIR has a better fire-resistance property than XEPS or PUR. Other uses of XEPS, PUR and PIR boards is in wall sheathing, above-grade wall insulations, foundation walls and perimeter insulation under slabs-on-grade, see Section 4.10.4.

### 4.9.6 Cellular Glass

Another rigid board foam product is cellular glass made by expanding molten glass into a closed cell structure and cooling it to form boards. Cellular glass boards have high compressive strength. They are impermeable to water vapor and water, and are suitable as insulation in roofs which carry heavy loads such as roof plazas and roof top parking areas, and as perimeter insulation under concrete slabs-on-grade.

### 4.9.7 Plastic Foam Inserts as Masonry Wall Insulation

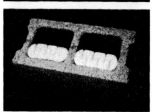

Plastic foam inserts are an alternative to granular loose-fill insulation for concrete masonry walls. Foam inserts require less on-site labor and are more resistant to water absorption than loose-fill granular insulation. The inserts are molded EPS shapes which are friction fitted into standard concrete blocks at the concrete block manufacturing plants, Figure 4.36. In another version of the same concept, specially designed blocks with cut-down webs allow foam insulation to be inserted into masonry cores at construction site, Figures 4.37(a) and (b).

In a more recent version, a specially designed block has two insulation pieces fitted at the manufacturing plant, one against each face of the block and a third piece inserted at the site between two adjacent blocks, Figure 4.37(c) The remaining cavity of the core can be site packed with an additional foam insert to increase thermal resistance or reinforced and grouted for higher strength.

**FIGURE 4.36** EPS inserts in concrete blocks installed at the block manufacturing facility.

### 4.9.8 Foamed-in-place Insulations

Foamed-in-place insulation is formed at the site by a mixture of two liquid chemical reactants. As the two chemicals combine, they rapidly expand into foam with volumes nearly 30 times the original combined volumes of the two chemicals. After expansion, the foam solidifies into a closed cell structure

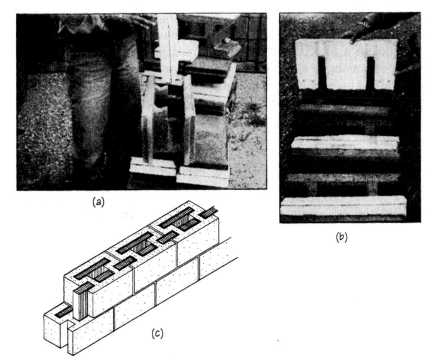

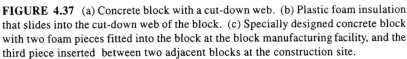

**FIGURE 4.38** Foamed-in-place insulation in masonry walls. Courtesy of: Tailored Chemical Products, Hickory, North Carolina.

**FIGURE 4.37** (a) Concrete block with a cut-down web. (b) Plastic foam insulation that slides into the cut-down web of the block. (c) Specially designed concrete block with two foam pieces fitted into the block at the block manufacturing facility, and the third piece inserted between two adjacent blocks at the construction site.

in a few minutes. The advantage of foamed-in-place insulation lies in the fact that it can be provided in preexisting cavities of odd shapes where other types of insulations would be less desirable or impossible to use. In a masonry wall, foamed-in-place insulation is either injected in cavities by drilling small holes (usually $5/8$ in. diameter) or poured in cavities from the top of the wall, Figure 4.38. Note that these applications require the skills of specialized and manufacturer-trained personnel.

## 4.10 AMOUNT OF INSULATION REQUIRED

From an economic standpoint, the amount of insulation required in the envelope is a function of the relationship between the price of energy and the cost of providing and installing insulation. If the energy prices are low, the cost of heating or cooling the building is low. In that case, a lower level of insulation is economical. On the other hand, if energy prices are high, a greater amount of insulation is justified. This is precisely why the levels of insulation provided in buildings increased when the world energy prices were suddenly quadrupled in 1973.

The climate of the location is another factor that affects the amount of insulation required. In a severe climate, a greater amount of insulation is required than in a mild climate. Thus, there is an optimum level of envelope insulation for a particular climate. This is defined as that level of insulation at which the savings in energy consumption realized by using the insulation balances the cost of providing and installing the insulation.

Since the energy prices and the cost of providing and installing insulation vary over time, no hard and fast rule can be laid down for the optimum amount of insulation for a location. With current energy prices, one source[4.4] recommends R-values for single family dwellings as given in Table 4.9. These values are related to the number of heating degree days (HDD) of the location. For the definition of HDD and the HDD data for various locations in the United States and Canada, refer to Appendix V.

**Table 4.9   Recommended R-values of  Walls and Roof-ceiling Assemblies for Single Family Dwellings**

| Envelope assembly | HDD < 5,000 | HDD between 5,000 and 7,500 | HDD > 7500 |
|---|---|---|---|
| Walls | R-25 to R-30 | R-30 to R-35 | R-35 to R-40 |
| Roof-ceiling | For unheated attics, R-value to be nearly 2 times the R-value of walls. <br> For flat roofs, R-value to be between 1 and 1.5 times the R-value of walls. | | |

### 4.10.1  Code Required Minimum Envelope Insulation

Since energy conservation in buildings is becoming increasingly important, more and more cities are requiring compliance with energy codes. The most referenced code for energy conservative design in the United States is the *Model Energy Code* (MEC)[4.5] published by the Council of American Building Officials (see Section 1.6.1). Compliance with the code can be achieved by either satisfying its prescriptive or its performance provisions.

The prescriptive provisions of the MEC, as applicable to residential structures, require that the envelope of the building contain a minimum amount of insulation. This is specified in terms of the $U_o$-values of external walls and roof-ceiling assemblies of the building. Since the U-value is the inverse of the R-value, the code specifies the maximum $U_o$-values that can be provided in the envelope.

For example, the maximum $U_o$-values specified by the MEC for the external walls of residential buildings are given in Table 4.10. Note that these values refer to the overall U-values of walls, as defined by Equation 4.9. The code-mandated maximum $U_o$-values for roof-ceiling assemblies of residential buildings are given in Table 4.11.

Since the code provisions are based on a certain permissible amount of heat loss or gain through the envelope, it allows a trade-off between the U-values of walls with those of the roof-ceiling assembly. In other words, a decrease in wall insulation can be compensated for by an increase in roof-ceiling insulation, or vice versa. For additional details, the reader should refer to the code.

**Table 4.10  Maximum $U_o$-Values for Walls of Residential Buildings**

|  | Heating degree days | $U_o$ |
|---|---|---|
| Detached one or two family residences | 0 | 0.265 |
|  | 0 - 2,500 | 0.265 - HDD $(34 \times 10^{-6})$ |
|  | 2,500 - 7,000 | 0.2188 - HDD $(15.55 \times 10^{-6})$ |
|  | 7,000 - 13,000 | 0.11 |
|  | > 14,000 | 0.10 |
| All other residential structures | 0 - 500 | 0.38 |
|  | 500 - 3,000 | 0.38 - (HDD - 500) $(66 \times 10^{-6})$ |
|  | 3,000 - 6,000 | 0.215 |
|  | 6,000 - 8,200 | 0.215 - (HDD - 6,000) $(30.5 \times 10^{-6})$ |
|  | 8,200 - 9,500 | 0.148 |
|  | 9,500 - 10,000 | 0.148 - (HDD - 9,500) $(55.8 \times 10^{-6})$ |
|  | >10,000 | 0.12 |

**Table 4.11  Maximum $U_o$-Values for Roof-ceiling Assemblies of Residential Buildings**

| Heating degree days | $U_o$ |
|---|---|
| 0 | 0.05 |
| 0 - 2,500 | 0.05 - HDD $(5.6 \times 10^{-6})$ |
| 2,500 - 3,900 | 0.036 |
| 3,900 - 6,000 | 0.036 - (HDD - 3,900) $(4.78 \times 10^{-6})$ |
| 6,000 - 16,000 | 0.026 |
| > 16,500 | 0.025 |

Tables 4.10 and 4.11 are reproduced from the 1993 edition of the *CABO Model Energy Code*[TM], copyright © 1993, with the permission of the publisher, the International Code Council.

**Example 4.8**

Determine the required minimum attic insulation, as specified by the MEC, for a single family dwelling in Minneapolis, Minnesota.

*Solution*: From Appendix V, HDD for Minneapolis = 8,382. From Table 4.11, maximum $U_o$ = 0.026. Thus, the minimum R-value of the roof-ceiling assembly must be 1/0.026 = 38.5. Assuming that R-2 will be provided by the attic cavity (see Table 4.7) and an additional R-1 by surface resistances, the attic insulation must be at least R-35.5, i.e., R-36.

**Example 4.9**

Determine the code-required minimum insulation in the opaque portions of the walls of a single family dwelling in Minneapolis. The area of the opaque portions of walls = 1,300 ft$^2$ and the glazed area = 200 ft$^2$. The U-value of glazed areas = 0.6.

*Solution*: From Table 4.10, the maximum $U_o$ of a wall assembly = 0.11. If the U-value of opaque portion of the wall is given by $U_w$, then from Equation (4.9):

$$0.11 \ = \ \frac{1300 \ U_w \ + \ 200 \ (0.6)}{1300 \ + \ 200}$$

Thus, $U_w$ = 0.035. In other words the minimum required R-value of the wall is = 1/0.035 = 28.6. Assuming R-1 is to be provided by surface resistances, the wall insulation must be a minimum of R-27.6, i.e., R-28.

### 4.10.2  Crawl Space Insulation

In a cold climate, the heat loss from a ground floor can be substantial. If the ground floor is a suspended floor with a crawl space, it should be insulated with insulation placed between floor joists, Figure 4.39. Note that the insulation is required under the entire floor. The maximum U-value of a floor over a crawl space, as per the MEC, are given in Table V.2, Appendix V.

### 4.10.3  Basement Wall Insulation

If the floor separating the superstructure from the basement is not insulated, the exterior basement walls must be insulated. The MEC requires that the basement walls be insulated to a depth of 10 ft below grade or to the level of the basement floor, whichever is less. The maximum U-values for basement walls are given in Table V.2, Appendix V.

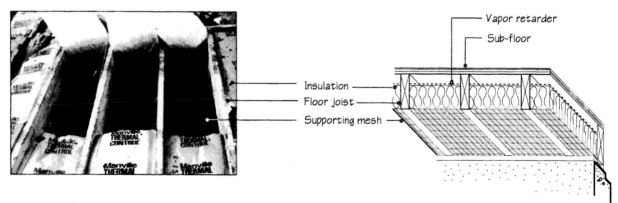

**FIGURE 4.39**  Insulation in the floor over a crawl space.

### 4.10.4 Insulation Under a Concrete Slab-on-grade

If the floor is a concrete slab resting on the ground (a slab-on-grade), it needs to be insulated only along its exposed perimeter. There is no need to place insulation under the entire slab because the heat loss from a slab-on-grade occurs only from the perimeter of the slab which is exposed to the outside. The portion of the slab away from the exposed perimeter does not contribute to heat loss. This is explained below.

In Section 4.4, we noted that the resistance of an element is directly proportional to its thickness L. In fact, the quantity L in Figure 4.6 refers to the length of the heat flow path through the element. The longer the path, the greater the resistance provided by that path to heat flow. Thus, when we assumed in Figure 4.6 that heat flows only along the thickness of the element, we in fact assumed that the heat flow along other paths (along the length or the width of the element) is zero. This is simply another way of stating that the length and width of the element is much larger than the thickness of the element.

Let us now examine the heat flow paths in a concrete slab-on-grade. A simplified visualization of heat loss from a slab-on-grade shows that there are three possible paths along which heat can flow from the slab.
- Vertically — through the thickness of the slab and into the ground;
- Horizontally through the slab; and
- Along several curved paths through the slab into the ground, as shown in Figure 4.40.

As for the vertical path, it is clear that the length of this path is extremely long, being the diameter of the earth. Thus, the vertical path presents an extremely large (an almost infinite) resistance to heat flow, implying that no heat will flow in the vertical direction.

Heat losses through the other two paths are functions of their respective lengths. The longer a path length, the greater the resistance of the path and hence, the smaller the heat loss through that path. Since the region of the slab away from an exposed edge has long path lengths, it does not contribute much to heat loss from the slab. Only the region which is close to the edges will affect heat loss. That is why a slab on the ground is best insulated around its exposed perimeter. Very little is gained by insulating under the entire slab.

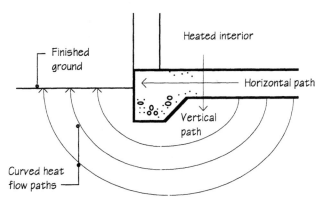

**FIGURE 4.40** Various heat flow paths through a slab-on-grade.

The standard practice is to insulate under the slab with either horizontal or vertical insulation. A few commonly used details for insulating a slab-on-grade are shown in Figure 4.41. In all these details, the location of the insulation is meant to insulate the horizontal and curved heat flow paths.

The minimum R-value of insulation is a function of the climate of the location and whether the slab is heated or unheated. This is given in Table V.3, Appendix V. The minimum width or height of the insulation (dimension "X" in Figure 4.41) is recommended to be 2 ft for a location with HDD less than 6,000, and 4 ft for a location with HDD greater than 6,000. Perimeter insulation is not required in a location with HDD less than 2,500.

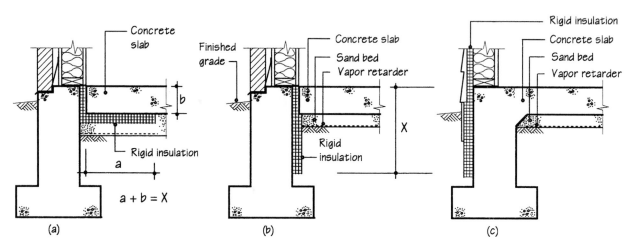

**FIGURE 4.41** Alternative details of insulation under a slab-on-grade.

## 4.11 THERMAL CAPACITY

The concepts of heat transfer and related thermal properties of materials discussed in earlier sections apply to the *steady state* heat transfer. The steady state is defined as the state in which the temperatures at all points within an assembly remain constant over time. The reverse of a steady state is an unsteady state, more commonly referred to as the *dynamic state*.

With particular reference to the building envelope, a steady state implies that the temperatures on both sides of the envelope are constant over time. In practice, a perfect steady state does not occur since although the internal air temperature may be kept constant by heating or cooling, the external temperature of the envelope varies over time.

The external temperature of the envelope is a function of the external air temperature and the intensity of solar radiation. On days when the sun's rays are absent, i.e., when the sky is cloudy, the diurnal variation in external temperature is small. Thus, an approximation of a steady state is obtained when: (i) the indoor temperature of the building is kept constant, and (ii) the outdoor temperature registers little diurnal variation for several days due to cloudy skies.

Cloudy skies generally occur during the winter season in northern Europe, Canada and the northern United States, resulting in nearly constant external

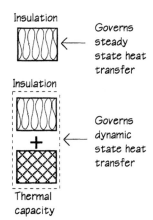

Insulation

Governs steady state heat transfer

Insulation

Governs dynamic state heat transfer

Thermal capacity

**FIGURE 4.42** Envelope characteristics that govern heat transfer under a steady state and a dynamic state.

temperatures. If the internal temperature of the building is kept constant by heating, then the heat transfer through a building envelope in these locations is a good approximation of a steady state. A similar situation may occur during periods of overcast skies in the warm-humid tropics if the indoor temperature is kept constant by air conditioning.

A dynamic state is a more commonly occurring condition than a steady state. In the dynamic state, the temperature at a point within a component varies with time due to the variation of temperature on the internal and external boundaries of the component. This occurs in climates where solar radiation intensities are high, resulting in large diurnal and seasonal variations in air temperature.

The distinction between steady and dynamic states has an important bearing on a building envelope's thermal properties. The property of the envelope which governs heat transfer under a steady state is its U-value. In other words, under a steady state, it is the insulation provided in the envelope that governs heat transfer through the envelope. Under a dynamic state, both the U-value (insulation) as well as the envelope's ability to store heat come into play, Figure 4.42.

The ability of a component to store heat is given by its *thermal capacity*, defined as the amount of heat required to raise the temperature of one square foot of the component by 1 °F. The greater the thermal capacity of the component, the greater the heat it will absorb for a given rise in its temperature. The units of thermal capacity are $Btu/(ft^{2.0}F)$. *Thermal mass* and *thermal inertia* are other terms that are used instead of thermal capacity.

The thermal capacity (TC) of a component is given by the product of its surface density and the specific heat of the material. Thus:

$$TC = (Surface\ density)\ (Specific\ heat) \qquad (4.10)$$

Surface density is the weight of the component per unit surface area. Hence, the units of surface density are pounds per square foot (psf). Surface density is obtained by multiplying the thickness of the component by its (volume) density. Thus, if the density of concrete is 145 pcf, the surface density of a 4 in. thick concrete wall is 145(4/12) = 48.3 psf. Values of surface densities of commonly used components are given in Appendix IV.

The specific heat is defined as the amount of heat required to raise the temperature of 1 lb of a material by 1 °F. Note that specific heat is a property of the material, while thermal capacity is a property of the component. The units of specific heat and thermal capacity in both the U.S. system and the SI system are given in Table 4.12. However, in the following discussion, we shall omit the use of units of thermal capacity so as to be consistent with our practice of omitting the units for R-values and U-values. The values of specific heat of a few commonly used materials are given in Table V.4, Appendix V.

An examination of Table V.4 shows that the range of variation of specific heats of commonly used building materials is fairly small. For most materials, specific heat varies between 0.15 and 0.20 Btu/(lb·°F). Water has the highest specific heat — 1.0 Btu/(lb·°F). The relatively high specific heat of wood is due to its large moisture content.

Since the difference in the values of the specific heat of materials is small,

**Table 4.12 Units of Specific Heat and Thermal Capacity**

| U.S. system | SI system |
|---|---|
| **Specific heat** | |
| Btu/(lb·°F) | kJ/(kg·°C) |
| To convert values given in U.S. system to SI system multiply by **4.19** | |
| **Thermal capacity** | |
| $Btu/(ft^{2.0}F)$ | $kJ/(m^{2.0}C)$ |
| To convert values given in U.S. system to SI system multiply by **20.44** | |

Low density material    High density material

Low thermal capacity    High thermal capacity

**FIGURE 4.43** The thermal capacity of a material is directly proportional to its surface density.

the variation in the TC values of components is mainly governed by their surface densities. Therefore, heavyweight materials (concrete, brick, stone etc.) have higher TC values than lightweight materials, such as insulating materials, wood and plastics, Figure 4.43.

## Example 4.10

Determine TC values of: (a) 4 in. (nominal) thick brick wall, and (b) 4 in. thick fiberglass insulation. Density of fiberglass insulation = 1.5 pcf.

*Solution*: (a) From Table IV.2, Appendix IV, surface density of 4 in. thick brick wall = 39 psf. Specific heat of brick = 0.19 Btu/(lb·°F), Table V.4, Appendix V. From Equation (4.10), TC value of a brick wall = 39 (0.19) = 7.4 Btu/(ft$^2$·°F).

(b) Density of fiberglass = 1.5 pcf. Surface density of 4 in. thick fiberglass = (1.5)(4/12) = 0.5 psf.

Specific heat of fiberglass = 0.17 Btu/(lb·°F). Hence, TC value of fiberglass insulation = 0.5 (0.17) = 0.085 Btu/(ft$^2$·°F).

From Example 4.10, note the large difference in thermal capacity values of a brick wall and fiberglass insulation. Although they both are of the same thickness, the brick wall has nearly 90 times greater thermal capacity than fiberglass insulation. Thus, a brick wall has a 90 times greater capacity to store heat as compared with fiberglass insulation of the same thickness. Stated differently, the brick wall will require a 90 times greater amount of heat for a given rise in temperature as compared with fiberglass insulation of the same thickness.

### 4.11.1 Thermal Capacity and the Dynamic State

Since the heat stored by a building envelope affects the thermal properties of the building, thermal capacity is an important envelope property. Together with the U-value of the envelope, it determines the heat gain or loss of a building. As stated earlier, thermal capacity comes into play only when the building envelope is subjected to dynamic thermal conditions. Its effect is substantial when the dynamic range of external temperature is large. When the range is small, thermal capacity plays a less important role. Thus, thermal capacity has no effect on heat transfer through the envelope when the dynamic range is zero — the steady state.

Where external conditions vary greatly over a 24-hour period, a large thermal capacity of the envelope improves the internal environment of an unconditioned building. This is due to the ability of heavyweight materials to store large quantities of heat during the heating part of the cycle (daytime), and to release the stored heat during the cooling part (nighttime).

Thermal capacity, therefore, has the effect of delaying the impact of external conditions on the interior of the building. This delay, which is called the *time lag*, is most useful in climates in which the need to cool and heat the building exists in a 24-hour cycle, i.e., the external temperatures are above the comfort temperature during the day and lower than the comfort temperature at night. Such conditions occur in some desert areas where the early morning temperature may be nearly 50 °F and the afternoon temperature in excess of 90 °F.

The adobe construction of Native Americans and various other cultures exploited the thermal capacity of walls and roofs to provide comfort conditions inside buildings. Thick walls coupled with a few small openings provided cool interiors during the summer and warm interiors during the winter. This is precisely what the temperature graphs of Figure 4.1 show.

### 4.11.2 Thermal Capacity vs Insulation

Since both thermal capacity and insulation affect heat transfer through the building envelope, the question arises as to what is the relative importance of thermal capacity and the insulation (U-value) of the envelope in determining the energy consumption in the heating and cooling of buildings. It has already been stated that thermal capacity affects heat transfer through the envelope only under dynamic conditions. Under steady state conditions, thermal capacity has no effect. On the other hand, insulation impacts heat transfer under both dynamic as well as steady state conditions.

Now let us examine the relative impact of insulation and thermal capacity on energy consumption in heated or cooled buildings. It has been demonstrated (mathematically as well as experimentally) that the amount of energy consumed in heating or cooling buildings is independent of the thermal capacity of the envelope, provided the heat flow through the envelope remains unidirectional (i.e., if heat flows from the inside to the outside, or from the outside to the inside).

Under unidirectional heat flow, only the U-value of the envelope (i.e., the insulation) determines the rate of energy consumption. The greater the insulation, the smaller the energy consumption. Thermal capacity of the envelope has no impact on energy consumption under unidirectional heat flow conditions. This is true even if the unidirectional heat flow represents dynamic condition.

On the other hand, if heat flow changes direction over time (from the outside to the inside for some time and from the inside to the outside at other times), it is both the insulation and the thermal capacity of the envelope that determine energy consumption. The statement of Figure 4.42 can, therefore, be modified as shown in Figure 4.44.

An obvious example of unidirectional heat flow is cold storage rooms in which the heat flow is generally from the outside to the inside. Thus, it is the insulation in the envelope of a cold storage building that determines its energy consumption.

Since in the cold climates of Canada, Europe and the northern United States, the heat transfer path remains unidirectional (heat flows from the inside

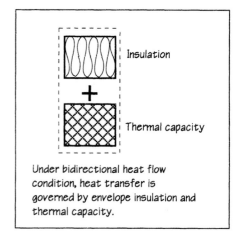

**FIGURE 4.44** Relative importance of insulation and thermal capacity on heat transfer.

to the outside) for most of the year, it is the insulation of the envelope that is significant. Thermal capacity plays an insignificant role in such climates. The same is true in most warm humid tropics where the heat flow is from the outside to the inside in air-conditioned buildings.

### 4.11.3 Location of Insulation in the Envelope

The relative locations of insulation and thermal capacity in the envelope are also important. It has been shown by tests on full-scale buildings that the outside placement of insulation is more effective in reducing energy consumption than if the insulation is placed in the middle of the envelope section or toward the interior of the building. The placement of thermal capacity (heavyweight materials) on the interior side of the envelope helps to moderate interior temperature fluctuations.

**REVIEW QUESTIONS**

**4.1**  Explain the three modes of heat transfer: conduction, convection and radiation.

**4.2**  What is the most commonly used unit of energy in the SI system? What is its relationship with the British thermal unit?

**4.3**  In which unit does an electric utility company charge its customers?

**4.4**  Determine the amount of energy consumed by a 200 watt lamp in 24 hours.

**4.5**  Determine the R-values of the following materials:
(i) 4 in. nominal (3.625 in. actual) brick wall,
(ii) $^5/_8$ in. thick gypsum board, and
(iii) 2 in. thick extruded polystyrene board.

**4.6**   Draw a plan of the following wall assembly and determine its total R-value: 4 in. brick veneer, 2 in. air cavity, 1 in. thick expanded polystyrene sheathing, 2 x 6 wood studs at 16 in. on center with full thickness fiberglass insulation, and $^5/_8$ in. thick gypsum wallboard.

**4.7**   What is the U-value of the assembly of Question 4.6.

**4.8**   What is an "aged R-value"? To which materials does it apply? Explain.

**4.9**   Determine the overall U-value of a roof whose opaque portion, with an area of 2500 ft$^2$, has an R-value of 35, and the area under skylights (100 ft$^2$) has an R-value of 1.0.

**4.10**  What is surface resistance? Explain.

**4.11**  What is the difference between solar radiation and radiation emitted by building surfaces? Explain.

**4.12**  Which material is commonly used to retard heat transfer in buildings by radiation? How does it function?

**4.13**  What is the wavelength region of:
(i) Solar radiation,
(ii) Visible radition,
(iii) Ultraviolet radiation, and
(iv) Radiation emitted by building elements.

**4.14**  With the help of sketches and notes, show the various ways in which a concrete masonry wall can be insulated.

**4.15**  With the help of a three-dimensional sketch, show how a wood frame wall is generally insulated.

**4.16**  What is insulating concrete? Where is it commonly used?

**4.17**  List various plastic foam insulations. What is the difference between extruded polystyrene foam board and expanded polystyrene foam board?

**4.18**  Refer to Sweet's Catalog and list at least:
(i) Three manufacturers of fiberglass insulation,
(ii) Two manufacturers of rock wool insulation,
(iii) Two manufacturers of slag wool insulation
(iv) Three manufacturers of extruded polystyrene insulation
(v) Three manufacturers of polyisocyanurate insulation.

**4.19**  Determine the minimum insulation required, as per the Model Energy Code, in the roof of an apartment building in: (i) Houston, Texas and (ii) Ancorage, Alaska.

**4.20**  Determine the minimum insulation required, as per the Model Energy Code, in the opaque portions of a wall in an apartment building in: (i) Houston, Texas, and (ii) Anchorage, Alaska. The walls have 20% glazed area whose U-value is 0.65.

**4.21**  Repeat the problem in Question 4.20(ii) if all other data are the same but the U-value of glazing is 0.45.

**4.22**  Under which climatic conditions will you recommend the use of insulation under concrete slabs-on-grade?

**4.23**  With the help of a sketch and notes, explain why it is not necessary to place insulation under an entire concrete slab-on-grade.

**4.24**  Which building materials have high thermal mass? In which climates is thermal mass in the building envelope beneficial from an energy performance point?

**REFERENCES**   4.1   Baird, George, et al: *Energy Performance of Buildings*, CRC Press, 1984, p. 2.

4.2   American Society of Heating, Refrigeration and Air Conditioning Engineering, Atlanta, Georgia: *Handbook of Fundamentals*, 1989, p. 22.6

4.3   Peterson, Wayne: "Foamed Plastic Roof Insulation", *The Construction Specifier*, November 1987, p. 66.

4.4   Nisson, Ned J.D. and Dutt, Gautam: *The Superinsulated House*, John Wiley and Sons, 1985, p. 74.

4.5   Council of American Building Officials, Falls Church, Virginia: *Model Energy Code*, 1993.

# 5

# AIR LEAKAGE AND WATER VAPOR CONTROL

## 5.1 INTRODUCTION

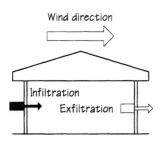

**FIGURE 5.1** Air leakage consists of infiltration and exfiltration of air through the building envelope.

In addition to thermal insulation and the thermal mass of the envelope, discussed in Chapter 4, another factor that affects the heat loss or gain of a building is the leakage of conditioned (heated or cooled) air through cracks and unsealed joints in the building envelope, and its replacement by the outside air. The leakage of air through the building envelope, which consists of air infiltration and exfiltration, is unwanted ventilation of the building, Figure 5.1. This increases energy consumption since the infiltrating air must be heated or cooled to the required inside air temperature. In extremely hot or cold climates where the temperature difference between the inside and the outside air is large, air leakage can add significantly to energy consumption of a building. In this chapter, we shall study materials and construction practices employed to control air leakage in buildings.

Air always contains some water vapor. In fact, air is not only a mixture of nitrogen, oxygen and carbon dioxide but also of water vapor. The leakage of air through the building envelope is, therefore, always accompanied by water vapor transmission from the inside to the outside of a building, and vice versa.

Air leakage is not the only means of water vapor transmission through the building envelope. Water vapor also moves through the envelope independent of air movement. This is due to the vapor pressure difference between the inside and the outside air. In this chapter, we shall examine the magnitude of the vapor pressure difference that commonly occurs in buildings.

The presence of water vapor in buildings or its movement through the building envelope is of little or no significance in building construction.

141

However, water vapor has the potential to convert into (liquid) water, a phenomenon known as *condensation*. Water causes a great deal of damage to construction assemblies. In this chapter, we shall examine the causes of condensation and the construction practices employed to control it.

## 5.2 AIR INFILTRATION

It is estimated that air leakage accounts for 20 to 40% of the heat loss in buildings in Canada and North America[5.1]. Although the absolute values of air leakage have declined in recent years because of tighter envelopes and better workmanship, the decline is roughly of the same order as the decline in heat loss due to the use of greater amounts of insulation. Thus, the relative values of heat loss due to air leakage have remained virtually unaltered.

Two factors that affect air leakage in a building are: (i) the leakage area, and (ii) the pressure difference between the inside and the outside air. The greater the leakage area or the pressure difference, the greater the rate of air leakage.

The leakage area is a measure of the relative tightness of the envelope. It is the area of cracks, holes and openings in the envelope and is a function of the type of construction, design and workmanship. The leakage sites in the envelope usually occur at the joints of various components. Thus, external doors, windows, skylights, fireplaces, electrical outlets, plumbing and duct penetrations represent typical leakage sites.

The pressure difference between the inside and the outside air depends on wind speed and direction. Since wind speed increases with height above the ground, the pressure differences at the upper floors of a building are greater than those at the lower floors, causing greater air leakage at upper floors. We observed in Section 2.8.3 that the windward face of a building is under positive pressure and the other faces, under suction. Therefore, air infiltrates through the windward face and exfiltrates through the nonwindward faces of the building.

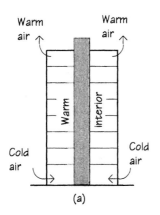

Another factor affecting the pressure difference is the temperature difference between the inside and the outside air. Since the density of air decreases with increasing temperature, warmer air exerts lower pressure than cooler air. The consequence of this fact is that, during the heating season, outside air infiltrates through the lower floors of a building due to its higher pressure and pushes the warm (low pressure) air out of the building from the upper floors, Figure 5.2(a). During the cooling season, the flow directions are reversed. Thus, cool inside air exfiltrates from the lower floors of the building, and the warm outside air infiltrates from the top, Figure 5.2(b).

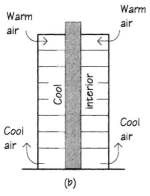

The infiltration-exfiltration of air due to temperature difference is called *stack action* because of its similarity to the movement of air in a chimney stack. In tall office buildings, the effect of stack action on energy consumption is significant[5.2]. Although the floors in a tall building tend to inhibit stack action, air movement takes place through stairwells, elevator shafts and other openings between floors.

**FIGURE 5.2** Infiltration and exfiltration due to stack effect.

Since the inside-outside pressure difference is a function of the external climate (wind speed and air temperature), there is little that can be done to control it. Thus, the only means of reducing air leakage in a building is to reduce the leakage area. This requires sealing all joints between building components and weatherstripping doors and windows. Weatherstripping is available in many forms, some of which are shown in Figure 5.3. They consist of foam rubber, tubular plastic (neoprene, vinyl or polyurethane), and spring bronze strips. Another type commonly used is pile weatherstrip which consists of fine bristles made from synthetic fibers with high wear characteristics. Due to its low friction, pile weatherstrip is popular in sealing the joints in sliding doors and windows, and in meeting stiles of doors.

Weatherstrips are resilient and compressible. In closed position, the door or window frames compress the weatherstrips, reducing air leakage. An additional advantage of weatherstrips lies in their ability to reduce dust and noise penetration, and the entry of insects.

Entry doors are another source of air leakage. If they are subject to frequent opening and closing, double doors or revolving doors are recommended. The joints between components, such as between door or window jambs and walls are usually sealed by a sealing compound which is a nonhardening synthetic material applied usually by a pumping gun (refer to Section 10.6).

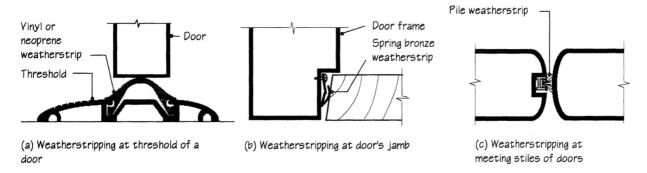

(a) Weatherstripping at threshold of a door

(b) Weatherstripping at door's jamb

(c) Weatherstripping at meeting stiles of doors

**FIGURE 5.3** Some examples of weatherstripping of doors.

### 5.2.1 Air Leakage Rate

Air leakage rate is measured in terms of the rate at which the air goes in and out through building envelope. Thus, an obvious unit of air leakage is cubic feet per hour ($ft^3/h$), or $m^3/h$ in the SI system. However, since we are usually interested in comparing the air leakage rate of one building with another, the unit most commonly used for air leakage is air change per hour (ach). Thus, if the air leakage rate of a building whose volume is 20,000 $ft^3$ is 0.5 ach, it means that it will leak 10,000 $ft^3$ of air per hour. This is equivalent to saying that the inside air is completely replaced by the outside air in two hours.

Based on tests conducted on several houses, it is estimated that the air leakage rate in recently constructed energy efficient houses in the United States varies between 0.1 ach to 0.7 ach, the average rate being 0.5 ach[5.3]. The leakage rate in older houses is of the order of 3.0 ach.

Since a great deal of air leakage in buildings occurs through doors, windows and curtain walls, limits are placed on their maximum permissible air leakage rates. The rate for windows (and curtain walls) is specified in terms of air leakage from a unit area of the window when the window is subjected to a standard air pressure difference.

Thus, the air leakage rate for windows is measured in $ft^3/(h \cdot ft^2)$. For example, the American Architectural Manufacturers' Association (AAMA) specifies a maximum air leakage rate of 9.0 $ft^3/(h \cdot ft^2)$ under a pressure difference of 1.57 psf for fixed (inoperable) residential or commercial windows [Reference 5.2, page 45]. In other words, the maximum air leakage rate in an AAMA-approved 2 ft x 5 ft fixed window assembly is 90 $ft^3$ of air per hour. In the SI system, the corresponding maximum air leakage rate through AAMA windows is 2.7 $m^3/(h \cdot m^2)$ under a pressure difference of 75 Pa. This means that no more than 2.7 $m^3$ of air should leak through 1 $m^2$ of an AAMA approved window in 1 hour.

Note that a pressure difference of 1.57 psf (75 Pa) corresponds to the pressure produced by a wind speed of nearly 25 mph (40 km/h), refer to Equation 2.2. This is well above the average annual wind speed in most locations. Therefore, the actual in-service leakage of a building envelope is usually less than its rated leakage.

### 5.2.2 Air Leakage in Wood Frame Construction

Air leakage is a particularly serious concern in wood or steel frame buildings because their envelope is inherently more leaky than other types of construction such as concrete or masonry. Additionally, nearly 60% of all energy consumed in buildings in the United States and in other industrialized countries is in the residential sector — individual houses, apartment buildings and motels[5.4]. Most of these buildings are constructed of wood frame. Thus, a small percentage decrease in energy consumption in residential buildings translates into large energy savings at the national level.

The leakage sites in a typical wood frame building are shown in Figure 5.4. The more important of these sites are: (i) the junction between the sill plate and wall foundation, (ii) the joints between external wall sheathing, and (iii) the joints between framing members at rough openings for doors and windows.

The joint between the sill and the foundation is typically sealed by installing a compressible material such as a rubber or fiberglass gasket under the sill plate, Figure 5.5.

As for the joints in external wall sheathing, they can be sealed in several ways. A somewhat labor intensive method is to caulk all joints in sheathing panels, and subsequently tape them. Another choice is to staple an asphalt saturated felt (building paper) over external wall sheathing, so that the sheathing is fully covered with building paper[1], Figure 5.6. The joints between the building paper are lapped and sealed with an asphalt-based mastic. Since the building paper is available in 36 in. wide rolls, sealing the joints of building

---

[1] Building paper is more commonly used as a water-resistant layer under external wall sheathing, to provide a second line of defense against water penetration.

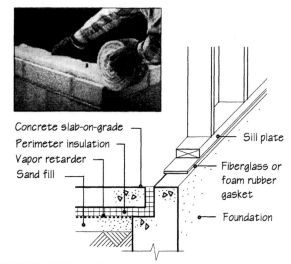

**FIGURE 5.4** Typical leakage sites in a wood frame building.

**FIGURE 5.5** One of the several ways to seal the joint between the sill plate and the foundation of a wood frame building.

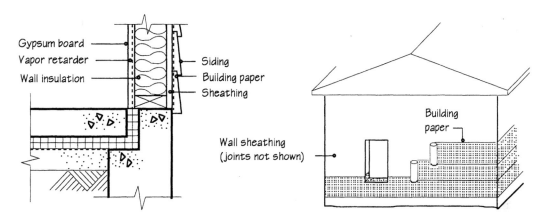

**FIGURE 5.6** Air leakage through a wood frame building is reduced by covering its walls with building paper applied over the external wall sheathing.

paper can also involve a great deal of labor. Another disadvantage of building paper is its low permeability to water vapor. As we shall see in Section 5.8, a high vapor permeability is an important requirement of any material that covers the external wall sheathing.

### 5.2.3 The Air Retarder

A more recently introduced alternative to building paper is a continuous air infiltration barrier, Figure 5.7. An air infiltration barrier, or simply an air barrier (also called a house wrap) is like the building paper except that it has greater tear resistance and a higher vapor permeability. Air barriers are available in rolls of up to one story high so that they can wrap over the walls of a wood frame building with very few joints.

First introduced in the United States in 1979, an air barrier is typically a 5 to 10 mil thick plastic sheet with micropores so that it allows very little air

FIGURE 5.7 Air retarder wrapped over external wall sheathing. Courtesy of: Tyvek Housewrap, DuPont, Wilmington, Delaware. (Tyvek ® is a registered trademark of the Dupont Company for its spun-bonded olefin).

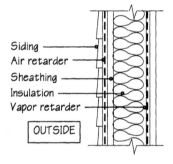

FIGURE 5.8 Locations of an air retarder in a wall assembly.

to pass through but has a high degree of permeability to water vapor (1 mil = 0.001 in.). Depending on the manufacturer, it is made from plastic fibers which are either woven or spunbonded into a sheet. One manufacturer makes an air barrier out of a microperforated plastic sheet.

Note that although the term "air barrier" is commonly used in the industry, a more correct term is *air retarder*, since most commercially available air barriers retard the flow of air through them, rather than completely stopping it. Therefore, in the following discussion, the term air retarder will be used.

An air retarder is usually wrapped over the wall sheathing and secured to the studs through sheathing with staples or broad head nails, Figure 5.8. Like the building paper, the air retarder is water resistant. Thus, an additional advantage of using the air retarder is that it protects the sheathing from any rainwater that may accidentally enter the wall through the external wall finish. Joints in the air retarder are lapped and sealed with a self adhesive tape, Figure 5.9.

FIGURE 5.9 Taping the joints of an air retarder improves its airtightness. Courtesy of: Tyvek Housewrap, DuPont, Wilmington, Delaware. (Tyvek® is a registered trademark of the Dupont Company for its spun-bonded olefin).

By virtue of its location in the envelope, the air retarder has a great deal of continuity since, being on the outside face of the wall, it is not interrupted by utility service penetrations such as the electric and water supply outlets. The vapor retarder (see Section 5.7), on the other hand, may have several penetrations as it is usually installed on the inside face of the wall.

The air retarder not only reduces heat gain or loss by reducing air leakage but also reduces air movement in the wall cavity in the vicinity of the insulation, thereby increasing the effectiveness of the insulation. Low density, loose-fill and fibrous insulations, such as fiberglass or mineral wool, are more susceptible to increased convective heat transfer from infiltration as compared to closed-cell foam insulations such as extruded polystyrene or polyisocyanurate foam insulation.

The use of air retarders is becoming a standard practice in residential construction in climates where the winters are long and severe. This is due to the relatively large difference between the inside and the outside air temperatures in cold climates, and hence a greater loss of energy by leakage. For example, the difference between the inside and outside air temperatures may be 60 °F or more on a typical winter day in a cold climate (70 °F inside air temperature and 10 °F outside air temperature). The corresponding difference in air temperatures in hot climates is much smaller. For example, the difference in air temperatures during the summer in a hot climate seldom exceeds 30 °F (70 °F inside air temperature and 100 °F outside air temperature). Therefore, in warm or mild climates, the use of air retarders is relatively less critical.

### 5.2.4 Air Leakage in Steel, Concrete and Masonry Construction

Airtightness in a steel, concrete or masonry building can be provided in the same way as in a wood frame building. The only difference is that an air retarder, as described above, must be secured to the external sheathing of a steel frame building or to a concrete or masonry wall by an adhesive. Usually, strips of adhesive at nearly 3 ft on centers are used. On a wood frame wall, the air retarder is secured by staples or nails.

In a well-constructed masonry building, air leakage is relatively small. However, if the mortar joints in the walls are not completely filled, leakage of air through joints may result, particularly through vertical mortar joints. An alternative to the use of an air retarder is a coat of hot asphalt or a coat of cold applied asphalt emulsion on the masonry back-up wall as shown in Figure 5.10. Plastic foam insulation in the cavity further reduces infiltration. Since asphalt has low vapor permeability, it also functions as a vapor retarder, so that a separate vapor retarder in the assembly may be unnecessary. Being water resistant, the mastic/asphalt coating also protects the back-up wall against any accidental water penetration.

### 5.2.5 Indoor Air Quality and Air Retarders

The quality of indoor air in buildings has come under much scrutiny in the

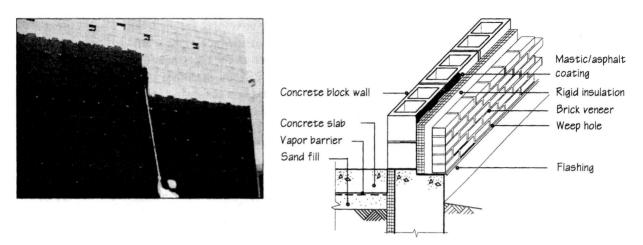

**FIGURE 5.10**   The air-tightness of a masonry wall is enhanced by coating the wall with mastic/hot asphalt.

last few years due to several complaints from the occupants — of headache, eye and nasal irritation, fatigue and unacceptable odors. Studies conducted by the Environmental Protection Agency (EPA) in the United States have concluded that the indoor air may become excessively polluted, creating what has come to be known as "sick building syndrome". According to the EPA, indoor air pollution is responsible for nearly 26,000 deaths annually in the United States[5.5].

In addition to dust, pollen and microorganisms, contaminants routinely added to indoor air are carbon dioxide, generated from combustion and human metabolism, and carbon monoxide from combustion and smoking. Several volatile organic compounds (VOC) are present due to the use of aerosols, cleaning chemicals and disinfectants. Formaldehyde, a colorless gas, is another major source of indoor air pollution. Although a VOC, it is generally listed separately because of its widespread use in building products in the form of urea formaldehyde. Urea formaldehyde is an adhesive used in wood veneer and wood fiber products such as plywood, particleboard, fiberboard, etc. Other sources of formaldehyde are carpet pads and underlayments, ceiling tiles, upholstery and wall coverings.

Another dangerous source of indoor air pollution is radon, a colorless, odorless, radioactive gas present in some soils which may leak into the interior through cracks in the floors. Radon is produced by the decay of radium, a substance that occurs in most soils. However, it is dangerous only when its concentration is high. Higher concentrations of radium are found in soils that contain uranium, phosphorous, shale and granite. Radon gas particles affect human lungs in the same way as smoking. Estimates indicate that radon is responsible for nearly 10% of deaths from lung cancer in the United States[5.6].

If the buildings are adequately ventilated, the above pollutants are generally of little concern. However, due to the relative airtightness of the envelope (doors, windows, walls etc.) of modern energy efficient houses and the use of air retarders, concern about indoor air quality in buildings has grown. A supply of fresh air is necessary to dilute airborne contaminants. In older houses in which the inside air was continuously replaced by the outside air every 20 to 30 minutes by leakage/ventilation, there was more than adequate amount of fresh air.

### 5.2.6 Air-to-air Heat Exchangers

In order to provide the necessary amount of fresh air with a minimum impact on energy consumption, a system of controlled ventilation is used. In this system, an optimum quantity of fresh air required to maintain a good indoor air quality is provided. Standards have been established for minimum ventilation in buildings to provide acceptable indoor air quality[5.7], which is roughly equivalent to 0.3 air changes per hour for an average size house in the United States or Canada.

Controlled ventilation not only saves energy but also provides a healthier environment. Air leakage is unpredictable and uneven. In a controlled ventilation system, stale air is exhausted from one vent in the building and fresh air drawn through another vent. The heat from the stale air is used to warm up the fresh air through a device called the *air-to-air heat exchanger*.

In addition to consisting of two air blowers and an air filter, the most important component of a typical air-to-air heat exchanger is a bank of parallel metal plates. The fresh and stale air pass through alternate spaces between the plates, and the heat is conducted from one side of the plate to the other, as shown in Figure 5.11.

Although air-to-air heat exchangers (also called energy recovery ventilators) are more commonly used in colder climates, they are equally appropriate in warm climates if the building envelope is relatively airtight.

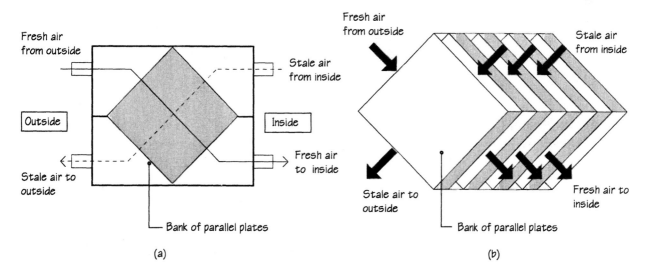

**FIGURE 5.11** (a) The primary component of an air-to-air heat exchanger is a bank of parallel plates contained inside an enclosure. (b) A bank of parallel plates, illustrating the principles of an air-to-air heat exchanger.

## 5.3 PERFORMANCE OF AIR RETARDERS

Several methods are available for testing the air leakage rate of materials or assemblies. Therefore, in comparing the effectiveness of various air retarders, it is important that their air leakage rates be obtained from the same test method since different methods will give different results. In the United States, ASTM Standard E 283: "Standard Test Method for Determining the Rate of Air Leakage Through Exterior Windows, Curtain Walls and Doors ..." has been adopted for measuring the air permeability through wall assemblies consisting of air retarders[5.8]. In ASTM E 283, a test specimen of wall measuring not less than 8 ft x 8 ft is sealed into an opening of the test chamber, Figure 5.12. The test specimen must include the air retarder material over 2 x 4 studs and sheathing, so as to simulate actual construction of the wall. *0.02 1/(ce)   75 pa*

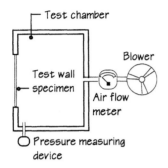

The test chamber consists of a fully sealed room, connected to an air blower which can create a constant positive or negative pressure in the chamber. The chamber is pressurized to the required pressure and the resultant air flow measured by a flow meter which is connected between the blower and the test chamber. Since no leakage can occur through the test chamber, the measured flow rate is the air leakage rate of the test specimen.

**FIGURE 5.12** Air permeability measuring set-up.

*Table A5  4.1.2
         A BC*

### 5.3.1 Criteria for the Selection of an Air Retarder

Since a low air leakage is the primary reason for which an air retarder is used, it is obvious that the air leakage rate of an air retarder should be as low as possible. ASTM E 1677 "Standard Specification for an Air Retarder Material or System for Low Rise Frame Building Walls" requires that the air leakage rate of an air retarder, measured according to ASTM E 283, should not exceed 0.06 ft$^3$/(min.ft$^2$) under a pressure difference of 1.57 psf[5.9]. Air leakage rates of a few selected materials are given in Table 5.1.

In addition to air permeability, other factors such as water vapor permeance, tear strength, resistance to water penetration and durability against ultraviolet deterioration must also be considered in the selection of an air retarder. An air retarder must have a high water vapor permeability and a high resistance to water penetration.

## 5.4 PROPERTIES OF WATER VAPOR

It is an observable fact that air contains water vapor. If water in a container is left exposed to air, we observe that the water disappears after some days. The disappearance of water is referred to as the *evaporation* of water, which is in fact the conversion of water into water vapor. It is because of water's property of converting to water vapor and mixing with the surrounding air that wet clothes and other materials dry.

Water vapor is like steam existing at temperatures below the boiling point of water. It mixes readily with air and is invisible. In fact, air is not only a mixture of nitrogen, oxygen and carbon dioxide but also of water vapor. Air without water vapor generally does not exist. Water vapor content in air is usually higher in coastal areas than inland locations.

The air can hold only a limited amount of water vapor. This limit increases

**Table 5.1  Air Leakage Rates of Selected Materials[1]**

| Material | Air leakage ft³/(min·ft²) | Material | Air leakage ft³/(min·ft²) |
|---|---|---|---|
| Plywood ($^3/_8$ in. thick) | 0.001 | 15 lb nonperforated felt | 0.053 |
| Particle board ($^1/_2$ in. thick) | 0.003 | 15 lb perforated felt | 0.078 |
| Gypsum board ($^1/_2$ in. thick) | 0.004 | Glass sheet | 0.000 |
| Expanded polystyrene board (1 in. thick) | 2.410 | Metal sheet | 0.000 |
| Extruded polystyrene (1 in. thick) | 0.005 | Air retarders (as per ASTM | |
| Fiberglass insulation | 7.240 | E 1677 requirement) | 0.060 (maximum) |

[1] Values given in this table are approximate and are for unjointed components.  Joints in components will increase air permeability.

as the temperature of air increases.  The greater the temperature of the air, the greater the amount of water the air can hold as vapor.  When the air at a certain temperature holds water vapor to its maximum capacity, it is called *saturated air*.  For example, one pound of saturated air at 70 °F (at standard atmospheric pressure) holds 110.4 grains of water in the form of water vapor.  [1 lb = 7000 grains (gr), see Appendix I].  This is another way of saying that 1 lb of air at 70 °F can hold a maximum of 110.4 gr of water vapor.  Wet objects exposed to saturated air will not dry because saturated air is unable to hold additional water.

### 5.4.1  Vapor Pressure and Relative Humidity

Being a gas, water vapor exerts pressure on the surfaces of the enclosure in which it is contained.  Although water vapor is mixed with air, the pressure that it exerts is independent of (dry) air pressure[2].  Vapor pressure is directly proportional to the amount of water vapor present in air.  Thus, the maximum vapor pressure occurs when the air is saturated.  This is called the *saturation vapor pressure*.

The ratio of the pressure of water vapor actually present in the air at a certain temperature to the saturation vapor pressure at the same temperature is called the *relative humidity* (RH) of air.  This ratio is generally expressed as a percentage.  Thus:

$$RH = \frac{\text{Vapor pressure of air}}{\text{Vapor pressure of saturated air}} \times 100 \qquad (5.1)$$

However, since vapor pressure is a function of the amount of water vapor present in air, relative humidity is more conveniently defined as the ratio of the weight of water vapor actually present in air to the weight of water vapor

[2] This fact is derived from Dalton's Law of Partial Pressures.

present in saturated air at the same temperature. Thus relative humidity may also be defined as:

$$RH = \frac{\text{Weight of water vapor held in air}}{\text{Weight of water vapor in saturated air}} \times 100 \qquad (5.2)$$

From the above equations, we see that a 100% relative humidity means that the air is saturated. A 50% relative humidity means that the air holds half its saturation water vapor content. The weights of water vapor in saturated air at different temperatures and the corresponding saturation vapor pressures are given in Table 5.2.

**Table 5.2  Amount of Water Vapor in Saturated Air and Saturation Vapor Pressure**

| Temperature (°F) | Water vapor (gr/(lb dry air) | Vapor pressure (psf) | Temperature (°F) | Water vapor (gr/(lb dry air) | Vapor pressure (psf) |
|---|---|---|---|---|---|
| -20 | 1.8 | 0.89 | 50 | 53.4 | 25.65 |
| -10 | 3.2 | 1.56 | 60 | 77.3 | 36.92 |
| 0 | 5.5 | 2.66 | 70 | 110.4 | 52.31 |
| 10 | 9.2 | 4.45 | 80 | 155.7 | 73.07 |
| 20 | 15.0 | 7.27 | 90 | 217.4 | 100.64 |
| 30 | 24.1 | 11.65 | 100 | 301.0 | 136.84 |
| 40 | 36.4 | 17.52 | 110 | 414.2 | 183.80 |

## Example 5.1

Determine the amount of water present as water vapor in a single family dwelling whose volume is 30,000 ft³. Air temperature = 70 °F and RH = 50%.

*Solution*: The amount of water vapor in 1 lb of saturated air at 70 °F = 110.4 gr, Table 5.2. From Equation (5.2), the amount of water vapor in 1 lb of air at 70 °F and 50% RH = 0.5 (110.4) = 55.2 gr.
   Since air weighs nearly 0.075 lb/ft³ (see Appendix IV), the weight of 30,000 ft³ of air = 2,250 lb. Hence, the amount of water in the air = 2,250(55.2) = 124,200 gr = 17.74 lb = 2.1 gal (1 U.S. gallon of water weighs 8.34 lb).

## Example 5.2

Determine the vapor pressure difference between the inside and the outside air for the following conditions. Inside air temperature = 70 °F, RH = 40%; outside air temperature is 10° F, RH = 60%.

*Solution*: From Table 5.2, the saturated vapor pressure (at 70° F) = 52.31 psf. From Equation (5.1), inside vapor pressure (at 70 °F and 40% RH) = 0.4 (52.31) = 20.92 psf. Similarly, the outside vapor pressure (at 10 °F and 60% RH) = 0.6 (4.45) = 2.67 psf.

Vapor pressure difference = 20.92 - 2.67 = 18.3 psf.

### 5.4.2 Magnitude of Prevailing Vapor Pressure

From Example 5.2, note that the vapor pressure difference of 18.3 psf is of the same order as the pressure produced by a wind speed of nearly 85 mph, which is almost a hurricane wind speed (see Equation 2.2). In other words, commonly obtained vapor pressure difference between the inside and the outside of a building can be quite high.

This is an important result since it is because of the large vapor pressure difference that water vapor is able to pass through building materials with relative ease as compared to the air. Several building materials such as gypsum board, plywood, concrete, etc., are vapor permeable but not air permeable. In fact, air retarders are materials which are meant to let the water vapor through but not the air. The air pressure difference between the inside and the outside is generally much smaller than the corresponding vapor pressure difference because the prevailing wind speed of 5 to 20 mph creates an air pressure difference of 0.06 to 1.0 psf respectively.

**5.5 CONDENSATION OF WATER VAPOR**

Consider air at a certain temperature and relative humidity. If no moisture is added to the air but the temperature of the air is raised, the result will be a decrease in the relative humidity of the air. For example, 1 lb of air at 70 °F and 50% relative humidity contains 55.2 grains of water vapor (see Table 5.2). If this air is sealed in a container so that no moisture enters or leaves the container, and the temperature of the air is progressively increased, we see that its relative humidity will decrease as shown in Figure 5.13. At 80 °F, the relative humidity of air will fall to 35.4%, since 55.2 gr is 35.4% of 155.7 gr — the saturation vapor content at 80 °F (see Table 5.2). At 90 °F, the relative humidity of this air will be 25.4%; and so on.

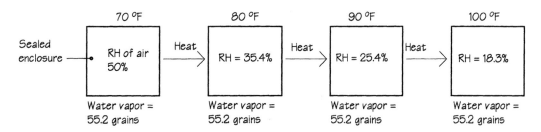

**FIGURE 5.13** If no moisture is added or subtracted from the air, and its temperature is increased, the relative humidity of the air will progressively decrease.

Conversely, when the air temperature is decreased, the capacity of air to hold water decreases, resulting in an increase in the relative humidity of air. If the decrease in air temperature is continued without adding or subtracting moisture, a temperature is reached when the air becomes saturated, i.e., its relative humidity becomes 100%. This air temperature is known as the saturation point temperature, but more commonly called the dew point temperature, or simply the *dew point*.

The dew point of air is different for every air mass. The dew point of very humid air is not too different from its temperature, which is the same as saying that very humid air will not require much cooling to reach 100% relative humidity.

If the temperature of air is decreased below the dew point, the amount of water vapor in excess of the saturation water vapor content changes into liquid water — a phenomenon called *condensation*. Thus, condensation is the reverse of evaporation.

Consider once again 1 lb of air at 70 °F and 50% relative humidity sealed in a container. As noted earlier, the amount of water vapor in this air mass is 55.2 gr. As the temperature of the air is decreased, its relative humidity increases. It can be shown (see Appendix VI) that the dew point of the above air mass is 50.8 °F. If the temperature of this air is lowered to less than 50.8 °F, the excess water vapor will condense into water. For example at 50 °F, the excess water vapor in this 1 lb air mass is 1.8 gr, which is obtained by subtracting 55.2 gr from 53.4 gr — the saturation water vapor content at 50 °F (see Table 5.2). At 40 °F, the condensed water is (55.2 - 36.4) = 18.8 gr, Figure 5.14.

Condensation occurs commonly in nature. The outer surface of a glass containing ice or cold water becomes wet because the (warm and humid) air in contact with the surface of the glass becomes cool enough to drop below its dew point. At this point, the air sheds excess water vapor, converting it into water which deposits on the surface of the glass.

In building interiors, condensation is commonly observed during the winter on hard impervious surfaces such as glass panes, metal window frames and glazed tiles. Hard and impervious surfaces do not absorb moisture so that any vapor that condenses on them is visible. Additionally, the glass sheet (or metal frame) has a lower thermal resistance than the surrounding wall. Therefore, the interior surface temperature of a glass sheet is much lower than that of the surrounding wall in heated buildings. If the interior

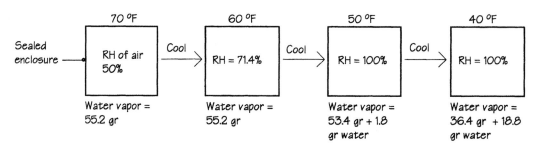

**FIGURE 5.14** If no moisture is added or subtracted from the air, and its temperature decreased, the relative humidity of the air will progressively increase until it becomes 100%.

surface temperature of glass is below the dew point of inside air, water vapor will condense on the glass. If the inside air is very humid, water drops will gradually grow in size and fall on the sill of the window, or the floor, forming puddles of water.

For condensation to occur in buildings, air must contain water vapor. In fact, water vapor is generally present in the inside air. Humans produce water vapor as they exhale and perspire. In health clubs and gymnasiums, considerable quantities of water vapor are released through human perspiration and breathing. In several industrial buildings such as bakeries and paper mills, the manufacturing processes produce large quantities of water vapor. In homes, a great deal of water vapor is produced in kitchens and bathrooms.

Water vapor can also arise from the drying of construction materials. Water added to concrete may take a year or more to dry. To a smaller extent, the same is true of masonry mortar, several flooring materials and plasters. Although this source of water vapor is temporary, it may last several months after the occupation of the building, depending on the climate of the location.

Conditions for human comfort require that air must be moist. Air with a low humidity can create discomfort and respiratory health problems. In some carpeted enclosures, low humidity air can create annoying static electricity. On the other hand, high relative humidity reduces skin evaporation and body cooling. High relative humidity coupled with high temperature gives rise to discomfort and a feeling of fatigue in humans. Air conditioning systems installed in buildings are designed to provide the required humidity levels. The relative humidity value commonly specified for office buildings is between 40% and 50%.

### 5.5.1 Surface and Interstitial Condensation

The condensation of water vapor on the surfaces of a building envelope such as on window panes or metal frames is called *surface condensation*. Condensation may also occur within the envelope assembly. This type of condensation is called *interstitial condensation*. Interstitial condensation is usually invisible unless it is of such magnitude that water drips out of the assembly in a visible manner.

Although water in vapor form is not damaging to construction assemblies, liquid water is. Out of the two types of condensation, interstitial condensation is more damaging because interstitially condensed water takes much longer to evaporate. Consequently, interstitial condensation causes corrosion of metals such as screws, nails and bolts, decay of wood, mold growth and the wetting of materials. The wetting accelerates the deterioration of materials. For example, gypsum board loses strength on wetting. Wetting of insulation reduces its R-value, and the extra weight of water may cause it to sag, particularly the fibrous insulation. The sagging of insulation may lead to uninsulated areas, creating thermal bridges. If the condensed water freezes within the assembly, disintegration of materials may occur because of the freeze-thaw effect.

Interstitial condensation occurs when water vapor moves into and through materials and building assemblies. If the temperature at any location within the assembly is below the dew point of air, condensation will take place at that location. Design to control interstitial condensation is important, particularly in cold climates where the potential for condensation is high.

**5.6 TRANSMISSION OF WATER VAPOR THROUGH AN ASSEMBLY**

There are two modes by which water vapor can move through an assembly, Figure 5.15. The first mode is due to the movement or leakage of air through the assembly. If the air can pass through a material or assembly, water vapor will also pass through it since water vapor and air are mixed together. The reverse, however, is not true, that is materials or assemblies which allow water vapor to pass through, may not allow air to pass through them. Most water vapor transmission through building assemblies takes place by this first mode, i.e., through air infiltration or ventilation.

The second mode of water vapor transmission occurs independently of air movement. This mode of transmission is called *vapor diffusion*. Vapor diffusion occurs because of the difference in vapor pressures across the two sides of a component. Vapor diffuses from a region of higher vapor pressure to that of lower vapor pressure in precisely the same way as heat travels from a higher temperature region to that of a lower temperature. In heated buildings, the inside air has a higher vapor pressure than the outside air (see Example 5.2). In these buildings, water vapor moves from the inside to the outside. In air-conditioned buildings in hot humid climates, water vapor moves from the outside to the inside.

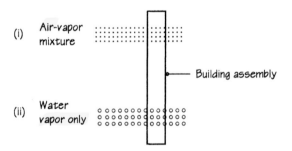

**FIGURE 5.15** Two modes of water vapor transmission through an assembly: (i) by air transmission, and (ii) by vapor (only) transmission. The second mode of water vapor transmission is called vapor diffusion.

### 5.6.1 Water Vapor Diffusion

The equation which governs the rate of water vapor diffusion through a component is similar to Equation (4.2), which gives the rate of heat conduction through a component. Thus:

$$w = \frac{m}{L} (P_2 - P_1) \tag{5.3}$$

In the above equation w is the weight of water vapor transmitted through a unit area of the component in unit time, measured in gr/(h·ft²). L is the thickness of the component (in inches), and $(P_2 - P_1)$, the vapor pressure difference across the component, Figure 5.16. In the U.S. system of units, vapor pressure is generally specified in inches of mercury (Hg). (1 in.Hg = 70.72 psf, see Table I.3, Appendix I).

The quantity m is called the coefficient of vapor permeability, or simply the *permeability*. Like thermal conductivity, permeability is a property of the material and therefore a constant for a given material.

If the quantity (m/L) is replaced by M in Equation (5.3), it becomes:

$$w = M (P_2 - P_1) \qquad (5.4)$$

M is called the *permeance* of the component. It is a property of the material and the thickness of the component. Permeance is similar to thermal conductance, and is obtained by dividing the permeability of the material by the component's thickness, i.e.:

$$\text{Permeance, M} = \frac{\text{Permeability of material, m}}{\text{Thickness of component, L}} \qquad (5.5)$$

From Equation (5.4), the unit for permeance is gr/(h·ft²·in.Hg). Since this is a complicated unit, it is abbreviated as the *perm,* and hence the property "permeance" is also called the *perm rating*. Thus, 1 perm = 1 gr/(h·ft²·in.Hg). In other words, a component having a perm rating of 1 perm will transmit 1 grain of water vapor per square foot per hour under a pressure difference of 1 in. of mercury. Since m = ML, the unit of permeability is called *perm-inch*. 1 perm-inch = 1 (gr·in.)/(h·ft²·in.Hg).

In the SI system, the unit of permeance is nanogram per second per square meter per Pascal. Thus, 1 SI perm = 1 (ng/(s·m²·Pa). The units of permeance and permeability in both the U.S. system and the SI system are given in Table 5.3.

Typical values of permeability of a few selected materials are given in Table 5.4, from which the values of permeance (M) can be calculated for a given thickness of the component by using Equation 5.5.

**Table 5.3 Units of Permeance and Permeability**

| Permeance |
| --- |
| U.S. system: gr/(h·ft²·in.Hg), called perm. |
| SI system: ng/(Pa·m²·s), called SI perm. |
| To convert from perm to SI perm, multiply value by 57.2. |

| Permeability |
| --- |
| U.S. system: gr·in./(h·ft²·in.Hg), called perm·in. |
| SI system: ng/(Pa·m·s), called SI perm·m. |
| To convert from perm·in. to SI perm·m, multiply value by 1.46. |

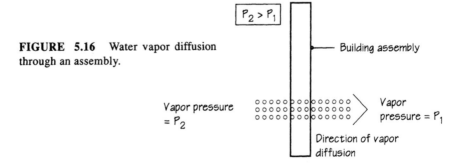

**FIGURE 5.16** Water vapor diffusion through an assembly.

Materials of low perm rating restrict the migration of water vapor. Plastics have low permeability. Hence, plastic membranes have low perm ratings. Metals and glass have zero permeability and hence zero perm ratings, i.e., they do not allow any water vapor to pass through. Note that when the perm rating is given, the thickness of the component must be stated. Perm ratings of a few materials are given in Table 5.5.

**Table 5.4  Vapor Permeability of Materials[1]**

| Material | Permeability (perm-inch) | Material | Permeability (perm-inch) |
|---|---|---|---|
| Concrete | 3.2 | Aluminum foil (unpunctured) | 0.0 |
| Brick wall | 3.2 | Fiberglass or mineral wool | 116.0 |
| Gypsum board | 20.0 | Extruded polystyrene insulation | 1.2 |
| Plywood (exterior glue) | 0.2 | Expanded polystyrene insulation | 5.0 |
| Plywood (interior glue) | 0.5 | Polyurethane/polyisocyanurate | 0.5 |
| Metals | 0.0 | Air cavity | 240.0 |

[1]  Permeability = Permeance of 1 in. thick material.

**Table 5.5  Perm Ratings of Components[1]**

| Component | Perm rating (perm) | Component | Perm rating (perm) |
|---|---|---|---|
| Aluminum foil (unpunctured) | 0.0 | Brick masonry, 4 in. thick | 0.8 |
| Aluminum foil on gypsum board | 0.1 | Concrete block masonry, 8 in. thick | 2.4 |
| Built-up roofing, 3 to 5 ply | 0.0 | Plaster on metal lath | 15.0 |
| 15 lb asphalt felt | 4.0 | Building paper, grade A | 0.25 |
| PVC (plasticized), 4mil thick | 1.2 | Building paper, grade B | 0.38 |
| Polyethylene sheet, 4 mil thick | 0.08 | Interior primer plus 1 coat flat oil | |
| Polyethylene sheet, 6 mil thick | 0.06 | paint on plaster | 1.6 - 3.0 |
| Polyethylene sheet, 8 mil thick | 0.03 | Exterior oil paint, 3 coats on wood | 0.3 - 1.0 |

[1]  Manufacturers' data should be consulted for more precise values.

**5.7 VAPOR RETARDERS**

From our previous discussion, we see that in terms of air and water vapor transmission, building materials may be classified under two types:

- *Air Permeable Materials*: Being air permeable, these materials are vapor permeable also. Porous materials and assemblies with unsealed joints fall into this category.
- *Air Impermeable Materials*: These are materials which restrict the flow of air. Most building materials fall in this category. Metals, plastics, concrete, masonry with pressed and tooled mortar joints and

sheet materials with sealed joints such as gypsum board, plywood, fiberboard, etc., are air impermeable.

Air impermeable materials can be further subdivided into two types depending on whether or not they allow water vapor to pass through, Figure 5.17. If they (air impermeable materials) allow the water vapor to pass through, they are called air barriers (retarders). For example, gypsum board is air impermeable but allows water vapor to pass through. Air retarders (discussed in Section 5.2) are materials that are specifically made to resist air flow but allow water vapor to pass through.

Materials that do not allow water vapor to pass through are called *vapor barriers*. The term "vapor retarder" is a more correct description since most such materials retard the flow of water vapor; they do not completely stop it. Thus, vapor retarders are materials which have a low perm rating. In practice, a material whose perm rating is less than 1 perm is considered a vapor retarder. A good vapor retarder is, however, one whose perm rating is less than 0.1 perm. A polyethylene sheet, 4 mil or thicker, provides that perm rating (see Table 5.5). Since only an air impermeable material can be a vapor retarder, vapor retarders are also called *vapor-air retarders*.

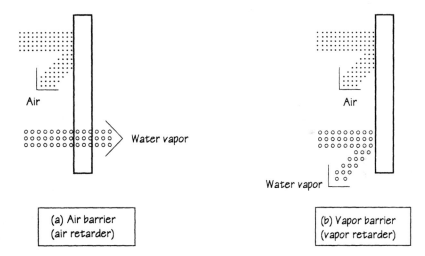

**FIGURE 5.17** Air impermeable materials are of two types: (a) those that allow vapor to pass through, called air barriers, and (b) those that do not allow vapor to pass through, called vapor barriers.

Vapor retarders may be classified as: (i) rigid vapor retarders, (ii) membrane vapor retarders and (iii) coatings.

### 5.7.1 Rigid Vapor Retarders

The rigid type vapor retarders are sheets or boards which are self supporting. Window glass and metal sheets are perfect vapor barriers since they have a zero perm rating. However, joints between sheets must be fully sealed if their zero perm rating is to be achieved. Cellular glass and plastic foam insulations such as extruded polystyrene, polyurethane and polyisocyanurate, have a low perm rating because of their closed cell structure.

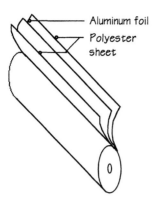

**FIGURE 5.18** Aluminum foil bonded between two polyester sheets makes a vapor retarder with nearly a zero perm rating.

### 5.7.2  Membrane Vapor Retarders

Materials that are specifically used as vapor retarders in building construction are of the membrane type.  These are thin and flexible sheets of materials which have a low vapor permeability.  Aluminum foil, polyethylene sheet and asphalt-saturated (building) paper are the most commonly used vapor retarders.  Aluminum foil is an excellent low-cost vapor retarder.  It has a zero perm rating provided it is without holes and (or) punctures.  However, aluminum foil does not have the strength required to be stretched over framing members such as studs and joists and is readily damaged during handling.  It is, therefore, laminated to another material which provides the necessary strength.

Several manufacturers exploit the zero permeance of aluminum foil in producing vapor retarders.  One manufacturer produces a vapor retarder consisting of 1 mil thick aluminum foil sandwiched between two 0.5 mil thick sheets of polyester, Figure 5.18.  In this composite product, the aluminum foil provides zero permeance and the polyester sheet provides tensile strength and puncture resistance.  Since the polyester sheet also has a low permeability, any small holes in the aluminum foil are sealed by the polyester sheet so that the composite product has nearly a zero perm rating.  The polyester sheet also helps to reduce the corrosion of the aluminum foil.  Another manufacturer uses aluminum foil with building paper and fiberglass scrim.  The scrim provides tear strength, and the building paper provides puncture resistance and the property to seal small holes in the foil.

Polyethylene sheet and building paper are some of the other commonly used vapor retarders.  They can be used independently since they have the required tensile strength to be stretched over framing members.  Polyethylene sheet is normally used in 6 mil thickness.  Thicker sheets (10 mil or thicker) may be used where greater tear or puncture resistance is desired.

Building paper is available in various grades  —  A, B, C and D.  Grade "A" building paper has the lowest perm rating, Table 5.5.  It is grade A building paper that is recommended for use as a vapor retarder.  Building paper is also used as a laminate on some insulating materials, see Figure 4.27(b).

The effectiveness of any vapor retarder is substantially reduced if it has holes or if it is not properly installed with a good seal.  To achieve good performance, a vapor retarder must be placed over structural supports, lapped, folded over and/or sealed to eliminate gaps before being stapled.

### 5.7.3  Coatings as Vapor Retarders

Coatings are field-applied, semiliquid compositions of low permeance.  The most commonly used coating is hot asphalt.  Other coatings used are coal tar, resins and polymeric compounds.  Depending on the manufacturer, they may either be brushed on or spray applied.  Oil paints also provide a low permeance, Table 5.5.  It is important that the substrate on which paints and coatings are applied is dimensionally stable since substrate movement will give rise to cracks, substantially increasing the permeance of coatings.

**5.8 CONDENSATION
CONTROL**

Surface condensation is easily controlled by increasing the R-value of envelope assembly. The more insulated the assembly, the less likely will surface condensation occur. Thus in a heated building, surface condensation is less likely to occur on the inside surface of an insulating glass unit (or on an insulated wall or roof) because the inside surface temperature of an insulated assembly is higher than that of an uninsulated assembly. In fact, the insulation increases the temperature on the warm side and decreases the temperature on the cold side of an assembly. This is shown in Figure 5.19 which gives the temperature gradients[3] in two wall assemblies under identical conditions.

The two wall assemblies are similar; the only difference between them is that the assembly of Figure 5.19(a) is uninsulated, and that of Figure 5.19(b) is insulated. Comparing the temperature gradients of Figures 5.19(a) and (b), we notice that the temperature of the inside surface of the uninsulated assembly is lower than that of the insulated assembly. If this surface temperature is lower than the dew point of inside air, condensation will occur on the inside surface of the uninsulated assembly. The dew point of the inside air is shown by dashed line in Figure 5.19.

In the insulated assembly, the dew point lies inside the assembly. Thus, we see that insulation prevents surface condensation but creates interstitial condensation. That is why interstitial condensation in buildings is a modern problem. It was rarely a problem in older buildings in which little or no insulation was used. Additionally, older buildings were not as air tight as modern buildings so that water vapor could move in and out of the interior of the building freely, causing no build-up of moisture within envelope assemblies. Chimney stacks were additional source of ventilation in old buildings.

Thus, an obvious solution to eliminating interstitial condensation is to provide a large amount of continuous ventilation in the building — much larger than that required for acceptable indoor quality[4]. But this is

**FIGURE 5.19** Temperature gradients in two wall assemblies under identical internal and external conditions: (a) wall without insulation, and (b) wall with insulation. (The dew point temperature of indoor air, given here, is with respect to a relative humidity of 50%, see Appendix VI).

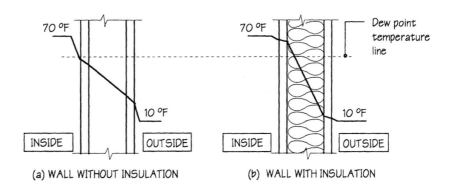

(a) WALL WITHOUT INSULATION          (b) WALL WITH INSULATION

---

[3] A temperature gradient is a graph which gives the variation of temperature through the cross-section of the assembly.

[4] Currently, the acceptable indoor air quality requirement for residential living areas is 0.35 air changes per hour but not less than 15 ft$^3$/min per person [ASHRAE Standard 62-1989].

unacceptable in view of its impact on energy consumption. Therefore, the solution commonly used to control interstitial condensation consists of two parts:

- Use a vapor retarder in the envelope. The purpose of a vapor retarder is to reduce the amount of vapor that passes into the assembly so that the minimum amount of vapor reaches the region of lower temperature where it may condense.

- Provide vapor permeability between the vapor retarder and the lower vapor pressure region (cold side) of the assembly. The purpose of this requirement is to ensure that any vapor that passes through the vapor retarder does not collect within the assembly where it may condense and/or freeze, Figure 5.20. One way of achieving this objective is to provide adequate ventilation routes in the assembly on the cold side of the vapor retarder (referred to as the *cold side venting*[5]) so that any vapor that has crossed the vapor retarder is able to mix freely with the air in the colder region of the assembly, thus preventing condensation. If some vapor condenses within the assembly, it will evaporate in due course because of venting of the assembly.

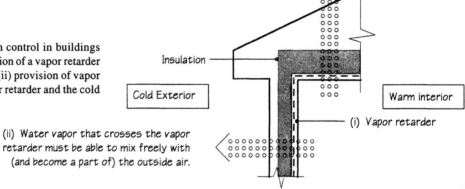

**FIGURE 5.20** Condensation control in buildings consists of two parts: (i) provision of a vapor retarder in the envelope assembly, and (ii) provision of vapor permeability between the vapor retarder and the cold side of the assembly.

(ii) Water vapor that crosses the vapor retarder must be able to mix freely with (and become a part of) the outside air.

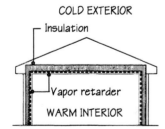

**FIGURE 5.21** Vapor retarder must be installed on the warm side of insulation.

### 5.8.1 Location of Vapor Retarder in an Assembly

Since the purpose of a vapor retarder is to reduce the transmission of water vapor through the envelope assembly, it implies that a vapor retarder must be located toward the region of higher vapor pressure. Since the higher vapor pressure generally occurs on the warm side of the assembly, the vapor retarder must be located toward the warm side of the insulation. In heated buildings, it is the side which faces the interior space, Figure 5.21. When both the air

---

[5] Excessive cold side venting should be avoided as it can reduce the effectiveness of insulation.

retarder and the vapor retarder are used in the assembly (see Figure 5.8), the vapor retarder acts as the second line of defense against air infiltration since a vapor retarder is also an air retarder.

In cold storage facilities and ice skating rinks, the vapor retarder must be placed toward the outside face of the insulation, since the outside vapor pressure is higher than the inside vapor pressure. For the same reason, a vapor retarder should be placed toward the outside of the assembly in a hot humid location. Any water vapor that travels into the building from the outside must be removed by the air-conditioning system. However, in most regions of the United States and Canada (except in coastal southeastern United States), a vapor retarder is installed toward the inside since the heating season is longer and more critical than the cooling season.

In buildings which are not mechanically heated or cooled (using natural ventilation), a vapor retarder is unnecessary. As a general rule, if insulating materials are not used in the envelope, a vapor retarder is unnecessary. A vapor retarder is also unnecessary in a hot-arid location since the difference between the inside and outside vapor pressures is generally small. In such a location, condensation is rare; therefore a vapor retarder is unnecessary. In fact, the use of a vapor retarder is discouraged in hot-arid climates.

### 5.8.2 Vapor Retarders in Wall Assemblies

In conventional wood frame buildings in the United States and Canada, the vapor retarder is generally secured to the inside face of the studs and covered with an interior finish such as gypsum board. In mild climates, 3.5 in. thick fiberglass or mineral wool batt insulation is used between 2 x 4 studs. The vapor retarder is either provided as building paper laminated to insulation (Figure 4.27) or as a separate polyethylene sheet over unfaced insulation. The polyethylene sheet functions as a better vapor retarder since it has fewer seams. Building paper, on the other hand, has seams at each stud. In colder climates, 2 x 6 studs are used to accommodate a 5.5 in. thick insulation.

Concern for energy conservation has led to the use of larger thicknesses of insulation, particularly in cold regions, which cannot be accommodated in the conventional 2 x 4 or 2 x 6 studs. Additional insulation in a conventional wall can be provided by fixing 2 x 3 or 2 x 4 horizontal spacers on the outside face of the wall, Figure 5.22.

Another alternative is the use of a double stud wall which consists of two parallel walls with an intervening space. By varying the depth of the intervening space, any amount of insulation can be provided in the wall, Figure 5.23. Each wall is made from 2 x 4 studs with insulation between studs and in the intervening space. The inner wall is a structural wall, the outer wall a curtain wall. The two walls are joined at the top and bottom by plywood plates. An additional advantage of a double wall is the absence of thermal bridges that are present in a single wall or a wall with horizontal spacers.

In a double wall, the vapor retarder is sandwiched between two layers of insulation. This arrangement ensures the continuity of the vapor retarder, free of penetrations created by electric and water supply outlets. However, since the vapor retarder must be on the warm side of the assembly, the thickness of insulation toward the warm side should be less than one-third the total insulation thickness (as a rough guide), Figure 5.24. The one-third rule ensures that if condensation occurs in the assembly, it will occur between the vapor retarder and the outside of the assembly.

Regardless of the method used to insulate the wall, it is important to ensure that the space between the vapor retarder and the outside is vapor permeable. If the outside finish of the wall is a siding material, the joints between the siding panels provide adequate vapor permeability. In the case of a masonry veneer, weep holes do the same job (see Figure 6.27).

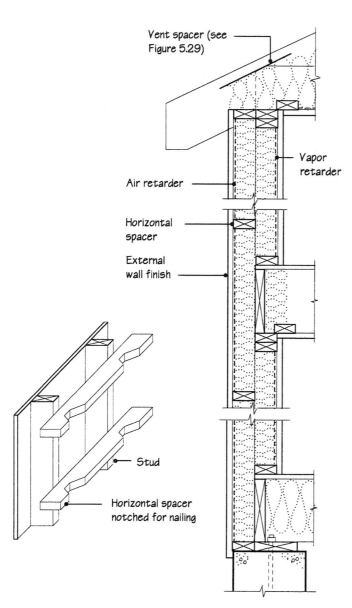

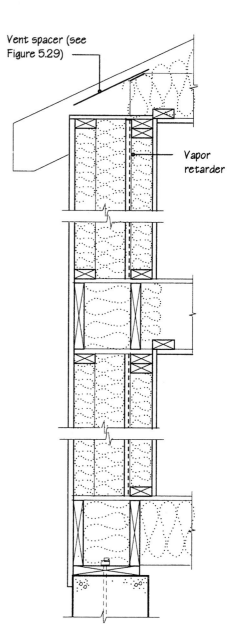

**FIGURE 5.22** Section through a wall with horizontal spacers. (Insulation is shown by dotted curves for the sake of clarity).

**FIGURE 5.23** Section through a double wall. (Insulation is shown by dotted curves for the sake of clarity).

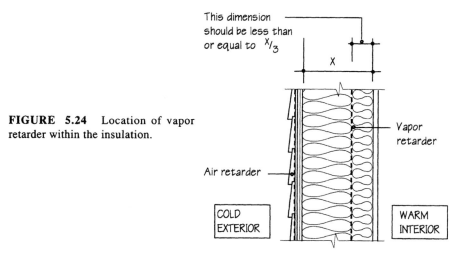

**FIGURE 5.24** Location of vapor retarder within the insulation.

### 5.8.3 Vapor Retarder in a Roof-ceiling Assembly and Attic Ventilation

In a sloping roof with a flat ceiling, the vapor retarder is provided below the insulation and above the ceiling finish in a cold climate, see Figure 5.26. The space between the roof and ceiling (attic space) must be ventilated to provide vapor permeability. An unventilated (or inadequately ventilated) attic will lead to condensation at the underside of roof sheathing

Ventilation of attic space is also required for reasons other than condensation control. In cold climates, ventilation prevents the formation of ice dams at roof eaves. If the attic is not ventilated, it remains relatively warm because of the entry of heat into the attic from the warm interior, but the eave overhangs are cold. This melts the snow in the middle of the roof which freezes again at the eaves, forming ice dams. The problem is worse in an uninsulated roof-ceiling assembly, Figure 5.25.

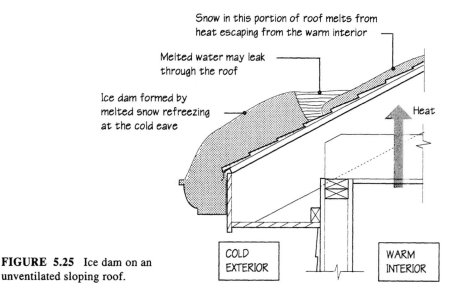

**FIGURE 5.25** Ice dam on an unventilated sloping roof.

Ice dams can substantially load the roof at the eaves and the gutter. They also prevent water from draining off the roof, which may cause roof leakage. Ceiling insulation, coupled with the ventilation of the attic, helps to eliminate ice dams in addition to preventing the build-up of water vapor.

The ventilation of the attic is also required in warm climates since it helps to reduce heat transmission from the ceiling into the interior of the building. The temperature of the air in an unventilated attic becomes much higher than the outside air because of the ability of air and the materials of the roof to store heat. This is particularly critical during the summer. Temperature differences in excess of 40 °F between the outside air and the attic air have been reported. The higher attic temperature increases heat transfer to the interior of the building. Attic ventilation coupled with a radiant barrier in the attic (see Figure 4.25) helps to reduce the temperature of the air in the attic to nearly that of the outside air.

Ventilation can be provided through openings at the soffit, Figure 5.26. The openings must be covered with a mesh or screen to prevent the entry of insects. Building codes mandate a minimum "net free area" of openings to be $\frac{1}{300}$ of the total attic area if a vapor retarder (with a perm rating of at least 1.0 U.S. perm) is provided in the ceiling. The "net free area" refers to the area of vents excluding the area of the solid part of the mesh or screen.

Thus, if the ceiling measures 60 ft x 50 ft, the net free area of vents must be (60 x 50)/300 = 10 sq ft. This vent area must be distributed throughout the soffit.

Although the soffit ventilation alone is adequate to satisfy building code requirements, effective attic ventilation requires cross ventilation, which is best provided through inlets at the soffit and outlets at a higher level. The soffit vent and higher level vent areas should be nearly equal. Four different alternatives are commonly used for (higher level) outlets: gable ventilation, ridge ventilation, turbine ventilators, and gable fans, Figure 5.27.

The code requirement for net free attic ventilation as being $\frac{1}{300}$ of the total attic area is the minimum requirement. Effective ventilation requires a much greater area. For a combination of soffit vents with a continuous ridge

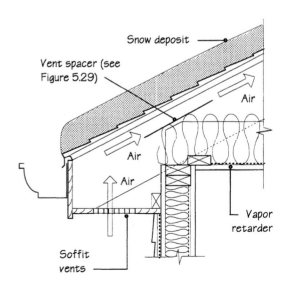

**FIGURE 5.26** Ventilation of the attic prevents the formation of ice dams over the eaves.

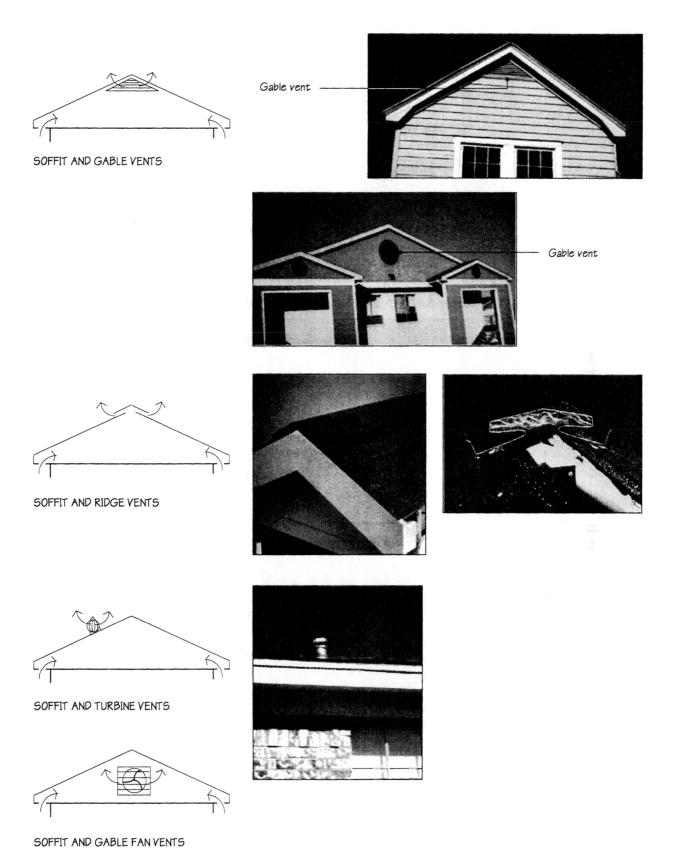

**FIGURE 5.27** Various alternatives for providing attic ventilation.

vent, gable vents or turbine vents, a minimum of $^1/_{100}$ of the total attic area is generally recommended. One half of this area should be provided by soffit vents, and the other half by high level vents. Approximate values of net free vent areas of various ventilating options are given in Table 5.6.

In a flat or a sloping roof with a ceiling secured to rafters (cathedral type ceiling), ventilation must be provided in each rafter space. This requires continuous soffit and ridge ventilation, Figure 5.28. To ensure that the insulation does not obstruct the space between the rafters and the ceiling, continuous vent spacers are used between rafters. This allows free ventilation below the roof, Figure 5.29. Larger rafters may be required to allow for both the insulation and the ventilating space. Vent spacers are also required at the eaves of a conventional roof where the insulation may tend to close the gap under the roof (see Figures 5.22, 5.23 and 5.26).

**Table 5.6 Net Free Vent Areas of Various Attic Ventilators**

| Vent type | Net free vent area (sq ft) |
|---|---|
| Ridge vent (one 8 ft long piece) | 1.0 |
| Gable vent (1 sq ft gross area) | 0.5 |
| Turbine vent (each) | 1.0 |
| Screened soffit vent (1 sq ft gross area) | 0.4 |

For more precise values refer to manufacturers' data.

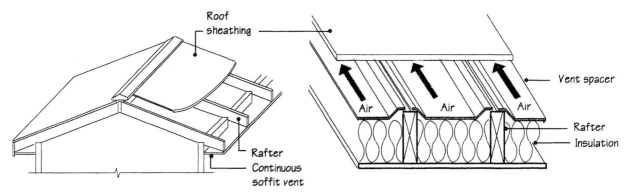

**FIGURE 5.28**  Continuous ridge and soffit ventilation in a cathedral type ceiling.

**FIGURE 5.29**  Vent spacers between rafters in a cathedral type ceiling.

### 5.8.4 Vapor Retarder Under a Slab-on-grade

A vapor retarder is also required under a concrete slab-on-grade in all climates to prevent subsoil moisture diffusing through the slab to the interior of the building, Figure 5.30. A 10 mil (0.25 mm) thick polyethylene sheet with joints overlapped is recommended as a vapor retarder under the slab. A layer of coarse sand below the vapor retarder drains water away from the vapor

## VAPORTIGHT CONSTRUCTION VS ATTIC VENTILATION IN COLD CLIMATES

Although preventing condensation in an attic by providing attic ventilation is perhaps the safest approach, and one that is currently mandated by building codes, it must be appreciated that it is not without disadvantages. In extremely cold climates, which are subjected to frequent blowing snow and rain, venting can cause serious problems by permitting snow and rain to infiltrate through the vents. Experience in cold Canadian climates has demonstrated that if indoor humidity levels are controlled, and if the ceiling is provided with a well-installed vapor retarder with an extremely low vapor permeance (vaportight construction), it is possible to prevent attic condensation without providing attic ventilation[5.11]. A major advantage of eliminating attic ventilation lies in improving the effectiveness of insulation.

However, if attic ventilation is not provided, the problem of ice dam formation should be investigated, or prevented by not providing eave overhangs. Damage due to ice dam formation in eaves and valleys can also be prevented by the use of waterproof shingle underlayment of sufficient width under the shingles.

Vaportight construction as an alternative to ventilation is particularly effective in a cathedral ceiling in a cold climate. Since each rafter cavity is independent in a cathedral ceiling, providing adequate ventilation under the entire roof can be problematic.

**FIGURE 5.30** Polyethylene sheet vapor retarder under a slab-on-grade (slab yet to be poured).

retarder by eliminating capillary action. Additionally, the sand functions as a protective cushion for the vapor retarder.

A vapor retarder is not required under a slab-on-grade if the migration of moisture is not detrimental to the occupancy of the building. Such buildings include garages, carports and other unheated spaces. A vapor retarder is also not required under driveways, walkways, patios, etc.

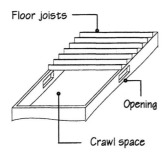

**FIGURE 5.31** Ventilation openings in a crawl space are required to prevent accumulation of water vapor.

### 5.8.5 Vapor Retarder and Ventilation in a Crawl Space

Since the crawl space has a dirt floor, water vapor accumulation in a crawl space can take place due to the evaporation of water present in the ground. To prevent water vapor accumulation, the ground should be covered with a vapor retarder, preferably a 10 mil (0.25 mm) thick polyethylene sheet. The vapor retarder is usually sandwiched between two layers of sand, the lower layer to provide a cushion for the vapor retarder and the upper layer of sand to hold down the vapor retarder.

In addition to the provision of a vapor retarder, the crawl space must be ventilated, Figure 5.31. Ventilation not only relieves the crawl space of excessive vapor build-up but also reduces the decay of wood and the concentration of radon gas, if present. Building codes require a minimum of 1 sq. ft. (0.09 m$^2$) of net free ventilation area for every 1,500 sq ft (135 m$^2$) of crawl space area. Thus, if the crawl space area is 3,000 sq ft, the ventilation opening area must be a minimum of 2 sq ft. If no vapor retarder is provided in the crawl space, the ventilation area must be increased tenfold.

### 5.9 PERFORMANCE OF VAPOR RETARDERS

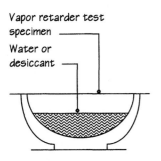

**FIGURE 5.32** Equipment for obtaining the perm rating of a material.

The suitability of a material to function as a vapor retarder is indicated by its perm rating which is measured according to ASTM Standard E 96 "Standard Test Methods for Water Vapor Transmission of Materials". The test describes two alternative methods for determining the perm rating: (i) desiccant method; and (ii) water method. Perm ratings obtained from the two methods are generally different. Therefore, in comparing the effectiveness of vapor retarders, it is important that perm ratings be obtained from the same method.

In both methods, the test specimen is sealed to the open mouth of a test dish, Figure 5.32. The only difference between the two methods is that in the desiccant method, the dish contains a desiccant and in the water method, it contains water. The sealed dish is placed in a controlled atmosphere. Periodic weighings of the dish determine the rate of water vapor movement. In the desiccant method, the vapor moves from outside the dish into the desiccant. In the water method, the vapor moves from inside the dish to the controlled atmosphere outside.

#### 5.9.1 Criteria for the Selection of Vapor Retarders
Obviously the perm rating is the primary property on which the selection of a vapor retarder should be based. However, as in the case of an air retarder, other properties such as the vapor retarder's tear strength, resistance to water penetration and durability must also be considered. For a detailed discussion of the criteria for the selection of vapor retarders, refer to Reference 5.10.

| REVIEW QUESTIONS | | |
|---|---|---|
| | **5.1** | What is stack action?  How does it affect air infiltration and exfiltration in a building? |
| | **5.2** | What does the acronym "ach" stand for? |
| | **5.3** | Approximately how much is the typical infiltration rate in contemporary residential construction in the United States?  How does it compare with the infiltration rate in older buildings? |
| | **5.4** | What is the purpose of using an air retarder in buildings?  Explain. |
| | **5.5** | With reference to Sweet's Catalog, list at least three manufacturers of air retarders. How do their products differ from each other? |
| | **5.6** | With the help of a sketch plan, show the location of an air retarder in a wood frame building. |
| | **5.7** | With the help of a three-dimensional sketch, explain the functioning of an air-to-air heat exchanger.  Where would you suggest its use? |
| | **5.8** | Explain what relative humidity of air is.  What is the approximate relative humidity of air  in air-conditioned buildings? |
| | **5.9** | Explain why building materials are usually more vapor permeable than air permeable. |
| | **5.10** | Explain the two modes by which water vapor permeates through building assemblies. |
| | **5.11** | List the three most commonly used vapor retarders for wall assemblies and their perm ratings. |
| | **5.12** | Draw a section through a typical wall assembly of a residential building in your area and show the location of insulation and vapor retarder. |
| | **5.13** | Explain the importance of attic ventilation.  Sketch the two most commonly used ways in which attic ventilation is provided. |
| | **5.14** | Explain the importance of crawl space ventilation.  What is the building code requirement for crawl space ventilation? |

| REFERENCES | | |
|---|---|---|
| | 5.1 | Harrje, David et al: "Tracer Gas Measurement Systems Compared in a Multifamily Building", *Air Change Rate and Airtightness in Buildings*, edited by Sherman, M.H., American Society of Testing and Materials Publication No. STP1067, 1989, p. 5. |
| | 5.2 | American Architectural Manufacturers Association, Palatine, Illinois: *Window Selection Guide*, 1988, p. 5. |
| | 5.3 | American Society of Heating, Refrigeration and Air Conditioning Engineers, Atlanta, Georgia: *Handbook of Fundamentals*, 1993, p. 23.10. |
| | 5.4 | Office of the Technology Assessment of the United States: *Residential Energy Consumption*, Allenheld, Osman and Co., 1980, p. 4. |
| | 5.5 | Altman, Roberta: *The Complete Book of Home Environmental Hazards*, Facts on File Publications, 1990, p. ix. |
| | 5.6 | Lonowski, Laura J: " Indoor Air Quality: The Role of Building Design, Materials and Construction",  Construction Specifier, May 1991, p. 149. |
| | 5.7 | American Society for Heating, Refrigeration and Air Conditioning Engineering, Atlanta, Georgia: ASHRAE Standard 62-1981. |
| | 5.8. | American Society for Testing and Materials, Philadelphia, Pennsylvania: "Standard Test Method for Determining the Rate of Air Leakage Through Exterior Windows, Curtain Walls, and Doors Under Specified Pressure Difference across the Specimen", ASTM E 283. |
| | 5.9 | American Society for Testing and Materials, Philadelphia, Pennsylvania: "Standard Specification for an Air Retarder Material or System for Low Rise Framed Building Walls", ASTM E 1677. |
| | 5.10 | American Society for Testing and Materials, Philadelphia, Pennsylvania: "Standard Practice for Selection of Vapor Retarders for Thermal Insulation", ASTM  C 755. |
| | 5.11 | TenWolde, Anton: Private communication with the author. |

# 6 WATER LEAKAGE CONTROL

**6.1 INTRODUCTION**

Apart from controlling heat flow, air infiltration and water vapor transmission, another important function of the building envelope is to exclude the entry of water. Despite its importance, water infiltration (or leakage) is the most frequently occurring complaint in buildings. It is also the most common cause of building construction litigation. For instance, in the United States 60 percent of all legal disputes in buildings are related to water leakage.

Apart from its obvious nuisance and damage to interiors, water deteriorates the building envelope. It corrodes metal components, fosters decay of wood, disintegrates masonry and concrete, and causes staining of building facades. Water leakage increases humidity levels and the potential of condensation in buildings.

Two major sources of water leakage in buildings are rainwater and subsoil water, although some water may also originate from defective water supply and plumbing systems. Since rainwater may leak through any part of the building envelope (roof, walls, windows, and external doors), the control of rainwater penetration into buildings is an extensive area of study. It includes the consideration of materials and construction details of various envelope assemblies such as roofs, external walls and windows, as well as the interfacing and transitional elements between them. Similar observations apply to subsoil water, which may infiltrate through slabs-on-grade, basement walls and floors.

In view of the extensive and varied nature of the water leakage problem, we shall restrict the coverage of the subject to its essential principles, and

173

explain them through a few selected assemblies. Brick veneer wall assembly will be discussed in greater detail because of its extensive use and versatility. (Although roofing is an important component of building envelope and is responsible for a majority of water leakage problems in buildings, it is too specialized to be covered in this introductory text).

## 6.2 ELEMENTS OF RAINWATER LEAKAGE CONTROL

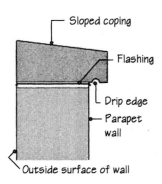

FIGURE 6.1 A coping over a parapet wall.

Some of the important strategies to control rainwater penetration through the building envelope involve elementary details that have been used for centuries. The most obvious one is to provide a nominal slope in all exposed horizontal surfaces. The purpose of the slope, which is usually 1:12, is to drain rainwater away from vulnerable parts of the building using the force of gravity. Thus, in external window sills and thresholds under entrance doors, the slope is provided away from the building. In copings over parapets, the slope is generally provided toward the roof, so that the rainwater falling on coping drains on the roof, Figure 6.1.

Another elementary strategy is to provide a drip mechanism at the underside of all exposed horizontal surfaces. A drip mechanism consists of a continuous overhanging edge, called the *drip edge*, or a continuous cut at the underside of the member. In the absence of a drip mechanism, rainwater will travel along soffit lines by surface tension, Figure 6.2(a). Surface tension creates forces of adhesion between the building surface and water, which the drip mechanism counteracts, Figure 6.2(b).

Surface tension is also responsible for creating capillary forces. Capillary forces are suction forces that occur in tiny spaces. Thus, porous materials such as brick and concrete block suck water because of the capillary action of their tiny pores. Note that capillary forces occur only in tiny spaces. Thus, where tiny spaces cannot be avoided, such as in a joint between two members, capillary suction can be prevented by introducing a larger space, nearly $^1/_4$ in. (6 mm) or more, immediately after the capillary space. This space is referred to as the *capillary break*, Figure 6.3(a).

Providing an *overlap* between members meeting at a joint is another commonsense measure. The force of wind can impart kinetic energy to water, causing the water to travel horizontally as well as vertically in the joint. Therefore, the overlap must be sufficiently large so that it presents a reliable baffle against wind-driven rain, Figure 6.3(b). A lapped horizontal joint

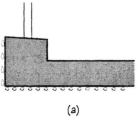

(a)

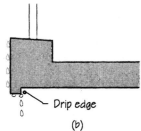

(b)

FIGURE 6.2 A drip edge at the soffit of a balcony prevents water travelling along the soffit.

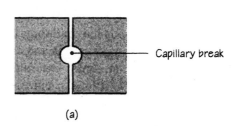

(a)

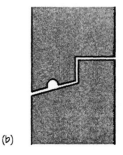

(b)

FIGURE 6.3 (a) Capillary break at the joint between two elements. (b) A lapped joint with capillary break.

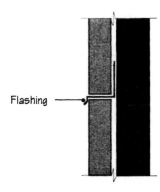

**FIGURE 6.4** Flashing at a horizontal butt joint.

performs better than a lapped vertical joint, since water has to work against the force of gravity to get across the overlap in a horizontal joint.

A horizontal butt joint can be made leakage resistant by incorporating a flashing, Figure 6.4. Flashing consists of an impervious membrane that provides a barrier to water and directs it to the outer surface. Galvanized steel, stainless steel, copper, lead and polyethylene sheets are commonly used as flashing materials.

Flashing is the most versatile item in all water-resisting strategies. It has so many uses that it is difficult to describe its function completely. It is used in roofs, in walls, under copings (Figure 6.1) and under window sills (Figure 6.5). Additional applications of flashing are presented later in this chapter.

Caulking the joints with sealing compounds, which are generally called *sealants* (see Section 10.6), is another commonly used strategy. Since sealants degrade over time from exposure to environmental factors, particularly direct solar radiation and water, they should not be relied upon as the only water-resisting element. A certain amount of redundancy must be built into the detail if the sealant is directly exposed to the environment.

Usually all or most of the above strategies are used in a single detail, as shown in Figure 6.5, which is a section at the sill level of a typical wood window.

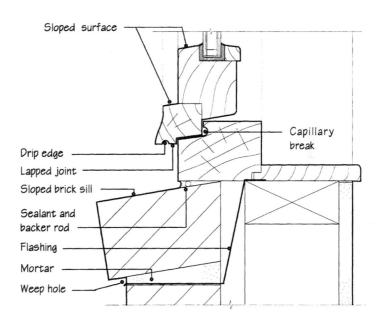

**FIGURE 6.5** Typical detail at a window sill showing elementary rainwater-resisting strategies.

## 6.3 WATER-RESISTANT EXTERIOR WALLS

Water-resistant exterior walls may be divided under the following three types:
- Walls with roof and intermediate floor overhangs
- Barrier walls
- Drainage walls  • Mass or storage wall systems

The first type of wall system depends on protective overhangs to prevent rainwater leakage, Figure 6.6. It has limited application as the overhangs required to completely shield the wall from wind-driven rain must be extremely deep. In addition, the overhangs pose economic as well as design constraints on the exterior envelope, particularly that of a multistory building. However, small overhangs at the roof level of a single story building can provide a great deal of protection against water penetration at the wall-roof junction, and are commonly used.

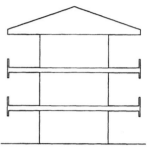

**FIGURE 6.6**   Horizontal overhangs to shield external walls from wind-driven rain.

**6.4 THE BARRIER WALL**

A barrier wall is one that resists rainwater leakage by providing an impervious barrier to water. Ideally, such a wall should be made of an impervious material, such as metal, glass or plastic. If the wall is made of a porous material, its water absorptivity should be so limited that the absorbed water does not seep up to the interior surface of the wall. In addition to the above requirements, a barrier wall should not develop through-the-wall cracks which may be caused by weathering, thermal or moisture expansion, or foundation settlements. If these cracks occur, leakage will result.

A good example of a barrier wall is a thick masonry (brick or stone) wall. A thick masonry wall resists rainwater leakage by virtue of the redundancy inherent in its large thickness. The thicker the wall, the greater the redundancy. In such a wall, the water penetrates the wall from absorption by masonry units and penetration through mortar joints. To function as a barrier wall, a wall must be of large thickness — 18 in. (450 mm) or thicker depending on the porosity of the wall material. In such a wall, water, even under a long rainy spell, cannot penetrate the entire thickness of the wall, so that the interior part of the wall remains dry. When the rain stops, the absorbed water begins to evaporate, and given a sufficiently long dry spell, the entire wall becomes dry again.

### 6.4.1 Lapped Wood Siding as a Barrier Wall

Another simple barrier wall system that has been used successfully for a long time in wood frame buildings is lapped siding. A lapped siding consists of horizontal wood boards, secured to studs through wall sheathing. The watertightness of the wall results mainly from the overlaps in joints, as shown in Figure 6.7. Boards are usually 4 in. (10 mm) to 12 in. (300 mm) wide, and are usually beveled.

The above wall is vulnerable to leakage at points where the siding boards terminate. Therefore, at terminations the ends of siding boards abut against a cover trim and the (vertical) joints between the siding and the trim are sealed. Intermediate vertical joints between two siding boards are similarly sealed. A waterproof felt under the boards provides the required redundancy should leakage from sealed joints occur. Each siding board is nailed with a single line of nails a little above the lower board to allow the boards to expand or contract.

Siding boards can also be applied vertically, as shown in Figure 6.8. Several versions of the above two simple walls are in common use. Regardless

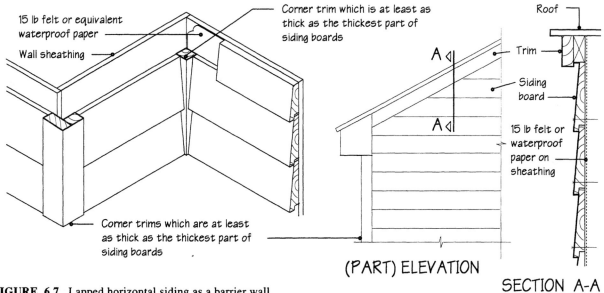

**FIGURE 6.7** Lapped horizontal siding as a barrier wall.

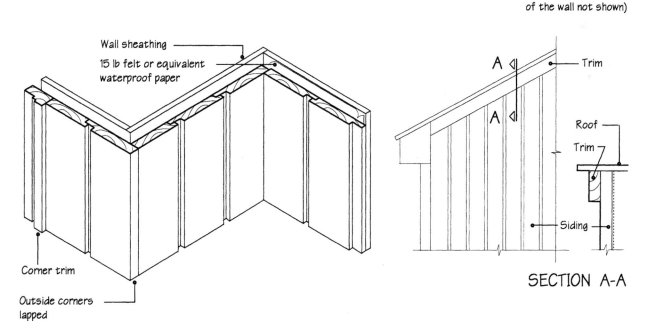

**FIGURE 6.8** Lapped vertical siding as a barrier wall.

of the version used, note that these walls derive their water-resistiveness from joint overlaps, sealants and the waterproof felt back-up (as the second line of defense).

In view of the combustibility of wood and its lack of durability, the walls of Figure 6.7 or 6.8 are used only for one or two story residential buildings. Additionally, because of the large number of joints in the walls, their water-resistiveness can be ensured only under low to moderate wind loads.

### 6.4.2 Precast Concrete Curtain Wall as a Barrier Wall

A barrier wall system used in high-rise buildings is the concrete curtain wall consisting of precast reinforced concrete wall panels. Since concrete is a porous material, a concrete wall absorbs water, though less than that of a brick wall. Therefore, concrete wall panels must be of sufficient thickness to present a barrier against water penetration. If the concrete is reasonably dense, a nearly 6 in. (150 mm) thick panel will generally provide the required water-resistiveness in the wall.

Since the panels are precast, insulating materials can be laminated to them during the precasting process, Figure 6.9. The commonly laminated insulating materials are plastic foams such as extruded polystyrene or polyisocyanurate. External panel finish and color can also be integral to the panel and are usually provided in the precasting plant. Interior finish materials can be also be laminated to panels, but for better workmanship and detailing they are provided separately. Gypsum board on light gauge steel stud framing is commonly used as the interior finish.

Windows can be accommodated by leaving openings in panels. A punched opening, as shown in Figure 6.9, weakens the panel structurally. Therefore, a panel with a large punched opening is prone to developing diagonal cracks at corners[6.1], particularly during lifting and erection processes. Although concrete panels are provided with extra reinforcement to reduce diagonal cracking, the size of punched openings must be limited. A better alternative to punched openings is to provide strip openings. This simplifies panel geometry so that each panel is rectangular, without any opening.

Concrete curtain wall panels with punched openings are usually one floor high so that one panel covers one story. The width of panels depends on elevational considerations and the capacity of lifting equipment. Extremely large panels should be avoided to prevent their cracking due to thermal and handling (lifting) stresses. Since the panels are nonloadbearing, they need to be supported by the building's structural frame.

The support system must be such that it allows differential movement between the building's structural frame and the panel. This is usually achieved by supporting the panel on one of its two horizontal edges, so that the other edge is free to move. In such a support system, the panel's load is transferred to the spandrel beam at the supporting edge. The other edge is also connected to the spandrel beam, but this connection is detailed in such a way that the panel can move in its own plane, but not laterally. The restriction to lateral movement ensures that lateral loads are transferred to the spandrel beam without any mechanical play at the connection. A commonly used concrete

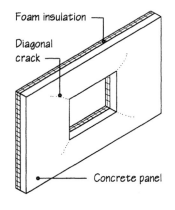

**FIGURE 6.9** Plastic foam insulation laminated to concrete panels during the precasting process.

curtain wall system is shown in Figure 6.10.

The above two panel connections are referred to as *dead load connection* and *wind load connection* respectively. The dead load connection is shown in Detail A, and the wind load connection in Detail B, Figure 6.10. The weight of the panel is transferred to the spandrel beam at the dead load connection. Note that this connection also resists the wind load, so that the dead load connection resists both the dead load and the wind loads on the panel. The wind load connection resists the wind loads only.

The joints in panels are critical in ensuring the watertightness of the wall. Apart from following the simple strategies of Section 6.2, the joints should be so detailed that they can be sealed separately from both the inside and the outside of the building. The double-sealed joint imparts redundancy in the system, so that the outside seal works as the first defense against water penetration, commonly referred to as the *deterrent seal*. The inside seal functions as the back-up seal. Double seal ensures that the inside seal is protected from severe weathering.

Double seal strategy requires the provision of weep holes at regular intervals in the outer seal to drain water that may enter the cavity between the two seals. Failure to provide weep holes will cause the water to be trapped within the wall, producing leakage in the wall and accelerating the deterioration of seals.

Weep holes should be located in the horizontal joints immediately above the flashing (see Figure 6.10, Detail B). The purpose of flashing is to collect water at each horizontal joint. If the flashing is not provided, water entering through the outside seal from any height in the building will drop to the ground floor level, causing a build-up of water at that level.

Double seal strategy also requires that the joints are accessible from the inside. In other words, the joints in panels should be so located that they are not covered by the building's structural frame — the spandrel beams and columns.

Horizontal joints in panels should preferably be lapped as shown in Figure 6.10, Detail B. Vertical joints may be lapped, but butt joints will also work.

## 6.5 THE DRAINAGE WALL

To qualify as a barrier wall, the wall should be impervious to water. There are several commonly used wall materials that are not impervious. A one wythe thick brick wall and thin (2 to 3 in. thick) concrete or stone panels are examples of water permeable materials, which are commonly used in modern curtain walls. Watertightness in such wall assemblies is provided by constructing them as drainage walls.

A drainage wall is a cavity wall which consists of an outer cladding connected to an inner back-up wall through a cavity space. In a drainage wall, the outer cladding is the first defense against water leakage. Therefore, it is made as water resistant as possible. However, the drainage wall concept recognizes that some water will inevitably leak through the cladding. The water that leaks through the cladding collects in the cavity from where it is drained out through small openings at the bottom of the cladding, called *weep holes*, Figure 6.11.

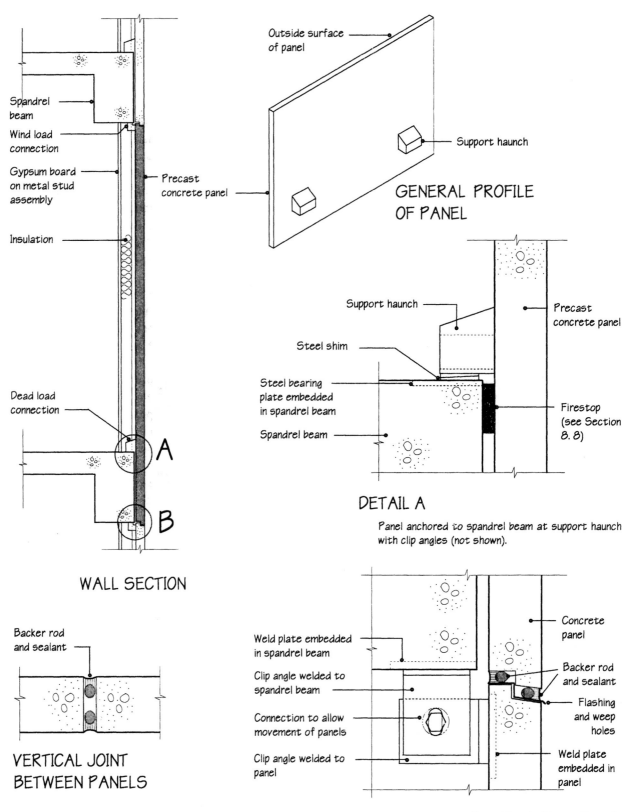

**WALL SECTION**

**GENERAL PROFILE OF PANEL**

**DETAIL A**

Panel anchored to spandrel beam at support haunch with clip angles (not shown).

**VERTICAL JOINT BETWEEN PANELS**

**DETAIL B**

Note the double sealing of joints in panels -- from the inside as well as the outside.

**FIGURE 6.10** Wall section and general construction details of a precast concrete curtain wall.

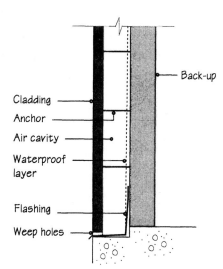

Back-up

Cladding

Anchor

Air cavity

Waterproof
layer

Flashing

Weep holes

**FIGURE 6.11** Section through a drainage wall showing its important components.

Weep holes, metal anchors and flashing are three important components of a drainage wall. Anchors tie the back-up and the cladding together. In doing so, the anchors transfer the lateral loads from the cladding to the back-up wall. It is the back-up wall that is usually designed to function as the structural wall.

As stated in Section 6.2, flashing is a continuous waterproof membrane that functions as a gutter. In other words, the purpose of flashing is to collect the water that penetrates into the cavity through the cladding and weep it to the outside. Therefore, it is laid at the bottom of the cladding, upturned a few inches and anchored to the back-up.

Another important component of a drainage wall is the continuous waterproof layer on the back-up wall. The waterproof layer[1] protects the back-up from small amounts of water that may accidentally reach the back-up by traveling over metal anchors or unintentional cavity obstructions. Because the waterproof layer is shielded by the cladding, its environmental degradation is much slower than an exposed surface.

The combination of cladding, cavity separation and the waterproof back-up provide sufficient redundancy in a well-designed drainage wall to make it leak-free for the entire life of the building. It is because of the greater redundancy in a drainage wall that makes it less problematic as compared to a barrier wall.

Although the drainage wall concept was introduced with reference to a water absorptive outer cladding such as the brick wall, or thin concrete and stone panels, it applies equally with an impervious outer cladding such as glass, metal, plastic or thick concrete panels. Note that the underlying philosophy of the drainage wall is the redundancy of its two water-resistant layers. If the outer layer is made of an impervious material, the redundancy is all the greater. Thus, the concrete curtain wall assembly shown in Figure 6.10 can also be designed on the drainage principle.

---

[1] The waterproof layer is usually an asphalt-saturated felt.

## 6.6 PRESSURE-EQUALIZED DRAINAGE WALL

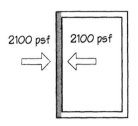

**FIGURE 6.12** Outside and inside wind pressures on a wall under zero wind speed.

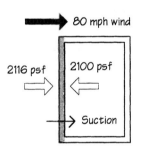

**FIGURE 6.13** Outside and inside wind pressures on a windward wall under a wind speed of 80 mph.

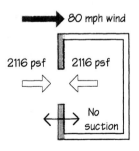

**FIGURE 6.14** Outside and inside wind pressures, if the enclosure has a large opening on the windward facade.

Weep holes in external cladding of a drainage wall, provided for the escape of rainwater, can become sources of water penetration into the cavity under conditions of wind-driven rain. This occurs at the windward face of the wall because of the suction forces created at the outer surface of the cladding. Consequently, rainwater is sucked into the cavity. Under conditions of heavy rain combined with high wind speed, cavity suction can be so large that water may be forced into the cavity, lift vertically in cavity space and soak the back-up wall.

To fully appreciate the phenomenon of cavity suction, let us review the fundamentals of wind loads on buildings. When there is no wind (zero wind speed), the air pressure on the inside and outside surfaces of the walls of an enclosure are the same, equal to the atmospheric pressure[2] — 2,100 psf (101 kPa). Since the atmospheric pressure works on both sides of a wall equally, the wall is under perfect equilibrium, and there is no wind load on the wall, Figure 6.12.

The above equilibrium is disturbed by wind, which creates additional pressure on the outside surface of a windward wall, while the pressure in the enclosure is equal to the atmospheric pressure. For example if the wind speed is 80 mph, we see from Example 2.6 that the wind pressure is nearly 16 psf. This means that the outside surface of the windward wall is under a pressure of 2,116 psf while the enclosure is under a pressure of 2,100 psf, Figure 6.13. It is this differential between the inside and outside pressures that we refer to as the wind load. It is also this pressure differential that causes suction of water through the windward wall.

If the windward wall has large openings and the rest of the enclosure has no openings at all, the wind will move into the enclosure and the air pressure inside the enclosure will be equal to the outside pressure, as shown in Figure 6.14. In the case of perfect equalization of pressures, the windward wall will not be subjected to any wind load, and there will be no suction created at the windward wall.

Understanding the above concept is essential to designing a watertight drainage wall. If the openings in the cladding of a drainage wall, such as the weep holes, are few and small in area, the pressure equalization between the cavity space and the external cladding will not take place. In such a wall, while the cavity space is under atmospheric pressure, the outside surface of the cladding is subjected to a pressure greater than the atmospheric pressure. This will cause the rainwater to be sucked into the cavity through weep holes. Rainwater will also be sucked into the cavity through joints in cladding that are inadequately sealed, or have become leaky over time.

Note that water suction will take place on the windward facade only since it is at this facade that the cavity pressure is lower than the outside pressure. On the other facades, the cavity pressure is higher than the outside pressure. Hence, no suction takes place from nonwindward facades.

In order to reduce the suction of water in a drainage wall, the pressure between the cavity space and the outside should be equalized as much as

[2] The reader should note the large magnitude of atmospheric pressure (2100 psf) in comparison with other loads on buildings. The live load on buildings seldom exceed 100 psf, and the weight of a 6 in. thick concrete slab is only 75 psf!

possible. Pressure equalization is accomplished by not completely sealing the cladding. In fact, providing weep holes and purposely incorporating other openings in the cladding help to create pressure equalization.

Since there is no pressure differential between the inside and the outside faces of cladding in a pressure-equalized drainage wall, the cladding is not subjected to any wind load. In such a wall, all the wind load acts on the back-up, and the cladding functions as a nonstructural element whose primary function is to control rainwater penetration by allowing free movement of air for pressure equalization. Therefore, the cladding in a pressure-equalized wall is referred to as a screen — more commonly as the *rain screen.*

### 6.6.1  Practical Limitations of Rain Screen Principle

Although the cladding in a pressure-equalized drainage wall should not be subjected to any wind load, in practice it is not possible to achieve a completely load-free cladding. The reason is that pressure equalization does not occur instantaneously. It takes some time for pressure equalization to take place depending on how rapidly the outside air can move into the cavity. If the area of openings in the windward wall is large, pressure equalization will be rapid; in the case of a small opening area, pressure equalization will be slow.

In other words, there is a time lag between a change in the outside pressure and the corresponding change in cavity pressure. During this period (when pressure equalization is taking place), the cladding is subjected to wind loads. If there is no further change in outside pressure, the cavity space and the outside will continue to be under equal pressures.

However, wind in a storm or hurricane occurs in gusts whose speed and pressure change continuously, which disturbs pressure equalization in a drainage wall. Therefore, the cladding is constantly subjected to wind loads, although the magnitude of this wind load is smaller than it would have been in the absence of any pressure equalization.

### 6.6.2  Airtight Back-up and Cavity Compartmentation

Once the cavity is pressure equalized, no air movement will occur in the cavity, because any movement of air implies the existence of pressure differential. The consequence of this fact is that the rain screen principle works only if the back-up is completely airtight. If the back-up has openings, air will move through the cavity into the enclosure, implying the existence of pressure differential (hence, the absence of pressure equalization). If the air is able to move into the enclosure through the back-up wall, water may be sucked into the enclosure. Therefore, in a pressure-equalized wall, the back-up wall must be made airtight. This is usually achieved by sealing all the joints in the back-up wall, and (or) providing an air retarder. The air retarder is usually placed on the outside face of the back-up wall so that it can also function as the waterproof layer.

Another cause of air movement in a wall cavity is shown in Figure 6.15. Under the action of wind, the windward wall is under positive pressure, and

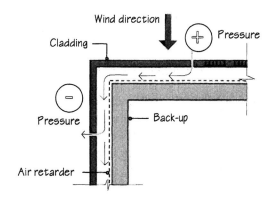

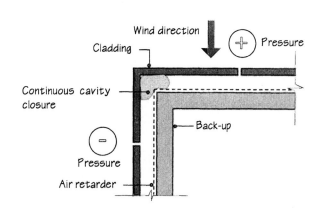

**FIGURE 6.15** Since wind produces positive pressure on the windward facade and negative pressure on other facades, air in a continuous cavity will move in the cavity as shown.

**FIGURE 6.16** To stop air movement in the cavity, the cavity must be closed at wall corners.

the side walls under negative pressure. If the cavity space is continuous from one facade to the other, air will move through the cavity as shown, negating attempts at pressure equalization. Therefore, the cavity space of a pressure-equalized drainage wall must be closed at wall corners. This is usually achieved by using a continuous vertical closure at the corners of the cavity, Figure 6.16. A closed cell compressible filler, such as the neoprene sponge, is commonly recommended as closure material.

In addition to providing vertical closures at wall corners, the wall cavity should also be closed by horizontal closures. In fact, the cavity should be subdivided into independent compartments. The compartmentation is in response to the variation of wind pressure over the building facade. Wind pressure is greater at upper floors of a building than at lower floors, and at edges and corners of the building than in the middle (see Section 2.8.4). If the cavity is not compartmented, the pressure inequality over the facade will generate air movement in the cavity.

Each compartment should have openings in the cladding at the top and bottom so that pressure equalization may take place. The openings should preferably be at the same height in order to avoid airflow short circuiting in the cavity.

Each compartment should be of small dimensions, and should be independently drained by weep holes. One recommendation[6.2] suggests that the compartment size should not exceed 400 ft² (37 m²) if the design wind load is less than 15 psf (0.7 kPa). If the design wind load is between 15 to 25 psf (0.7 to 1.2 kPa), the compartment size should not exceed 250 ft² (23 m²). For a design wind load in excess of 25 psf (1.2 kPa), the maximum recommended area of compartments is 100 ft² (9 m²), Table 6.1. Closures should be spaced more closely at corners and edges of buildings to account for greater wind loads at these locations.

Although preferable, it is not necessary that cavity closures must form absolutely airtight compartments. Therefore in a multistory building, shelf

**Table 6.1 Design Wind Load and Cavity Compartment Size**

| Design wind load (psf) | Compartment size (ft²) |
|---|---|
| 0 - 15 | 400 |
| 15 - 25 | 250 |
| > 25 | 100 |

angles (see Section 6.7.3), which are usually provided at each floor level, can be used as horizontal closures. Thus, in practice we need only provide vertical closures in the cavity.

## 6.7  BRICK VENEER CURTAIN WALL

Among the most commonly used drainage walls is the brick veneer wall assembly. In this assembly, the cladding consists of one wythe[3] of brick, connected to a back-up wall which may be of wood studs, metal studs or concrete masonry. Wood stud back-up, Figure 6.17, is generally used in residential construction. Metal stud back-up, Figures 6.18 and 6.19, and concrete masonry back-up, Figure 6.20, are generally used in commercial construction. Brick veneer may also be used with a reinforced concrete back-up wall.

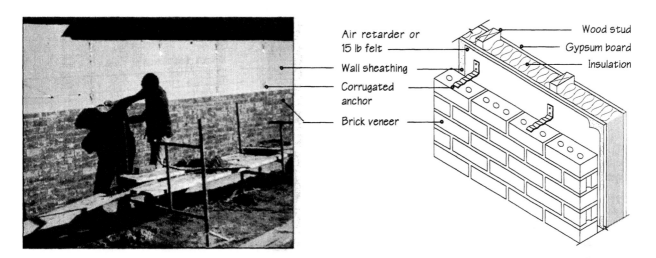

**FIGURE 6.17** Elements of a brick veneer with a wood stud back-up — a commonly used external wall assembly for residential buildings.

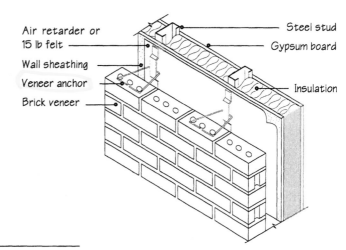

**FIGURE 6.18** Elements of a brick veneer with a steel stud back-up.

---

[3] A wythe is a vertical layer of masonry one masonry unit thick. In the case of brick masonry, this amounts to a thickness of $3^5/_8$ in.

Shelf angle and
flashing

Gypsum sheathing
with taped joints

Brick veneer

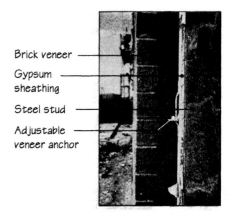

Brick veneer

Gypsum
sheathing

Steel stud

Adjustable
veneer anchor

**FIGURE 6.19** Photographs taken during the construction of a ten story building with a brick veneer on steel stud back-up in external walls. The completed building is shown at the top of the page.

The popularity of the brick veneer wall assembly lies in the aesthetic appeal of the brick facade, the durability of brick and virtually no requirement for maintenance. It may be used in both low-rise and high-rise buildings. In fact, brick veneer with concrete masonry back-up is the wall assembly of choice for many building types, particularly schools, offices and campus buildings.

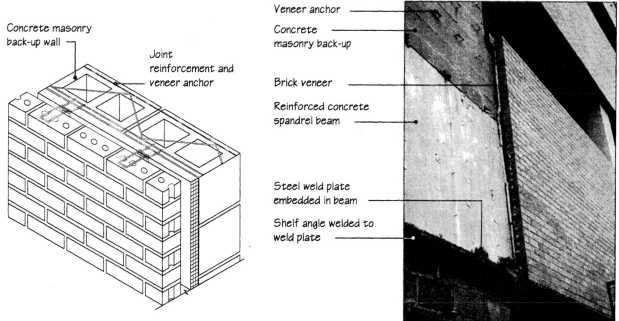

**FIGURE 6.20**  Brick veneer with concrete masonry back-up.

### 6.7.1 Metal Anchors and Cavity Depth

In a brick veneer assembly, the veneer is tied to the back-up wall with metal anchors. The primary purpose of anchors is to transfer lateral loads from the veneer to the back-up wall, since it is the back-up wall that is designed to resist all the wind load. Therefore, the anchors are subjected to either axial compression or tension depending on whether the wall is subjected to positive wind pressure or suction. The anchors must, therefore, have sufficient rigidity, and no mechanical play in the plane normal to the wall. However, since the veneer and the back-up will usually expand or contract at different rates in their own planes, the design of anchors must accommodate this relative movement.

Anchors for brick veneer wall assembly are, therefore, made of two pieces that fit into each other. One piece is secured to the back-up, and the other is set in the veneer. The two pieces can move with respect to each other in the plane of the wall, but not perpendicular to it. Typical anchors are shown in Figures 6.18 and 6.20.

The Brick Institute of America recommends that the anchors be made from a minimum of 9 gauge (4.7 mm) diameter wire or sheet metal of equivalent strength. Galvanized steel is commonly used for anchors but stainless steel is recommended where durability is an important consideration, or where the environment is unusually corrosive. Anchors should not be spaced more than 2 ft apart, and at least one anchor should be provided for each 2 ft$^2$ (0.2 m$^2$) of wall area[6.3]. Additional anchors are required at the ends and corners of walls in response to greater wind loads at these locations.

A cavity depth of 2 in. (50 mm) clear is recommended. In a smaller cavity depth, there is a possibility that if the mortar squeezes out into cavity *most times ends up 1"*

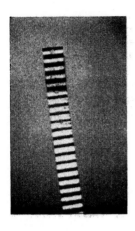

**FIGURE 6.21** Corrugated veneer anchor.

space during brick laying, it may bridge over the cavity and make a permanent contact with the back-up wall. Although, the waterproof layer is supposed to shield the back-up, the possibility of squeezed mortar bridging the cavity must be prevented. A 2 in. cavity depth reduces the above possibility.

In residential construction, however, a 1 in. cavity depth is commonly used. With a 1 in. cavity depth and a relatively low wind load, a 22-gauge one-piece corrugated galvanized sheet steel anchor, as shown in Figure 6.21, is commonly specified for one or two story wood frame construction in low wind speed and low seismic risk locations. Corrugated sheet anchors should not be used where the above conditions do not exist because of their relatively low compressive strength.

The corrugations in the anchor produce a better bond between the anchor and the mortar joint so that the anchor's pull out strength is enhanced by corrugations. But the corrugations weaken the anchor in compression so that the anchor has the tendency to buckle under a positive pressure on the wall.

Special veneer anchors are required in seismic zones 3 and 4, and high wind speed locations.

### 6.7.2 Flashing Materials

Flashing must be resistant to water penetration. Therefore, it must be resistant to corrosion, abrasion and puncture. Durability is also an important consideration since the replacement of flashing in the event of its failure is extremely expensive. In addition, the flashing material must be flexible enough to be easily shaped to the profile of the cavity, and should be able to retain that shape.

Polyvinyl chloride (PVC) sheet, 30 mil thick, is commonly used. However, for superior construction, stainless steel flashing is recommended. Copper sheet may also be used, but it can stain light-colored masonry due to the long-term corrosion of copper. Copper combination flashing which consists of a copper sheet laminated to asphalt-saturated felt and (or) fiberglass scrim combines the good qualities of copper and felt, and is an excellent flashing material. Another good combination flashing consists of mylar, fiberglass scrim and vinyl film bonded together into a sheet material. Lead or aluminum flashing should not be used since alkalies in mortar deteriorate these materials.

A flashing must be provided at all interruptions in the brick veneer, i.e., at the foundation level, over shelf angles and lintels, and at sill levels of windows. The joints in flashing must be lapped and sealed with an appropriate sealer. Additionally, the flashing must be turned up to form a dam at each end of a window sill, Figure 6.22. Weep holes should be provided under the sill to drain any water that enters the wall at the sill level, see also Figure 6.5.

### 6.7.3 Shelf Angles and Horizontal Expansion Joints

Brick veneer may be supported on foundations without any support at

**FIGURE 6.22** End dams in a flashing at the window sill.

intermediate floors up to a maximum height of 30 ft above the ground. This is what is commonly done in a one to three story wood frame building. In this case, the cavity extends uninterrupted from the foundation to the roof level, and the entire load of the veneer is carried directly on the foundation. A step of nearly $1^1/_2$ in. (39 mm) in height, referred to as the *brick ledge*, is commonly created in the foundation to receive the first course of brick, Figure 6.23, Detail B.

In a multistory steel or reinforced concrete frame building, however, brick veneer should be supported at each story on steel shelf angles. Shelf angles are supported by and anchored to the building's spandrel beam, and sized to carry the load of a one floor high veneer.

Flashing should be placed directly on the shelf angle (without a mortar bed under the flashing). The flashing should project out of the veneer face to ensure that the water will drain to the outside of the veneer. If the flashing is of a rigid material, the projection should be shaped to form a *drip edge*, as shown in Figure 6.23, Details A and B. If a flexible material is used, such as PVC sheet flashing, it should be trimmed flush with the wall. In either case, it is necessary that the flashing should not be stopped short of the wall face, as that will allow the water to back up into the wall.

Below the shelf angle, there should be a minimum of $1/_2$ in. (13 mm) air space between the veneer and the shelf angle, to allow differential vertical movement between the veneer and the back-up wall or the structural frame of the building. This expansion joint should be finished with a backer rod and sealant on the wall's face, so that it looks like a horizontal mortar joint. The air space may be filled with a compressible filler, if desired. The veneer may project over the shelf angle, as shown in Figure 6.23, Detail A, but this projection should not exceed one-third the thickness of the brick.

Shelf angles may either be welded to the structural frame of building as shown in Figure 6.20, or bolted to the frame. In the bolted connection, a steel wedge insert is embedded in concrete spandrel beam at 2 to 3 ft ( 600 to 900 mm) on centers, and the shelf angle bolted to the insert as shown in

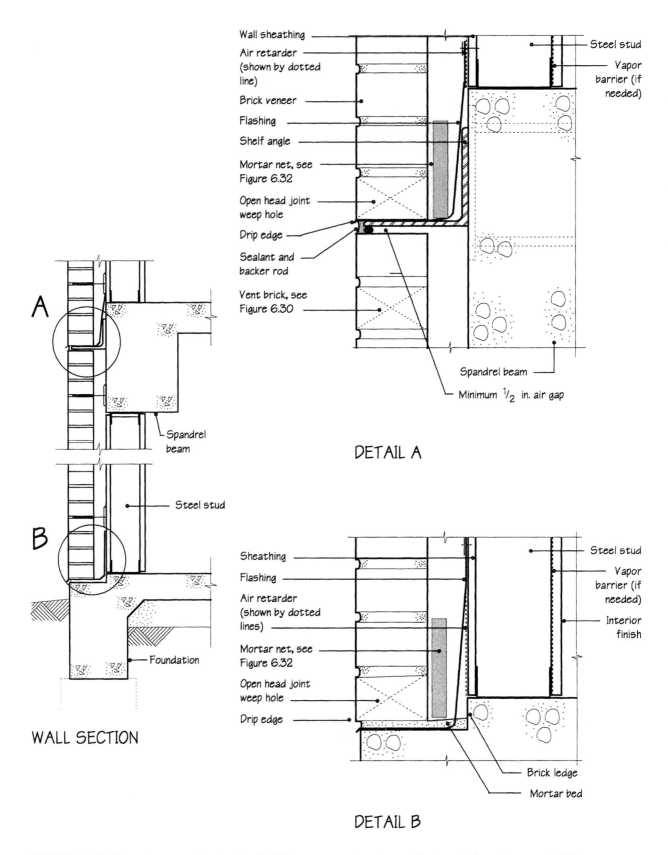

**FIGURE 6.23** General construction details of a brick veneer steel stud assembly in a reinforced concrete building.

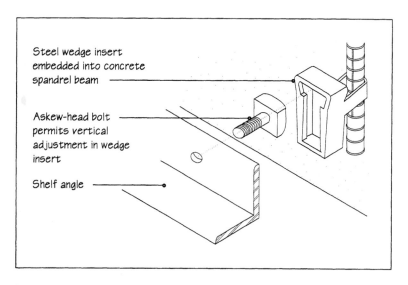

FIGURE 6.24 Details of a shelf angle bolted to a concrete spandrel beam.

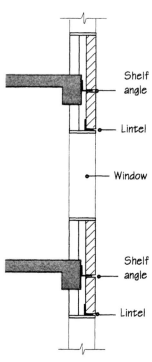

FIGURE 6.25 Section through a multistory building showing the location of shelf angles and lintels.

Figure 6.24. The shelf angles are usually provided at each floor level. In that case, additional steel angle lintels are required over window openings to support the overhead brick veneer, Figure 6.25. The lintels are usually not anchored to the building's frame but are simply built loose into the brick veneer. Flashing and weep holes must be provided over lintels in exactly the same way as on shelf angles.

In order to avoid using lintel angles as well as shelf angles, shelf angles may be placed at the level of window heads instead of floor levels. In such a design, shelf angles are hung off the spandrel beams, as shown in Figure 6.26. Shelf angles should be no more than 12 ft (4 m) in length with nearly $1/2$ in. (13 mm) space at ends to provide for their expansion. Shelf angles must not be continuous.

FIGURE 6.26 Shelf angles suspended from the spandrel beam.

**FIGURE 6.27** Open head joint as a weep hole.

### 6.7.4 Weep Holes and Vents

Weep holes must be provided immediately above the flashing. There are several different ways of providing weep holes. The simplest and the most commonly used weep hole is an open vertical joint (head joint) in a brick veneer, Figure 6.27. However, if an open head joint is objectionable because it allows insects to enter and lodge in the cavity, joint screens may be used. A joint screen is an L-shaped element, Figure 6.28, whose vertical leg has small louvered openings to let the water out, and whose horizontal leg is embedded into a horizontal mortar joint (bed joint). The joint screen has the same width as the head joint, so that in the finished wall it has the appearance of a mortar joint. An alternative to a joint screen is to lightly pack the open head joint with fiberglass (insulation).

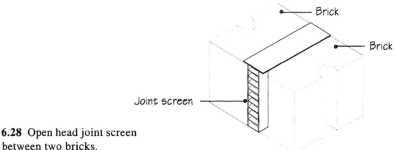

**FIGURE 6.28** Open head joint screen embedded between two bricks.

**FIGURE 6.29** Wick as a weep hole.

Instead of the open head joint, wicks and plastic tubes may be used in a an otherwise mortared head joint. Wicks, which are fiberglass ropes embedded in the veneer's head joints, Figure 6.29, absorb water from the cavity by capillary action, and drain it to the outside. They do not make efficient weep holes and should be avoided. Tubes are better than wicks but do not function as well as open head joints.

Since the two functions of weep holes are to provide drainage and pressure equalization, a sufficient number of weep holes must be provided. The Brick Institute of America recommends weep holes at a maximum of 24 in. (600 mm) on center (16 in. on center with metal stud back-up). Sufficient vent area at the top of the veneer, under shelf angles, should be provided to assist in pressure equalization. Although not commonly used, this may be provided by a metal vent brick which is of the same dimensions as a clay brick, Figure 6.30. The vent brick consists of inclined louvers so that any water that enters the vent brick is captured by its base and finally drained to the outside. One vent brick per cavity compartment may provide adequate top ventilation in the cavity.

### 6.7.5 Mortar Joint Profile and Mortar Droppings in Cavity

In addition to the requirements mentioned above, there are some other features

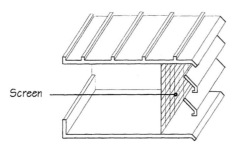

CROSS-SECTION THROUGH
A VENT BRICK

FIGURE 6.30 Vent brick. Sample of vent brick provided by Sunvent Industries, Pelham, New Hampshire.

FIGURE 6.31 Tooling of mortar to produce a water-resistant joint.

that must be incorporated to obtain a leak-free brick veneer wall assembly. Since most of the leakage in a veneer occurs through mortar joints, they should be tooled with a concave joint tooler as soon as the mortar has become thumbprint hard, Figure 6.31. The joint tooler compresses the mortar into the joint, making the joint more water resistant.

Weep holes will function well only if they do not get clogged by mortar droppings in the cavity. Poor bricklaying practice can result in substantial accumulations of mortar on the flashing. Care in bricklaying to reduce mortar droppings is, therefore, essential. A cavity width of 2 in. (50 mm) or more makes it easier to control mortar droppings.

In addition to good bricklaying, other measures must be incorporated to ensure that mortar droppings do not clog the weep holes. Laying a nearly 2 in. thick bed of pea gravel over the flashing may help to keep the weep holes free from blockage.

A better alternative, however, is to use a mortar debris collection device in the cavity immediately above the flashing. A mortar debris collection device is a fibrous mesh, Figure 6.32(a), that captures the droppings and suspends them permanently above the weep holes, Figure 6.32(b). The water in the cavity can freely percolate through mortar droppings and the net to reach the weep holes.

(a)

(b)

Figure 6.32 The use of mortar debris collection device in cavity. Courtesy of: Mortar Net USA Ltd., Highland, Indiana, producers of the The Mortar Net™.

### 6.7.6  Vertical Expansion Joints in Brick Veneer

In Section 6.7.3, we mentioned the need for a horizontal expansion joint immediately below each shelf angle to permit vertical movement of the veneer. In addition to the vertical movement, the veneer should also be able to expand horizontally. This provision is in recognition of the fact that brick walls expand after construction, as discussed in Section 10.3.2. Therefore, a brick veneer must be provided with vertical expansion joints at intervals, Figure 6.33.

The recommended interval for vertical expansion joints is 25 ft (7.5 m) on center in the center portion of the wall and not more than 10 ft (3 m) from the wall's corner. The joints should be detailed so that there is an air space between adjacent bricks which should be finished on the outside with sealant and a backer rod.

### 6.7.7  Testing Brick Veneer Walls for Water Penetration

Brick veneer wall assembly is such a well-established assembly that it is usually not tested for water penetration. However, if new materials are used such as new types of mortar or brick units, then the walls should be tested for water penetration. The standard for testing brick veneer walls is ASTM E

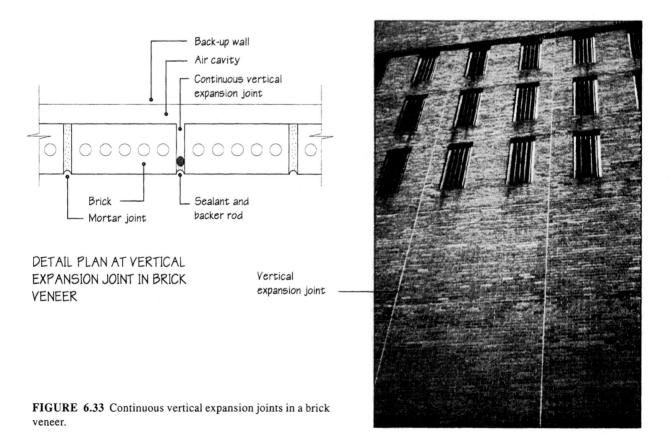

**FIGURE 6.33** Continuous vertical expansion joints in a brick veneer.

514: Standard Test Method for Water Penetration and Leakage Through Masonry[6.4].

The test procedure uses a continuous water spray on brick veneer specimens under static air pressure of 10 psf (500 Pa). Consequently, the procedure does not simulate actual conditions of wind-driven rain. However, the method is useful in comparing the water penetration of one wall assembly with another.

## 6.8 GLASS CURTAIN WALL AND WATER LEAKAGE

The design and detailing of a glass-aluminum curtain wall is complex. Therefore, unlike brick or concrete curtain walls, glass curtain walls are fabricated and installed by specialist contractors who have developed their products after considerable testing and experience. An architect has little control in detailing a glass curtain wall, unless the design requires the development of new details due to the uniqueness of the building. Even in such a case, the architect will usually work with a curtain wall supplier or a curtain wall consultant in developing the design. A mock-up of the wall will be constructed and tested for water penetration, wind resistance, etc., according to ASTM standard.

Despite its complexity, the basic principles of a glass curtain wall detailing are simple. The manufacturers of these walls realize that it is impossible to make a barrier wall out of a glass-aluminum curtain wall. Therefore, they are designed as pressure-equalized drainage walls, with some difference from the cavity wall system of Section 6.5, or the brick veneer curtain wall of Section 6.7.

The most commonly used glass-aluminum curtain wall utilizes the *stick system* in which the vertical framing members of the wall are connected to floor slabs, followed by the horizontal members which span between adjacent vertical members. This design accentuates the vertical members. If the horizontal members are to be accented, they should be installed first and the vertical members will span between them.

Single glass sheet or insulating glass units are installed in the rectangular panels formed by horizontal and vertical members, and are sealed with rubber gaskets or liquid applied sealant. Since leakage may occur at the outside seal between the glass and the metal frame, each glass lite is provided with a pressure-equalization chamber and weep holes, Figure 6.34. A pressure-equalization chamber is an air space adjacent to the outside seal and connected to outside air through weep holes. The purpose of a pressure-equalization chamber is to reduce the suction force at the outside seal-glass interface.

The weep holes are provided in the horizontal members supporting each lite so that this member acts as a gutter. Weep holes are so located that rainwater cannot gain entry into the wall through them.

A vertical section through a typical glass curtain wall is shown in Figure 6.35. Note the double seal between the glass and the metal frame. The outside seal is the deterrent seal. If the water goes through this seal, it will drain out through the weep holes. The inside seal provides the airtightness required for pressure equalization. Remember that the pressure-equalization principle requires an airtight back-up.

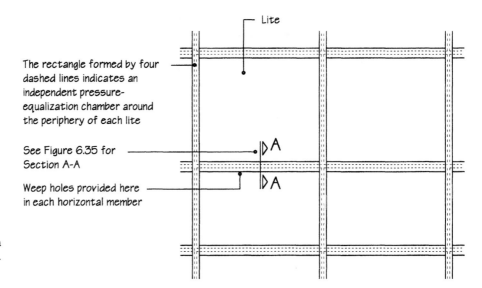

The rectangle formed by four dashed lines indicates an independent pressure-equalization chamber around the periphery of each lite

See Figure 6.35 for Section A-A

Weep holes provided here in each horizontal member

Lite

**FIGURE 6.34** Elevation of a typical glass-metal cutain wall.

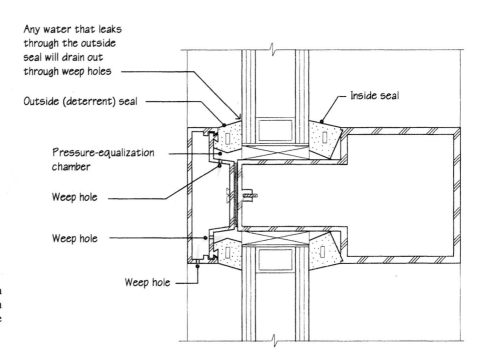

Any water that leaks through the outside seal will drain out through weep holes

Outside (deterrent) seal

Pressure-equalization chamber

Weep hole

Weep hole

Weep hole

Inside seal

**FIGURE 6.35** Section through a typical glass curtain wall (Section A-A, Figure 6.34).

## 6.9 BELOW-GRADE WATER LEAKAGE CONTROL

The first defense against subsoil water leakage in buildings is the control of surface water which includes direct run-off rainwater and that discharged from roofs. It is controlled simply by sloping the finished grade away from the building. A minimum gradient of $1/2$ in. per foot (1:24) is generally recommended. This prevents percolation of water directly into the building foundation. For the same reason, the topsoil around the perimeter of the building should be a low permeability soil such as clay, or concrete or brick paving.

The second line of defense against subsoil leakage is the waterproofing of below-grade structure — basement walls and the basement floor. Waterproofing consists of two parts: (i) the application of a waterproofing layer to basement walls and floor, and (ii) incorporating a drainage system.

*Above + Below grade*

### 6.9.1 Waterproofing Layer

The waterproofing layer is applied on the outside surface of the basement wall and below the basement floor, so that it forms a continuous and an unbroken barrier to the entry of water. Layers of hot coal tar pitch or hot asphalt alternating with fiberglass felts to yield a 3 to 5 ply membrane used to be the most common waterproofing material. The material and the waterproofing technique was precisely the same as that used with the built-up roofing.

However, while a hot tar or asphalt system is easily applied on a horizontal surface, its application on a vertical surface is extremely difficult. Safety concerns are critical in underground waterproofing because of the limited working space available. Therefore, the hot waterproofing system has generally been replaced by the cold application process.

The simplest and the most commonly used cold waterproofing system for below-grade applications consists of a rubberized asphalt sheet system. *Pell + Stick* The sheets, usually 60 mil (1.5 mm) thick, are available in self adhering rolls with a release paper attached. Before applying the sheets, the basement wall and floor surfaces are cleaned and primed with the manufacturer's primer. Since the sheets are self adhering, they form a continuous waterproof membrane. Chemically compatible liquid sealants are available from manufacturers to seal protrusions and terminations. *Mostly get others professionals to do the work.*

### 6.9.2 Drainage System

The drainage system is an important component of subsoil water leakage control. Its purpose is to collect, drain and discharge subsoil water away from the building. The drainage system consists of drainage mats and a drain *weeping tile* pipe. The drainage mats are installed directly against the waterproof layer. They have a thick open weave structure that allows the subsoil water to drain downward by gravity. Thus, the drainage mats eliminate or reduce water pressure acting on the basement walls. An additional purpose of drainage mats is to protect the waterproof layer from any damage that might be caused by the backfill. Some manufacturers provide the drainage mat laminated to expanded polystyrene board which provides insulation.

The drain pipe is simply a 4 to 6 in. (100 to 150 mm) diameter perforated pipe set in a bed of crushed stone that allows the water to seep into the pipe. Drain pipes are most commonly made of PVC or corrugated polyethylene. The pipe is first covered with a synthetic filter fabric before being covered with crushed stone. The fabric captures fine soil particles and prevents them from getting into the pipe and clogging its perforations.

The drain pipe runs all around the basement and is installed a little above the foundation level. If installed below the foundation, it may tend to wash away the soil below the foundation, causing foundation settlement or foundation failure. The water collected by the drain must be discharged to a lower ground or drained into a sump pit, from where it can be pumped up to the storm water drain. A section through a typical basement wall is shown in Figure 6.36.

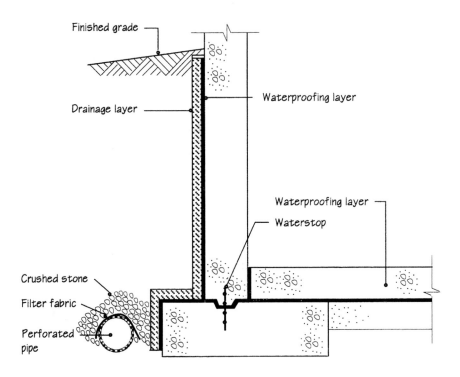

**FIGURE 6.36** Section through a typical basement showing the details of waterproofing.

### 6.9.3 Waterstop

In addition to the waterproof layer and the drainage system, leakage control requires that all "cold joints" in concrete members must be provided with a waterstop. A cold joint is a joint formed by two concrete pours in which the previous pour had hardened and cured before the subsequent pour. A waterstop is a continuous plastic section, half of which is embedded in the first pour, and the other half in the second pour. It comes in long length rolls, so that a seamless waterstop can be provided.

**REVIEW QUESTIONS**

**6.1** What is capillary suction? With the help of a sketch and notes describe how it can be prevented.

**6.2** Sketch in detail a drip edge under a reinforced concrete balcony floor.

**6.3** With the help of sketches, explain how a barrier wall resists water leakage.

**6.4** Explain the principles of a drainage wall.

**6.5** What is the rain screen principle? Discuss its importance in the detailing of a drainage wall.

**6.6** Draw a wall section showing all the important components of a brick veneer wall with a wood stud back-up.

**6.7** Draw a wall section showing all the important components of a multistory brick veneer curtain wall with a metal stud back-up.

**6.8** Draw a wall section showing all the important components of a brick veneer wall with a concrete masonry back-up.

**6.9** Sketch in three dimensions typical anchors for use in the walls of Problems 6.7 and 6.8.

**6.10** Discuss the importance of vertical expansion joints in brick veneer wall. Sketch the detail of this joint.

**6.11** With the help of sketches and notes, explain the waterproofing of a basement wall.

**REFERENCES**

**6.1** Ruggiero, S and Meyers, J: "Water in Exterior Bearing Walls — Problems and Solutions", ASTM STP 1107, American Society of Testing and Materials, Philadelphia, Pennsylvania, 1991.

**6.2** Brick Institute of America, Reston, Virginia: "Brick Masonry Rain Screen Walls", Technical Note No. 27, 1994.

**6.3** Brick Institute of America, Reston, Virginia: "Brick Veneer Steel Stud Panel Walls", Technical Note No. 28B, 1987.

**6.4** American Society for Testing and Materials, Philadelphia: "Standard Test Method for Water Penetration and Leakage Through Masonry", ASTM E 514-90.

# TRANSPARENCY IN BUILDINGS – The Material Glass

**7.1 INTRODUCTION**

The introduction of daylight into buildings has always been an important design requirement. In early buildings, this requirement was satisfied through simple voids in walls. Subsequently, windows made of wood shutters were used which had to be opened to let daylight in. The use of oiled paper panels or muslin cloth in wooden frames, which provided some light without opening the windows, was the next step in providing transparency in buildings.

With the discovery of glass, the window's performance (as well as its appearance) changed dramatically. It was now possible to obtain daylight without admitting other environmental constituents such as wind, rainwater, dust and insects. The earliest use of glass in openings is usually traced to the Roman Empire, where it was employed in small sizes.

The real use of glass, however, occurred during the middle ages as stained glass windows gained popularity with the Church. Staining (or painting) of the glass was not only used as decoration but also to hide several defects, such as air bubbles and colored impurities that were integral to the glass made at that time. During the Middle Ages, church windows were particularly large. They not only provided daylight but also explained Biblical stories to people who could not read using dramatic pictures made from brightly stained glass.

Transparency of glass improved greatly with the perfection of the *crown glass* process around the 14th century[7.1] which provided glass with fewer air bubbles and other defects. In this process, molten glass was first converted to a globe by blowing through a long pipe, transferring the globe from the blow pipe to a rod, and then cutting the globe open. The cut globe was subsequently flattened into a disc by repeated heating and vigorous spinning, Figure 7.1.

In a similar process, called the *cylindrical process*, molten glass was first blown into a globe and subsequently enlarged into a cylinder by swinging the pipe back and forth. The cylinder was later cut along its length, flattened by heating and converted to sheets, Figure 7.2.

**FIGURE 7.1** Crown glassmaking process. Courtesy of Corning Museum of Glass, Corning, New York.

**FIGURE 7.2** Cylindrical glassmaking process. Courtesy of Corning Museum of Glass, Corning, New York.

Clear glass, as we know it today, came into commercial use at the end of the seventeenth century with the invention of the glassmaking process by Bernard Perrot[7.2]. In Perrot's process, molten ingredients of glass were first cast in a mold and later spread into sheets by rollers. When the glass solidified fully, it was ground and polished with abrasives from both sides. The mechanization of rolling and grinding operations brought down the price of glass sufficiently so that it could be used commercially in mirrors and store fronts. Although, the process of manufacturing modern glass is substantially different from the cast or cylindrical glass of several centuries ago, its ingredients are virtually the same.

The transparency of glass, coupled with modern manufacturing techniques that provide large sheets of glass inexpensively, are responsible for the extensive use of glass in modern buildings. Although major innovations have recently taken place in most building materials, the developments in glass have outstripped every other material. These developments have not only led to the use of glass as the primary material for the cladding of buildings but also to its use in daring and dramatic designs, Figure 7.3.

In this chapter, we shall discuss the process of manufacturing glass, its various types and their properties.

### 7.1.1 Transparency of Glass

Although glass is a solid substance, its molecular structure resembles that of a liquid. A typical solid is composed of numerous tiny crystals. Each crystal has a definite geometric form at the atomic level which reflects the arrangement of its constituent atoms. In a typical solid, the crystals are packed together in a regular manner to form repeating networks or lattices. For example, the crystalline structure of ordinary sand (silicon dioxide) is a

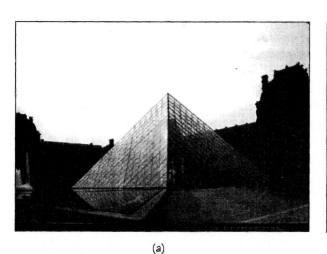

(a)

(b)

**FIGURE 7.3** (a) The Louvre, Paris, France. (b) Interior view, King Saud University Building, Riyadh, Saudi Arabia.

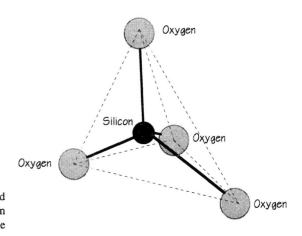

**FIGURE 7.4** Arrangement of atoms in the crystal of ordinary sand (silicon dioxide, $SiO_2$). Each crystal is a tetrahedron in shape. Oxygen atoms lie at the vertices, and the silicon atoms at the center of the tetrahedron.

tetrahedron in which four oxygen atoms surround a central silicon atom, Figure 7.4. The tetrahedrons are networked in such a way that each oxygen atom is shared between two silicon atoms, so that there are twice as many oxygen atoms as the silicon atoms to provide the chemical composition of silicon dioxide, $SiO_2$.

Crystals are formed when the material changes from its molten state to a solid state. Crystallization occurs abruptly at a specific temperature for the material, called the *freezing point* (or the crystallization temperature). In the molten (liquid) state, a material has an amorphous (noncrystalline) structure. An amorphous structure is one in which the constituent atoms are joined to one another but not in a regular three-dimensional pattern — rather in a random pattern.

Glass is a material that has never crystallized. It becomes hard while still retaining its liquid structure. Thus, glass is sometimes called an amorphous solid or a *supercooled liquid*. Because of its amorphous structure, glass does not have a definite melting point like a crystalline solid.

In a crystalline solid, the material melts at a specific temperature and the temperature of the material remains constant until all the material has melted. For instance, ice melts at a temperature of 32 °F (0 °C). During the melting process, the temperature of the ice-water mixture continues to be at 32 °F.

Glass, on the other hand, softens gradually into a liquid at an increasing temperature. On cooling, the reverse occurs and glass hardens gradually. The reason is that the chemical bonds between the constituent atoms of glass are not all of the same type as in a crystalline material. Thus, there is no single temperature at which all the bonds break at once. The bonds break within a range of temperature, and glass softens as this process continues. Once all the bonds have broken, glass turns into a liquid.

The amorphous structure of glass is responsible for its transparency. All solids except glass and clear plastics are opaque to light. The opaqueness of a crystalline solid is explained by the fact that light, in its passage through the solid, is reflected at each crystal boundary. At each reflection, some light is lost. Since there are numerous such crystal boundaries, even within a small thickness of a solid material, light goes through a large number of reflections, losing some light at each reflection. This makes the material behave as an opaque material. Glass is virtually one large crystal containing no internal boundaries, which is why it is transparent. Several crystalline impurities, however, can make glass translucent or opaque.

The amorphous structure of glass is not merely a property of the materials of which the glass is made since many other materials can also be made to produce an amorphous structure on solidification. The amorphous structure of a solid material is also a property of the rate at which molten ingredients are cooled. If cooled slowly, the atoms in the molten mass have sufficient time to organize into a regular pattern to become a crystalline solid. Therefore, in the manufacturing of glass, the ingredients are cooled rapidly to below the crystallization temperature to prevent their crystallization. If the ingredients are cooled slowly, crystallization will occur, causing the ingredients to lose their "glassy" character.

## 7.2 MANUFACTURE OF MODERN GLASS

The primary raw material for making glass is sand, which is also called *silica*. Sand used for glass manufacturing is obtained from sandstone deposits. Seashore sand is unsuitable for glassmaking since it has too many impurities.

Although silica is all that is needed to make glass, other ingredients are added to modify several properties[1]. The two major ingredients added to silica for making (window) flat glass are sodium oxide and calcium oxide (lime). That is why flat glass is called *soda-lime glass*. Soda-lime glass consists of nearly 72% silica, 15% sodium oxide, 9% calcium oxide and 4% other minor ingredients. One of the minor ingredients in glass is iron oxide which occurs naturally in sand. It is the iron oxide which gives a clear glass sheet its bluish-green tinge when viewed from its edge.

Sodium oxide works as a *flux*. A flux is an additive which lowers the melting point of the main ingredient — in this case, the silica. The melting point of pure silica is very high — nearly 3,100 °F (1,700 °C). When sodium oxide is added to silica, the mixture melts at a much lower temperature which reduces the cost of glassmaking. There are other ingredients that can be used as flux, but sodium oxide, which is obtained from soda ash (sodium carbonate), is commonly used because of its lower cost. Sodium oxide also makes the molten mixture more workable. Pure silica in its molten form is highly unworkable. It is so viscous that any bubbles of air or gas produced during melting do not readily escape from the molten mass.

The mixture of silica and sodium oxide yields glass that is not too durable. It slowly dissolves in water and has low resistance to chemical attack. The addition of calcium oxide stabilizes the mix so that the resulting glass is durable and is also more easily worked.

---

[1] Pure silica is used for glassmaking only where its higher resistance to heat and higher transmissivity to radiation is required such as in mercury vapor lamps and telescope mirrors. Glass made with pure silica is called *silica glass*.

### 7.2.1 Float Glass Process

Although the raw materials for making flat glass have remained virtually unchanged, the manufacturing process has evolved considerably over the years. In the process that is commonly used today, the raw materials are granulated, mixed together and loaded into a furnace where they melt. Broken pieces of glass from an earlier batch and scrap glass are also loaded in the furnace at this stage. From the furnace, the molten material goes to a molten glass tank and then to a bed of molten tin. Since the specific gravity of tin is higher than that of molten glass, the latter floats on a molten tin bed.

The above process is continuous and controlled so that a predetermined thickness of molten glass travels continuously over the molten tin tank, called the *float bath*, Figure 7.5. In the float bath, the molten glass is cooled at one end. In order to prevent crystallization, the cooling of glass in the float bath is controlled. There, the molten glass solidifies into a sheet and then travels over rollers to the annealing chamber, called the *annealing lehr*. The glass that enters the annealing lehr has internal stresses locked within its body. This is due to the thermal gradient that is set up between the external surfaces and the interior of the glass because of its relatively rapid cooling in the float bath.

In the annealing lehr, the glass is first heated sufficiently to relieve it of any stresses created during the solidifying process. It is then cooled very slowly so that every glass particle cools at the same rate to ensure that no stresses are frozen in the glass. The annealing lehr is, therefore, several hundred feet long. At the end of the annealing lehr, the glass sheet emerges as a continuous ribbon at room temperature, free of any internal stresses, Figure 7.6. It is then cut into desired lengths by automatic cutters, packed and transported to its destination, Figure 7.7.

Since the top surface of a liquid must be horizontal due to gravity, the floating of molten glass over molten tin ensures that the top and bottom surfaces of glass are horizontal. This provides a uniform thickness of glass sheet — an important requirement to ensure distortion-free vision through glass.

The glass obtained from the above process is called *float glass* to distinguish it from sheet glass and plate glass, which were the two types of flat glass used before the discovery of the float glass manufacturing process. The float glass process was first used in 1959 by Pilkington Brothers Limited

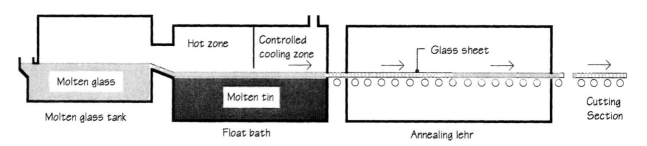

**FIGURE 7.5** Outline of float glass manufacturing process.

**FIGURE 7.6** In the float glass process, glass emerges as an endless ribbon at room temperature. Courtesy of: PPG Industries Inc., Pittsburgh, Pennsylvania.

**FIGURE 7.7** Glass is cut by automatic cutters to required sizes before packing and shipping. Courtesy of: PPG Industries Inc., Pittsburgh, Pennsylvania.

near Liverpool, England, and has since become a worldwide standard for the manufacturing of glass. Virtually all flat glass manufactured in the industrialized world is produced by the float glass process. Discounting a few exceptions, plate glass is no longer commercially produced and sheet glass is produced in extremely small quantities. Only float glass is used in modern windows and curtain walls.

Float glass is available in standard thicknesses ranging from $3/_{32}$ in. (2.5 mm) to 1 in. (25 mm). Manufacturers must be consulted for the availability of certain thickness before specifying it for a project. Glass of $3/_{32}$ in. thickness is commonly referred to as a single strength (SS) glass and that of $1/_8$ in. (3 mm) thickness, as a double strength (DS) glass.

**7.3 HEAT TREATMENT OF GLASS**

The glass obtained from the float glass process, without any further treatment, is the basic glass, referred to as the *annealed glass*. Annealed glass, which may be clear or tinted, is the most commonly used glass type in buildings. However, where a stronger glass is required, annealed glass is heat treated before use. Heat treatment increases the bending strength and the temperature resistance of glass. Two types of heat treated glass are used: tempered glass (also referred to as fully tempered glass) and heat strengthened glass.

### 7.3.1 Tempered Glass

Tempering is the exact opposite of annealing. While annealing reduces or eliminates locked-in stresses, tempering produces them. Tempering involves heating the glass below its softening point, to a temperature of nearly 1,300 °F (700 °C), and suddenly cooling (quenching) it by blowing a jet of cold air on all surfaces of the glass simultaneously. This causes the outer layers of glass to harden quickly while the interior of the glass is still soft. The interior of the glass begins to cool next. As the interior cools, it has a tendency to shrink but is prevented from doing so by the already-hardened outer surfaces, Figure 7.8. Consequently, the exterior of the glass comes under a state of compression and the interior, under a state of compensating tension.

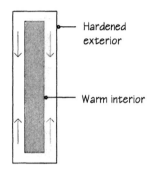

**FIGURE 7.8** During the tempering process, as the warm interior of glass shrinks, it produces compressive stress in the already hardened exterior surface of glass

The compressed layers, in a tempered glass sheet, are nearly one-fifth its total thickness, Figure 7.9. Between the zones of compression and tension, there are two neutral surfaces where the glass is unstressed. As per ASTM C 1048 specification[7.3], tempered glass must have an extreme surface and edge compression of at least 10 ksi (69 MPa).

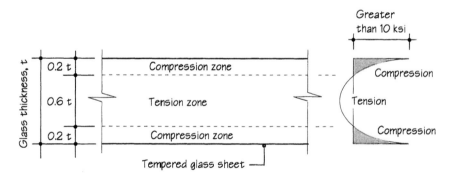

**FIGURE 7.9** Stress distribution in a tempered glass sheet.

Like all brittle materials, glass is weak in tension. Therefore, a glass sheet is weak in bending also, because bending creates tensile (and compressive) stresses in the sheet, see Section 3.8. The locked-in compressive stresses in the outer layers of a tempered glass cancel (or reduce) the tensile stresses produced by bending. Consequently, tempered glass is four times stronger than annealed glass in bending. It can withstand greater deflection than annealed glass of the same thickness, Figure 7.10, and is far more resistant to impact and thermal stresses.

Tempering does not affect other properties of glass such as solar heat gain, U-value or the color of glass. However, because of bowing and warping

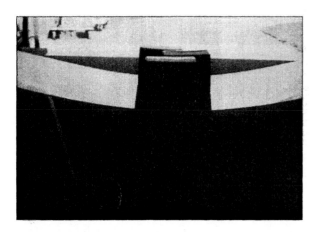

**FIGURE 7.10**  Deflection of a tempered glass sheet under load. Note the ductility of tempered glass — its ability to deflect substantially prior to failure.

**FIGURE 7.11**  Breakage patterns of tempered glass and annealed glass.

caused by the shrinkage of glass during heat treatment, tempered glass produces noticeable optical distortion.

Tempering is done after the glass has been cut to size. A tempered glass sheet must not be cut, drilled or edged since these processes release the locked-in stresses, causing the glass to disintegrate abruptly. Sand blasting and etching may be done with some care. However, both sand blasting and etching reduce the thickness of outer compressed layers, reducing the effectiveness of tempering.

When tempered glass breaks, it breaks into tiny square-edged cubicle-shaped granules — a breakage pattern usually referred to as *dicing*, Figure 7.11. Annealed glass, on the other hand, breaks into long sharp-edged pieces. Tempered glass is, therefore, used in hazardous locations provided it meets the requirements of safety glazing, as described in Section 7.9.

Another important use of tempered glass is in the openings of high-rise buildings to provide safe access to firemen. Because tempered glass is generally more expensive than annealed glass, only a few lites of tempered glass in selected locations are provided. Such lites carry a clear identification on the outside, such as the letter "T" adhered to the lite, Figure 7.12. A fireman wanting access to the interior of such a building during a fire may break the tempered glass lite without undue fear of injury resulting from the breakage of glass. Tempered glass is used in rear walls of squash and racquetball courts[2] and other large glass areas where its greater impact resistance and safety is required.

Nickel sulfide stones and certain other impurities present in glass ingredients do not fully melt during glass manufacture. They are known to expand after days or even years of glass manufacture. When this expansion

---

[2] Some experts suggest the use of heat strengthened laminated glass in place of tempered glass for the glazed rear walls of racquetball or squash courts because of the possibility of spontaneous breakage of tempered glass.

**FIGURE 7.12** In a glass curtain wall building, a few lites of tempered glass are generally incorporated. These lites are so identified by the letter "T". In the event of a fire, the firemen can break these lites to gain safer access into the building.

occurs in tempered glass, it creates excessive tensile stress in the glass, resulting in its spontaneous breakage. This breakage, although rare, occurs abruptly and can be a safety hazard.

### 7.3.2 Heat Strengthened Glass

Heat strengthened glass falls in between annealed glass and tempered glass. It is heat treated in exactly the same way as tempered glass but to a lower temperature of nearly 1100 °F (600 °C). It is nearly twice as strong as annealed glass in bending. It breaks into pieces which are sharper than those of tempered glass, but more blunt than those obtained from the breakage of annealed glass. In other words, heat strengthened glass does not "dice" on breakage. Therefore, heat strengthened glass is not a safety glass. Like tempered glass, heat strengthened glass cannot be cut or drilled after heat treatment.

The primary use of heat strengthened glass is in spandrel areas of an all-glass curtain wall, Figure 7.13. A spandrel area is an area of a wall which is between the head of a window on one floor and the sill of the window on the floor above. A spandrel area includes edge beams and the floor slab. In fact, the purpose of spandrel glass panels is to hide edge beams and floor slabs behind them. Thus, an all-glass curtain wall consists of two distinct areas of glass: vision glass and spandrel glass, Figure 7.14.

It is common practice to opacify the spandrel glass panels and place insulation behind them. Insulation reduces heat transfer through the wall and opacification prevents insulation from being seen from the outside. Opacification is accomplished by either an integral ceramic frit coating on glass or a polyester or polyethylene film adhered to glass.

**FIGURE 7.13** An example of an all-glass curtain wall building.

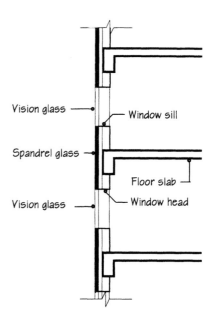

Vision glass

Window sill

Spandrel glass

Floor slab

Vision glass

Window head

**FIGURE 7.14** Section through an all-glass curtain wall showing spandrel and vision areas.

In an all-glass curtain wall, the vision glass is directly exposed to air circulation on both sides while the spandrel glass is exposed to air from the outside only. Consequently, the spandrel glass is not able to dissipate heat as quickly as the vision glass, and is therefore subjected to much greater thermal stress than the vision glass. Because of its greater strength as compared to annealed glass, heat strengthened glass is usually specified for spandrel panels and annealed glass for vision panels.

To obtain a measure of uniformity between the vision and the spandrel areas of an all-glass curtain wall, a shadow-box space behind the spandrel glass may be created. This is accomplished by using exactly the same type of glass in both the vision and the spandrel panels, except that the spandrel glass is heat strengthened while the vision glass may be annealed glass. Note that spandrel glass is not opacified in this construction. The shadow-box effect is obtained by using a dark-colored rigid insulation at least 1 in. (preferably more) away from the spandrel glass. The space between the spandrel glass and the insulation simulates the depth of view of vision glass. Using a tinted-reflective glass adds to the blend between the vision and the spandrel panels.

Because of the insulation, shadow box spandrel design is particularly susceptible to interstitial condensation (see Section 5.8) and consequent corrosion of metals in the space immediately behind the glass, and the wetting of insulation. Therefore, it is recommended for use where condensation effects are minimal.

Condensation effects can be reduced by the use of an insulating glass unit (refer to Section 7.6 for the description of insulating glass unit). Both lites of glass in the insulating glass unit of spandrel panels must be heat strengthened, Figure 7.15. In this detail, the glass toward the exterior is of the same color and type as the vision glass and the glass toward the interior is an opacified glass.

A reasonable uniformity between vision and spandrel panels is obtained if the glass used is tinted or tinted-reflective glass so that the visible light transmittance of glass is less than 25 percent. The all-glass effect becomes nearly impossible to achieve if visible light transmittance of glass exceeds 40 percent. A mock-up of an all glass curtain wall constructed at the actual building site is recommended before finalization of design.

In spandrel areas, heat strengthened glass is preferred over tempered glass because: (i) heat strengthened glass is cheaper than tempered glass, (ii) heat strengthened glass does not break spontaneously like tempered glass, and (iii) when heat strengthened glass breaks, most of it stays within the opening, similar to annealed glass. Tempered glass, on the other hand, fractures in small pieces and tends to evacuate the opening[3].

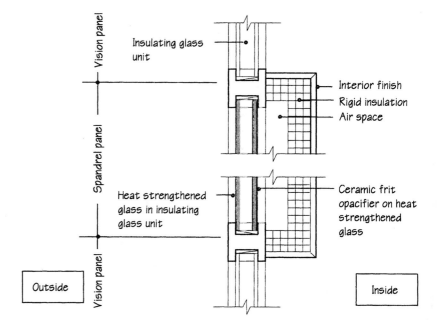

**FIGURE 7.15** Section through a spandrel glass panel (several details not shown for the sake of clarity).

### 7.3.3 Chemically Strengthened Glass

Glass can also be strengthened by chemical process. In this process, glass is placed in a time-and-temperature controlled molten potassium salt bath. This causes the smaller sodium ions in glass to be replaced by larger potassium

---

[3] In skylights and overhead glazing, building codes require the use of protective screens below the glazing in which tempered or heat stengthened glass is used.

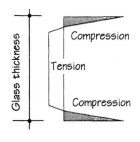

**FIGURE 7.16** Stress distribution in a chemically strengthened glass.

ions which increases surface compression as the larger ions wedge into the smaller spaces left by the sodium ions.

The compressed outer layers in a chemically strengthened glass are much thinner than those in a heat treated glass, Figure 7.16. Consequently, much thinner sheets of glass can be strengthened. This is particularly advantageous where reduction of dead load is a major consideration, such as in skylights and overhead glazings. In such situations, chemically strengthened laminated glass may be specified. However, chemically strengthened glass is more expensive than heat strengthened glass and should be used only where its higher cost can be justified.

The primary use of chemically strengthened glass is in ophthalmic and aeronautical industries. In buildings, chemically strengthened glass is not generally used as monolithic glass sheets, but as a laminate in laminated glass sheets. By virtue of the process, chemically strengthened glass is inherently flatter than heat treated glass. It has better optical properties than heat strengthened glass which is a desirable property in a laminated glass with multiple layers of glass.

The level of compressive stress commonly obtained in chemically strengthened glass is usually between 6.5 to 10.0 ksi (45 to 69 MPa). Chemically strengthened glass is not a safety glass.

### 7.3.4 Bent Glass

Bent glass is made from float glass which has been heated sufficiently to become plastic so that it can be bent to shape. Various forms of bent glass shapes have been used in windows and skylights. Bent tempered glass is also available and is commonly used in revolving doors, curved glass handrails, elevator cars, office partitions and skylights.

## 7.4 GLASS AND SOLAR RADIATION

When solar radiation falls on a glass surface, a part of it is transmitted through glass, a part reflected and a part absorbed by the glass. A $^1/_8$ in. (3 mm) thick clear (DS) glass sheet transmits nearly 86%, reflects 9% and absorbs nearly 5% of solar radiation. In other words, the transmissivity, reflectivity and absorptivity of clear glass for solar radiation are 0.86, 0.09 and 0.05 respectively. Thus, if 100 units of solar energy falls on a clear glass sheet, 86 units are transmitted to the interior, 9 units reflected to the exterior, and 5 units are absorbed by the sheet, Figure 7.17.

The 5 units of solar radiation absorbed by a clear glass sheet increase its temperature and the glass becomes a low temperature (longwave) radiator. It radiates $R_i$ units of absorbed heat to the inside and $R_o$ units to the outside, so that $R_i + R_o = 5$ units. The relative values of $R_i$ and $R_o$ depend on the internal and external air temperatures. A greater amount of heat is radiated toward the cooler side. Thus, if the inside air is cooler than the outside air, $R_i$ is greater than $R_o$. Conversely, if the outside air is cooler than the inside air, $R_o$ is greater than $R_i$.

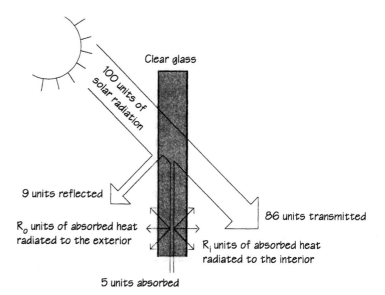

**FIGURE 7.17** Transmission, reflection and absorption characteristics of $^1/_8$ in. thick (DS) clear glass sheet. Note that the total solar heat gain through this glass = (86 + $R_i$) units.

### 7.4.1 Shading Coefficient

From Figure 7.17, it may be seen that the solar heat gain through a glass is equal to the sum of transmitted solar energy plus a fraction of the absorbed solar energy that is subsequently emitted by the glass toward the interior. A commonly used measure of how well a glass sheet performs with respect to solar heat gain is the *shading coefficient*. The shading coefficient of a glass sheet is defined as the ratio of solar heat gain through a given glass to the solar heat gain through an unshaded clear DS glass under the same internal and external conditions. In other words:

$$\text{Shading coefficient} = \frac{\text{Solar heat gain of glass}}{\text{Solar heat gain of clear DS glass}} \tag{7.1}$$

Thus, the shading coefficient is the total amount of solar energy that passes through a glass relative to a clear DS glass under the same design conditions. It includes solar energy transmitted directly plus any absorbed solar energy subsequently radiated or convected to the interior of the room.

Equation (7.1) shows that the shading coefficient of a clear DS glass is 1.0. This is practically the maximum possible value of shading coefficient. The shading coefficient of a clear SS glass is nearly 1.01. The shading coefficient of a tinted glass is less than 1.0 because it absorbs more radiation and transmits less. The same is true for reflective glass because of its high reflectivity. The deeper the tint, or more reflective the coating, the smaller the shading coefficient. Thus, if the shading coefficient of a certain glass is 0.3, it means that solar heat gain through that glazing is 30% of the heat gain through a clear DS glass.

Note that shading coefficient describes the property of glass with respect to direct solar beam. A glass with a lower shading coefficient is more efficient in reducing solar heat gain. Since most of the solar heat gain through a glass is by direct transmission of solar beam, the shading coefficient is a relatively insignificant property for a glass on which direct solar beam does not fall. Thus, the shading coefficient is not an important property for glass which is protected from the direct sun by shading devices, or a glass facing the north direction (in the northern hemisphere), or facing the south direction in the southern hemisphere. For the same reason, the shading coefficient does not apply to heat transfer at nighttime.

### 7.4.2 Tinted (or Heat Absorbing) Glass

Glass can be tinted to a desired color by adding metallic pigments to molten constituents of glass before the glass is annealed. The most commonly used colors are bronze, gray and blue-green. Tinted glass is also called *heat absorbing glass* since it absorbs more heat than clear glass under identical conditions. A thicker glass, made with exactly the same concentration of pigment and the same batch of molten constituents as a thinner sheet, appears to be deeper in color because a greater amount of light is absorbed by a thicker sheet. For the same reason, a thicker tinted glass absorbs more heat than a thinner glass.

As a result of greater heat absorption, the temperature of tinted glass is higher than that of clear glass, particularly if direct solar beam is incident on the glass. Tinted glass sheets of large thickness that may be exposed to intense solar heat should be heat strengthened to withstand greater thermal stresses.

### 7.4.3 Visible and Ultraviolet Transmittance

Since transparency is the primary reason for using glass in buildings, another important property of glass is its ability to transmit light (the visible part of the solar spectrum — wavelengths from 0.4 micron to 0.7 micron). While the transmissivity of clear DS glass averaged over the entire solar spectrum is 0.86, its transmissivity averaged over the visible region, called *visible light transmittance*, is nearly 0.90.

Visible light transmittance of tinted glass is obviously lower than that of clear glass. Among tinted glasses, green tint is most efficient in transmitting light and gray tinted glass, the least efficient. For example, the visible light transmittance of $^1/_8$ in. (3 mm) thick green and gray tinted glasses are 84% and 62% respectively, Table 7.1.

Radiation, in general, has an adverse effect on human skin and eyes, and is also responsible for fading the colors of drapes, carpets, paintings and art works. Ultraviolet radiation (radiation below 0.4 micron wavelength) has a higher energy content than radiation at longer wavelengths. Thus, although it is only 3 percent of the total solar radiation, the material degradation potential of ultraviolet radiation is far greater than that of visible or longwave

**Table 7.1  Solar Properties of Clear and Tinted Glass**

| Type of glass | Shading coefficient | Visible transmittance | UV transmittance |
|---|---|---|---|
| $^1/_8$ in. thick clear glass | 1.0 | 90% | 77% |
| $^1/_8$ in. thick green tinted glass | 0.82 | 84% | 57% |
| $^1/_8$ in. thick blue tinted glass | 0.84 | 71% | 59% |
| $^1/_8$ in. thick bronze tinted glass | 0.85 | 69% | 49% |
| $^1/_8$ in. thick gray tinted glass | 0.84 | 62% | 49% |

Values given in this table are representative only.  Manufacturer's data must be consulted for precise values.

radiation.  For example, ultraviolet radiation at 0.35 micron wavelength has a degradation potential 50 times greater than visible radiation at 0.5 micron. Manufacturers of glass quote the ultraviolet transmittance of their products. A glass with lower ultraviolet transmittance is obviously preferable.

### 7.4.4  Reflective Glass

Reflective coatings may be added to clear as well as tinted glass.  The coating may be of metal or metal oxide bonded to one surface of the glass.  Some of the metals used are chrome, stainless steel, titanium, gold and copper oxide. The coating is extremely thin so that sufficient light can pass through the glass.  Reflective glass works as a mirror from the outside during the day, hiding interior activity.  At night, however, the interior activity is visible from the outside when the interior space is lit.

The coating is deposited on glass by one of the two methods: magnetic sputtering and pyrolytic deposition.  The magnetic sputtering method requires a large vacuum chamber in which atoms of metal or metal oxide are dislodged from the original material by an induced electrical charge.  These atoms impinge on the surface of the glass placed in the chamber, creating a thin layer of coating.  If the glass is required to be tempered or heat strengthened, it should be done prior to the application of the sputtered coating.

In the pyrolytic deposition process, a metal or metal oxide coating is applied to hot glass.  This can be done either in the heat strengthening furnace, or at the hot end of the annealing lehr, or at the cool end of the float bath.  In the pyrolytic deposition process, the reflective coating is virtually impregnated into the glass sheet since the glass constituents are in a semisolid state when the coating is applied.  Consequently, pyrolytically deposited film is more durable than magnetically sputtered film.  Pyrolytically coated glass can be heat treated without adversely affecting the coating.

A coating exposed to the external surface is more effective in reflecting solar radiation but less durable.  Sputtered coating is too soft to withstand the abrasive effects of wind and rain.  Therefore, a sputtered coating should be exposed only to the interior.  A more protected location, such as surface 2 or surface 3 of an insulating glass unit, is preferred for sputtered coating (see Section 7.6 for the description of insulating glass unit).  A pyrolytic coating may be exposed to the outside but the manufacturer's recommendations must be followed for cleaning the glass.

If the reflective coating is on the interior surface of the glass, the heat absorbed by the glass is larger than if the coating is on the outside. This is due to the fact that in an inside-coated glass, the solar beam passes through the glass twice and hence it goes through two absorptions instead of one absorption in an outside coated glass, Figure 7.18. Therefore, an inside coated reflective glass may require heat strengthening because of its greater heat absorption, and consequently greater stress produced in the glass. This is particularly true if the glass is also tinted.

A reflective coating reduces the shading coefficient of glass. A reflective-tinted glass can provide a fairly low shading coefficient value. This is why a reflective-tinted glass is commonly used in glass curtain walls in tropical or sub-tropical climates. However, a reduction in the shading coefficient is generally accompanied by a corresponding reduction in visible light transmittance which may be undesirable.

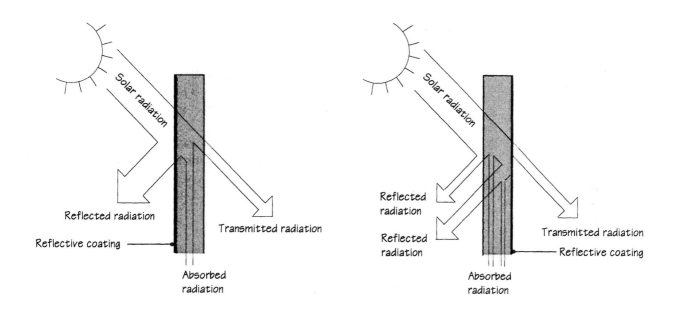

(a) Reflective coating on the outside surface         (b) Reflective coating on the inside surface

**FIGURE 7.18** Transmission, reflection and absorption characteristics of reflective glass with: (a) reflective coating on the outside surface, and (b) reflective coating on the inside surface.

One of the disadvantages of using reflective glass is that it reflects the solar beam toward the street and the surrounding buildings. The glare created by reflection is known to have temporarily blinded passing motorists. Several high-rise buildings located on opposite sides of a street with reflective coated glass facades may make the street unduly warm in the summer due to multiple reflections of solar beam between opposite facades, Figure 7.19. For these reasons, some cities do not allow the use of reflective glass on building exteriors[7.4].

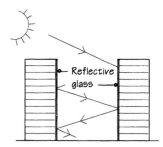

**FIGURE 7.19** Multiple reflections of solar beam from reflective glass on opposite facades of buildings.

**7.5 GLASS AND LONGWAVE RADIATION**

Although the transmissivity of clear glass for solar radiation is nearly 0.86, its transmissivity falls sharply for radiation in wavelengths greater than 2.0 microns, Figure 7.20[7.5]. In fact, the transmissivity of clear glass is practically zero at wavelengths greater than 3.0 microns, implying that glass is virtually opaque to longwave radiation. This explains why a glass enclosure becomes hot on a sunny day even when the external air temperature is low.

Because of the relatively high transmissivity of clear glass, solar radiation can easily penetrate the interior through glass. Having penetrated the interior, solar radiation heats room surfaces and the contents of the room. The radiation emitted by interior surfaces and room contents is longwave radiation. Since glass is opaque to longwave radiation, solar heat is trapped in the enclosure — a phenomenon called the *greenhouse effect*.

The properties of glass with respect to longwave radiation (wavelengths greater than 3.0 microns) are shown diagrammatically in Figure 7.21. Of the 100 units of longwave radiation incident on glass, 90 units are absorbed, 10

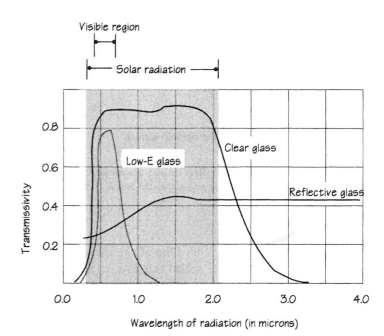

**FIGURE 7.20** Transmissivity-wavelength relationships of clear glass, low-E glass and reflective glass.

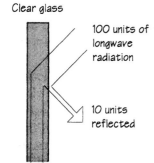

Clear glass

100 units of longwave radiation

10 units reflected

90 units absorbed

**FIGURE 7.21** Reflection, absorption and transmission characteristics of glass with respect to longwave radiation.

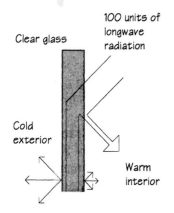

Clear glass

100 units of longwave radiation

Cold exterior

Warm interior

**FIGURE 7.22** Emission of absorbed radiation by glass.

units reflected and practically nothing is transmitted through glass. In other words, the longwave absorptivity of glass is 0.90, reflectivity, 0.10, and transmissivity, zero. These properties are listed in Table 7.2 which also gives the corresponding properties of glass for (shortwave) solar radiation, as a comparison. Since the absorptivity is equal to emissivity[4], the emissivity of glass is also 0.90.

Of the 90 units of longwave radiation absorbed by glass, some will be emitted toward the interior and some toward the exterior. Once again, the relative proportions of emitted radiations depend on the interior and exterior air temperatures.

Now imagine that the longwave radiation incident on glass comes from surfaces and the contents of a warm and heated enclosure. Imagine also that the outside air temperature is low — a typical winter condition. Ninety percent (90%) of the room's radiation will be absorbed by glass which will then be emitted to the inside as well as the outside. Since the outside temperature is low, a large portion of the absorbed radiation will be emitted toward the outside. In other words, the glass is soaking 90% of the heat incident on it from the enclosure, most of which is being dissipated by radiation to the outside, Figure 7.22.

At this stage, it is important to appreciate that this (radiation) is not the only mode by which heat from the inside is being lost to the outside. The other important mode of heat loss through the glass is conduction, which from Equation (4.2) is proportional to the difference between the inside and the outside surface temperatures of glass. Convection becomes an important mode if the outside air speed is large. In fact, the conduction and convection heat losses, together with the radiant heat loss, are the determinants of the U-value of glass.

### 7.5.1 Low Emissivity Glass

Consider once again the longwave radiation incident on the glass from the room interior. A simple way to reduce its loss to the exterior is to coat the surface of the glass with a low emissivity film. When the emissivity of the surface of a material is lowered, its absorptivity also gets lowered[4]. Consequently, the reflectivity of the surface increases. Thus, if the interior

### Table 7.2 Transmissivity, Reflectivity and Absorptivity of Clear Glass

| Type of radiation | Transmissivity | Reflectivity | Absorptivity |
|---|---|---|---|
| Solar radiation | 0.86 | 0.09 | 0.05 |
| Longwave radiation | 0.0 | 0.10 | 0.90 = Emissivity |

[4] Note that absorptivity = emissivity (see Section 4.6.2). Note also that since ground and building surfaces emit only longwave radiation, the concept of emissivity applies only to longwave radiation. The emissivity of most building surfaces, except metals, is equal to 0.9, see Table 4.6.

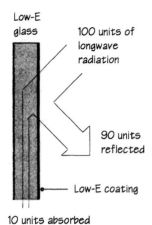

**FIGURE 7.23** Reflection, absorption and transmission characteristics of a low-E glass with respect to longwave radiation.

surface of a glass is coated with a film whose emissivity is 0.1, 10% of the radiant heat from the room interior will be absorbed and 90% reflected back to the interior, Figure 7.23. This will considerably reduce heat loss from the room.

A glass with a low emissivity coating is called a *low-E glass*. The process of producing a low-E glass is exactly the same as producing a reflective glass, i.e., a low-E glass is also made by depositing a metal or a metal oxide coating on one of its surfaces, either by magnetic sputtering or pyrolytic deposition. The sputtered coating has lower abrasion resistance than the pyrolytically deposited coating but gives a lower emissivity value — nearly 0.10. Low-E glass produced by the pyrolytic process has an emissivity value of nearly 0.3. Because of its lower abrasion resistance, sputtered coating is referred to as *soft coat low-E* and pyrolytically coated glass as *hard coat low-E*. Sputtered coated low-E glass can be used only in an insulating glass unit where the coating is applied to either surface 2 or surface 3 of the unit.

A low-E glass is extremely useful in cold climates. It originated in the 1970s in Europe where it is used extensively in the cold climate of Northern Europe. It functions much like reflective glass does in the tropics. While a reflective glass reflects (shortwave) solar beam back to the exterior, a low-E glass reflects (longwave) interior heat back into the enclosure.

Although a low-E glass is very effective in cold climates, it is also useful in the tropics. A low-E coating placed on the interior surface of a glass reduces the inward emission of solar heat absorbed by glass. However, it is more common to place the low-E coating on surface 3 of an insulating glass unit. In such a unit, the solar heat absorbed by the outer lite of the glass is reflected back to the exterior.

Unlike reflective glass, the low-E coating is almost invisible to the eye. Reflective coating, on the other hand, is clearly visible because of its mirror-type effect. Thus, a low-E coating leaves glass virtually transparent. It cuts out very little of the visible part of solar radiation which is hardly noticeable. This is obvious from Figure 7.20. Notice the fairly high transmissivity of low-E glass in the visible region and its low transmissivity elsewhere.

## 7.6 THE INSULATING GLASS UNIT

In Section 4.8.1, we noted that the U-value of a clear glass sheet is nearly 1.0. This is an extremely high value as compared to the opaque portions of a wall. Consequently, most heat transfer in a building occurs through glazed areas.

Since air is a good insulator, the U-value of glass can be decreased by providing a cavity space between two sheets of glass. To avoid problems with the cleaning of the surfaces of glass facing into the cavity, it is necessary that the cavity space be hermetically sealed. An unsealed cavity traps dust and moisture, both of which fog the view through the glass.

A sealed assembly consisting of two glass sheets with an intervening cavity space is called an *insulating glass unit* (IGU). As stated in Section 4.7, the optimum width of cavity to minimize heat transfer is 0.75 in. However, IGUs of various cavity widths, usually less than 0.75 in., are generally used.

The most commonly used IGU in commercial construction is a 1 in. (25 mm) unit in which the total width of the unit — thickness of two glass sheets plus the width of the cavity — is 1 in. In such a unit, the width of the cavity varies depending on the thickness of the glass. If the two sheets of glass are each $1/4$ in. (6 mm) thick, the width of cavity is $1/2$ in. (13 mm). On the other hand, if the thickness of each glass sheet is $3/16$ in. (5 mm), the width of the cavity is $5/8$ in. (16 mm). In residential windows, a $5/8$ in. IGU is common. An IGU used for sound control requires a larger cavity width.

The construction of an IGU is shown in Figure 7.24. It consists of two sheets of glass with a metal spacer, sealed to the glass at the sides — the primary seal. The entire assembly is further sealed around all four edges — the secondary seal. The cavity space is filled with dry air. However, as an extra precaution, the metal spacer is filled with a desiccant to absorb any incidental moisture that was not fully evacuated from the cavity. The spacer may be of a clear silvery finish or any other required color. The four glass surfaces of an IGU are numbered as 1, 2, 3 and 4 starting from the outside.

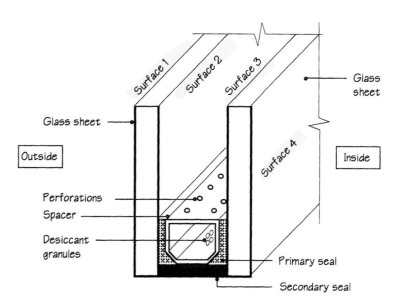

**FIGURE 7.24** Cross-sectional detail of an insulating glass unit.

Since argon has a higher insulating value than air (see Table 4.4), several manufacturers provide argon-filled units. Krypton is another gas that is used as a filling in IGUs. Krypton has better insulating properties than even argon but is more expensive. Some IGU manufacturers use a krypton-argon mixture.

Air, argon or krypton are filled in the cavity with the pressure of one atmosphere to prevent any loading of glass due to pressure differences. Note that if vacuum were to replace air or gas filling, the glass would be subjected to the atmospheric pressure (nearly 2,100 psf), which is several times greater than the wind load expected on a window glass, even under a hurricane.

A special type of IGU is shown in Figure 7.25. It is manufactured with a patented process in which the two sheets of glass are fused together at the edges. The unit contains no spacer or desiccant. The cavity space is filled

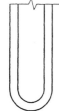

**FIGURE 7.25** An insulating glass unit made by fusing two lites of glass.

with dry air or dry nitrogen. These units are available in small sizes and are primarily used in residential windows.

## 7.7 THE U-VALUE OF GLASS

The U-value of an IGU is a function of several factors. Manufacturer's data must be consulted for a precise value. However, an approximate value of U can be obtained by referring to Table 7.3. From this table, we observe that an air-filled cavity space provides an R-value of approximately 1.0. Since a single glass sheet has an R-value of approximately 1.0, which is mainly due to the internal and external surface resistances, an IGU with one air space has an R-value of nearly 2.0 (1.0 for the R-value of inside and outside surface resistances and 1.0 for the R-value of the cavity. The two sheets of glass add negligibly to the total R-value of the unit). Since the U-value is the inverse of the R-value, the U-value of this unit is nearly $^1/_2$, i.e., 0.5. The R-value of an IGU with two air spaces is nearly 3.0 (U = 0.33), and so on, Figure 7.26.

It has been observed that a low-E coating also adds an R-value of nearly 1.0 to the unit. Thus, a low-E coated insulating unit with one air space has an R-value of nearly 3.0 (U = 0.33).

A reflective coating also helps to reduce the U-value in the same way as a low-E coating since a reflective coating is of similar material as the low-E coating. The contribution of a reflective coating to the R-value is nearly 0.2. Thus, a reflective coated monolithic glass will have an R-value of nearly 1.2 (U-value = 0.83). The tinting of glass has a negligible effect on the U-value.

Argon-filled units have lower U-values as compared with units that contain air. Approximately, argon filling will add an R-value of 1.6 to the unit. Thus, an argon-filled low-E coated reflective insulating unit will have a total R-value of nearly 3.8 (1.0 for internal and external surface resistances, 1.6 for argon-filled cavity, 1.0 for low-E coating and 0.2 for reflective coating). The U-value of such a unit will, therefore, be approximately $^1/_{3.8}$, i.e., 0.25.

Reduction of U-value beyond 0.25 can be achieved only by adding a second cavity space in the insulating unit but if this is accomplished by adding a third sheet of glass, it makes the unit heavier and costlier. One manufacturer makes a low-E insulating unit by using a patented system in which a clear plastic film is suspended half way into the cavity, Figure 7.27. The film divides the cavity space in two spaces decreasing the U-value of the unit without making it heavier. The low-E coating is placed on the plastic film.

**Table 7.3 Factors That Affect the R-value of an Insulating Unit**

| Item | Contribution to R-value of glass |
|---|---|
| Air-filled cavity | 1.0 |
| Argon-filled cavity | 1.6 |
| Low-E coating | 1.0 |
| Reflective coating | 0.2 |

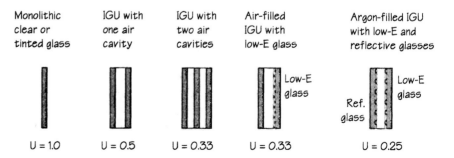

**FIGURE 7.26** Approximate U-values of various types of insulating glass units.

**FIGURE 7.27** An insulating glass unit with a low-E coated plastic film in cavity space. Courtesy of Southwall Technologies, Palo Alto, California.

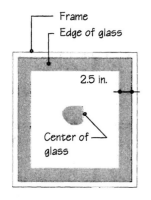

**FIGURE 7.28** Three parts of a glazing.

**FIGURE 7.29** Polyurethane connector between the inside and outside parts of an aluminum frame.

Being transparent, the film is not visible so that the unit is indistinguishable from the standard one cavity unit. The U-value of this unit with argon filling is reported to be 0.19, and 0.16 with krypton filling.

Because of the intervening plastic, there is a limitation on the ability of the above unit to withstand high temperature. Manufacturer's recommendations should be followed if this unit is exposed to high temperatures. Insulating glass units with U-values of nearly 0.1 are available. These units use two low-E coated plastic films with krypton gas filling, giving three cavity spaces.

### 7.7.1 U-values for Summer and Winter Conditions

In the previous discussion, we have assumed that the U-value of glass is constant for a given type of glass or an insulating unit. In fact, the U-value of glass depends, to some extent, on the external and internal environmental conditions. Thus, glass manufacturers quote separate U-values for summer and winter conditions. The difference between the two values is significant only if a detailed analysis of the energy performance of a building is required.

### 7.7.2 Difference Between the U-value of Glass and the U-value of Glazing

The U-values discussed above refer to glass only. In practice, however, we are interested in the U-values of glazing which includes the glass and the frame in which the glass is held. Due to the high thermal conductivity of framing material, such as aluminum, the overall U-value of glazing is higher than that of glass[5].

The overall U-value of a glazing is obtained by averaging the U-values of the three parts of the glazing: the center of glass, the edge of glass and the frame, using WINDOW — a computer program developed by Lawrence Berkeley Laboratory[7.6]. The center of the glass constitutes most of the glazing, Figure 7.28. The U-value of the center of the glass is the U-value of glass itself. The approximate U-values given in Figure 7.26 refer to the U-values of the center of the glass.

The edge of glass is an area surrounding the frame which has a width of 2.5 in. A greater amount of heat is conducted through this area than the center of the glass because of its proximity to the frame (and the presence of aluminum spacer in an IGU).

The U-value of the frame depends on the dimensions of the frame, its material and its configuration (whether or not there is a thermal break in the aluminum frame). A thermal break consists of a plastic connector, usually polyurethane, between the two parts of the aluminum frame, Figure 7.29. Polyurethane has excellent rigidity as well as strength to withstand loads on the frame. The frames of most aluminum windows used in contemporary commercial construction are thermally broken.

---

[5] Because of the widespread use of insulating glass and its relatively low U-value, the overall U-value of glazing, even with wood frame, may be higher than that of glass.

In comparing the thermal performance of various types of windows and curtain walls, an architect must obtain the U-value of the entire glazing, not just the glass. As stated earlier, the U-value of a window or curtain wall is usually different from the U-value of the glass. The size of window may also affect its U-value. A small window will generally have a higher U-value than a large window although the materials used in both windows are the same. This is due to the relatively larger area of frame and edges in a small window. In commercial curtain walls where the framing members are spaced farther apart, the difference between the U-values of the glass and the glazing is usually small.

### 7.7.3 Relative Heat Gain

In addition to data on the shading coefficient, U-value, visible light transmittance and ultraviolet transmittance, glass manufacturers also provide data on the relative heat gain (RHG) through glass. The purpose of RHG data is to compare the performance of various types of glass during the summer. RHG is defined as the total heat gain through glass when a certain amount of solar radiation (assumed as 200 Btu/h·ft$^2$ as the ASHRAE standard) is incident on glass. Relative heat gain is the sum of direct solar radiation transmitted through glass plus heat gain due to inside-outside temperature difference. Thus:

RHG = Shading coefficient (200) + U (Inside-outside air temperature difference)

The inside-outside temperature difference is assumed as 14 °F (assuming that the external temperature is 89 °F and internal temperature, 75 °F ). The U-value used in the above equation is the summer U-value, ($U_s$). Thus:

$$RHG = SC(200) + U_s(14)$$                                        (7.2)

A glass with a lower RHG value will obviously be more energy conservative in warm climates. Manufacturers list various thermal properties of glass in a comprehensive table. A representative listing is shown in Table 7.4.

### 7.7.4 Luminous Efficacy of Glass

While RHG is a measure of the net solar heat gain through glass, luminous efficacy (LE) is a measure of how effective the glass is in reducing solar heat gain with respect to its ability to admit daylight. The luminous efficacy of glass is defined as the ratio of its visible transmittance to its shading coefficient. Thus:

$$\text{Luminous efficacy} \quad = \quad \frac{\text{Visible transmittance}}{\text{Shading coefficient}}$$

**Table 7.4  Solar-Optical Properties of Selected Types of Glass**

| Product | Thickness (in.) | Transmittance (%) | | | Reflectance (%) | Relative heat gain (Btu/h·ft²) | U-value (Btu/h·ft²·°F) | | Shading coefficient |
|---|---|---|---|---|---|---|---|---|---|
| | | Solar | Visible | UV | | | Summer | Winter | |
| Clear float | 3/32 | 87 | 91 | 84 | 9 | 220 | 1.02 | 1.12 | 1.03 |
| | 1/8 | 86 | 90 | 83 | 9 | 217 | 1.02 | 1.11 | 1.00 |
| | 1/4 | 81 | 89 | 79 | 8 | 210 | 1.02 | 1.09 | 0.98 |
| | 1 | 55 | 82 | 59 | 5 | 163 | 0.95 | 0.95 | 0.75 |
| Blue-green | 1/4 | 51 | 76 | 51 | 6 | 162 | 1.02 | 1.09 | 0.73 |
| Bronze | 1/4 | 50 | 54 | 36 | 6 | 161 | 1.02 | 1.09 | 0.73 |
| Reflective: Blue-green | | | | | | | | | |
| Coated surface 1 | 1/4 | 28 | 33 | 11 | 36 | 103 | 1.07 | 1.09 | 0.44 |
| Coated surface 2 | 1/4 | 28 | 33 | 11 | 18 | 115 | 1.09 | 1.08 | 0.50 |
| Insulating unit, 1 in. | | | | | | | | | |
| Clear | 1 | 65 | 82 | 62 | 11 | 179 | 0.55 | 0.48 | 0.85 |
| Bronze | 1 | 41 | 51 | 28 | 7 | 127 | 0.57 | 0.48 | 0.59 |
| Clear, low-E on surface 3 | 1 | 55 | 80 | 50 | 13 | 167 | 0.38 | 0.35 | 0.79 |
| Bronze, low-E on surface 3 | 1 | 34 | 49 | 23 | 8 | 115 | 0.39 | 0.35 | 0.53 |

Values given in this table are approximate.  Manufacturer's data must be consulted for precise values.

Being a recently introduced parameter, LE values are not directly available in glass manufacturers' tables.  A glass with a higher LE value will admit more daylight for the same amount of solar heat gain as a glass with a lower LE value.  Because of its high transmission in the visible region, a low-E coated glass will generally provide higher LE value than an uncoated or reflective glass.  Since green and blue tints (in that order) are relatively more efficient in admitting daylight, they give a higher LE value as compared to gray or bronze tints.  Thus, a green tinted low-E coated glass has a high LE value.  A glass with a high LE value is particularly desirable for office buildings in the tropics.  An LE value of 1.5 and above is considered a high value.

## 7.8 STRUCTURAL PROPERTIES OF GLASS

Glass is a brittle material, i.e., it fails at a relatively low strain.  Like all brittle materials, glass is weak in tension and bending but relatively strong in compression.

Although glass is not considered a structural material, glass in windows must be able to withstand wind, earthquake loads and thermal loads.  Glass in skylights must be able to withstand snow loads in addition to wind and earthquake loads.  Glass used in the rear walls of squash and racquetball courts is subjected to impact loads, and the glass used in aquariums must be able to withstand hydrostatic pressure. All these loads cause bending in glass. Thus, the most important structural property of glass that is of interest to us is its bending strength.

The bending strength of glass is a function of the flaws such as surface and internal cracks which are present in large numbers in a glass sheet (see Figure 3.36). Furthermore, the edge conditions of glass affect its strength. Clean-cut edges provide the maximum strength. If the edges are damaged, the ability of the glass to resist the load is reduced. The actual breakage of glass results from a complex interaction between the size, orientation, distribution and severity of cracks and edge defects.

Because of the unusually large number of flaws and their random orientation, the strength of glass is highly variable. Therefore, the strength of an individual glass sheet cannot be predicted with any reasonable accuracy. In other words, if several identical sheets of glass are tested, there will be an unusually large variation in their breaking loads. Thus, glass strength can be expressed only in statistical terms.

The statistical nature of glass strength is expressed in terms of the probability of its breakage under the load. The probability of breakage is directly related to the average bending strength of glass. The "average" bending strength of glass means that 50% of the lites of glass will (probably) break when the glass is subjected to this stress. Thus, if the average bending strength of a glass is 6,000 psi, it means that half the number of lites of this glass will break when the imposed loads create a stress of 6,000 psi.

Since 50% probability of breakage is an extremely high probability to be used in buildings, the maximum actual stress to which the glass is subjected in buildings is well below its average bending strength. In other words, a large factor of safety is necessary in establishing the maximum allowable stress for glass.

**Table 7.5 Safety Factor and Probability of Glass Breakage Under Wind Load**

| Safety factor | Number of lites that may break (of each 1,000 lites loaded) |
|---|---|
| 1.0 | 500 |
| 2.0 | 22 |
| 2.5 | 8 |
| 3.0 | 4 |
| 4.0 | 1.3 |
| 5.0 | 0.7 |
| 8.0 | 0.2 |
| 10.0 | 0.15 |

Source: Reference 7.7 with permission.

### 7.8.1 Wind Loads and Glass Thickness

The greater the factor of safety[6] provided, the smaller the allowable stress and the lower the probability of breakage. The glass industry has determined a relationship between the factor of safety and the probability of breakage of glass due to bending caused by wind loads, Table 7.5. The probability of breakage is expressed in terms of the number of lites that are likely to break per one thousand lites. Thus, a probability of breakage of $3/_{1000}$ (three per thousand) means that 3 out of a total of 1,000 lites will (probably) break.

The most commonly used probability of breakage for determining glass thickness in windows and curtain walls is 8 per thousand ($8/_{1000}$). In fact, this is the maximum probability of breakage allowed by building codes for determining glass thickness to withstand wind loads. From Table 7.5, the factor of safety corresponding to $8/_{1000}$ probability of breakage is 2.5. Thus, if the average bending strength of a certain glass used in windows is 6,000

---

[6] The term "design factor" is more commonly used with statistically less reliable materials such as glass instead of the "factor of safety", although both these terms relate to the same basic concept.

psi and the probability of breakage is $^8/_{1000}$, then the maximum bending stress that can be imposed on the glass is 6,000/2.5 = 2,400 psi. Stated differently, if 1,000 lites of this glass are subjected to the same but increasingly larger loads, then as soon as the stress in lites reaches 2,400 psi, 8 lites will probably break.

Although a probability of breakage of $^8/_{1000}$ (factor of safety = 2.5) is commonly used for the design of window glass, a lower probability of breakage may be required in high-rise buildings and other critical situations. For instance, a factor of safety of 10.0 is used in the design of glass in aquariums.

Based on the data obtained from test-to-destruction of 2,000 new glass lites, an empirical glass strength chart has been developed by the glass industry[7.8]. This chart is shown in Figure 7.30.

Since the tests were designed to determine the strength of glass to withstand wind loads, a one-minute duration of loading was considered adequate. The reason is that design wind loads on buildings are based on peak wind speeds which generally last only a few seconds.

The chart of Figure 7.30 is intended for the selection of glass thickness to withstand a given wind load. In other words, the chart gives the maximum

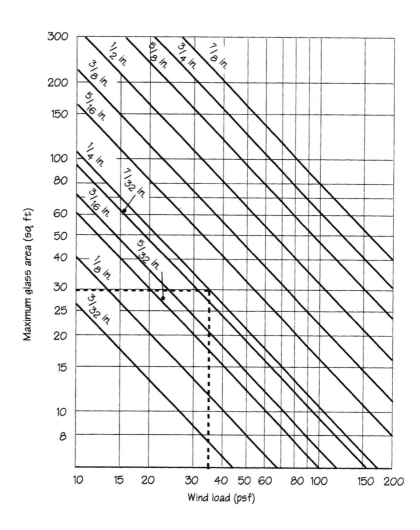

**FIGURE 7.30** Maximum allowable glass area to resist wind load for a four-side supported annealed glass. Probability of breakage $^8/_{1000}$. Ratio of long to short dimension of glass not to exceed 5. Source: Reference 7.8 with permission.

wind load that a glass of a given thickness and area can withstand. For instance, if a $1/4$ in. thick glass is to be used in a window whose area is 30 ft$^2$, we note (from broken lines in Figure 7.30) that it will withstand a maximum wind load of 35 psf. The following conditions must be satisfied for the use of Figure 7.30.

- The glass used is annealed glass.
- The glass is rectangular and supported on all four sides, i.e., the glass is enclosed within a frame on all four sides.
- The aspect ratio (the ratio of long to short dimension of the glass) does not exceed 5:1.
- Probability of breakage is $8/1000$ lites.

Figure 7.30 can also be used for a probability of breakage other than $8/1000$ by using the appropriate safety factor from Table 7.5, and one of the following equations.

$$\text{Maximum permissible wind load} = \frac{2.5}{\text{Safety factor}} \left[ \text{Wind load from Figure 7.30} \right] \quad (7.3)$$

$$\text{Maximum permissible glass area} = \frac{2.5}{\text{Safety factor}} \left[ \text{Glass area from Figure 7.30} \right] \quad (7.4)$$

Figure 7.30 can also be used for glass types other than the annealed glass by using the strength adjustment factors given in Table 7.6. The use of the chart is illustrated in Examples 7.1 to 7.3. The glass strength chart for a two-side supported glass is given in Figure 7.31. Note that a two-side supported glass[7] requires greater thickness than a four-side supported glass under the same conditions.

### Table 7.6  Strength Adjustment Factors

| Glass type | Adjustment Factor |
|---|---|
| Annealed glass | 1.0 |
| Heat strengthened glass | 2.0 |
| Tempered glass | 4.0 |
| Laminated glass (annealed) | 0.75 |
| Laminated glass (heat strengthened) | 1.5 |
| Laminated glass (tempered) | 3.0 |
| Insulating unit: | |
|    Annealed/annealed | 1.8 |
|    Heat strengthened/heat strengthened | 3.6 |
|    Tempered/tempered | 7.2 |

Values given in this table have been extracted from Reference 7.9. For complete details, see the original table. Printed with permission.

---

[7] A two-side supported glass is weaker than a four-side supported glass and hence requires greater thickness for the same area.

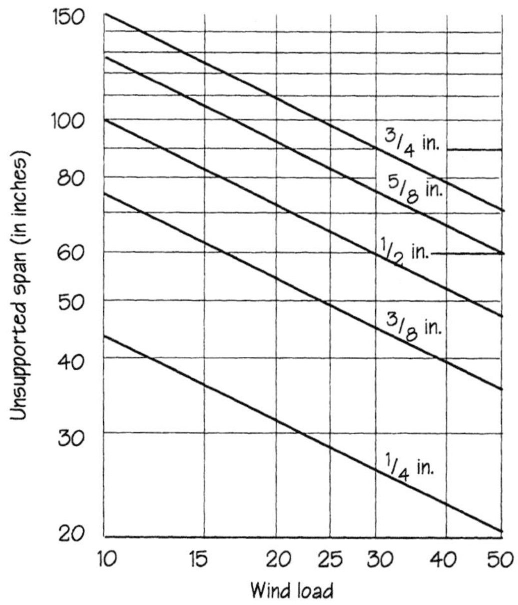

**FIGURE 7.31** Maximum allowable glass span to resist wind load for a two-side supported glass. Probability of breakage $8/_{1000}$. Source: Reference 7.8 with permission.

In addition to Figures 7.30 and 7.31, there are other charts that may be used for selecting glass thickness. One such set of charts is given in ASTM Standard E 1300[7.9]. ASTM E 1300 charts were developed using sophisticated computer analyses and are considered to represent more realistic conditions than those assumed in charts of Figure 7.30. However, they do not currently represent glass industry consensus.

**Example 7.1**

Determine the maximum permissible wind load on a $1/_4$ in. thick annealed glass. The glass is supported on all four sides and measures 4 ft x 7 ft-6 in. The required probability of breakage is one per thousand lites.

*Solution*: Area of glass = 4 x 7.5 = 30 ft$^2$. From Figure 7.30, maximum permissible wind load = 35 psf. The safety factor corresponding to a probability of breakage of $8/_{1000}$ is 2.5, Table 7.5. The safety factor required for a probability of breakage of $1/_{1000}$ is 4.5 (obtained by interpolation from the values given in Table 7.5). From Equation 7.3,
   Maximum permissible wind load = (2.5/4.5)(35) = 19.4 psf

**Example 7.2**

Determine the maximum permissible area of a $3/_{16}$ in. thick glass supported on all four sides to withstand a wind load of 30 psf. Probability of breakage is 4 per 1,000 lites.

*Solution*:  From Table 7.5, safety factor corresponding to a probability of breakage of 4 per 1,000 lites = 3.0.  Glass area from Figure 7.30 = 24 ft$^2$. From Equation 7.4,

Maximum permissible glass area = (2.5/3.0)24 = 20 ft$^2$.

**Example 7.3**

Determine the maximum wind load for the Example 7.1 if the glass used is: (a) $^1/_4$ in. thick laminated glass, (b) insulating glass unit with both sheets of $^1/_4$ in. thick annealed glass.  Required probability of breakage is $^1/_{1000}$.

*Solution*: (a) From Example 7.1, the maximum wind load that a $^1/_4$ in. thick annealed glass can withstand is 19.4 psf.  For laminated glass, the strength adjustment factor is 0.75 (Table 7.6).  Hence, the maximum permissible wind load on a $^1/_4$ in. thick laminated glass  = 19.4(0.75) = 14.6 psf.

(b) For an insulating glass unit made of two sheets of $^1/_4$ in. thick annealed glass, the strength adjustment factor is 1.8 (Table 7.6).  Hence, the maximum permissible wind load = 19.4(1.8) = 34.9 psf.

**7.8.2  Strength of Glass Under Sustained Loads**

The strength of a material is not only related to the magnitude of load but also to the length of time during which the load acts on the material.  Most materials can withstand greater load if the load acts for a brief interval than if the load acts for a long duration due to the effect of fatigue on the material. That is why building codes permit greater magnitude of short-term loads (wind and earthquake) in comparison to sustained loads such as dead loads, live loads and snow loads.

The load duration factor is all the more important in the case of glass. The strength of glass is smaller for sustained loads as compared to wind or earthquake loads.  Therefore, the charts of Figures 7.30 and 7.31 cannot be used directly for determining the thickness of glass for sustained loads.  For example, in determining the thickness of glass for skylights (to resist snow loads), annealed glass strength is usually reduced to 60% of its strength for wind loads.  The strengths of heat strengthened glass and tempered glass are reduced to 80% and 95% respectively of their strengths for wind loads.

Thus, the tempered and heat strengthened glasses are not only stronger than annealed glass, they have greater ability to resist sustained loads than annealed glass.  It is because of their higher strengths and better performance in resisting sustained loads that tempered glass and heat strengthened glass are used in situations where excessive thermal stresses may be present.  Note that thermal stresses cause sustained loading as compared with short-term loads caused by wind or earthquake.

### 7.8.3 Modulus of Elasticity and Deflection of Glass

From Table 7.6, we observe that tempered glass is four times stronger than annealed glass. This implies that a tempered glass lite can withstand four times as much load as an annealed glass lite of the same thickness and size. However, the modulus of elasticity of tempered glass (and heat strengthened glass) is the same as that of annealed glass. This important fact implies that the deflection of tempered glass and annealed glass lites, of the same size and thickness, will be equal under a given load.

Thus, if tempered glass is made to withstand a greater wind load because of its higher strength, a greater deflection will be produced in lites. Greater deflection can cause poor long-term performance of gaskets, leading to premature failure of lites. Therefore in practice, tempered glass and heat strengthened glass are designed to withstand the same wind load as annealed glass. In other words, the higher strengths of tempered glass and heat strengthened glass are usually not exploited. Tempered glass and heat strengthened glass are used primarily for their greater impact resistance, greater thermal stress resistance and safer breakage pattern.

In addition to the deflection of glass, the deflection of the frame in which the glass is held is an important consideration. Glass strength charts are based on the premise that the framing system is rigid. If there is an excessive deflection in framing members, lack of support for glass will result, leading to its premature breakage.

### 7.9 SAFETY GLASS

Because of the transparency of glass, a large glazed opening without an intermediate horizontal framing member may be mistaken for a clear (unglazed) opening. In such situations, there is a likelihood that a person may tend to walk through the glass. In these and several other situations, the use of annealed glass may be hazardous because of the sharp pieces it produces on breakage. Building codes require the use of safety glass in locations where accidental human impact is expected. Such locations are called *hazardous locations*. Some examples of hazardous locations are: glazing in sliding patio doors, swinging doors, main entry doors, storm doors, bath tub and shower doors, and stair and balcony railings.

Two types of glass are commonly used as safety glass: tempered glass and laminated glass. However, all tempered or laminated glass is not safety glass. To be recognized as safety glass, the glass must meet the requirements of Consumer Product Safety Commission's (CPSC) "Safety Standard for Architectural Glazing Materials", 16 CFR 1201.

Compliance with CFR 1201 is based on the glass passing the impact test. In this test, the glass specimen is mounted in a test frame as shown in Figure 7.32. The test frame has an impactor suspended from the top. The impactor, which weighs 100 pounds, consists of a leather punching bag filled with lead shots. The impact on the test specimen is produced by moving the impactor away from its rest position and releasing it. In its rest position, the impactor is at the center of the test specimen.

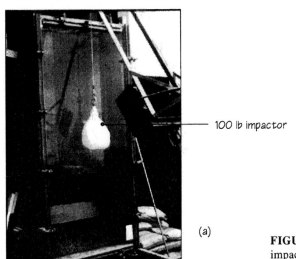

— 100 lb impactor

(b)

(a)

**FIGURE 7.32**  (a) Glass specimen mounted in the test frame, ready for impact testing.  (b) After the test, broken glass collects in the tray at the bottom of the frame.

---

XYZ Glass Co.

Tempered Safety Glass

16 CFR 1201 Category I

ANSI Z97.1-1984

**FIGURE 7.33**  Example of permanent label etched on a tempered safety glass.

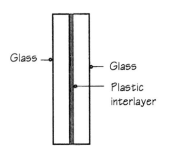

Glass

Glass

Plastic interlayer

**FIGURE 7.34**  Section through a laminated glass sheet.

CFR 1201 divides safety glazing into two categories.  Category I glass must be able to withstand an impact of 150 lb.ft which is produced when the impactor is dropped from a drop height of 18 in.  For Category II glass, the drop height is 4 ft, so that the impact delivered to glass is 400 lb.ft.  Category I glass can be used only in lites which are 9 ft$^2$ or less in area and Category II, for lites greater than 9 ft$^2$.

The test simulates the impact of a person running into a glazing.  Although 100 pounds is less than the average weight of a human being, it is considered adequate since, in an impact with a glazing, the entire weight of the person is not likely to be involved.  The glass is assumed to have passed the test provided the specimen satisfies the breakage criteria outlined in CFR 1201.

CFR 1201 came into effect in 1977.  Prior to this, a less stringent standard, ANSI Z97.1, was used by codes.  The difference between ANSI and CPSC tests is that the latter requires greater impact resistance.  Usually, a glass that satisfies CPSC test will also satisfy the less stringent ANSI standard.  The reverse, however, is not true.  For instance, wired glass satisfies ANSI standard, but not CPSC standard.

Building codes require that every lite of tempered glass used in hazardous locations be certified by the Safety Glass Certification Council (SGCC) and bear a label identifying its compliance with 16 CFR 1201.  The label similar to the one shown in Figure 7.33 must be a permanent label which is usually etched on the glass before the glass is tempered.

### 7.9.1  Laminated Glass

In its simplest form, a laminated glass is made from two layers of glass laminated under heat and pressure to a plastic interlayer so that all three layers are fused together, Figure 7.34.  In the event of an impact, the glass layer in laminated glass may break but it will not fall off the building.  The glass will tend to remain bonded to the interlayer. This minimizes the hazard of shattered glass.

Laminated glass has been used for automobile windshields for a long time. In architectural applications, laminated glass is the product of choice for skylights, sloped and overhead glazing, zoos, and aquariums. Since the glass remains in the opening even after breakage, laminated glass is also recommended in windows in earthquake-prone areas to reduce injury from abrupt shattering of glass.

The plastic interlayer may be clear or tinted. It comes in three standard thicknesses: 15 mil (0.38 mm), 30 mil (0.75 mm) and 60 mil (1.5 mm). Where greater safety or security glass is required, a greater thickness of the interlayer (0.090 or thicker) may be obtained on special order. One major advantage of the plastic interlayer is that it blocks out most of the ultraviolet radiation. The plastic interlayer also improves sound transmission properties of glass.

If used in hazardous locations, laminated glass must pass the same impact resistance test of 16 CFR 1201 as tempered glass. Laminated glass with a 15 mil thick interlayer readily passes this test in Category I, and that with a 30 mil thick interlayer passes the same test in Category II. However under 16 CFR 1201, laminated glass must also pass the boil test. The boil test determines the ability of glass to withstand resistance to high temperature. In this test, 12 in. by 12 in. (300 mm x 300 mm) specimens of laminated glass are immersed in boiling water for two hours. The specimens are deemed to have passed the test if bubbles or other defects more than $1/_2$ in. (13 mm) from the outer edges of glass do not develop.

Any type of glass — annealed, heat strengthened, or tempered — can be used in making laminated glass. Laminated glass can also be use in insulating units.

Tempered laminated glass provides the highest impact resistance, and is commonly specified in zoos[7.10] where impact from large agile animals such as lions, tigers and gorillas is expected, Figure 7.35. Laminated glass is also specified in aquariums, Figure 7.36.

**7.10 PLASTIC GLAZING**

Clear plastic sheets have gained popularity in some applications as alternative glazing materials. Three important advantages of plastic over glass are:

- Plastic can be bent to curves far more easily than glass. Plastic is the material of choice in specially curved skylights, particularly doubly curved shapes such as domes.
- Plastic is several times stronger than glass of the same thickness, and is also more impact resistant. It does not shatter or crack like glass. It is therefore specified in fenestration where the breakage of glass due to vandalism is a concern, or where a high degree of security is required.
- Plastic glazing is lighter than glass.

However, the disadvantages of plastic glazing far outweigh its advantages. That is why its use is limited to such applications where glass cannot be used. Some of the disadvantages of plastic glazing are:

- It is usually costlier than glass.

**FIGURE 7.35** Laminated glass window in St. Louis Zoo, St. Louis, Missouri. Courtesy of: The Monsanto Company, St. Louis, Missouri.

**FIGURE 7.36** Laminated glass in the Aquarium of the Americas, New Orleans, Louisiana. Courtesy of: The Monsanto Company, St. Louis, Missouri.

- Plastic has a much greater coefficient of thermal expansion than glass. If the movement of plastic glazing is restricted, it will visibly bow out in the direction of higher temperature. Framing details must, therefore, allow linear movement as well as the rotation of glazing. Consequently, framing details are more complex with plastic glazing which further adds to its cost.
- Humidity changes also affect the dimensional stability of plastics. Plastic expands with increasing humidity, creating the same problems as thermal expansion.
- Plastic is not abrasion resistant, although abrasion resistant coatings on plastic glazing considerably improve the abrasion resistance of plastics.
- Plastic is vapor permeable so that sealed insulating units are not possible.
- Plastic yellows with age (ultraviolet degradation), reducing its clarity and light transmission.
- The most serious disadvantage of plastic is its combustibility. It will contribute fuel in a building fire. That is why building codes place severe limitations on the area of plastic glazing and the height of the building above which it cannot be used. For example, the Uniform Building Code does not allow the use of plastic glazing in wall openings more than 65 ft above the ground level.

### 7.10.1 Acrylic vs Polycarbonate Glazing

At the present time, two types of plastics are used for glazing: acrylic and polycarbonate. Acrylic has better resistance to ultraviolet radiation than polycarbonate. It yellows more slowly and has greater resistance to abrasion

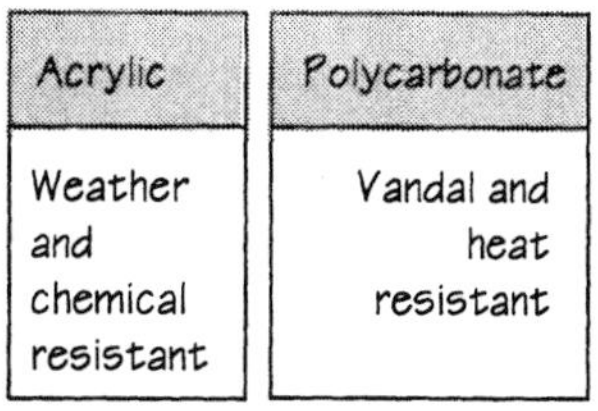

| Acrylic | Polycarbonate |
|---------|---------------|
| Weather and chemical resistant | Vandal and heat resistant |

**FIGURE 7.37** Differences between acrylic and polycarbonate glazing.

and scratching than polycarbonate. It also has greater resistance to chemicals such as household and glass cleaners.

Polycarbonate, on the other hand, has greater impact resistance than acrylic. It can withstand 30 times greater impact than acrylic and 250 times greater impact than glass, making it the most vandal resistant glazing. Polycarbonate is therefore commonly specified for bus shelters and school windows where vandalism is a problem. Polycarbonate can also withstand greater temperatures than acrylic. Therefore, polycarbonate is commonly used in signs which are exposed to high temperatures from light sources.

Acrylic is commonly used in curved skylights and greenhouses where its greater durability and weatherability is required. The primary differences between acrylic and polycarbonate glazing are highlighted in Figure 7. 37.

## 7.11 GLASS FOR SPECIAL PURPOSES

The types of glass and clear plastics described so far are the ones that are commonly used. A few of the glass types used for special purposes are described below.

### 7.11.1 Security Glazing

Security glass refers to a glass which is resistant to burglary and forced entry, and bullet penetration. Since burglary and bullet resistance is a function of both the glass and the frame in which the glass is held, the term security glazing is commonly used. Typically, security glazing is composed of single or multiple panes of glass fused with a single or multiple sheets of plastic.

Burglary resistant glazing must withstand repeated impacts from such hand-held weapons as hammers, crowbars and bricks, as specified in Underwriters Laboratory Test UL 792. Laminated glass with two sheets of glass and a 90 mil thick interlayer usually meets UL 792 requirements.

Bullet resistant glazing must withstand bullet penetration. It is specified for drive-in bank windows, armored vehicles and any other application where a high degree of security is required. Laminated glass or glass clad polycarbonate are commonly used for bullet resistant glass. By increasing the thickness of plastic layers, increasingly greater security may be obtained from bullet penetration, as shown in Figure 7.38.

### 7.11.2 Radiation Shielding Glass and Plastic

Radiation shielding by building materials is generally a function of their density. The greater the density and the thicker the material, the greater its radiation shielding capability. Metals, concrete and masonry materials (provided there are no cracks in concrete and masonry) provide excellent radiation protection. However, lead because of its highest density among building materials and its flexibility is the most commonly used radiation shielding material. Where transparency is not required, lead curtains are commonly used, and lead aprons are worn for additional protection.

| Type of gun | | Overall approximate laminate thickness |
|---|---|---|
| | Medium power -- small arm | $1^3/_{16}$ in. |
| | High power -- small arm | $1^1/_2$ in. |
| | Super power -- small arm | $1^3/_4$ in. |
| | High power -- rifle | 2 in. |

**FIGURE 7.38** Bullet resistant laminated glass capabilities. Courtesy of: The Monsanto Company, St. Louis, Missouri.

Radiation shielding glass is made by the addition of lead (usually in the form of lead oxide) to the same ingredients as those of soda-lime glass. Lead acrylic is made from lead-acrylic polymer. Lead glass and lead acrylic have much greater radiation shielding potential than ordinary soda-lime glass.

Lead glass or lead acrylic is commonly used in observation windows, port holes and transparent partitions in medical X-ray facilities, Figure 7.39. Its primary purpose is to protect the X-ray equipment operator, observer and other people in the vicinity of X-ray equipment from stray radiation.

Radiation shielding potential of lead glass or lead acrylic is related to its lead content which is measured by lead equivalency. For instance, a $^7/_{16}$ in. (11 mm) thick lead glass has nearly $^3/_{32}$ in. (2.5 mm) equivalent thickness of lead. Lead glass and lead acrylic of various lead equivalencies are made by manufacturers to provide different radiation protection capabilities. The

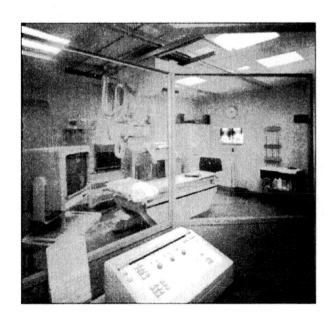

**FIGURE 7.39** Lead acrylic partition between the operator's room and the X-ray room. Courtesy of: Nuclear Associates, Carle Place, New York.

addition of lead reduces the transparency of glass somewhat depending on the lead equivalency.

### 7.11.3 Fire-Resistant Glass

Ordinary soda-lime glass (whether annealed, tempered or laminated) is not resistant to fire. When subjected to a typical building fire, it shatters in two or three minutes. The glass that is commonly used as a fire-resistant glass is wired glass. Wired glass is made by the rolling process — not by the float glass process. During the rolling process, welded wire mesh (which looks like chicken wire mesh) is embedded in the middle of glass thickness so that the resulting product is a steel wire reinforced glass, Figure 7.40.

Square or diamond shape wire mesh is commonly used. In a square mesh, the wires are nearly $5/_8$ in. (16 mm) apart, and in a diamond mesh, the diagonals do not exceed 1 in. in length. The wire diameter is nearly 0.020 in. (0.5 mm). The minimum thickness of glass recognized as fire rated glass is $1/_4$ in. (6 mm). When subjected to fire, wired glass also breaks in two to three minutes, but unlike annealed glass which falls off, wired glass is held within the opening because of the wire mesh.

Because of the embedded wires, wired glass is often confused as safety glass, which it is not. Unlike tempered glass, wired glass is not impact resistant. Additionally, its bending strength is only half that of annealed glass, see Table 7.6. On impact, wired glass breaks into sharp pieces and the broken wires will generally project out of the glass causing injury to the person. The wires can even act as a spider web on human impact and catch a victim rather than permit the person to pass through safely. Thus, although wired glass is fire resistant, it is not a safety glass.

The question arises as to which type of glass should be used in a hazardous location (subjected to human impact) which also requires fire rating. In such locations, building codes require the use of wired glass because fire-resistance requirements are generally considered by codes to override safety requirements. Although wired glass does not meet the safety requirements of CFR 1201, it has some safety features, such as the steel reinforcement. Lately however, fire rated safety glass has been introduced, which is described in Section 8.16.

**FIGURE 7.40** Wired glass in a fire rated window.

## 7.12 CRITERIA FOR THE SELECTION OF WINDOW GLASS

With so many factors to consider, the selection of glass, particularly for windows and curtain walls, is not an easy task. Evidently, the selected glass must be structurally adequate. Note once again that although tempered glass and heat strengthened glass are stronger than annealed glass, their higher strength is not generally exploited in determining glass thickness to withstand wind loads. In other words, the required glass thickness will be the same for an annealed glass or a tempered glass, or a heat strengthened glass, although the tempered and heat strengthened glasses are stronger than annealed glass. The tempered glass and heat strengthened glass are used primarily where their higher impact and (or) thermal stress resistance are required. Where greater safety or security is required, laminated glass must be considered.

Energy performance of glass usually plays an important role in its selection. For buildings with large glazed areas, the selection of a glass type should be based on detailed energy calculations by an expert. However, a general understanding of the shading coefficient, luminous efficacy, U-value and relative heat gain is normally sufficient to make the correct decision. Summarized below are some of the important features of the energy performance parameters that affect the selection of glass.

The shading coefficient describes the property of glass with respect to direct solar beam. If the direct solar beam does not fall on the glass, the shading coefficient is of no relevance. The smaller the shading coefficient, the smaller the heat transmitted through the glass from direct solar beam. A tinted or reflective glass has a low shading coefficient, and a tinted reflective glass has an even lower shading coefficient. For warm climates, a glass with a low shading coefficient is desirable. However, in extremely cold climates, it may be advantageous to use clear glass to admit a greater amount of solar radiation provided it does not cause excessive glare and fading of interior colors.

The reduction of shading coefficient by reflective coatings and tinting of glass is usually accompanied by a reduction of visible (light) transmittance. Thus, although a smaller shading coefficient reduces the transmission of solar heat, it also reduces the entry of daylight through glass. This is generally undesirable since it increases the need for artificial lighting, thereby increasing the energy use. A glass with a high luminous efficacy provides a good balance between the need to increase daylight admission and reduce the shading coefficient.

While shading coefficient comes into effect only when a direct solar beam is incident on glass, the U-value is responsible for heat transfer through the glass at all times. Remember, the U-value is an index of heat transfer through a component with respect to the difference in external and internal air temperatures. A larger U-value means that a greater amount of heat will pass through the glass. Obviously, a glass with as low a U-value as economically feasible should be selected in all climates.

It is the U-value of an entire glazing that is important, not just that of the glass. In comparing the U-values of different glazings, the architect should ensure that their U-values are obtained from the same procedure. The computer program, WINDOW, is now an accepted procedure for determining the U-value of glazing.

Economic and aesthetic factors are other important considerations.

Sometimes, the decision may be based mainly on the aesthetic consideration. For example, the color of glass may be one of the most important criteria in some glazing decisions. Finally, building code constraints and the availability of the product must be reviewed before a final decision is made.

### 7.12.1  Energy Ratings of Fenestration

In view of the number of options, the complexity of variables, and the rapid development of new products, a need to simplify the selection of glazing products has been felt. In the United States, this task has been undertaken by the National Fenestration Rating Council (NFRC)[7.11], which rates the energy performance of windows, skylights and doors based on a single number criterion. The objective of NFRC rating is to compare one fenestration product with another. NFRC publishes a directory of rated windows, skylights and doors.

**REVIEW QUESTIONS**

| | |
|---|---|
| **7.1** | Explain why glass is referred to as a supercooled liquid. |
| **7.2** | With the help of a sketch and notes, describe the float glass manufacturing process. |
| **7.3** | Why is the glass obtained from the float glass manufacturing process called "annealed glass"? |
| **7.4** | What is tempered glass? How does it differ from annealed glass? Where is it commonly used? |
| **7.5** | What is spontaneous breakage of glass? How does it occur? |
| **7.6** | What is heat strengthened glass? Where would you recommend its use? Explain with the help of a sketch. |
| **7.7** | What is shading coefficient? On what factors does it depend? |
| **7.8** | With the help of a sketch, show how the solar beam is reflected, transmitted and absorbed by clear glass. Give also the approximate relative values of reflected transmitted and absorbed components. |
| **7.9** | Repeat the above sketch for a reflective glass in which the reflective coating is on (i) the inside surface, (ii) the outside surface of glass. |
| **7.10** | Why do some cities ban the use of reflective glass on building exteriors? |
| **7.11** | Explain the greenhouse effect as related to a glass enclosure. |
| **7.12** | Explain what a low-E glass is. On which surface of an insulating glass unit is the low-E coating usually applied, and why? Explain with the help of a sketch. |
| **7.13** | With the help of a sketch, explain the construction of an insulating glass unit. |
| **7.14** | What is the approximate U-value of: (i) a single glass sheet, (ii) an insulating glass unit with an air cavity, (iii) an insulating glass unit with argon filling and low-E coating. |
| **7.15** | Describe the following properties of glass: (i) luminous efficacy and (ii) relative heat gain. |
| **7.16** | In a glass curtain wall, the supporting vertical framing members are spaced 4 ft on center and the horizontal members at 7 ft on center. Determine if $1/4$ in. thick annealed glass is adequate for the wall. Wind load is 35 psf and the required probability of glass breakage is 8/1000. |
| **7.17** | In the curtain wall of Question 7.16, what is the maximum wind load that can be imposed on the wall if the probability of breakage is 1/1000? |
| **7.18** | Determine the maximum glass area for a $1/2$ in. thick window glass subjected to a wind load of 40 psf. Probability of breakage is 1/2000. |
| **7.19** | What is safety glass? Which types of glass qualify as safety glass? |

**7.20**   With the help of a sketch, show the construction of laminated glass. Where is it commonly used?

**7.21**   Name the two types of plastics that are used as glazing materials. What are their relative advantages and disadvantages?

**7.22**   With reference to Sweet's Catalog, list three manufacturers of flat glass in the United States.

**REFERENCES**   7.1   Newman, Harold: *An Illustrated Dictionary of Glass*, Thames and Hudson, Publishers, London, 1977, p. 82.

7.2   Peter, John: *Design With Glass*, Reinhold Publishing Corporation, 1964, p. 9.

7.3   American Society for Testing and Materials, Philadelphia, Pennsylvania: "Standard Specifications for Heat Treated Flat Glass" ASTM C 1048-92.

7.4   Valdes, Noel: "Low-E Glass", The Construction Specifier, Vol. 44, No. 8, 1988, p. 74.

7.5   American Society of Heating, Refrigeration and Air Conditioning Engineers, Atlanta, Georgia: *ASHRAE Handbook of Fundamentals*, 1989, p. 27.21.

7.6   Schuman, Jennifer: "Cool Daylight", Progressive Architecture, April 1992.

7.7   International Conference of Building Officials, Whittier, California: *Uniform Building Code Standards*, 1988, p. 1216. Reproduced from the 1994 edition of the *Uniform Building Code* TM, copyright© 1994, with the permission of the publisher, the International Conference of Building Officials.

7.8   American Architectural Manufacturers Association, Palatine, Illinois: *Structural Properties of Glass*, 1984, p. 87.

7.9   American Society for Testing and Materials, Philadelphia, Pennsylvania: "Standard Practice for Determining the Minimum Thickness of Annealed Glass Required to Resist a Specified Load", ASTM E 1300-94.

7.10   Kellman, Cheri: "Selecting Glass for Zoos and Aquariums", The Construction Specifier, Volume 44, No.3, March 1991, p. 102.

7.11   Berger, Robert: "NFRC's Energy Rating System for Windows and Patio Doors", The Construction Specifier, Vol. 44, No. 3, March 1991, p. 87.

# 8

# FIRE-RELATED PROPERTIES

**8.1 INTRODUCTION**

Fires that used to engulf an entire neighborhood or a city[1] are rare these days. Fires, in the modern time, are generally limited to individual buildings or a small group of buildings. This is due to sustained improvements in fire safety and zoning regulations, and several advances in fire detection and suppression equipment used in buildings. If fire safety considerations were less stringent than those currently in use, the fire of the severity shown in Figure 8.1 would have not only caused the total destruction and collapse of this building but a domino effect that would have burnt and destroyed a large area of the city.

However, despite various improvements in fire-safe design and construction, the frequency of building fires and the resulting property losses are still substantial. In the United States, approximately 1.2 million fires occurred in 1988, resulting in a total property loss of nearly 11.5 billion dollars[8.1]. The actual losses are in fact much greater since indirect losses resulting from interruptions in business operations cannot be accurately estimated and are not included in these figures. In certain cases, such as libraries and museums, fire causes irreparable damages.

The statistics of deaths and injuries resulting from fires are equally appalling. Fire continues to be the single largest killer of building occupants.

---

[1] Although forest fires are fairly common in contemporary times, the types of fires such as the Great Fire of London of 1666 which lasted several days and nights and destroyed virtually half the city of London, are thankfully a thing of the past.

Fire-gutted floors

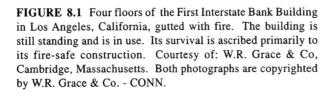

**FIGURE 8.1** Four floors of the First Interstate Bank Building in Los Angeles, California, gutted with fire. The building is still standing and is in use. Its survival is ascribed primarily to its fire-safe construction. Courtesy of: W.R. Grace & Co, Cambridge, Massachusetts. Both photographs are copyrighted by W.R. Grace & Co. - CONN.

By comparison, natural disasters, such as earthquakes, hurricanes and floods, account for a much smaller toll of lives, and deaths caused by structural failures of buildings are rare these days. For instance, in the United States, an average of nearly 6,000 civilians (excluding fire fighters) die and nearly 31,000 individuals are injured annually in building fires[2]. Some of the injured suffer from life-long disabilities and many find it difficult to recoup from psychological and emotional aftereffects of fire.

It is because of the above facts that fire-related provisions are the most important provisions in modern building codes. Fire is the biggest hazard to life safety in modern buildings and the codes recognize this fact by making fire protection an important objective. For example, the classification of buildings in various occupancy groups, as provided in building codes, is based primarily on the degree of fire hazard present in buildings. The maximum permissible area and the height of a building are also based on the ability of various components of the building to withstand fire. In fact, if the structural engineering provisions are disregarded, then nearly three-quarters of building code regulations, in one way or another, relate to fire safety considerations.

Fire safety in buildings is a function of several variables, which may be grouped under the following four headings: (i) architectural design, (ii) construction materials and systems, (iii) fire detection and suppression, and (iv) public education, Figure 8.2.

---

[2] Fire death rates in the United States and Canada are nearly twice as high as those in Europe (Reference 8.2, p. 1-4).

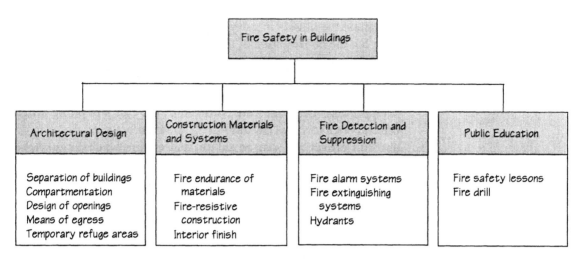

**FIGURE 8.2** Elements of fire safety in buildings.

Fire-safe architectural design, an extensive area of study in itself, is outside the scope of this text. Briefly, it involves the design of all such features of a building which reduce fire hazard and assist in speedy evacuation of people in the event of a fire. These features include: separation of one building from another; compartmentation of building to contain the fire within the enclosure of its origin; design of openings in walls and floors to inhibit vertical spread of fire; design of the means of egress such as corridors, foyers, aisles, stairways, ramps and exterior balconies; and the location of temporary refuge areas in critical buildings such as high-rise structures and hospitals where the occupants can wait in relative safety until evacuated through external help or until the fire is extinguished.

Fire detection and suppression covers fire alarm systems, fire sprinklers, fire hydrants, stand pipes and other firefighting equipment.

In this text, we are concerned only with the elements of fire-safe materials and construction which includes the study of fire endurance of materials, fire resistive construction and the characteristics of interior finishes.

## 8.2 FIRE CODES AND BUILDING CODES

In addition to the building code, a building is also regulated by the jurisdiction's fire code. As mentioned in Section 1.2, a building code contains provisions which relate to the the design and construction of buildings. With the exception of aesthetic issues, every aspect of a building's design and construction is regulated by building codes. But once the building has been built and occupied, it must be maintained to remain safe against fire and other hazards. The regulations that cover aspects of fire safety in a building during its use and occupancy are dealt with in a *fire prevention code*, or simply a *fire code*.

Thus, a fire code regulates such items as the location, maintenance and installation of fire protection appliances, maintenance of exit ways, and the storage of combustible and (or) hazardous materials. For example, the storage of flammable liquids in a dry cleaning establishment is regulated by the fire code but the construction of the enclosure to store the flammable liquids and the requirement for an automatic fire suppression system are contained within the appropriate building code.

The building code and the fire code are two arms of a city's building safety ordinances. They are enforced by the city's building official and fire official respectively. Because the distinction between fire-safe construction and fire prevention can be subtle, and at times indistinguishable, there is always a certain amount of overlap between the fire code and building code provisions. The fire department and building department of a city are expected to work in close cooperation, since the aims of both are the same — to ensure public safety.

The principal fire code in the United States is the Fire Prevention Code published by the National Fire Protection Association (NFPA). However, in order to ensure compatibility and correlation between the building code and the fire code, each model code organization publishes its own fire code which is usually based on the NFPA code. A jurisdiction will generally adopt the building code and fire code of the same model code organization.

## 8.3 COMBUSTIBLE AND NONCOMBUSTIBLE MATERIALS

In the context of fire-safe construction, building materials are divided in two categories: *combustible* and *noncombustible materials*. Metals used in construction (iron, steel, aluminum, copper, etc.), and ceramic materials (concrete, brick, stone, gypsum, etc.) are noncombustible materials. Wood, paper, wool and plastics are combustible materials.

While the distinction between a combustible and a noncombustible material is generally obvious, it is not always so. For example, it is not clear whether fire retardant treated wood is a combustible or a noncombustible material. Additionally, some materials may contain a small combustible content which may not contribute appreciably to fire, such as concrete made with polystyrene beads as aggregate. Are these materials to be considered as combustible or noncombustible materials?

Building codes define a noncombustible material as one of which no part will ignite when subjected to fire. More precisely, a noncombustible material is one which passes ASTM Test E 136: "Test Method for Behavior of Materials in a Vertical Tube Furnace at 750 °C". In this test[8.3], a pre-dried specimen of the material measuring 1.5 in. x 1.5 in. (38 mm x 38 mm) in cross-section and 2 in. (50 mm) in length is placed in a cylindrical furnace measuring 3 in. (75 mm) in diameter and 10 in. (260 mm) in length.

The furnace has a transparent fire-resistant top so that the specimen can be visually inspected during testing. Before placing the specimen in the furnace, the furnace is raised to a temperature of 1,382 °F (750 °C). The specimen is weighed before and after the test.

The material is reported as noncombustible if it satisfies all the following conditions:

- The temperature of the furnace or of the specimen does not increase by 54 °F (30 °C) above the initial temperature of the furnace at any time during the test.

- No flaming of the specimen occurs after the first 30 seconds.
- If the weight loss of the specimen during the test exceeds 50% of its original weight, then the recorded temperature of the specimen at any time during the test shall not rise above the initial temperature of the furnace, and there shall be no flaming of the specimen.

The restrictions of 30 seconds and 54 °F recognize that a brief period of flaming and a small increase in temperature are not serious limitations of a material which may otherwise satisfy the test. It has been found that if a material remains within the above limitations, its combustible fraction is less than 3 percent.

The 50% weight loss restriction is included because some low density materials burn so rapidly that the temperature rise of the furnace is less than 54 °F and the flaming, if it occurs, is also limited to the first 30 seconds. Thus, although the material is combustible, it satisfies the first two conditions. The weight loss condition is to identify such materials as combustible materials.

Fire retardant treated plywood and solid lumber which have been pressure treated with fire retardant chemicals do not satisfy the above conditions and are therefore classified as combustible materials. However, recognizing that fire retardant treated wood makes reduced contribution as fuel in the early stages of fire, building codes permit its use in some limited situations where only the noncombustible materials are allowed. For example, permanent partitions in commercial buildings which may otherwise be required to be of noncombustible materials (metal stud and gypsum board assemblies) may be constructed of fire retardant treated wood framing.

ASTM E 136 test is applicable only to elementary materials, not to laminated or coated materials. In recognition of the fact that a material with a noncombustible core as defined by the above test, but with a facing of a combustible material or a combustible paint, does not contribute greatly to fire, building codes classify such materials as noncombustible materials, Figure 8.3. The constraints placed on the combustible paint or laminate are that its thickness shall not exceed $1/_8$ in. (3 mm) and its flame spread rating shall not exceed 50 (see Section 8.9 for the explanation of flame spread rating).

Note that noncombustibility refers only to the fact that a noncombustible material will not add fuel to the fire. Noncombustibility is not related to the ability of the material to withstand fire. For example, wood is a combustible material and steel, a noncombustible material, but a structure constructed of heavy sections of wood is better able to withstand fire than the one constructed of unprotected steel members.

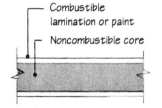

**FIGURE 8.3** A material with a noncombustible core but with a combustible lamination of less than $1/_8$ in. thickness is regarded as a noncombustible material.

## 8.4 FIRE BASICS

Fire or combustion is a chemical reaction between a fuel and oxygen. In this reaction, which is also called oxidation, the molecules of fuel (combustible material) react with the molecules of oxygen to produce flammable gaseous oxides. The reaction is exothermic, implying that heat is produced during the reaction. Thus:

$$\text{Combustible material (fuel)} + \text{Oxygen} \longrightarrow \text{Flammable gases} + \text{Heat}$$

The oxidation of a combustible material, as shown above, is not unique to fire but occurs commonly in nature. The corrosion of iron is caused by the oxidation of iron. Human metabolism, in which the body converts food into energy, is also through the process of oxidation. The food we eat reacts with the oxygen we inhale. This reaction produces the energy that sustains us. The only difference between the oxidation within our bodies and the oxidation of a combustible material is that in the latter case, the oxidation is so rapid that it produces fire.

The oxidation reaction in the case of fire is not self starting. It will not start just because the combustible material and oxygen are in contact with each other. At normal temperature and pressure, the combustible material (except a few flammable liquids and gases) and oxygen do not react with each other. The application of heat to the mixture is required to start the reaction. Once the reaction has continued for some time with the aid of an external heat source, a stage is reached when the heat given off by the reaction increases the temperature of the material so that the reaction becomes self sustaining, and the external heat source is no longer required.

The chemical reaction between the material and oxygen is necessary before the material will ignite. But the presence of a chemical reaction alone is not enough to ignite the material. For ignition to occur, a pilot flame, spark or a glowing object is usually required. After ignition has started, the heat given off by combustion is usually more than the heat required to sustain the combustion. This cycle continues until all the fuel has been oxidized.

### 8.4.1 Growth of Fire in an Enclosure

In its initial stage, a building fire is always localized to a small area of the enclosure. As the fire progresses, various combustible items in the enclosure get heated and give off flammable gases. These gases diffuse and collect in the upper portion of the enclosure. When the concentration of gases and their temperature reach appropriate levels, a stage is reached when the gases suddenly ignite and the fire which was previously localized now engulfs the entire enclosure. This stage is called *flash-over* and is characterized by its abruptness. After the flash-over, the fire grows rapidly. When all the contents in the enclosure have been consumed, the fire begins to decay.

Flash-over is highly dangerous and is accompanied by: (i) an extremely rapid increase in the temperature of the enclosure, (ii) a sudden decrease in the quantity of oxygen, and (iii) an increase in the levels of carbon monoxide to lethal levels. Thus, an escape from the enclosure after the flash-over is virtually impossible. Firefighters have to be constantly aware of this phenomenon when fighting fires in buildings.

Sometimes, a change in room condition, such as the breaking of a window (due to heat) or the opening of a door in a sealed room, may trigger flash-over. This happens in a room where the conditions are otherwise ripe for a flash-over except the availability of sufficient oxygen. The opening of the door or window provides that necessary oxygen for flash-over.

Large enclosures such as those found in industrial structures or atriums in modern shopping malls may not experience flash-over during a fire because an adequate amount and concentration of gases to fill the entire enclosure is not obtained. In such enclosures, the fire may fully develop in an area without involving the entire enclosure.

### 8.4.2 Products of Combustion

We have seen that heat is always produced in a combustion reaction. The other product of combustion is smoke. Smoke consists of (i) fire gases, (ii) solid particulate matter, representing finely divided particles of solid matter suspended in the atmosphere, and (iii) liquid particulate matter, representing condensed vapors dispersed in the atmosphere as tiny liquid droplets, Figure 8.4. While fire gases in smoke are generally transparent, the solid and liquid particulate matter form an opaque cloud and diminish visibility in a fire.

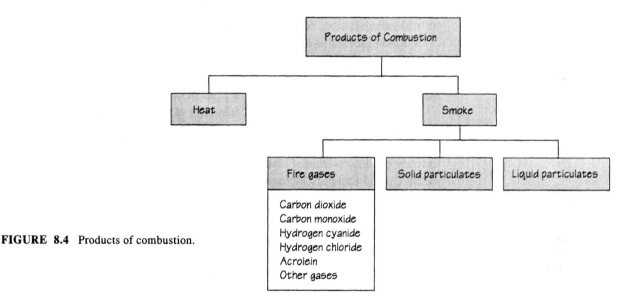

**FIGURE 8.4** Products of combustion.

Several different types of fire gases are produced in a combustion reaction depending on the type of material that burns. Carbon dioxide and carbon monoxide are produced in almost all fires. If a sufficient supply of oxygen (air) is available during the fire, the carbon which is present in almost every combustible material such as wood, cotton, silk, wool, plastics, etc., is converted to carbon dioxide ($CO_2$). This type of combustion is called complete combustion. However, most fires take place under conditions of incomplete combustion. In an incomplete combustion, the amount of oxygen available is less than that required for complete combustion. In such a case, carbon monoxide (CO) is produced.

Other gases produced in a fire may include hydrogen cyanide, hydrogen chloride, acrolein, etc. Hydrogen cyanide is produced from the burning of wool, silk, leather, rayon, and plastics containing nitrogen. Hydrogen chloride is produced from polyvinyl chloride (pvc). Acrolein is produced from wood and paper.

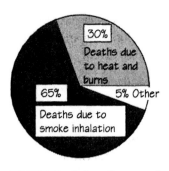

**FIGURE 8.5** Causes of deaths in a building fire.

Both products of combustion — smoke and heat — are responsible for human deaths and injuries. In other words, deaths and injuries in a building fire may occur due to burns, or smoke inhalation, or both. The statistics based on autopsies conducted on people who died in building fires indicate that smoke inhalation accounts for nearly 65% of all deaths[8.4]. The burns account for 30%, and the remaining 5% of deaths are caused by emotional shock and heart failure, Figure 8.5.

### 8.4.3 Toxic Effects of Smoke

All gases produced in a combustion reaction are toxic to humans in varying degrees. However, carbon monoxide is considered the major threat to human life in building fires. Although not the most toxic of fire gases, it is always present in such large quantities that its overall toxic effect is most devastating. It is estimated that nearly 50% of fatalities in building fires which are caused by smoke inhalation, occur due to the effect of carbon monoxide.

Carbon dioxide is also present in large quantities in a fire but its toxicity is 50 times lower than that of carbon monoxide. For example, 5,000 parts per million (ppm) concentration of carbon dioxide in the atmosphere has the same toxic effect on humans as 100 ppm of carbon monoxide[8.5].

At the present time, building codes do not regulate the toxicity of smoke produced by the burning of building materials and interior finishes. Statistics, however, indicate that if the total fatalities in building fires are to be reduced, toxicity of materials must be curbed. The state of New York is the first state in the United States to have compiled a fire gas toxicity database for nearly 500,000 building products such as electrical wire insulation, electrical conduit pipes, thermal insulation and interior finish products[8.6]. In this database, records of toxicity have been obtained from a standard toxicity test which measures toxicity based on the $LC_{50}$ criterion. The $LC_{50}$ measurement gives the mass of the tested product which when heated as per the standard test, produces fire gases lethal to 50% of test animals. The smaller the $LC_{50}$ value, the more toxic the material.

It is expected that the toxicity data will help design professionals to specify safer products. It will also help identify materials which are relatively more hazardous so that manufacturers will take measures to improve their performance or withdraw them from the market.

### 8.4.4 Effect of Smoke on Visibility

The solid particulate matter in smoke consists primarily of unoxidized carbon in the form of extremely small particles suspended in the atmosphere. Incomplete combustion produces greater amounts of solid particles. The liquid particulate matter comprises mainly water vapor and tar droplets. Both the solid and liquid particles scatter light and hence reduce visibility.

Although reduced visibility has no direct effect on fire fatalities, it impedes the escape of a building's occupants and prolongs their exposure to toxic gases and heat. This often results in panic conditions which are known to have caused several deaths in building fires. Smoke also has irritating effects on eyes and lungs and this may result in serious medical problems.

**8.5 FIRE-RESISTANCE RATING OF A BARRIER**

One of the important design strategies employed to reduce fire hazard in a building is to subdivide it into small compartments so that the fire is limited to the compartment of origin. This strategy is based on the fact that the fire will either extinguish itself after a while due to the lack of oxygen in the compartment or take some time to spread to other compartments. During this period, the occupants can be relocated to a place of safety.

The concept of compartmentation, as shown in Figure 8.6, assumes that the barriers (walls, floors and roofs) bounding the compartment will be of such construction that a burn-out of the fuel in the compartment will not seriously affect the adjacent compartments. To meet this criterion, a barrier should satisfy the following three requirements:

- The barrier should be able to perform its structural function without collapse, i.e., it should be able to sustain the loads for which it has been designed throughout the duration of the fire.
- The barrier should remain firetight, i.e., it should develop no cracks during the duration of the fire. The purpose of this requirement is to ensure that smoke and flames will not spread to adjacent compartments.
- The temperature of the unexposed face of the barrier during a fire should be so low that the heat received by radiation and (or) conduction from the barrier will not ignite combustibles in adjacent compartments.

When exposed to a fire for a sufficient length of time, all barriers regardless of their material will eventually crack, disintegrate and collapse. Thus, a barrier can satisfy the above requirements for a limited duration only. The ability of a component to endure fire for the duration during which it satisfies all the above requirements, is called the *fire-resistance rating*, or simply the *fire rating* of the component.

Requirements of a fire-resistive barrier

- Structural integrity
- Fire tightness
- Low temperature of unexposed surfaces

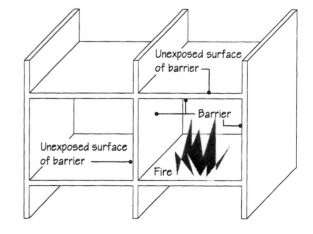

**FIGURE 8.6** The concept of compartmentation and the requirements of a barrier to withstand fire.

In other words, the fire rating is the ability of the barrier to confine the fire to the enclosure of its origin for a particular duration. Accordingly, it is measured in the units of time, i.e., in hours or fractions thereof. Thus, a one-hour fire rating means that the assembly can endure a typical building fire for at least one hour. A two-hour fire rating means that it can endure fire for two hours or more. Note that by virtue of its definition, fire rating is a property of building components such as walls, floors, roofs, doors and windows, and not simply of the materials of which the components are constructed. Thus, the fire rating of a material, such as concrete or wood, is meaningless.

### 8.5.1 Building Code Requirements for Fire Rating

The fire rating of walls, floors, roofs and columns, as required by building codes, varies with the type of construction. In fact, the classification of buildings by the type of construction is based on the fire rating of walls (loadbearing and nonloadbearing), and the structural components of the building (floors, roofs and the structural frame). The higher the fire rating of these components, the better the type of construction. For a given occupancy (see Section 1.7), building codes allow greater area and greater height for a more fire-resistive type of construction.

The fire rating requirement of building components (walls, floors, roofs, structural frame and permanent partitions) is generally given in terms of integral (whole number) hours. Thus, the building codes require these components to be rated as 0, 1, 2, 3 or 4 hours. The maximum fire rating required by building codes for any component is 4 hours.

A building is classified in one of the nine different types of construction, as shown in Table 8.1 These nine categories are subcategories of the five basic construction types: Type I, Type II, Type III, Type IV, and Type V in decreasing degree of fire resistiveness[3]. In Types I and II, walls and structural components must be of noncombustible materials (concrete, steel or masonry). In Type V, all components may be of wood. In Types III and IV, external walls must be of noncombustible materials while other components may be of wood. That is why Type III and IV are grouped as noncombustible/ combustible construction types.

Type I is the most fire-resistive construction and Type V-N, the least fire-resistive. Although not expressly mentioned, Type III and Type V are of wood light frame construction. The difference between them is that, in Type III, external walls are required to be of noncombustible materials and if they are loadbearing, they must have a minimum of 4-hour fire rating. In Type V, the external walls may be of combustible or noncombustible materials.

Type IV is called *heavy timber* (HT) construction. In this construction, floors, roofs and the structural frame are of heavy sections of wood without any added gypsum board or similar protection. In other words, in heavy timber construction, the wood members are exposed. Heavy timber construction is slow burning and is assumed to provide an equivalent of one

---

[3] The classification described here is as per the Uniform Building Code. The other two model building codes follow a similar classification.

hour fire protection, see Section 8.12.1. Thus, the overall fire endurance of HT construction type is generally considered equivalent to Type III-1 hr. Examples of a few construction types are shown in Figures 8.7, 8.8 and 8.9.

For a building to be classified as a given type of construction, the fire ratings of various components must either be equal to or greater than those given in Table 8.1. Note that fire ratings given in Table 8.1 are minimum fire ratings. A building cannot be designated as a particular type unless it meets all the minimum fire rating requirements for that type of construction.

**Table 8.1  Classification of the Types of Construction According to the Fire-Resistance Rating of Building Components**

| Component | Noncombustible types | | | | Noncombustible/ combustible types | | Combustible types | | |
|---|---|---|---|---|---|---|---|---|---|
| | Type I | Type II | | | Type III | | Type IV (HT)[1] | Type V | |
| | FR[2] | FR[2] | 1-hr. | N[3] | 1-hr. | N[3] | | 1-hr. | N[3] |
| Bearing walls (Exterior) | 4 | 4 | 1 | N[3] | 4 | 4 | 4 | 1 | N[3] |
| Bearing walls (Interior) | 3 | 2 | 1 | N[3] | 1 | N[3] | 1 | 1 | N[3] |
| Nonbearing walls (Exterior[4]) | 4 | 4 | 1 | N[3] | 4 | 4 | 4 | 1 | N[3] |
| Structural frame[5] | 3 | 2 | 1 | N[3] | 1 | N[3] | 1 or HT | 1 | N[3] |
| Permanent partitions | 1 | 1 | 1 | N[3] | 1 | N[3] | 1 | 1 | N[3] |
| Floors and floor-ceilings | 2 | 2 | 1 | N[3] | 1 | N[3] | HT | 1 | N[3] |
| Roofs and roof-ceilings | 2 | 1 | 1 | N[3] | 1 | N[3] | HT | 1 | N[3] |

[1] "HT" stands for heavy timber.
[2] "FR" stands for fire-resistive type.
[3] "N" stands for non-fire-rated construction, i.e., no general requirements for fire resistance.
[4] The fire-resistance rating of exterior nonbearing walls may be reduced if the wall is adequately spaced away from adjacent buildings or property line. In most cases, if the exterior nonbearing wall fronts on a sufficiently wide street or open space, as required by the code, it may be of non-fire-rated construction, but must be of noncombustible material for Types I, II, III and IV.
[5] Structural frame includes columns and beams.
Source:  This table is an abridged version of Table 6-A, *Uniform Building Code*, 1994, printed with permission. See original table for complete details. Reference 8.16.

---

**Example 8.1**

Using Table 8.1, determine the type of construction of a building in which the materials and fire ratings of different components are as given in the following table.

| Component | Material used | Fire rating (hrs) |
|---|---|---|
| Bearing walls (exterior) | None provided | - |
| Bearing walls (interior) | None provided | - |
| Nonbearing walls (exterior) | Concrete and brick masonry | 4 |
| Structural frame | Reinforced concrete | 2 |
| Permanent partitions | Metal studs and gypsum board | 1 |
| Floor-ceiling assembly | Reinforced concrete | 2 |
| Roof-ceiling assembly | Steel deck | 2 |

*Solution*: Since all components are of noncombustible materials, the building will be classified as Type I or Type II. Comparing the fire ratings of the building's components with those of Table 8.1, the building is classified as Type II-FR.

**Example 8.2**

What changes must be made in the materials and fire ratings of components to upgrade the construction of Example 8.1 to Type I -FR?

*Solution*: Examining the fire ratings required for Type I-FR construction in Table 8.1, we see that if the fire rating of structural frame of the building of Example 8.1 is increased to a minimum of 3 hours, it will be classified as Type I-FR construction.

**Example 8.3**

What will be the construction type of building of Example 8.1 if permanent partitions are constructed of 2 x 4 wood studs (instead of metal studs) with a 1-hr fire rating?

**FIGURE 8.7** Unprotected steel frame construction — an example of a Type II-N construction.

*Solution:* Since partitions are of combustible construction, the building can no longer be classified as Type II. Note that to qualify as Type I or II, all components must be of noncombustible materials. From Table 8.1, the revised classification for this building is Type III-1 hr.

However, if the partitions were constructed of fire retardant treated wood, the building will be able to retain its classification as Type II-FR since building codes allow the substitution of fire retardant treated wood for noncombustible materials in partition walls.

## Example 8.4

Determine the type of construction for the building in which the materials and fire ratings of different components are as follows:

| Component | Material used | Fire rating (hrs) |
|---|---|---|
| Bearing walls (exterior) | Concrete and brick masonry | 4 |
| Bearing walls (interior) | Concrete masonry | 2 |
| Nonbearing walls (exterior) | Concrete and brick masonry | 2 |
| Structural frame | None provided | - |
| Permanent partitions | Wood studs and gypsum board | 1 |
| Floor-ceiling assembly | Wood joists and plywood floor | 1 |
| Roof-ceiling assembly | Wood trusses and plywood sheathing | 1 |

*Solution:* Since some components are of combustible materials, the building will be classified as Type III or Type V. Type IV is ruled out since the roofs and floors are not constructed of heavy timber. Comparing the given fire ratings with those of Table 8.1, we observe that the building can be classified as Type III-1 hr, provided the exterior nonbearing walls meet the code requirements with respect to their separation distances from adjacent buildings or property lines, see Note 4 under Table 8.1.

**FIGURE 8.8** A building with heavy timber structural frame — an example of a Type IV (HT) construction.

**FIGURE 8.9** Wood light frame protected by $1/2$ in. thick gypsum board on interior surfaces is a typical example of Type V-N construction.

### 8.5.2 Stair and Elevator Shafts

Stairways, ramps and elevators in buildings function as openings in floors. If not enclosed all around by a vertical enclosure (shaft), floor openings compromise the compartmentation ability of the floor, and hence its fire resistiveness. Stairways, ramps and elevators must therefore be enclosed all around by fire rated walls. In the case of stairways for example, building codes generally require shaft walls to have a minimum of 1-hour fire rating in buildings of up to three stories in height. In buildings of four or more stories in height, a 2-hour rating is required of stairway shaft walls. Requirements for elevator shafts are similar.

The only exception to the requirement of enclosing a stairway is a supplemental stairway between two adjacent floors which serves as a means of communication between two floors, and is not an exit stairway. Stairways in single family dwellings, and apartment buildings up to four floors in height, are also exempt from this requirement. Exceptions are also made in the case of escalators, but there are other requirements to ensure that escalator openings do not compromise the compartmentation ability of the floor.

Even when enclosed all around, a stairway functions as a chimney stack. This causes hot gases, smoke and particulate matter to flow upward and spread into the upper floors. Building codes, therefore, restrict the size of openings (doors and windows) and their fire ratings in stairway shafts.

**8.6 ASTM E 119 TEST**    Although analytical tools are available to calculate the fire rating of a few limited types of building assemblies, the most reliable approach to obtain a fire rating is to test the assembly according to the standard fire test. Several laboratories are equipped to conduct the test. In the United States, the two more commonly used laboratories are the Underwriters Laboratories Inc., and Inchtape Testing Services. In Canada, the Underwriters Laboratory of Canada is most commonly used.

The fire ratings of assemblies tested by the Underwriters Laboratories are given in its annual publication entitled the *Directory of Fire Resistance*[8.7]. Inchtape Testing Services and the Underwriters Laboratory of Canada publish similar directories[8.8, 8.9]. These are the most comprehensive sources available to obtain the fire ratings of assemblies. Additionally, model codes generally give tables listing the fire ratings of commonly used construction assemblies. For assemblies using gypsum board, the *Fire Resistance Design Manual* published by the Gypsum Association[8.10] is a valuable reference and is recognized by all three model building codes.

The test procedure that is used to measure the fire rating of a component is ASTM E 119 "Standard Test Methods for Fire Tests of Building Construction and Materials". This test procedure[8.11] is applicable to measuring the fire-resistance ratings of:

- Loadbearing and nonloadbearing walls;
- Floors and roofs; and
- Columns.

### 8.6.1 Test Furnace Used in ASTM E 119 Test

In this test procedure, the component is exposed to fire in a specially designed furnace whose temperature is controlled according to the standard time-temperature curve, Figure 8.10. The curve specifies the average furnace temperature as measured by several thermocouples placed in the furnace close to the test specimen. The temperature increase in the furnace is steep during the initial stages, rises to 1,000 °F (540 °C) in the first 5 minutes, and to 1,550 °F (840 °C) in the first 30 minutes. Subsequently, the rise is gradual so that the temperature at 4 hours is 2,000 °F (1,100 °C). The steep initial rise in the temperature curve simulates the build-up of temperature that occurs in an actual fire after the flash-over.

Two different types of furnaces are required, one for testing vertical components such as walls and columns, and the other for testing the horizontal members such as floors and roofs. Each furnace contains an opening in which

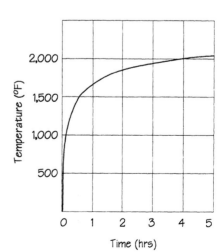

**FIGURE 8.10** Time-temperature relationship in ASTM E 119 standard fire test.

the test specimen is mounted, Figure 8.11.  If after mounting the specimen, there are any spaces left between the specimen and the opening, they are carefully sealed.  The opening for testing vertical members is obviously vertical and that for the horizontal members, horizontal.  The ASTM test neither specifies the opening size, nor the size of the furnace and its construction details, but prescribes minimum dimensions for test specimens.

The test specimen must duplicate as nearly as possible the conditions in which it is to be used in the actual building.  Thus, if the component is loadbearing, it should be loaded before heating and the load maintained throughout the test duration.  The load placed on the member is the maximum design load as specified in the structural design criteria.

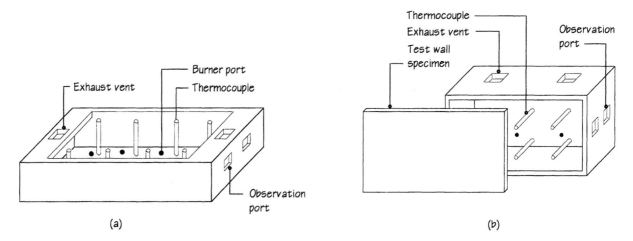

**FIGURE 8.11**  Test furnaces for: (a) floors and roof assemblies, and (b) wall assemblies and columns.

### 8.6.2 Test for Wall Assemblies

Only one face of the wall is normally exposed to fire in the test.  Obviously, this practice presents no problem with assemblies which are symmetrical in construction.  For example, a metal stud wall with $1/2$ in. (13 mm) thick gypsum board on both sides will have the same fire rating from both sides.  But what about an asymmetrical wall assembly, such as a wall with $1/2$ in. thick gypsum board on one side and $5/8$ in. (16 mm) thick gypsum board on the other side?  Asymmetrical walls will generally have two different ratings depending on the side that is exposed to the furnace.

In the test procedure, an asymmetrical wall or partition may be tested with either or both sides exposed to fire separately.  If both sides are tested, the fire rating of each side is indicated in the test report.  In the case of an interior unsymmetrical wall, building codes require that it be tested from both sides and the smaller of the two ratings be used as the fire rating of the wall.  The rationale for this provision is quite obvious since an interior wall may be exposed to fire from either side.

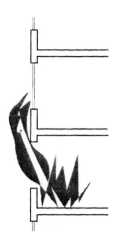

**FIGURE 8.12** A fire originating from inside a building may shatter the windows and thus expose the upper floor to fire.

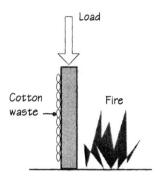

**FIGURE 8.13** Wall test specimen details in ASTM E 119 test.

Although an exterior wall is generally unsymmetrical and is not exposed to fire hazard from the outside, it may require testing from both sides. The reason is that the fire may emerge from the openings in an exterior wall to attack the unexposed side. Since the openings in an exterior wall are generally of lower fire ratings than the wall itself, the possibility exists for the exterior face of the wall to become exposed to fire, Figure 8.12. The Uniform Building Code, therefore, requires the external wall to be rated from both sides, and the smaller of the two values is considered to be the fire rating of the wall.

The BOCA National Building Code and the Standard Building Code permit the exterior walls to be tested for exposure from the inside face only provided that the wall is at least 5 ft away from an adjacent building or the property line. If the distance is less than 5 ft, the wall must be rated from both sides. The rationale is that if the distance between buildings is greater than 5 ft, hazard due to flames and radiant heat from one building to another are relatively insignificant.

The ASTM E119 test for walls is conducted until failure occurs or until the wall specimen has withstood the test for a period equal to that specified by the manufacturer of the assembly. The failure is defined to have occurred when any one of the following end point criteria are not met:
- The wall assembly continues to support the loads and maintain its structural integrity throughout the test period.
- The cotton waste placed on the unexposed face of the wall does not ignite, Figure 8.13. This criterion ensures that the assembly does not develop cracks or openings through which hot gases and smoke will pass to ignite the cotton waste.
- The average temperature of the unexposed face of the wall assembly does not exceed 250 °F (120 °C) above its initial temperature. This limitation ensures that heat does not ignite combustible materials placed in the room toward the unexposed face of the assembly.
- The wall is able to withstand the cooling and erosion effects of a stream of water from a hose directed at it from the exposed face immediately after the test.

The hose stream test assesses the ability of the wall to withstand thermal shock. Many assemblies explode under this test. The test simulates the effect of water sprinklers in an actual fire. It is conducted on a duplicate specimen after the expiry of a period equal to one-half the fire rating of the assembly, but not to exceed one hour. For instance, if the wall is rated at $1^1/_2$ hours, the specimen is exposed to the fire for 45 minutes only, immediately after which the hose stream is applied. If the wall is rated at 3 hours, the hose stream is applied at the end of one hour. The hose stream test is not required of walls whose fire rating is less than 1 hour.

### 8.6.3 Test for Floor Assemblies and Roof Assemblies

Floors and roof assemblies are tested under two different end support classifications:
- Restrained classification in which the assembly is restrained against expansion at the supports.

- Unrestrained classification in which the edges and ends of the assembly are free to expand and rotate at the supports.

Contrary to common belief, the restrained classification for a given assembly usually has a higher fire rating than the unrestrained classification. This is due to the greater structural redundancy present in restrained assemblies than in unrestrained ones. Restrained classification, therefore, should be assumed to exist only when the assembly is capable of resisting substantial thermal expansion. Since the degree of end restraints is difficult to assess, ASTM E 119 includes guidelines to determine whether the assembly will behave in a restrained or unrestrained manner in an actual construction.

Both floors and roofs are required to be tested from the underside only. Since heat and flame travel in space by convection and radiation, their direction of travel is upward. As such, exposure to fire from beneath the floor or the roof represents the worst case. If a floor or roof has a suspended or an attached ceiling, it should be included in the test assembly.

The ASTM E 119 test does not evaluate the performance of roof coverings such as a built-up roof covering, single ply roof covering, or shingle roof covering. Roof coverings are evaluated under ASTM E 108 "Standard Methods for Fire Test of Roof Coverings".

The failure of the assembly is assumed to have occurred when any one of the four end point criteria as given in Figure 8.14 are not met. The first three criteria are the same as those for wall assemblies. The fourth criterion refers to the temperature of structural steel members and steel reinforcement provided in reinforced concrete members. Since steel looses its strength substantially when heated, its temperature is monitored during the test.

The assembly must maintain its structural integrity throughout the test period.

Cotton waste placed on the unexposed face should not ignite.

The temperature of the unexposed face should not exceed 250 °F above the ambient temperature.

The temperature of structural steel members recorded at several points should not exceed an average of 1,100 °F.

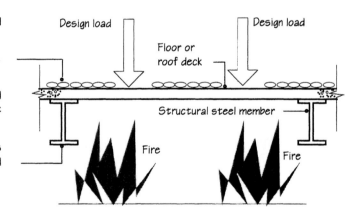

**FIGURE 8.14** Conditions of acceptance of a successful test for floor or roof assemblies.

### 8.6.4 Test for Columns

A column test specimen must, as far as possible, duplicate the construction details as contemplated in the design. The height of the column should be the same as in the actual design but not less than 9 ft (2.7 m). The column should be exposed from all four sides and tested under the full design load. The only criterion for a successful test is that the column should be able to withstand the loads throughout the test period.

## 8.7 FIRE-RATED OPENINGS

A fire-resistive wall or partition can serve as a barrier to the spread of fire only if the openings (doors and windows) installed in them also provide the same (or nearly the same) degree of fire protection. Building codes require a minimum level of fire protection of door or window assemblies that are provided in fire rated walls.

The fire protection ratings of openings in fire-rated walls is usually required to be lower than the fire ratings of walls in which they are installed. For example, in a 4-hour rated wall a 3-hour rated door is considered adequate. The provision of an opening with a lower fire protection rating than the wall in which it is installed does not greatly compromise the overall integrity of the wall. The reason is that, under normal conditions of use, there is usually a lower fire hazard in the vicinity of an opening as compared with the rest of the wall. For example in the case of a door, there is clear space on both sides of the door to provide for unobstructed traffic. Hence, the availability of fuel in close proximity to the door, and the resulting fire hazard, is less than in the rest of the wall. Another reason is that the total opening area in fire-rated walls is usually so limited by building codes, that a lower protection of openings does not greatly reduce the overall effectiveness of the wall.

Note that in referring to openings, we have used the term "fire protection rating" and not "fire-resistance rating". This is because the "opening protection" is not rated according to ASTM E 119 test, but according to ASTM E 152[8.12] and ASTM E 163[8.13]. However, there is great deal of similarity between ASTM E 119 test and the tests used for rating opening protection.

Reference to a "rated" opening implies that the entire assembly is rated. The assembly consists of the door (or window), door frame (or window frame), anchorages, sill, knobs, latches, hinges, etc. Building codes require that a fire-rated door or window and its frame bear an approved label or other identification showing its rating, Figure 8.15.

### 8.7.1 Fire Doors

Fire-rated door assemblies (or simply fire doors) are rated at 3 hours, $1^1/_2$ hours, 1 hour, and $^3/_4$ hour. In order for a fire door to be effective, it must remain in a closed position. Therefore, a fire door must be self closing. However, recognizing that a fire door may be required to remain in an open position for functional reasons, codes require that a fire door which is not self closing must be provided with an automatic closing device that activates in the event of a fire.

In addition to the hourly ratings, fire doors in exit enclosures, such as stairways and exit corridors and foyers, must meet the requirement of the temperature of the unexposed side. Codes require that the temperature of the

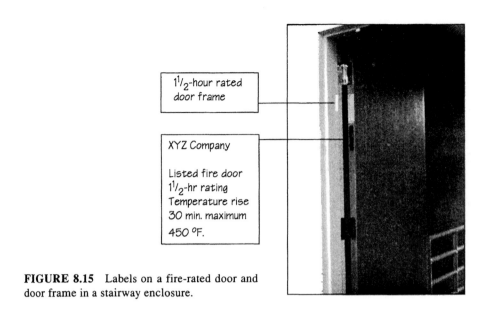

**FIGURE 8.15** Labels on a fire-rated door and door frame in a stairway enclosure.

unexposed side of a fire door in an exit enclosure not exceed 450 °F (230 °C) above the ambient temperature after a 30-minute exposure to the fire test.

In addition to 3-hour, $1^1/_2$-hour, 1-hour, and $^3/_4$-hour rated doors, there are 20-minute rated door assemblies. A 20-minute rated door assembly is, in fact, a smoke-and-draft control assembly. Its main purpose is to minimize the transmission of smoke from one side of the door to the other. A 20-minute door is usually required in a 1-hour rated corridor wall. A $1^3/_4$ in. (45 mm) thick solid-bonded wood core door usually gives a 20-minute protection. However, to be accepted as a 20-minute door, a $1^3/_4$ in. thick solid-bonded wood core door must pass the required test to substantiate performance.

### 8.7.2 Fire Windows

Glazed windows in external walls are usually not required to be fire rated if the building's distance from nearby buildings and property lines is sufficiently large, as explained in the following section. However, a glazing in a fire-rated interior wall, and a glazing in a fire door must be rated.

There is only one recognized rating for glazing — $^3/_4$ hour. Wired glass, $^1/_4$ in. thick, when used in an approved frame is recognized to provide a rated glazing — also referred to as a fire window. However, not all $^1/_4$-in. thick wired glass is accepted for use in a rated glazing. To be so accepted, the wired glass must satisfy the requirements of the fire test for a $^3/_4$-hour rating. Rated wired glass is required to be labeled.

A rated glazing can be a maximum of 9 ft² (0.8 m²), with neither side exceeding 6 ft (1.8 m). Since a rated glazing can have only a $^3/_4$-hour rating, the glazed area of 9 ft² is allowed only in a $^3/_4$-hour rated opening. If the rating of opening is higher than $^3/_4$ hour, the area of glazing allowed is smaller For example, in a 1-hour or $1^1/_2$-hour rated opening, the maximum area of rated glazing is 100 in². In a 3-hour rated opening, no glazing is allowed.

**Table 8.2 Maximum Area of Exterior Wall Openings**

| Separation distance | Opening area allowed |
|---|---|
| 0 - 3 ft | 0% |
| 3 - 5 ft | 15% (P) |
|  | 0% (UP) |
| 5 - 10 ft | 25% (P) |
|  | 10% (UP) |
| 10 - 15 ft | 45% (P) |
|  | 15% (UP) |
| 15 - 20 ft | 75% (P) |
|  | 25% (UP) |
| 20 - 25 ft | 100% (P) |
|  | 45% (UP) |
| 25 - 30 ft | 100% (P) |
|  | 70% (UP) |
| > 30 ft | 100% |

P = Protected opening, UP = Unprotected opening.
Source: Copyright 1993, Building Officials and Code Administrators International Inc., Country Club Hills, Illinois. 1993 BOCA *National Building Code.* Reprinted with permission of author. All rights reserved.

Until recently, wired glass was the only fire-rated glass. Today glazing materials which provide up to 2-hour protection are available, see Section 8.16. Since a fire window is defined as a $^3/_4$-hour assembly, any glazed assembly providing more than $^3/_4$-hour rating is treated as a wall assembly and is therefore tested as per ASTM E 119 test.

### 8.7.3 Openings in Exterior Walls

Building codes classify openings in exterior walls under two types: *protected* and *unprotected*. A protected opening is defined as one which has a minimum of $^3/_4$-hour opening protection in a wall required to have a rating of one hour or less. For an exterior wall required to have a rating of greater than 1 hour, the opening protection must be at least $1^1/_2$ hours.

Since openings in exterior walls pose a hazard to surrounding buildings, building codes restrict the area of openings in exterior walls depending on: (i) whether the openings are protected or unprotected, and (ii) the wall's separation distance — the distance of the wall from nearby buildings or property lines. For example, BOCA National Building Code does not allow any opening (protected or unprotected) in an exterior wall if its separation distance is 3 ft (0.9 m) or less. If the separation distance is between 3 ft to 5 ft, the openings may be a maximum of 15% of the wall area, but must be protected. Increasingly greater percentage opening areas are allowed as the distance of the wall from nearby buildings increases, Table 8.2.

If the separation distance is greater than 20 ft, the openings may be 100% of wall area but must be protected. With a separation distance of 30 ft or more, 100% unprotected openings may be used.

## 8.8 FIRESTOPPING AND DRAFTSTOPPING

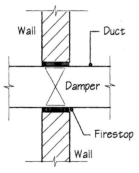

**FIGURE 8.16** A firestop consisting of a noncombustible material is required to seal a duct or pipe penetration in a wall or floor.

Walls, floors and roofs in buildings are often penetrated by service ducts, pipes, or electrical outlets. If these components (walls, floors and roofs) are to function as effective barriers to the spread of fire, the space around the ducts, pipes and outlets must be thoroughly sealed. The sealing of the space around a penetration is called *firestopping.* An unsealed space will allow heat, smoke and flammable gases to transmit from one side of the barrier to the other, compromising the fire rating of the barrier. Heating and air-conditioning ducts must be provided with dampers at fire-rated walls, which should automatically seal the duct in the event of a fire, Figure 8.16.

Firestopping materials must obviously be noncombustible. Several materials are in common use. They consist of sealants, putties and foams which are available in caulking guns and pails, Figure 8.17. Foamed fire stop is a two-component material which foams at room temperature and fills the space. Firestop materials also help to seal spaces against air and sound transmission.

In addition to sealing spaces around penetrations, firestops are also required in all concealed spaces in floors, walls and ceilings. Concealed spaces present considerable fire hazard because when a fire originates in a

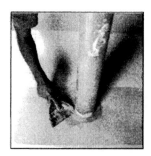

**FIGURE 8.17** Firestopping around a penetration in a floor. Courtesy of: U.S. Gypsum Company, Chicago, Illinois.

concealed space, it can grow and burn the structural members in the concealed space before being noticed from the outside.

Tests have shown that a fire originating from and spreading into concealed spaces can destroy a wood structure in less than 30 minutes. Although the structural components may have a high degree of fire rating due to the protective gypsum board lining on wood members, they are completely defenseless against fire that originates inside a concealed space. Building codes mandate that concealed spaces in wood frame walls must be firestopped where they meet concealed spaces in ceilings or attics.

A firestop cannot stop a fire from occurring. It simply breaks up the size of concealed space so that the fire remains localized to the area of origin and has a limited amount of oxygen available for growth.

Firestops in wood frame assemblies are permitted to be of wood. Usually $1^1/_2$ in. (38 mm) thick solid wood members are used as firestops. A few locations of firestops required in wood frame assemblies are shown in Figure 8.18.

The term *firestopping* is used when the concealed space being divided is a narrow space such as the space between studs or a space around pipe or duct penetrations. If the space is deep, the term used is *draftstopping*, although both firestopping and draftstopping serve the same purpose. Thus, a firestop is provided in a wall or floor assembly and a draftstop in plenum space or an attic space, Figure 8.19. Draftstopping is required only in wood frame

**FIGURE 8.18** Some examples of firestops provided in wood frame construction.

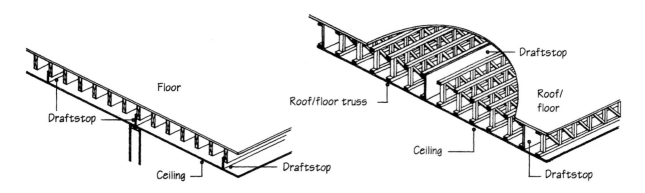

**FIGURE 8.19** Examples of draftstops.

assemblies. A $^1/_2$ in. (13 mm) thick gypsum board is commonly used as a draftstop. The codes generally limit the area between two draftstops to a maximum of 1,000 ft$^2$ (93 m$^2$).

## 8.9 FIRE PROPERTIES OF INTERIOR FINISHES

While fire rating is the property of the component to act as a barrier to the spread of fire to adjacent compartments, the properties of the component that determine the hazard posed by it to the development and spread of fire within the compartment of origin are a function of:

- the surface burning behavior of interior finish materials, and
- the toxicity and density of smoke generated by the burning of finish materials.

Experience with actual building fires and experimental investigations with full-scale fire tests have shown that apart from providing additional fuel, interior finishes contribute to fire hazard by: (i) flaming of the material, and (ii) producing smoke. The properties that are used to assess these hazards are *flame spread index* (FSI), and *smoke developed density* (SDD) respectively.

### 8.9.1 Flame Spread Index

FSI is a measure of the rate at which flames spread on the surface of an interior finish. It is an important index since a rapid spread of flames either prevents or delays the escape of occupants from the building. Its importance was realized in the 1940s when investigations revealed that the main cause for the loss of lives in three major building fires[4] that took place within a span of four years was the rapid spread of flames on the surfaces of interior finishes.

The FSI of a finish material is measured from the Steiner Tunnel Test[8.14] on a scale that begins at zero but has no upper limit. The FSI of (select

---

[4] These tragedies were: the Boston Coconut Grove Nightclub fire in November 1942, killing 490 people; the La Salle Hotel fire in June 1946, killing 61 people; and the Atlanta Winecoff Hotel fire in December 1946, killing 161 people.

grade) red oak has been arbitrarily fixed at 100 and that of a portland cement board at zero. In this respect, the FSI scale is similar to the Celsius scale in which the boiling point of water and the freezing point of water are arbitrarily fixed at 100 °C and 0 °C respectively.

Red oak has been chosen as the standard because: (i) the rate of flame travel on red oak is uniform, and (ii) the test results on red oak are reasonably repeatable.

A material whose FSI is 200 means that the rate of flame spread on this material is twice as fast as that on red oak. Similarly on a material whose FSI is 50, the rate of flame travel is half as rapid as on red oak. Table 8.3 gives typical FSI values of some commonly used building materials. Building codes limit the maximum value of FSI to 200 for an interior finish material.

### 8.9.2 Smoke Developed Density

SDD measures the visibility through smoke. The smaller the visibility through smoke, the greater the SDD value. SDD values of materials are obtained from the same test as the FSI. SDD is also measured on a scale that begins at zero but has no upper limit. Once again, the SDD value of red oak has been arbitrarily fixed at 100, and that of cement board as zero.

As mentioned in Section 8.4.3, building codes at the present time do not require a rating of the toxic effects of smoke except prohibiting the use of some materials as interior finishes because of the excessive toxicity of their smoke. The only building code requirement of the smoke generated by materials is that the SDD value of a material used as an interior finish should not exceed 450.

### 8.9.3 Building Code Requirements for Interior Finish Materials

Various types of interior finishes are used in contemporary buildings such as wood, plywood, plaster, gypsum board, acoustical tiles, and several decorative

**Table 8.3 Approximate FSI Values of Selected Materials**

| Interior finish material | FSI | Interior finish material | FSI |
|---|---|---|---|
| Fiberglass blanket | 15 - 30 | Red oak | 100 |
| Rock wool blanket | 10 - 25 | Southern pine | 130 - 190 |
| Shredded wood fiber board (treated) | 20 - 25 | Douglas fir | 70 - 100 |
| Spray-on cellulosic fibers (treated) | 20 | Plywood paneling | 75 - 275 |
| Cement board | 0 | Fire retardant treated lumber | Less than 25 |
| Bricks or concrete block | 0 | Cork | 175 |
| Concrete | 0 | Carpets | 10 - 600 |
| Gypsum board with paper lining | 10 - 25 | | |

furnishings. Only finishes applied on walls and ceilings are regulated for FSI and SDD values. Floor finishes such as carpets and floor tiles are not rated for flame spread index or smoke density. The reason is that since flames spread vertically upwards, floor finishes do not get involved in a fire until after the flash-over. In addition, carpets and rugs are regulated by the U.S. Department of Commerce under the Flammable Fabrics Act. Thus, they need no further evaluation for flame spread or smoke density. However, carpets placed on ceilings or walls must be rated for FSI and SDD.

Excluded from the evaluation of FSI and SDD values are: trims, picture molds, baseboards, handrails, and door and window frames. Since these elements cover a small area of interior surfaces, they do not present a great deal of fire hazard. Additionally, thin materials, thickness less than $1/28$ in., are also not regulated provided their surface burning characteristics are not worse than a paper of the same thickness. This provision is meant primarily to exclude materials such as gypsum board, wall papers and ordinary paint from testing. The reason is that the combustible content of such materials is so small that their flaming presents little hazard.

**Table 8.4 Building Code Classification of Interior Finish Materials**

| Flame spread class | FSI | SDD |
|---|---|---|
| Class I | 0 - 25 | < 450 |
| Class II | 26 - 75 | < 450 |
| Class III | 76 - 200 | < 450 |

Building codes classify interior finishes in three flame spread categories: Class I (or Class A), Class II (or Class B), and Class III (or Class C), Table 8.4. The objective of this classification is to regulate the use of interior finish materials according to the fire safety requirements of spaces. Since Class I (or A) materials are the least hazardous, building codes mandate that they be used in enclosed vertical exit ways — staircases and elevators. A minimum of Class II (or B) material is required in other exit ways — corridors, lounges, foyers etc. Class III (or C) material may be used in areas such as individual rooms, Figure 8.20. There are a few exceptions to the above rules, for which the applicable building code should be consulted. For example, Class III (or C) materials are allowed to be used in all areas of a single family dwelling, even in stair enclosures and corridors. No classification is given to materials with an FSI greater than 200, and a SDD greater than 450, as these materials are not allowed as interior finish materials.

**FIGURE 8.20** General building code requirements for minimum flame spread class for various areas of a building.

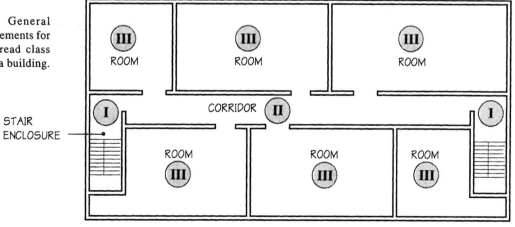

### 8.9.4 Fire Resistance and Surface Flammability

Note that the fire rating and the surface burning characteristics of interior finishes are entirely independent and unrelated properties. While fire rating is a measure of the structural integrity of a component during a fire, flame spread rating and smoke density measure the fire hazard of an interior material. For example, heavy timber construction may have one hour or more of fire rating but it presents a degree of hazard as an interior finish. A thin steel plate, on the other hand, is a poor fire barrier with virtually zero fire rating but it presents no hazard as an interior finish.

**8.10 FIRE ENDURANCE OF MATERIALS**

All materials are adversely affected by fire. However, some materials endure fire better than others. Consequently, assemblies constructed of these materials give higher fire ratings. In the following sections, we will discuss fire endurance properties of some of the commonly used materials. The procedures for calculating the fire ratings of assemblies are also examined in these sections. Calculation procedures should be used when test results for an assembly are not available.

**8.11 FIRE ENDURANCE OF GYPSUM**

Gypsum is a rock-like mineral found extensively on the earth's surface. Its chemical name is calcium sulfate dihydrate ($CaSO_4 \cdot 2H_2O$), which shows that every molecule of gypsum contains two molecules of water chemically combined with one molecule of calcium sulfate. The consequence of this fact is that 100 pounds of gypsum rock contains nearly 21 pounds of water.

When gypsum is heated it begins to give up water — a process called *calcination*[5]. At nearly 400 °F (200 °C), gypsum gives up all its water and the resulting product is called *dead burned gypsum* or *anhydrite*. Anhydrite[6] is pure calcium sulfate ($CaSO_4$).

Because of its chemically combined water, gypsum is an excellent material for providing fire resistance. Under the action of heat, gypsum calcines and the water is converted into steam. Steam not only helps in absorbing some of the heat, but also provides a cooling effect. Gradually, as the outer layer of a gypsum sheet or board calcines, heat penetrates into the next inner layer and as this layer calcines, heat penetrates further to calcine the next layer. Thus, given enough time, the entire board of gypsum will calcine layer by layer.

---

[5] The calcined gypsum, ground to a fine powder, is called *plaster of paris*, a material used for interior plastering on wood or metal lath. Chemically, plaster of paris is calcium hemihydrate ($CaSO_4 \cdot 1/2H_2O$). When water is added to plaster of paris, it returns to its original hard, rock-like form — gypsum (containing calcium sulfate and water molecules). Because plaster of paris reverts to gypsum on the addition of water and its subsequent setting, plaster of paris expands on setting — unlike portland cement which shrinks, and hence cracks, on setting and hardening. That is why plaster of paris is popular for casting in molds because it assumes the shape of the mold accurately without any shrinkage cracks.

[6] Anhydrite has a longer setting time than plaster of paris, and is marketed as Keene's cement, which is used as finish coat in interior plaster.

Calcined gypsum is much weaker than uncalcined gypsum and disintegrates easily. In other words, heat weakens and disintegrates gypsum. But the disintegration of gypsum under heat is a slow process. Gypsum's slow rate of disintegration is not only due to the presence of water in it but also because calcined gypsum is a better thermal insulator than uncalcined gypsum. Since water is a good thermal conductor, the absence of water in calcined gypsum improves its insulating properties.

Thus, gypsum derives its fire-resistance property in two ways: (i) by converting water into steam, and (ii) by producing calcined gypsum which, being a better insulator than uncalcined gypsum, retards the flow of heat to the inner layers of the material. Figure 8.21 shows the temperature gradient in a 6 in. thick gypsum wall which has been exposed to ASTM E 119 test fire for two hours. Note that after 2 hours, less than 2 in. thickness of gypsum has calcined, since at a distance of 2 in. from the exposed face, the temperature of the wall is only 220 °F — almost the boiling point of water. Beyond the calcined layers, the temperature is low. At the unexposed face, the temperature is only 130 °F.

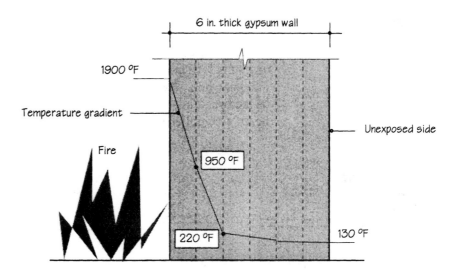

**FIGURE 8.21** Temperature gradient along a 6 in. thick gypsum wall after two-hour exposure to fire under ASTM E 119 test.

### 8.11.1 Gypsum Boards

As mentioned earlier, gypsum may be used as gypsum plaster but since plastering involves a great deal of on-site labor, it is more commonly used in the form of prefabricated boards, called *gypsum boards*. Some other terms used for the product are *wallboard, plasterboard,* or *drywall.*

Gypsum board is one of the most extensively used interior finish materials, not only in residential work but also in commercial construction. It is relatively inexpensive, easy to install and unlike plaster, does not require time to dry. In addition, being a dry form of construction, it leaves little mess as compared to on-site plastering.

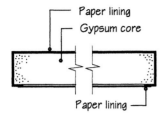

**FIGURE 8.22** Composition of gypsum board.

A gypsum board contains a core of gypsum which is sandwiched between special paper faces, Figure 8.22. The core is formulated with gypsum slurry, starch, water and some pregenerated foam to lower its density to obtain better insulating value. This type of core is called the regular core or *type "R" core*. Another type, called *type "X" core*, contains glass fibers in addition to the materials that are used in type R core. Glass fibers add reinforcement to gypsum so that after calcining, gypsum particles hold together and do not disintegrate as easily as in a type R board. Properly installed, a $^5/_8$ in. (16 mm) thick type X gypsum board on both sides of wood or metal studs provides a 1-hour fire rating from each side.

In fact, type X gypsum board is defined as one that gives a 1-hour fire rating to a wall assembly when used in $^5/_8$ in. (16 mm) thickness over wood or metal studs. If $^1/_2$ in. (13 mm) thick type X gypsum board is used, the assembly gives a 45-minute fire rating. Two $^5/_8$ in. (16 mm) thick type X gypsum boards on studs gives the assembly a 2-hour rating. Three such layers give a 3-hour fire rating, and so on, Figure 8.23. In fact, almost any fire rating can be obtained by adding the number of layers — another reason for the popularity of gypsum board as fire protection material.

Note that if the assembly is asymmetrical, the fire rating from each side will be different. For instance, if $^5/_8$ in. thick type X gypsum board is used on one side of studs and $^1/_2$ in. thick type X board on the other side, the assembly will have a 1-hour rating from one side and 45-minute rating from the other side. The lower of the two values, i.e. 45 minutes in this case, will be the fire rating of the assembly. Fire resistances of commonly used gypsum board assemblies may be obtained from Reference 8.10.

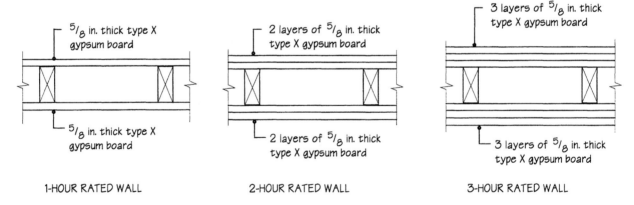

**FIGURE 8.23** One-, two- and three-hour rated wood frame wall assemblies. Fire rating remains unaltered if wood studs are replaced by metal studs.

**8.12 FIRE ENDURANCE OF WOOD**

The fire resistance of wood depends mainly on its size. Wood members of large cross-sectional dimensions have performed well in actual fires. This is due to the formation of char on the surface of burnt wood. Char not only protects the unburnt wood from direct flames but because char is a good thermal insulator, it helps to retard heat transmission beyond the char layer.

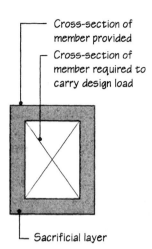

Cross-section of member provided

Cross-section of member required to carry design load

Sacrificial layer

**FIGURE 8.24** An additional thickness provided in a wood member gives it the required fire rating.

Tests conducted on wood with only one face exposed to the standard fire have revealed that wood chars at a constant rate of 1 in. to 2 in. (25 to 50 mm) per hour depending on the specie. Hence, unprotected wood light frame construction, which uses only $1^1/_2$ in. (38 mm) thick members, has negligible fire resistance.

On the other hand, if the dimensions of wood members are made larger than those required to carry the design loads, wood structures can have a fairly high degree of fire resistance without any added protection from gypsum board or similar protective finish. For example, assume that a wood column is required to be 6 in. x 8 in. in cross-section to support the design loads. If the specie of wood used in the column chars at the rate of 1.5 in. per hour, then a 9 in. x 11 in. wood column will be able to withstand fire for one hour. The 1.5 inches of additional thickness of wood all around the column cross-section works as a sacrificial layer in the event of fire, Figure 8.24. After an exposure of one hour, the column will still be left with a cross-section of 6 in. x 8 in., which is the size required to carry the design loads.

### 8.12.1 Heavy Timber Construction

In recognition of the charring characteristics of wood, building codes recognize heavy timber (HT) construction as an entirely separate classification (see Table 8.1). To qualify for heavy timber classification, building codes prescribe that the structural members such as columns, beams, floor joists and planks, must be of certain minimum dimensions. For example, a column is required to be a minimum of 8 x 8 nominal ($7^1/_4$ in. x $7^1/_4$ in. actual) and a beam must be a minimum of 6 x 10 nominal ($5^1/_2$ in. x $9^1/_4$ in. actual).

Although not explicitly mentioned in building codes, the structural components of heavy timber construction are assumed to provide a nearly 1-hour fire rating. If the code-prescribed minimum dimension criteria for heavy timber construction are followed, there is no need to provide an additional sacrificial perimeter of wood to achieve the 1-hour rating. These minimum dimensions are based on the fact that after one hour exposure to fire, the unburnt cross-sections of wood will still be sufficient to carry the building's dead loads.

The burnt layers of wood would no doubt reduce the safety margin in the structure to some extent, but this will be compensated for by the fact that a fire-damaged structure will be subjected to a much smaller live load than its design live load. It is also based on the fact that the damaged structure would require major repairs after the fire. Thus, the only structural requirement of the fire-damaged structure in heavy timber construction is that it should not collapse within a one-hour exposure to fire.

However, if more precise values of fire rating for exposed wood members are required, they may be calculated from the available procedures[8.16].

### 8.12.2 Fire Retardant Treated Wood

Fire retardant treatment on wood converts fire gases produced in the combustion of wood into harmless carbon dioxide and water vapor, rendering wood virtually flameless[7] and thereby reducing its fuel contribution. However, the treatment does not prevent wood from decomposing under exposure to fire. Therefore, the fire rating of components consisting of fire retardant treated (FRT) wood is not higher than those consisting of untreated wood.

However, because of reduced fuel contribution and improved surface flammability of FRT wood, building codes allow its use in (up to 1-hour rated) nonloadbearing partitions in Type I and Type II constructions, where otherwise noncombustible materials, such as metal studs, brick, concrete or masonry are allowed. FRT wood is also used as rough framing for exterior windows in noncombustible wall assemblies since ordinary wood is not allowed in such assemblies. Rough framing provides a base to which windows may be secured. FRT wood may be used as solid blocking in steel stud wall assemblies to support wall-hung fixtures.

### 8.12.3  Calculation of Fire-Resistance Rating of Wood Light Frame Assemblies

An approximate procedure has been developed to calculate the fire rating of wood light frame assemblies. This procedure is recommended for use in the case of assemblies for which actual test results are not available. The applicability of the procedure is limited to assemblies in which the framing members (studs, joists or rafters) have a maximum spacing of 16 in. on center. Thus, the procedure does not apply to assemblies in which the framing members are spaced 24 in. on center. Additionally, for floor and roof assemblies, the procedure is applicable only if floor or roof sheathing is a minimum of $^1/_2$ in. thick plywood or $^{11}/_{16}$ in. thick solid lumber boards.

According to this procedure, the fire rating of an assembly is equal to the sum of:

(i)   The time assigned to the fire-exposed membrane of the assembly, plus

(ii)  The time assigned to framing members, plus

(iii) The time assigned to insulation, as per Table 8.5.

The membrane on the unexposed side is not included in calculations.

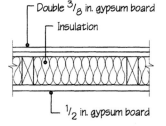

FIGURE 8.25  Wall assembly of Example 8.5.

### Example 8.5

Calculate the fire rating of the wall of Figure 8.25, which consists of two $^3/_8$ in. thick type R gypsum board on one side and $^1/_2$ in. thick type R gypsum board on the other side of 2 x 4 wood studs spaced 16 in. on center with intervening fiberglass insulation.

*Solution*: From Table 8.5, the fire rating of a wall assembly with fire exposure

---

[7] The flame spread index of FRT wood is less than 25 and its smoke developed density, less than 450.

on the side with double $^3/_8$ in. thick gypsum boards = time assigned to gypsum boards + time assigned to studs + time assigned to insulation = 25 + 20 + 15 = 60 minutes.

The fire rating of wall assembly with fire exposure on the side with $^1/_2$ in. thick gypsum board = 15 + 20 + 15 = 50 minutes.

Thus, the fire rating of the wall is 50 minutes, being the smaller of the two values.

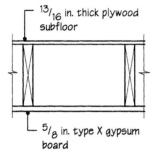

$^{13}/_{16}$ in. thick plywood subfloor

$^5/_8$ in. type X gypsum board

**FIGURE 8.26** Floor-ceiling assembly of Example 8.6.

### Example 8.6

Calculate the fire rating of the floor-ceiling assembly of Figure 8.26 consisting of: $^{13}/_{16}$ in. thick plywood subfloor supported on 2 x 12 floor joists spaced 16 in. on center, and $^5/_8$ in. thick type X gypsum board ceiling.

*Solution*: The fire rating of the assembly will be calculated by assuming that it is exposed to fire on the ceiling side. Thus, the fire rating of assembly = time assigned to gypsum board + time assigned to floor joists = 40 + 10 = 50 minutes.

**Table 8.5  Time Assigned to Various Materials Used in Wood Frame Assemblies**

| Material | Time (min.) | Material | Time (min) |
|---|---|---|---|
| $^3/_8$ in. exterior glue plywood | 5 | Double $^3/_8$ in. type R gypsum board | 25 |
| $^1/_2$ in. exterior glue plywood | 10 | $1/_2$ in. + $^3/_8$ in. type R gypsum board | 35 |
| $^5/_8$ in. exterior glue plywood | 15 | Double $^1/_2$ in. type R gypsum board | 40 |
| $^3/_8$ in. type R gypsum board | 10 | Wood studs @ 16 in. o.c. | 20 |
| $^1/_2$ in. type R gypsum board | 15 | Wood floor and roof joists 16 in or less o.c. | 10 |
| $^5/_8$ in. type R gypsum board | 30 | Rock wool insulation between studs | |
| $^1/_2$ in. type X gypsum board | 25 | (weighing not less than 1.0 psf) or | |
| $^5/_8$ in. type X gypsum board | 40 | fiberglass (weighing not less than 0.6 psf) | 15 |

Source:  Reference 8.16 with permission.

## 8.13  FIRE ENDURANCE OF CONCRETE

Although most of the water that is used in making concrete evaporates during the setting and hardening of concrete, a part remains in concrete permanently. The unevaporated water is approximately one-quarter the weight of portland cement, so that portland cement in concrete exists as water-cement gel. Under intense heat, this water is converted into steam — a phenomenon similar to the evaporation of water from gypsum. Like gypsum, concrete also loses strength, spalls and disintegrates under long-term exposure to fire.

As with all other materials, the primary factor that determines the fire rating of a concrete member is its thickness. The thicker the member, the higher the fire rating. Another factor that influences the fire rating of a concrete member is the type of aggregate used in concrete. The lighter the aggregate, the more fire resistive the concrete member. Structural lightweight concrete (density 85 to 115 pcf) made from lightweight aggregate such as expanded shale or slag, is more fire resistive than normal-weight concrete because of better thermal insulation provided by lightweight aggregate. Non-structural concrete (approximate density 30 pcf) made with perlite or vermiculite aggregate, gives yet greater fire resistiveness, and is commonly used as a spray-on fire protection on structural steel members.

Among the normal-weight concretes (approximate density 145 pcf), the one made with limestone is slightly more fire resistive than the one made with siliceous aggregate (aggregate other than limestone aggregate). As an illustration of the effect of aggregate, the fire ratings of reinforced concrete walls with different types of aggregate are given in Table 8.6.

Another factor influencing the fire rating of a concrete member is the cover provided to reinforcing steel. Because steel loses strength at higher temperatures, the cover provided to reinforcing steel, Figure 8.27, must be consistent with the fire rating of the member. A small cover reduces the fire rating of the member.

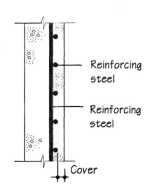

**FIGURE 8.27** Concrete cover to steel in a reinforced concrete member.

**Table 8.6 Fire Rating of Concrete and Reinforced Concrete Walls**

| Type of aggregate in concrete | Thickness of wall (in.) | | | |
|---|---|---|---|---|
| | 4-hr | 3-hr | 2-hr | 1-hr |
| Siliceous aggregate | 7.0 | 6.2 | 5.0 | 3.5 |
| Carbonate aggregate | 6.6 | 5.7 | 4.6 | 3.2 |
| Sand-lightweight concrete | 5.4 | 4.6 | 3.8 | 2.7 |
| Lightweight aggregate | 5.1 | 4.4 | 3.6 | 2.5 |

Fire ratings given in this table assume a concrete cover to steel of $^3/_4$ in. Source: Reference 8.16, with permission.

## 8.14 FIRE ENDURANCE OF MASONRY WALLS

Fire tests have shown that the fire rating of a masonry wall is determined by the temperature-rise criterion on the unexposed side. A masonry wall does not usually fail the E 119 test through structural collapse, or by developing cracks, or under the hose stream test. This fact allows the use of the theory of heat conduction to determine the fire rating of masonry walls. According to this theory, the fire rating of a wall (R), composed of several parallel layers of different materials, is given by:

**Table 8.7 Fire Ratings to Be Used in Equation 8.1**

| Element | Fire rating (hr) |
|---|---|
| Air cavity | 0.13 |
| $1/2$ in. plaster or gypsum board | 0.13 |
| $5/8$ in. plaster or gypsum board | 0.19 |
| $3/4$ in. plaster or gypsum board | 0.26 |

Source: Reference 8.16 with permission.

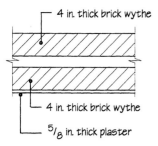

FIGURE 8.28 Brick cavity wall of Example 8.7.

$$R = \left[ (R_1)^{0.59} + (R_2)^{0.59} + (R_3)^{0.59} + \cdots \right]^{1.7} \qquad (8.1)$$

where $R_1$, $R_2$, $R_3$, . . . are the fire ratings (in hours) of the individual layers. If there is an air cavity in the wall, it can be treated as a separate layer. Tests have shown that the fire rating of a continuous air space (from 0.5 in. to 3.5 in. deep) may be assumed as approximately equal to 0.13 hour, Table 8.7. The effect of one or more layers of plaster in masonry walls can also be included by using the values given in the same table.

**Example 8.7**

Calculate the fire rating of a brick cavity wall which is composed of two wythes of 4 in. (nominal) thick clay bricks with a 2 in. deep air cavity, Figure 8.28. The inside face of the wall is plastered with $5/8$ in. thick plaster. Assume that the fire rating of a 4 in. thick wall = 1.25 hours.

*Solution*: $R_{\text{masonry wall}} = 1.25$. From Table 8.7, $R_{\text{cavity}} = 0.13$, $R_{\text{plaster}} = 0.19$. From Equation (8.1),

$$R = [(1.25)^{0.59} + (0.13)^{0.59} + (1.25)^{0.59} + (0.19)^{0.59}]^{1.7}$$
$$= 6.3 \text{ hours}$$

**8.14.1 Fire Rating of Solid Masonry Walls**

Equation (8.1) can also be used to calculate the fire rating of a wall of a certain thickness if the fire rating of a different thickness of the same material is known. For example, if the fire rating of a 3 in. thick wall is known, then we can calculate the fire rating of any other thickness of the wall provided both walls are of the same material. In such a case, Equation (8.1) becomes:

$$R_2 = R_1 \left[ \frac{V_2}{V_1} \right]^{1.7} \qquad (8.2)$$

where $V_1$ and $V_2$ are the volumes of solid materials per unit surface area in walls 1 and 2 respectively. $R_1$ and $R_2$ are the corresponding fire ratings of walls. If both wall 1 and wall 2 are fully solid, i.e., they have no voids, Equation (8.2) can be modified to:

$$R_2 = R_1 \left[ \frac{t_2}{t_1} \right]^{1.7} \qquad (8.3)$$

where $t_1$ and $t_2$ are the thicknesses of walls 1 and 2 respectively.

**Example 8.8**

Calculate the fire rating of an 8 in. thick clay masonry wall given that the fire rating of a 4 in. thick wall is 1.25 hours. The dimensions of walls are nominal dimensions and both walls are constructed of 100% solid units, i.e., there are no voids in the wall.

*Solution*: Since the wall is constructed of 100% solid units, Equation (8.3) can be used to calculate the required fire rating. The actual dimensions of 4 in. and 8 in. thick walls are 3.625 in. and 7.625 in. respectively. Since the fire rating of 4 in. thick wall $(R_1) = 1.25$ hours, the fire rating of an 8 in. thick wall $(R_2)$ is:

$$R_2 = 1.25 \left[ \frac{7.625}{3.625} \right]^{1.7} = 4.4 \text{ hours}$$

### 8.14.2 Fire Rating of Hollow Masonry Walls

Contemporary masonry walls are seldom solid. They are usually constructed of hollow masonry units  To obtain the fire rating of a wall comprising hollow units, we use the concept of *equivalent solid thickness*. Equivalent solid thickness is obtained by assuming that the hollow unit is recast into a 100% solid unit so that the amount of masonry material in the equivalent solid unit is equal to the amount of material in the original hollow unit. The fire rating of the wall built of hollow units is equal to the fire rating of wall of equivalent solid thickness. Table 8.8 gives the fire ratings of 100% solid concrete masonry walls, which, as seen from the table, is a function of the type of aggregate used in masonry units.

**Table 8.8  Fire Ratings of Concrete Masonry Walls**

| Type of aggregate in concrete masonry | Equivalent solid thickness of wall (in.) | | | |
|---|---|---|---|---|
| | 4-hr | 3-hr | 2-hr | 1-hr |
| Calcareous or silicious gravel | 6.2 | 5.3 | 4.2 | 2.8 |
| Limestone, cinder or slag | 5.9 | 5.0 | 4.0 | 2.7 |
| Expanded clay or shale | 5.1 | 4.4 | 3.6 | 2.6 |
| Expanded slag or pumice | 4.7 | 4.0 | 3.2 | 2.1 |

Source:  Reference 8.16, with permission.

**Example 8.9**

Determine the equivalent solid thickness of a concrete masonry wall which is constructed of hollow concrete masonry units. Each unit measures 8 in. x 16 in. x 8 in. (actual dimensions $7^5/_8$ in. x $15^5/_8$ in. x $7^5/_8$ in.). Face shell thickness of units is 1.35 in. and web thickness, 1.2 in., Figure 8.29.

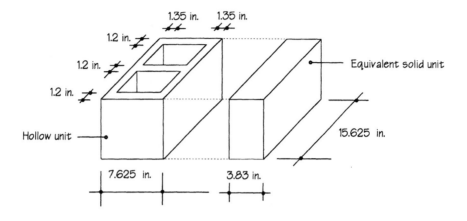

**FIGURE 8.29** Refers to Example 8.9. The equivalent solid thickness is obtained by assuming that the unit is recast into a solid unit of the same length and height as the original unit.

*Solution*: We can determine the equivalent solid thickness of the hollow unit by examining its plan view and calculating the ratio of the solid area to the total area of the unit. It may be seen that each cell in the unit measures 4.925 in. x 6.0125 in. Hence,

Area of each cell = 4.925 x 6.0125 = 29.61 in.$^2$
Gross area of unit = 15.625 x 7.625 = 119.14 in.$^2$
Hence, the area of solid in the unit = 119.14 - 2(29.61) = 59.92 in.$^2$
Ratio of solid area to the total area = 59.92/119.14 = 0.50
Hence, the equivalent solid thickness of unit = 0.50 (7.625) = 3.83 in.

**Example 8.10**

Determine the fire rating of the wall constructed of masonry units of Example 8.9. The aggregate used in units is expanded clay.

*Solution*: From Table 8.8, the equivalent solid thickness required to give a 3-hour fire rating is 4.4 in. and to give a 2-hour fire rating is 3.6 in. Since the equivalent thickness of the wall is 3.83 in., the fire rating of the wall is 2.28 hours, obtained by interpolating between the above values.

**8.15 FIRE ENDURANCE OF STEEL**

As stated previously, the fire rating of steel is extremely poor, and its inherent incombustibility gives a false sense of security. Exposed (unprotected) steel is in fact one of the worst construction materials when subjected to fire. At nearly 1,100 °F, steel's yield strength falls to approximately 60% of its value at normal temperature (70 °F). Since 60% of yield strength is commonly used as the allowable stress, the load-carrying capacity of a steel member is reduced to the design load at 1,100 °F, leaving no safety margin. This is why 1,100 °F is considered to be the critical temperature of structural members in ASTM E 119 test (see Figure 8.13).

Steel has a high coefficient of thermal expansion. From Example 10.1, we see that a 50 ft long beam, when subjected to a temperature rise of 1,100 °F will expand by nearly 4 in. in length. An expansion of 4 in. is a substantial expansion which may affect buildings in several ways.

If the steel beam is restrained, the attempted expansion will induce thermal stress which, coupled with the beam's reduced strength at an elevated temperature, may cause rapid failure of the beam. If the beam is unrestrained, it will expand and tend to push members attached to it. For instance, a steel beam resting on a masonry wall will push the wall laterally on expansion and may cause the wall to collapse.

It is important, therefore, that structural steel be protected against fire. Unprotected steel buildings may be used, but building codes severely limit the allowable areas and heights of such structures.

There are various ways in which protection to structural steel may be provided. The oldest method is to encase steel sections in concrete as shown in Figure 8.30. It is generally used in floor systems which consist of reinforced concrete slabs resting on steel beams so that the concrete-encased steel beams function monolithically with the slab. The thickness of concrete cover required to obtain a given fire rating depends on the type of aggregate in concrete. Recall that lightweight aggregate concrete provides a higher rating than normal-weight aggregate concrete.

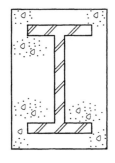

**FIGURE 8.30** Encasement of steel member in concrete.

As with all other materials, heavier and thicker steel sections give greater fire resistance as compared with lighter sections. Unprotected open web joists and trusses, which are constructed of light sections, seldom yield more than a 15-minute fire rating in E 119 test. Thus, another important factor that affects the fire rating of a steel member is its weight per unit length (W). In fact, fire tests have indicated that it is not just the weight but the weight-to-perimeter ratio of the section (W/D) that determines the fire rating of the section. The perimeter of a section (D) is simply the sum of all exposed dimensions of the section's profile, Figure 8.31.

The disadvantage of protecting steel by concrete encasement is the high cost of form work and the additional dead load it poses on the structure. It has, therefore, been replaced by more efficient techniques (lighter in weight and more economical) such as spray-applied fire protection and gypsum board facing.

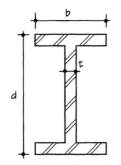

**FIGURE 8.31** The perimeter of a column section (D) = 4b - 2t + 2d.

### 8.15.1 Spray-Applied Protection

Spray-applied protection, Figure 8.32, is the most commonly used method of protecting steel. Two types of materials are used for spray-applied (or spray-on) protection: (i) mineral fiber and binder, usually fiberglass and portland cement, and (ii) cementitious mixture containing portland cement or gypsum mixed with lightweight aggregate such as perlite or vermiculite. Before

**FIGURE 8.32**  Spray-applied protection on structural steel.

spraying the protection, dirt, loose scale and oil are removed from the member in order to develop better adhesion.

In general, cementitious protection is more rugged, has better abrasion resistance, and is aesthetically superior to mineral fiber protection. After spraying, cementitious protection can be finished smooth with a trowel. Portland based cementitious protection is preferred over gypsum protection in high humidity areas because of portland cement's better resistance to moisture. Since the protection is always applied before the installation of duct work, piping and other equipment, any damage caused by such installation must be subsequently repaired.

Virtually any amount of fire resistance can be obtained by varying the thickness of spray-on protection. For a given fire rating, the thickness of spray-on protection depends on the spray-on material and the W/D ratio of the member to be protected. The heavier the member, the thinner the protection. However, a $^5/_8$ in. (16 mm) thickness per 1 hour of fire rating is a good rough estimate of the required thickness of protection. Thus, a 1-hour rating is obtained by nearly $^5/_8$ in. (16 mm) thick material, a 2-hour rating by $1^1/_4$ in. (32 mm) thick material, and so on.

Fire rating is not the only criterion that spray-on protection must meet. It must also meet the minimum requirements for damageability resistance, adhesion to steel, deflection (so that the protection does not delaminate when the steel member deflects under loads), air erosion resistance and corrosion resistance (spray-on protection protects steel from corrosion also). Spray-on protection must be carried out by specialist contractors who warranty its installation, fire resistance and other performance characteristics.

### 8.15.2 Gypsum Board Encasement

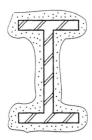

**FIGURE 8.33** Spray applied protection results in an unattractive profile of steel section.

The disadvantage of spray-applied protection is its relative unattractiveness, Figure 8.33, which usually necessitates that the protected component be covered. An alternative to spray-on protection is gypsum board encasement which provides a finished appearance to steel frame.

Gypsum board encasement consists of gypsum boards mechanically fastened to steel sections, usually screw attached to light gauge steel studs, Figure 8.34. The studs are tack welded to structural steel members. Almost any degree of fire rating can be obtained by varying the number of board layers. Gypsum plaster on a metal lath may be used in place of gypsum boards, but it requires greater on-site labor, and is relatively uncommon.

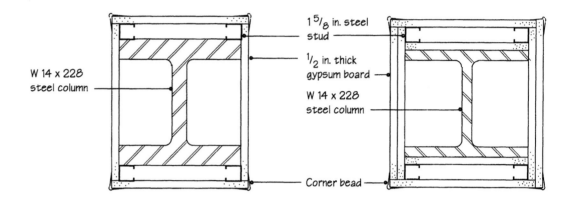

**FIGURE 8.34**  Steel columns encased by gypsum boards. Although the number of gypsum board layers are different in the two columns shown, their fire ratings are the same — 2 hours. The heavier steel section with a larger (W/D) ratio requires a smaller protection.

### 8.15.3  Intumescent Paints

An alternative to gypsum board encasement is intumescent paint on steel members. Intumescent paint is typically 20 to 50 mil (0.5 mm to 1.3 mm) thick. When exposed to the heat of fire, the paint intumesces or "swells" under high temperatures yielding an insulating char cover on steel, 2 in. to 4 in. thick. It is this char layer that protects steel from fire. However, the char layer is damaged under long-term exposure to fire, and hence this technique can be used only for low levels of fire rating, not exceeding two hours.

Being a thin film, intumescent paint does not alter the overall profile of steel sections. It gives the structure the look of exposed steel, and is commonly used in situations where the expression of exposed steel is required from an architectural and interior design perspective, Figure 8.35.

Intumescent paints are available in different colors. Thus, the painted structure can color coordinate with the overall character of the interior. Another advantage of intumescent paint protection is its abrasion resistance and relatively smooth surface which does not easily collect dust. It is, therefore, ideal for areas where dust free environment is required, such as laboratories and hospitals. If a washable top coat is provided on intumescent paint, the structure can be washed with water which is an advantage in food processing plants.

Intumescent paint protection, however, is far costlier than conventional

**FIGURE 8.35** Steel truss painted with intumescent paint providing a fire rating of 1 hour, Hospital for Sick Children, Toronto, Ontario. Courtesy of: AD Fire Protection Systems, Scarborough, Ontario. Architect: Zeidler Roberts Partnership. Photo: Lenscape Inc.

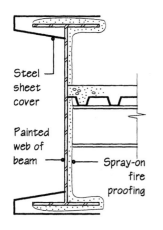

Steel sheet cover

Painted web of beam

Spray-on fire proofing

**FIGURE 8.36** Protection of an exposed spandrel beam by a steel sheet cover.

spray-on fireproofing. It is, therefore, not practical for buildings where economy is a major consideration. In buildings with large areas of steel deck supported on steel beams and columns, the intumescent paint may be used for beams and columns, but the deck may be protected by a more economical alternative.

### 8.15.4  Unpainted Exposed Steel

Unpainted exposed steel has also been used but mainly in spandrel beams. On the interior of the building, the spandrel beams are protected by conventional techniques but on the exterior, they remain exposed. To shield the exposed faces of beams from flames, a protruding steel sheet cover is fastened to bottom flanges of beams, Fig. 8.36. For aesthetic reasons, the steel sheet is designed as an integral part of the exterior cladding of the building.

### 8.15.5  Suspended Ceilings

Suspended ceilings consisting of gypsum lath and plaster, or gypsum boards or acoustical tiles, are used as fire protection to otherwise unprotected steel beams or trusses in roof-ceiling or floor-ceiling assemblies. The ceiling grid may be directly attached to, or hung from, the bottom flanges of beams or bottom chords of trusses. The effectiveness of such a system depends on how well the ceiling continues to perform as a barrier. Often the maintenance is not proper, resulting in a defective ceiling tile or gypsum board not being replaced properly so that hot gases enter the plenum space to attack the unprotected steel.

**8.16 FIRE ENDURANCE OF GLASS**

One-quarter inch thick labeled wired glass has traditionally been used in openings with a rating of $^3/_4$ hour or less. Lately a wireless glass product has been introduced which provides fire rating of up to 2 hours. This product comprises an insulating glass unit in which the intervening cavity is filled with a clear gel. In the case of fire, the gel absorbs the heat, transforming it into a heat-insulating crust.

A unit consisting of two sheets of $^1/_4$ in. (6 mm) thick tempered glass with $^3/_8$ in. (9 mm) gel provides a $^1/_2$-hour fire rating. The same construction with $1^1/_8$ in. (28 mm) gel provides a 1-hour rating. A 2-hour rating is obtained by a unit with two gel spaces of $1^1/_4$ in. (30 mm) and three sheets of glass. Under normal conditions (when there is no fire), this product appears as any other insulating glass unit with clear glass lites, Figure 8.37. Apart from being fire resistant, this product is also a safety glazing as it meets CPSC CFR 1200 requirements in Category II (see Section 7.9).

**FIGURE 8.37** Lobby at the Red Lion Inn, Costa Mesa, California. Glazed walls provide $1^1/_2$-hour rating. Courtesy of: SAFTI Division, O'Keeffe's Inc., San Francisco, California.

**REVIEW QUESIONS**

**8.1**    Explain the difference between a building code and a fire code.

**8.2**    Which ASTM test is used to determine whether a material is combustible or noncombustible? Is a material with a combustible lamination but with a noncombustible core classified as a noncombustible material?

**8.3**    Explain what flash-over is.

**8.4**    Explain the concept of compartmentation and its importance in buildings.

**8.5**    What is fire-resistance rating? Is the concept of fire-resistance rating applicable to materials or assemblies?

**8.6**    List the criteria that a wall must satisfy in ASTM E 119 test.

**8.7**    List the types of construction under which building codes classify buildings.

**8.8**  A building which is at a distance of nearly 50 ft from adjoining buildings and property lines has fire ratings as listed below. Determine the type of construction of the building.

| Component | Material used | Fire rating (hrs) |
|---|---|---|
| Bearing walls (exterior) | None provided | |
| Bearing walls (interior) | None provided | |
| Nonbearing walls (exterior) | Aluminum and glass curtain wall | 0 |
| Structural frame | Structural steel | 1 |
| Permanent partitions | Metal studs and gypsum board | 1 |
| Floor-ceiling assembly | Lightweight concrete on steel deck | 1 |
| Roof-ceiling assembly | Steel deck with spray-on protection | 1 |

**8.9**  Will the type of construction of the building of Question 8.8 change if permanent partitions are made of wood studs and gypsum board with a $3/_4$-hour fire rating? If so, to which construction type will the building belong?

**8.10**  What is a rated opening? Where is a rated opening required?

**8.11**  Locate a fire door in your school's building and sketch the label on the door.

**8.12**  Describe what a fire stop is. With the help of sketches show two locations where firestops are used in wood frame assemblies.

**8.13**  What is the difference between a firestop and draftstop? Explain with the help of sketches.

**8.14**  Explain what flame spread index and smoke density are. What maximum values of flame spread index and smoke density are allowed by building codes for building interiors?

**8.15**  List various classes in which building codes classify interior materials with respect to flame spread index and smoke density.

**8.16**  Explain why gypsum is commonly used as a fire-protective material.

**8.17**  Sketch in plan a 2-hour rated gypsum board metal stud assembly.

**8.18**  What is fire retardant treated wood?

**8.19**  Determine the equivalent thickness of a wall consisting of 10 in. ($9^5/_8$ in. actual) thick, two core hollow concrete masonry units. The thickness of the face shells of the units is $1^1/_2$ in. and web thickness is $1^1/_4$ in.

**8.20**  Determine the fire rating of the wall of Question 8.19, given that the units are made of expanded clay aggregate.

**8.21**  Describe the most commonly used method of protecting structural steel against fire.

**8.22**  With reference to Sweet's Catalog, list two major suppliers of structural steel fire protection materials. Briefly describe their products.

**REFERENCES**

8.1   Karter, M.J.: "Fire Loss in the United States in 1988", Fire Journal, Sep/Oct 1989, p. 29.

8.2   National Fire Protection Association, Quincy, Massachussetts: *Fire Protection Handbook*, 17th Edition, 1991, p. 1-5.

8.3   American Society of Testing and Materials, Philadelphia, Pennsylvania: *1992 Annual Book of ASTM Standards*, p. 352.

8.4   Harwood, B., and Hall, J.R.: "Smoke Inhalation or Burns", Fire Journal, May/June 1989, p. 29.

8.5   Butcher, E.G., and Parnell, A.C.: *Designing For Fire Safety*, John Wiley and Sons, 1983, p. 72.

8.6   Shaffer, G.S.: "Towards a Safer Built Environment", The Construction Specifier, March 1989, p. 118.

8.7   Underwriters Laboratory Inc., Northbrook, Illinois: *Directory of Fire Resistance*.

8.8   Underwriters Laboratory of Canada, Scarborough, Ontario.

8.9     Inchtape Testing Services — Warnock Hersey: *Certification Listings*.

8.10    Gypsum Association, Evanston, Illinois: *Fire Resistance Design Manual*, 14th Edition, 1994.

8.11    American Society for Testing and Materials, Philadelphia, Pennsylvania: "Standard Methods for Fire Tests of Building Construction and Materials", E 119-95.

8.12    American Society for Testing and Materials, Philadelphia, Pennsylvania: "Standard Methods of Fire Tests of Door Assemblies", E 152-81.

8.13    American Society for Testing and Materials, Philadelphia, Pennsylvania: "Standard Methods for Fire Tests of Window Assemblies", E 163-84.

8.14    American Society for Testing and Materials, Philadelphia, Pennsylvania: "Standard Methods for Surface Burning Characteristics of Building Materials", E 84-95.

8.15    International Conference of Building Officials, Whittier, California: *Handbook to the Uniform Building Code — An Illustrative Commentary*, 1991, p. 443.

8.16    International Conference of Building Officials, Whittier, California: "Methods For Calculating Fire Resistance of Steel, Concrete, Wood, Concrete Masonry and Clay Masonry Construction", UBC Standard 7-7, *Uniform Building Code*, Vol. 3, 1994.

# ACOUSTICAL PROPERTIES

**9.1 INTRODUCTION**

Acoustical and noise control problems exist in almost every modern building. Although an acoustical consultant will usually be required for the design of an auditorium or the solution of a complicated noise control problem, most building construction issues require a basic understanding of acoustic fundamentals. It is these fundamentals that are discussed in this chapter.

The chapter begins with a discussion of the physics of sound and the decibel scale, and then proceeds to describe the properties and use of sound absorbing materials. Reduction of noise affected by sound absorbing materials is discussed next. Finally, the chapter deals with sound insulating construction — a topic that is distinctly different from sound absorbing construction.

**9.2 FUNDAMENTALS OF WAVE MOTION**

Sound is the human ear's response to pressure fluctuations in the air caused by vibrating objects. For example, a tap on a wall produces sound because the tap makes the wall vibrate. The vibrating wall produces pressure fluctuations in the air. The same phenomenon occurs from the vibrations of a guitar string when the string is plucked.

Although most sounds in our environment are produced by vibrating objects, some sounds do not involve mechanical vibrations. They are produced by a sudden increase in air velocity, through turbulence in air flow. Thus, sound is produced when air escapes out of a compressed air line. Similarly, air escaping out of air-conditioning outlets produces sound because the outlets

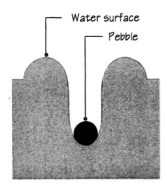

**FIGURE 9.1** Ripple produced on the surface of water by a pebble.

are smaller in cross-sectional area than the area of the duct, which increases the velocity of air at the outlets.

Sound travels in space by a phenomenon called *wave motion*. Wave motion in air is similar to the motion of a ripple produced by dropping a pebble into a pond. Imagine for a moment that you are sitting near a pond which is undisturbed by any air movement so that the surface of water is calm and free from all motion, and you drop a pebble in the pond. As soon as the pebble strikes the surface, a ripple radiates out from the point of impact in an ever increasing circular ring.

A closer examination of the ripple indicates that when the pebble strikes the surface of water, it creates a local depression on the surface. Since water, like most liquids, is incompressible, the particles of water adjacent to the point where the pebble strikes, are forced upwards. Thus, a ripple consisting of a trough and two crests, as shown in Figure 9.1, is formed at the surface of water.

Once the pebble has passed through the surface of water, the elasticity of bulk water tends to bring the water surface back to its normal state, causing the water particles to oscillate about their original undisturbed positions. This motion is transmitted to neighboring particles, so that the the ripple, and the energy contained in it, advances away from the point of the ripple's origin.

Observations of light floating objects in ponds indicate that while the ripple (or the wave) travels forward, the particles of water do not. The water particles simply oscillate up and down from their original positions. Thus in a wave motion, it is the energy contained in the wave that travels, not the particles of the medium.

Most waves in nature do not contain a single ripple, but rather a series of ripples, each following the preceding ripple after a constant time interval. The physical quantity that is related to the number of ripples generated in unit time is called the *frequency*. The other important quantities associated with wave motion are *wavelength* and the *speed* of wave travel. In fact, frequency, wavelength and the speed with which the wave travels are related to each other by a simple relationship. This relationship can be obtained with reference to the examination of multiple ripples produced in a liquid medium such as water.

Assume that the speed of travel of ripples (or waves) in a liquid medium is 100 ft per minute and the ripples are formed by dropping pebbles at the same location at a constant interval of 12 seconds, i.e., at a frequency of 5 pebbles per minute. Since the speed of wave travel is 100 ft per minute, the first ripple will have traveled a distance of 20 ft when the second pebble hits the surface of water, Figure 9.2(a). At the instant when the third pebble hits the surface of the water, the first ripple will be at a distance of 40 ft and the second ripple at a distance of 20 ft, Figure 9.2(b). Similarly, when the fourth pebble hits the surface, the first, second and third ripples will be at distances of 60 ft, 40 ft and 20 ft respectively, as shown in Figure 9.2(c). Thus we note that at any given instant, the distance between adjacent ripples is constant.

If the frequency is increased to 10 cycles per minute, we shall see that the distance between adjacent ripples is reduced to 10 ft. If the frequency is 2 cycles per minute, the corresponding distance between ripples increases to 50 ft.

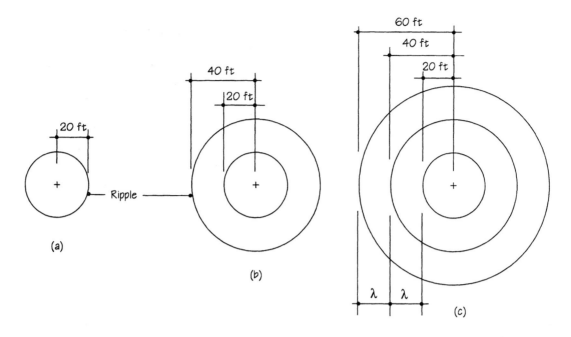

**FIGURE 9.2** Location of ripples at the instant when: (a) the second pebble hits the surface of water, (b) the third pebble hits the surface of water, and (c) the fourth pebble hits the surface of water.

The distance between two adjacent ripples at any instant is called the wavelength which is denoted by the Greek symbol "lambda" ($\lambda$). If the frequency is denoted by f, and the speed by v, the relationship between frequency, wavelength and the speed of a wave motion, as obtained from the above observation, is given by:

$$v = f\lambda \qquad\qquad (9.1)$$

Although the above relationship was obtained by considering ripples on the surface of a liquid, it applies to all kinds of wave motion including sound waves. Consider once again a wall set into vibration by an impact. As the wall moves to one side, say to the left, the air directly in contact with the left side of the wall is pushed to the left, creating compression in that layer of air. This compressed layer pushes the layer of air further to its left, which in turn pushes the next layer to the left, and so on. In this way, a compression ripple (or compression wave) travels away from the left of the wall in a domino-like manner.

When the wall reverses direction i.e., when it moves to the right, the opposite condition occurs. The layer of air to the left of the wall which was earlier in compression suffers a reduction in pressure, called *rarefaction*. The rarefaction is transferred to successive layers and a rarefaction wave travels away from the wall to the left exactly in the same way as the compression wave traveled.

Compression and rarefaction waves also travel to the right side of the wall. In fact when the air in contact with the left side of the wall is under compression, the air on the right side is under rarefaction, and vice versa.

**9.3 PROPERTIES OF SOUND WAVES**

It is the succession of pressure and rarefaction waves traveling away from a vibrating source that we refer to as the sound wave. A compression and rarefaction wave creates vibration (back-and-forth motion) of air particles. One back-and-forth motion of an air particle is called a *cycle*. Thus in one cycle, the particle starts from its original position of rest (shown by the black dot in Figure 9.3), moves to the extreme right, back to the particle's original position, to the extreme left, and finally back to its original position.

The above process repeats itself in the second and subsequent cycles. Note that the velocity of the particle in a cycle is maximum at its central position, and zero at extreme left and right, in the same way as the velocity of a pendulum is zero at extreme positions and maximum at the pendulum's central position. The maximum displacement of the particle from its rest position is called the *amplitude of vibration*.

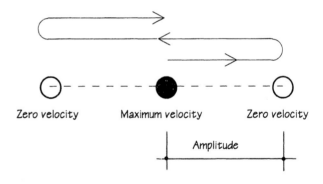

**FIGURE 9.3** Three cardinal positions of a vibrating particle and the corresponding particle velocities.

### 9.3.1 Frequency of Sound

The number of cycles that the air particles move back and forth in one second in a sound wave is called the frequency of the wave. Its unit is cycles per second (c/s) which is also termed *Hertz* (Hz) after the Austrian physicist Heinrich Hertz. Subjectively, the frequency of a sound wave is perceived as its pitch. A high pitched sound means that it has a high frequency. A female voice is slightly higher pitched than the male voice.

Frequency of sound is an important acoustical concept since the properties of building materials and construction assemblies vary with the frequency of sound. Additionally, the behavior of sound in an enclosure is also dependent on its frequency.

A normal young adult is capable of hearing sounds ranging from 20 Hz to 20 kHz. Frequencies below 20 Hz are called *infrasonic* frequencies. They are not heard but are perceived by humans as vibrations. Frequencies above 20 kHz, referred to as *ultrasonic* frequencies, are also not heard.

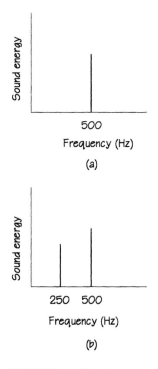

**FIGURE 9.4** Sound spectrum of (a) 500 Hz tuning fork, (b) 250 Hz and 500 Hz tuning forks sounding simultaneously.

Sounds in our environment do not generally consist of individual frequencies (a single note or pure tone) such as that produced by a tuning fork. If the frequency is represented on the horizontal axis and the energy contained in the sound is represented on the vertical axis, the graphical representation of a pure tone is a vertical line. For instance if a tuning fork of 500 Hz is struck, its representation will be as shown in Figure 9.4(a). The harder the tuning fork is struck, the louder the sound emitted by the tuning fork, i.e., the greater the sound energy produced. Therefore, the line representing the sound will be taller.

If two pure tones of different frequencies, say one at 250 Hz and the other at 500 Hz are produced simultaneously, their graphical representation will be two vertical lines, Figure 9.4(b). The two vertical lines will be of the same height if the energy content of each tone is the same. If the energy content of the two tones is different, their heights on the graph will be unequal.

The frequency-energy relationship of a sound is called the *sound spectrum*. Most sounds in our environment are complex, i.e., they consist of a continuum of frequencies, so that their spectrum is a continuous curve. For example, the human voice consists of sounds ranging from nearly 200 Hz to 5 kHz. The male voice peaks at nearly 400 Hz and the female voice at nearly 500 Hz, Figure 9.5.

**FIGURE 9.5** Approximate sound spectra of male and female speech.

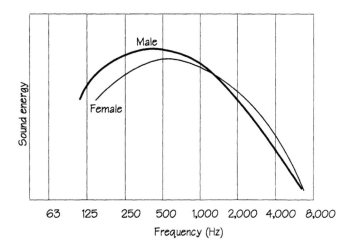

### 9.3.2 Octave Bands

Since the range of audible sound frequencies is rather large (20 Hz to 20 kHz), it is not possible to deal with individual frequencies. Therefore, we divide the entire range of audible sound frequencies into frequency bands, and study the properties of building materials, assemblies and enclosures with respect to these frequency bands.

A frequency band is simply a continuum of frequencies lying between two frequency limits. The width of the band is the difference between the lower frequency limit and the upper frequency limit. For example, if we arbitrarily choose a bandwidth of 200 Hz, the lower frequency limit of the first band will be 20 Hz and the higher frequency limit, 220 Hz. The lower

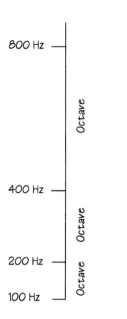

**FIGURE 9.6** Definition of an octave

and upper frequency limits of the next band will be 220 Hz and 420 Hz respectively, followed by a band ranging from 420 Hz to 620 Hz, and so on. In these frequency bands, the center frequency of the first band (the band extending from 20 Hz to 220 Hz) is 120 Hz, the center frequency of next band is 320 Hz, and so on. The center frequency of each band was obtained by averaging the upper and lower frequency limits, i.e., by adding the lower and upper frequency limits and dividing the sum by 2.

In architectural acoustics, we divide the entire range of audible frequencies into octave bands or simply *octaves*, a concept that has been borrowed from music. An octave is a band of frequencies whose upper frequency limit is twice the lower frequency limit. For example the frequency interval from 200 Hz to 400 Hz is an octave, the interval from 400 Hz to 800 Hz is the next higher octave, and so on, Figure 9.6.

The center frequency of an octave cannot be obtained by simply averaging the upper and lower frequency limits since the bandwidths of successive octaves are not constant, but increase by a factor of 2. For instance, the bandwidth of the octave ranging from 200 Hz to 400 Hz is 200 Hz, the bandwidth of octave ranging from 400 Hz to 800 Hz is 400 Hz.

The center frequency of an octave band is obtained by multiplying the upper and lower frequency limits and square rooting the product. Thus, the center frequency of an octave ranging from 200 Hz to 400 Hz is given by:

$$\sqrt{200 \times 400} \quad = \quad 283 \text{ Hz}$$

Since the lower and upper frequency limits of an octave are in the ratio of 1:2, the upper and lower frequency limits of an octave with a given center frequency is obtained by the following relationships.

$$\text{Upper frequency limit} \quad = \quad (\sqrt{2}) \text{ Center frequency}$$

$$\text{Lower frequency limit} \quad = \quad \frac{\text{Center frequency}}{\sqrt{2}}$$

In architectural acoustics, frequencies below 50 Hz and beyond 10 kHz are seldom important. Therefore, eight octaves with the following center frequencies are used: 63 Hz, 125 Hz, 250 Hz, 500 Hz, 1 kHz, 2 kHz, 4 kHz and 8 kHz. The upper and lower frequency limits of each octave are shown in Figure 9.7. For instance, the lower and upper frequency limits of the octave centered at 250 Hz are 177 Hz and 354 Hz. Octaves from 63 Hz to 250 Hz are generally referred to as low frequencies, 500 Hz and 1 kHz as mid frequencies, and 2 kHz to 8 kHz as high frequencies, Figure 9.7.

**FIGURE 9.7** Octaves, their center frequencies, and upper and lower frequency limits, given in Hz.

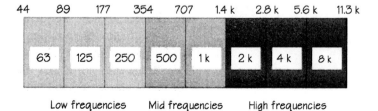

### 9.3.3 Frequency Ranges of Speech and Music

As indicated in Figure 9.5, the frequency range of speech extends from nearly 200 Hz to 5 kHz, covering nearly 4.5 octaves. Nearly 75% of sound energy in speech is contained in vowels which are low frequency components of speech. It is the sound in vowels that accounts for the distinguishing quality of an individual's speech.

The consonants are the high frequency components of speech. The energy contained in consonants is relatively small, but it is the consonants that provide intelligibility in human speech. Frequencies lower than 500 Hz contribute negligibly to speech intelligibility. The frequency range of speech is shown in Figure 9.8, which also gives frequency ranges for music and acoustic laboratory tests.

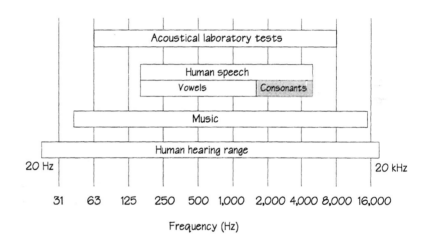

**FIGURE 9.8** Frequency ranges of acoustical laboratory tests, human speech, and music.

### 9.3.4 Velocity of Sound

The speed (or the velocity) of sound in air has been measured as 1,130 ft per second, ft/s (344 m/s). The speed of sound does not vary with the frequency of sound or its loudness. In other words, sounds at all audible frequencies, regardless of their loudness, travel at the same speed.

The velocity of sound in a solid medium is considerably larger than the velocity of sound in a gas or a liquid. For instance, the velocity of sound in steel is nearly fifteen times faster than in air. This explains why we are able to hear the vibrations of railroad tracks well before we receive the sound from the arriving train, which reaches us by traveling through the air.

### 9.3.5 Velocity of Air Particles

The reader should note that the velocity of sound is not the same as the velocity of air particles set into vibration by the sound. As seen from Figure 9.3, the velocity of a vibrating air particle varies with the distance of the particle from its central position. At the central position, the particle velocity is maximum; at the extreme positions, the particle velocity is zero.

The maximum particle velocity (as also the average particle velocity) is a function of two variables: the loudness of sound and the frequency of sound. The louder the sound, the greater the maximum (or the average) particle velocity. This can be realized by feeling a speaker cone. When the sound produced by the speaker is loud, the cone moves back and forth by a greater distance. At low sound levels, the speaker cone moves imperceptibly.

At normal conversation levels, the average velocity of air particles is approximately 0.1 mm/sec. In an extremely loud sound, the average particle velocity may reach nearly 1 cm/sec.

The frequency also affects velocity. If the frequency is high, the velocity also must be high because with a high frequency of vibration, the particle must return to its original position in a short duration. For a low frequency vibration, the particle velocity must be low. Thus, the particle velocity increases with increasing frequency.

## 9.4 PARTICLE VELOCITY AND WAVELENGTH OF SOUND

As stated in Section 9.2, the wavelength and the frequency of sound are related to each other according to Equation (9.1). The greater the frequency of sound, the smaller its wavelength. Thus, the wavelength of sound at 20 Hz is 1130/20 = 56.5 ft (17.2 m). At 20 kHz, the wavelength is 0.056 ft, or 0.7 in. (17 mm). The wavelength of sound corresponding to the center frequencies of various octaves is shown in Table 9.1.

Although the velocity of sound is 1,130 ft/sec, for most practical purposes it may be assumed as 1,000 ft/s. With that approximation, the wavelength of sound at 100 Hz is nearly 10 ft, at 1 kHz the wavelength is nearly 1 ft, at 2 kHz, the wavelength is 6 in., and so on.

Physically, the wavelength of a sound wave is the distance between adjacent compression peaks or adjacent rarefaction peaks, Figure 9.9. In fact, the wavelength of sound is the distance between two air particles which are in exactly the same vibrational situation.

**Table 9.1 Wavelength of Sound at Center Frequencies of Octaves**

| Frequency (Hz) | Wavelength (ft) | m |
|---|---|---|
| 63 | 18.0 | 5.5 |
| 125 | 9.0 | 2.8 |
| 250 | 4.5 | 1.4 |
| 500 | 2.3 | 0.7 |
| 1000 | 1.1 | 0.35 |
| 2000 | 0.6 | 0.17 |
| 4000 | 0.3 | 0.09 |
| 8000 | 0.15 | 0.04 |

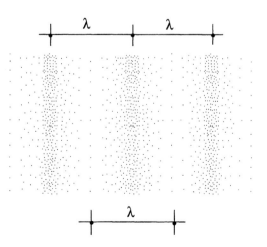

**FIGURE 9.9** The distribution of air particles at any instant in a sound wave. The wavelength ($\lambda$) of sound is the distance between adjacent compressions or adjacent rarefactions in air.

If we could somehow take a photographic picture of the vibrating particles of air in a sound wave, we would find that particles of air one wavelength apart are vibrating in phase, i.e., they both would either be moving to the left or the right at the same distance from their central positions. Thus if one particle is in the extreme right position, the other particle which is $\lambda$ away will also be in the extreme right position. Alternatively if one particle is in the extreme left position, the other particle will also be in that position, Figure 9.10(a). If one particle is moving to the left, the other particle will also move to the left. In other words, the particles of air $\lambda$ apart behave as if the two particles are connected together by a rigid bar. At any instant both particles are at the same distance from their central positions, are moving in the same direction, and have the same velocity.

Particles of air which are $0.5\lambda$ apart are completely out of phase with each other, i.e., if one particle is in the extreme right position, the other particle $0.5\lambda$ away will be in the extreme left position, Figure 9.10(b). These particles are either moving away from each other or moving toward each other. At any instant, both particles are at the same distance away from their rest positions, have the same velocity but are moving in opposite directions.

Particles of air which are $0.25\lambda$ apart are fifty percent out of phase which means that if one particle is at the central position, the other particle $0.25\lambda$ away will be in the extreme left or extreme right position, Figure 9.10(c) on the next page. At any instant, therefore, if one particle has zero velocity, the other particle which is $0.25\lambda$ away has the maximum velocity.

(a) Locations of two vibrating particles of air which are one wavelength apart.

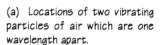

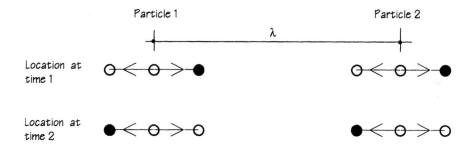

(b) Locations of two vibrating particles of air which are a half wavelength apart.

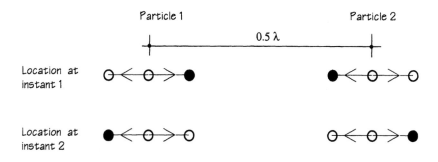

**FIGURE 9.10 (a) and (b)** Relative locations of vibrating air particles $\lambda$ and $0.5\lambda$ apart. A black dot indicates current particle location.

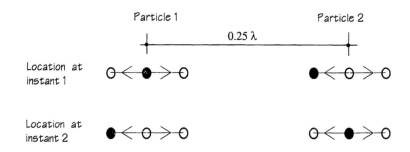

(c) Locations of two vibrating particles of air which are a quarter wavelength apart.

**FIGURE 9.10 (c)** Relative locations of vibrating air particles 0.25λ apart. A black dot indicates current particle location.

Since the velocity of air particles at the boundaries of an enclosure (interior surfaces of walls or ceiling) must obviously be zero, the maximum particle velocity in an enclosure occurs at 0.25λ away from the enclosure boundaries. This is an important fact since, as we shall see later, some of the sound absorption characteristics of building materials are influenced by this fact.

**9.5 THE DECIBEL SCALE**

The physical quantity associated with the loudness of sound is its intensity which is defined as the amount of sound power falling on (or passing through, or crossing) a unit area. Since the unit of power is Watt (see Section 4.2.1), the unit of sound intensity is Watts per square meter ($W/m^2$).

The sound intensity which is just audible, called the *threshold of audibility*, has been found to be $10^{-12}$ $W/m^2$, and the intensity that corresponds to the sensation of pain in the human ear[1] is approximately 10 W. Thus, the ear responds to a very large range of intensities since the loudest sound is 10,000,000,000,000 times ($10^{13}$ times) louder than the faintest sound.

In a situation, where one has to deal with a large range of the magnitudes of a given quantity, it is more convenient to express the magnitude as a ratio of a reference magnitude. In the case of sound intensity, the reference intensity is assumed as $10^{-12}$ $W/m^2$ and a given sound intensity is expressed as a multiple of the reference intensity. The multiple is obtained by dividing the given intensity ($I$) by the reference intensity ($I_{ref}$), i.e., the multiple is given by the ratio: ($I/I_{ref}$). For instance, $10^{-9}$ $W/m^2$ is 1,000 times (or $10^3$ times) the reference intensity. Similarly, $10^{-3}$ $W/m^2$ is $10^9$ times the reference intensity.

Dealing with a large range of magnitudes is further simplified if we express them as the logarithm of the above ratio. Thus, the intensity of a given sound can be expressed as:

$$\log \frac{I}{I_{ref}} \qquad \text{where } I_{ref} = 10^{-12} \ W/m^2$$

---

[1] The sound that produces pain in the human ear is not the loudest produceable sound. The sound intensity in the neighborhood of a space rocket during its liftoff exceeds $10^8$ $W/m^2$, which is equivalent of 200 dB.

Note that since the above logarithm is a ratio of two intensities, and since the ratio of two identical quantities has no units, the above logarithm is a unit-less (dimensionless) quantity. However, we arbitrarily assign to it the unit "Bel" in recognition of Alexander Graham Bell, the inventor of the telephone.

The numbers obtained from the above logarithmic manipulation are a little too small. Therefore, it is more common to use one-tenth of a Bel, called the decibel (abbreviated as dB) as the unit of this logarithm[2]. In other words, decibel is the unit of the following logarithmic ratio:

$$10 \, \log \frac{I}{I_{ref}}$$

The quantity defined by the above logarithm is called the *sound intensity level*, to distinguish it from sound intensity. Note once again that the unit of sound intensity level is dB, while the unit of sound intensity is $W/m^2$.

---

**Example 9.1**

Determine the sound intensity level of a sound whose intensity is (i) 0.0025 $W/m^2$, and (ii) 4.5 $W/m^2$.

*Solution:* (i) Sound intensity level = $10 \, \log \, (0.0025/10^{-12}) = 10 \, \log \, (2.5 \times 10^9) = 94$ dB.

(ii) Sound intensity level = $10 \, \log \, (4.5/10^{-12}) = 10 \, \log \, (4.5 \times 10^{12}) = 126.53$ dB, or 127 dB.

---

**Table 9.2 Perception of Change in Sound Intensity Levels**

| Change in level (dB) | Human perception |
|---|---|
| 1 | Imperceptible |
| 3 | Just perceptible |
| 5 | Clearly noticeable |
| 10 | Substantial change |

The above example shows that expressing the loudness of sound in dB is far more convenient than expressing it in $W/m^2$. For instance, it is easier to express the loudness of sound as 94 dB instead of expressing it as 0.0025 $W/m^2$. This fact may be further appreciated with reference to Figure 9.11 which gives the sound intensity and sound intensity levels of common environmental sounds.

Obtaining convenient numbers is not the only reason for the use of the decibel scale. The decibel scale also corresponds more directly to the ear's perception of loudness. For instance, a change of 1 dB in sound intensity level is hardly perceived by the human ear. That is why the sound intensity level is expressed in a whole number since expressing it as a decimal number indicates an unnecessary precision. Thus, a sound intensity level of 50.6 dB may be approximated to 51 dB without losing any accuracy. The minimum change in sound intensity level that is just perceptible is 3 dB. A 5 dB change is quite noticeable, and a 10 dB change is substantial, Table 9.2.

---

[2] The unit decibel is not unique to acoustics. It is used in all fields where the range of magnitude of a quantity is large.

| Sound intensity (W/m²) | Sound intensity level or sound pressure level (dB) | Noise in the environment |
|---|---|---|
| 10 | 130 | Threshold of pain |
| 1 | 120 | Near a jet aircraft at take-off |
| 0.1 | 110 | Riveting machine |
| 0.01 | 100 | Pneumatic hammer |
| 0.001 | 90 | |
| 0.0001 | 80 | Heavy truck at 50 ft |
| 0.00,001 | 70 | Vacuum cleaner at 10 ft / Busy office |
| 0.000,001 | 60 | Conversational speech at 3 ft |
| 0.0,000,001 | 50 | |
| 0.00,000,001 | 40 | |
| 0.000,000,001 | 30 | Bedroom at night |
| 0.0,000,000,001 | 20 | Quiet countryside |
| 0.00,000,000,001 | 10 | Human breathing |
| 0.000,000,000,001 | 0 | Threshold of audibility |

**FIGURE 9.11** Some typical noises in our environment, their sound intensities and sound intensity levels.

**FIGURE 9.12** Sound level meter by Bruel and Kjaer.

### 9.5.1 Sound Intensity Level and Sound Pressure Level

The loudness of sound is measured by a meter called the *sound level meter*. A typical sound level meter is shown in Figure 9.12. An important component of a sound level meter is the microphone in which the meter terminates. The microphone responds to the changes in air pressure created by the sound. A built-in amplifier converts the pressure changes into voltage changes. The voltage changes are then processed by the electronic circuitry of the meter into a quantity called the *sound pressure level* (SPL) which is displayed on the meter's panel.

Thus, in practice it is the sound pressure level, not the sound intensity level that is measured. However, in architectural acoustics, the sound pressure level is approximately equal to the sound intensity level. Therefore the two terms, sound pressure level and sound intensity level, are used synonymously.

## 9.6 BOUNDARY PHENOMENA IN ACOUSTICS

When sound energy falls on a boundary of an enclosure — a wall or ceiling — a part of the energy is reflected back into the enclosure, a part is absorbed within the material of the boundary and converted to heat, and a part is transmitted through the enclosure's boundary. The fraction of the total sound energy falling on a boundary element that is reflected by the element is called the *reflection coefficient* of the element, denoted by the Greek symbol "rho" ($\rho$). Since the reflected energy is always less than the total energy falling on the element, $\rho$ is always less than 1.0, and is generally expressed as a decimal number. For instance, if the reflected sound energy is 20% of the incident sound energy, $\rho = 0.2$.

The fraction of the incident sound that is transmitted through the element is called the *transmission coefficient* denoted by the Greek symbol "tau" ($\tau$). The fraction of the incident sound that is absorbed into the material of the element is called its *absorption coefficient*, represented by the Greek symbol "alpha" ($\alpha$). Since the sum of the reflected, absorbed and transmitted amounts of energy must be equal to the total incident energy, the following relationship must hold:

$$\rho + \alpha + \tau = 1.0$$

The most important property of a boundary element that affects sound reflection, absorption and transmission characteristics is its weight. Massive and heavy weight elements are more reflective than lightweight elements, i.e. the value of $\rho$ for heavy weight elements is high. Since a heavy weight element is more reflective, less sound is available to go through it. Thus, a heavy weight element transmits little sound, i.e., the value of $\tau$ for a heavy weight element is small. To appreciate the reason for the above fact, consider a wall with a sound source located as shown in Figure 9.13.

Before the sound source is turned on, the air on both the source side and the receiver side of the wall is calm. However, when the source is turned on, the air particles on the source side begin to vibrate. The vibrating air particles in proximity to the wall on the source side produce vibrations in the wall. The vibrating wall in turn produces vibrations in the air on the receiver side, which are perceived as sound.

If the wall is heavy, the amplitude of vibrations in the wall is small. Consequently, the vibrations in the air on the receiver side have a small

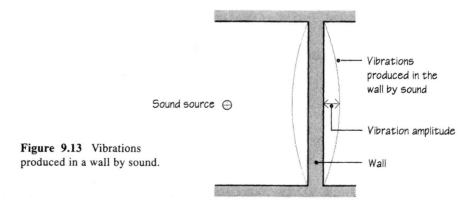

**Figure 9.13** Vibrations produced in a wall by sound.

amplitude, implying that very little sound transmits through the wall. On the other hand, a lightweight wall has large vibrations, producing large vibrations in the air on the receiver side. Therefore, a greater amount of sound transmits through the wall.

If we examine the reflection, absorption and transmission characteristics of sound from the perspective of an enclosure's interior, we find that both the absorbed and the transmitted parts of sound energy are lost from the enclosure. Therefore, the absorbed and the transmitted parts are grouped together and considered as the absorbed part. In other words, in considering the acoustics of an enclosure, we assume that of the sound energy that falls on an enclosure boundary, a part is reflected and a part absorbed, i.e:

$$\rho + \alpha = 1.0$$

In the above equation, the absorption coefficient ($\alpha$) also includes the transmission coefficient. Thus, the absorption coefficient is that fraction of incident sound energy that is not reflected by the enclosure. That is why the two walls shown in Figure 9.14 are considered to have the same absorption coefficient although the wall of Figure 9.14(a) transmits more sound than that of Figure 9.14(b). It is for the same reason that an open window, although not absorbing any sound, is considered a perfect acoustical absorber because all the sound falling on the window is transmitted to the outdoors. Thus, for an open window, the absorption coefficient = 1.0.

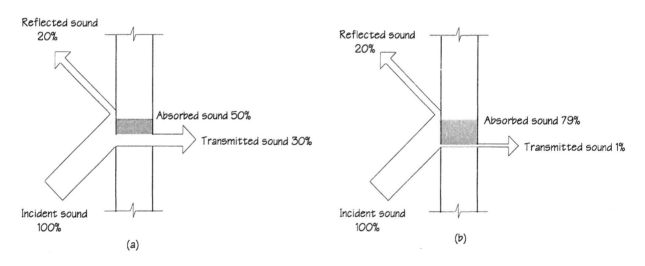

**FIGURE 9.14**  Two assemblies which have the same overall absorption and reflection characteristics.

**9.7 SOUND DIFFRACTION**

As stated in the previous section, a building element must be heavy to provide a strong reflection of sound. Another factor that affects the reflection of sound is the size of the element. If the element is small in relation to the wavelength of sound, most of the sound energy will bend around the edges of the element and travel forward without creating any reflection. The property of sound to bend around the edges of an obstacle is called *diffraction*. It is because of diffraction that we are able to hear the sound even when the sound source is not visible to us. If the size of the element is large compared with the wavelength of sound, most of the sound will be reflected from the element; only a small amount of sound will diffract.

Thus, we see that the degree of diffraction is influenced by the dimensions of the element in relation to the wavelength of sound. Diffraction effect is more pronounced if the wavelength of sound is large in comparison with the dimension of the obstacle , i.e., lower frequency sounds bend around a given obstacle more than high frequency sounds, as shown in Figure 9.15.

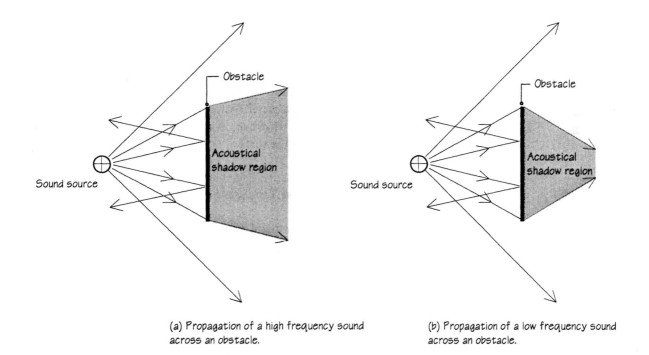

(a) Propagation of a high frequency sound across an obstacle.

(b) Propagation of a low frequency sound across an obstacle.

**FIGURE 9.15** Diffraction of sound produced by an obstacle.

### 9.7.1 Diffraction and the Size of Reflector

Experimental observations indicate that for a plane rectangular obstacle to reflect most of the sound impinging on it, both its dimensions must be at least $5\lambda$. For instance, the size of the panel must be at least 10 ft x 10 ft if it is to be used as a reflector for a 500 Hz sound, since $\lambda$ for a 500 Hz sound is approximately 2 ft. If the dimensions of the panel are progressively decreased so that it is less than $5\lambda$ on either side, increasingly greater diffraction will occur. If the panel size is equal to $\lambda$ in both directions, most of the sound will bend around the panel with very little sound reflected from the panel.

Diffraction is not unique to sound. In fact, it occurs in all kinds of wave motion including light, which is also a wave phenomenon. However, we usually do not experience the bending of light around the edges of objects because the wavelength of light is extremely small in comparison with the objects in our environment. For instance, the wavelength of light is less than 0.000003 in. ( 0.0007 mm). It is because of the relatively small wavelength of light with respect to the sizes of obstacles that light produces sharp shadows.

By comparison, the sizes of obstacles in our environment such as a column in a hall, a low height partition in an office, or a boundary wall between courtyards of two adjacent dwellings, are usually of the same order of size as the wavelength of sound. Remember that the wavelength of sound varies from nearly 50 ft at 20 Hz to nearly 1 in. at 10 KHz. It is because of the relatively large wavelength of sound that sound is able to bend around obstacles.

Because of its small wavelength, a high frequency sound behaves like light, producing sharper acoustical shadows than a low frequency sound. Thus, the region of acoustical shadow behind an obstacle is larger for a high frequency sound than for a low frequency sound, as shown in Figure 9.15.

Note, that regardless of the size of the panel, sound diffraction will always occur around the edges of a panel. In other words, reflection of sound from a panel is never complete. However, for a panel greater than $5\lambda$ in size, the amount of diffracted sound is small.

### 9.7.2 Sound Transmission Through Screens

It is because of diffraction that a much greater percentage of sound energy transmits through screens than the percentage of voids in the screen. For instance if the area of voids in a screen is 30% (i.e., a visual transparency of 30%), the amount of sound energy that transmits through the screen (acoustical transparency) is greater than 30%. In other words, the acoustical transparency is always greater than the visual transparency.

The acoustical transparency of a screen depends on the frequency of sound. The higher the frequency, the closer the acoustical transparency is to the visual transparency. As the sound frequency is decreased, the acoustical transparency of the screen increases. For low frequency sounds, virtually 100% of sound passes through a screen of 20% visual transparency.

The effectiveness of screens to transmit sound is used extensively in building interiors. Since most sound absorbing materials are fibrous, they need to be protected, and require that specially designed wood screens, perforated metal or plywood panels, or fabric coverings be used.

The acoustical transparency of a screen is not only a function of its visual transparency. It is also a function of the distribution of voids in the screen. For a given visual transparency, small closely spaced voids provide greater acoustical transparency than large voids spaced farther apart. For example, the screen of Figure 9.16(a) has a greater acoustical transparency than the screen of Figure 9.16(b), which in turn has greater acoustical transparency than the screen of Figure 9.16(c), although the visual transparency of all three screens is the same — 30%. Indeed, the acoustical transparency of all three screens increases with decreasing sound frequency.

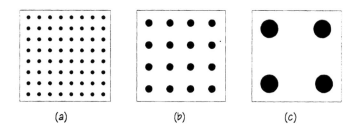

**FIGURE 9.16** Three perforated panel screens of equal (30%) visual transparency but different acoustical transparencies.

(a)                          (b)                          (c)

The reason for the above fact is provided by the diffraction phenomenon. In a screen with small closely spaced voids such as the one of Figure 9.16(a), the individual solid areas are small. Consequently, a large amount of sound is able to bend around the solid areas and pass through the screen. In a screen with only a few large voids such as the one of Figure 9.16(c), the solid areas are large. Hence, a large portion of sound is reflected from them, and a small amount passes through the screen

The diffraction phenomenon also explains why a thicker screen is less acoustically transparent than a thinner screen. Thus, of the two perforated panels, the one of Figure 9.17(a) is more acoustically transparent than that of Figure 9.17(b) although the visual transparency of both panels is the same. For perforated metal panels which are usually 30 to 60 mil thick, a visual transparency of 30% provides nearly 90% acoustical transparency at 8 kHz[9.1].

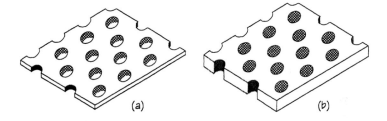

**FIGURE 9.17** Perforated panels of different thickness but same visual transparency.

(a)                                    (b)

**9.8 RATINGS OF SOUND ABSORBING MATERIALS**

All materials and objects absorb sound to some degree. However, materials whose sound absorption coefficient is greater than 0.2 are called *sound absorbing materials*, or *acoustical materials* although the former term is preferable. For the same reason, the term *acoustical treatment* usually implies sound absorptive treatment.

The sound absorption coefficient of a material varies with the angle of incidence of sound — the angle at which the sound strikes the surface of the material. However in a room, the sound strikes its surfaces from all angles with almost equal probability. Therefore, we are usually interested in the *random incidence absorption coefficient*. The random incidence absorption coefficient is the absorption coefficient averaged over all angles of incidence. In the following discussion, the random incidence absorption coefficient will be referred to simply as the absorption coefficient ($\alpha$) of the material.

The value of $\alpha$ varies with the frequency of sound. In architectural acoustics, we are normally concerned with the value of $\alpha$ in six octaves, ranging from 125 Hz to 4 kHz. Thus, the values of $\alpha$ are generally quoted at 125 Hz, 250 Hz, 500 Hz, 1 kHz, 2 kHz, and 4 kHz.

### 9.8.1 Noise Reduction Coefficient

The noise reduction coefficient (NRC) of a material is the average value of the absorption coefficients at 250, 500, 1,000 and 2,000 Hz, rounded off to 0.05. Thus:

$$NRC = \frac{\alpha_{250} + \alpha_{500} + \alpha_{1000} + \alpha_{2000}}{4}$$

For example, if the values of $\alpha$ for a material are:

| Frequency (Hz) | $\alpha$ |
|---|---|
| 125 | 0.16 |
| 250 | 0.31 |
| 500 | 0.52 |
| 1000 | 0.83 |
| 2000 | 0.91 |
| 4000 | 0.97 |

the NRC of the material is:

$$NRC = \frac{0.31 + 0.52 + 0.83 + 0.91}{4} = 0.65$$

We see from the definition of NRC that it is a single number rating of the sound absorptive property of a material. The convenience of NRC lies in its single number specification. However, since the low and high frequencies are not fully represented in the NRC value, the applicability of NRC data is limited to those noise control situations where most of the sound energy lies between 250 Hz and 2 kHz. Such situations include interiors where noise is primarily due to speech since most of speech energy lies in the four octaves ranging from 250 Hz to 2 kHz (see Figure 9.5).

Sound absorptive materials used in offices, restaurants, airport waiting areas, and such other assembly spaces are commonly specified based on the NRC value. In situations where a significant amount of sound energy lies outside the above four octaves, the values of $\alpha$ at these other frequencies must also be examined.

### 9.8.2 The Unit of Sound Absorption

The product of the area of an absorber and its absorption coefficient is called the *sound absorption* of the material. Thus, if the surface area of a material is S, and its absorption coefficient $\alpha$, then the sound absorption provided by the material (A) is:

$$A = S\alpha$$

(9.2)

The unit of absorption (A) is called *sabin*, after the American acoustician Wallace Cement Sabine. Thus, if the surface area of a material is 100 ft$^2$ and its absorption coefficient is 0.75, the amount of absorption provided by this material is 100 x 0.75 = 75 sabin.

Since the surface area may be in square feet or square meters, the unit "sabin" is either a foot sabin or metric sabin. One metric sabin = 10.76 ft sabins, since 1 m$^2$ = 10.76 ft$^2$.

## 9.9 SOUND ABSORBING MATERIALS

Sound absorbing materials may be classified under the following three types — a classification based on the mechanism by which they absorb sound:

- Porous absorbers
- Panel or membrane absorbers
- Volume absorbers

### 9.9.1 Porous Absorbers

Almost any material whose surface is porous may be considered a porous absorber. The porosity of the material may be either due to the fibrous composition, or due to voids between granules or particles of the material. Fiberglass and mineral wool are the most commonly used porous absorbers. Mineral fiberboards with fissured or pierced surfaces are used as ceiling tiles in most commercial interiors.

A sound wave falling on a porous absorber causes the air in the voids of the material to vibrate back and forth. As the air vibrates in the voids, the vibrational energy of air is converted into heat due to friction between air particles and void walls.

For frictional losses to occur, it is important that the voids in the material must be interconnected and continuous so that the air can pump back and forth within the material. Thus, only open-cell materials can be good sound absorbers. Plastic foams such as expanded polystyrene and polyisocyanurate which have closed unconnected cells are poor sound absorbers. On the other hand, urethane and melamine foams are good sound absorbers because of their open cell structure.

The effectiveness of a porous material, such as fiberglass, depends on its *flow resistance*, defined as the degree of difficulty by which the air will flow through the material. If the flow resistance is too low, the frictional losses are small. Consequently, the value of $\alpha$ is low. On the other hand, if the flow resistance is too high, the air flow through the material is so limited that the frictional losses are once again low. Thus, there is an optimum value of flow resistance that provides the highest value of $\alpha$ for the material.

The flow resistance depends on the density of fibrous material and the fiber diameter. In general, the greater the density and the thinner the fiber, the greater the flow resistance. A simple test to estimate the flow resistance of a fibrous material is to blow air through it. Materials which allow little or no air to pass provide little or no sound absorption. Fiberglass with a density ranging from 1 to 9 lb/ft$^3$ is commonly used as sound absorbing material.

The effectiveness of a porous absorber increases with the thickness of the absorber. The increase is relatively large at low frequencies (from 125 Hz to 1 kHz) and small at high frequencies, Figure 9.18. This is due to the fact that the particle velocity maximizes at a distance of 0.25$\lambda$ from the back-up wall or ceiling (see Section 9.4). Note that the particle velocity is zero at the surface of the back-up wall or ceiling because, being a heavy element, it is not set into vibration by the pressure fluctuations of sound. With a larger thickness of porous absorber, low frequencies (with their longer wavelengths) are more likely to be intercepted by the absorber in the region where the particle velocities are high, resulting in greater sound absorption at low frequencies.

Stated differently, the above fact implies that the layer of porous absorber which is in direct contact with the back-up is useless in absorbing sound since the particle velocity is zero there. The effectiveness of the layers increases as we move away from the back-up until it maximizes at 0.25$\lambda$ away from the back-up. After that, the effectiveness decreases again and maximizes at 1.25$\lambda$ away from the back-up. For example, for a 1 kHz sound ($\lambda$ approximately equal to 12 in.), the effectiveness of absorber maximizes at 3 in., and then at 15 in., 27 in., 39 in., etc. from the back-up.

Of course for reasons of economy and space utilization, we do not use a porous absorber with a thickness of 1.25$\lambda$. In fact, a material such as fiberglass is seldom used in thickness exceeding 2 in. At 4 in. thick, a fiberglass blanket provides fairly high values of $\alpha$ in both the low and high frequency regions,

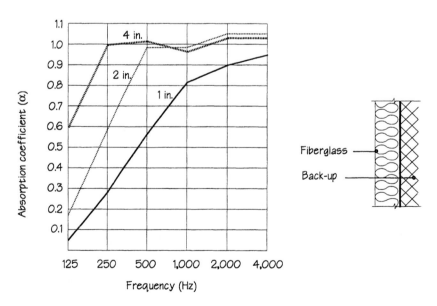

**FIGURE 9.18** Frequency-$\alpha$ relationships for 1 in., 2 in. and 4 in. thick fiberglass blankets (density 6 lb/ft$^3$).

as shown in Figure 9.18. An 8 in. thick fiberglass blanket gives a virtually flat frequency-α relationship.

It is precisely because of the above reason that for the commonly used thickness of 1 to 2 in., the absorption coefficient of a porous absorber increases with frequency. For the higher frequencies, the absorber thickness is comparable with 0.25λ, but for the lower frequencies, the absorber thickness is so small that the absorber is not available at locations of high particle velocities.

Note that the value of α may exceed 1.0. This apparent anomaly is due to the measuring procedure for determining the value of α. Values of up to 1.1 may be obtained for thick porous absorbers.

If a porous material is spaced away from the back-up wall or ceiling with an intervening air cavity, its frequency-α relationship is similar to that of a thicker material placed against the back-up without any cavity. In other words, the provision of air cavity increases the sound absorption of the material at low frequencies. At frequencies above 1,000 Hz, the increase in the value of α is usually insignificant, Figure 9.19. The slight decrease in the value of α at high frequencies is due to the presence of cavity space in locations of maximum particle velocity.

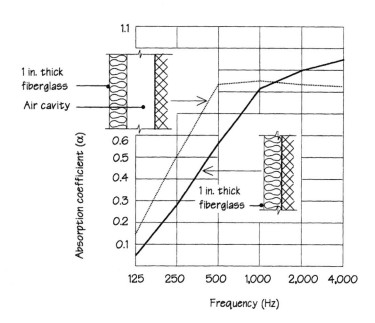

**FIGURE 9.19** The effect of cavity space on frequency-α relationship of a 1 in. thick fiberglass blanket.

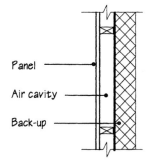

**FIGURE 9.20** A solid unperforated panel against a hard back-up with an intervening cavity space.

## 9.9.2 Panel or Membrane Absorbers

A solid unperforated panel installed against a hard back-up with an intervening air space acts as a panel absorber, Figure 9.20. When a sound wave impinges on such a panel, it sets the panel into vibration. Since the panel is never fully elastic, it looses some energy by damping.

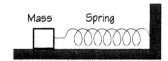

**FIGURE 9.21** A mass-spring assembly.

The vibration of the panel is similar to the vibration of a mass attached to a spring, Figure 9.21. Just as a mass-spring assembly loses energy and gradually stops oscillating due to damping forces, so does the panel. In the case of mass-spring assembly, the damping is caused by the viscosity of the medium. The more viscous the medium, the greater the energy loss by damping. Thus, the damping forces are larger if the mass-spring assembly oscillates in an oil medium than in air because of the greater viscosity of oil. Additional damping in a mass-spring assembly is provided by frictional losses at the surface on which the mass oscillates. Damping also exists within the material of the spring.

For a given mass-spring assembly, damping forces increase as the velocity of the mass increases. The velocity of the mass is maximum at resonant frequency. Therefore, the damping forces have the maximum effect at the *resonant frequency*. The resonant frequency of mass-spring assembly is its natural frequency — the frequency at which the mass will oscillate when it is pulled to one side and, thereafter, is left to oscillate on its own.

In the case of the panel, the damping is provided by the medium and at its edge fixing. An additional source of damping exists in the material of the panel which comes into play due to bending vibrations in the panel. Because the damping forces are maximum at the resonant frequency of the panel, a panel absorber has a maximum value of $\alpha$ at the resonant frequency. On both sides of the resonant frequency, the value of $\alpha$ decreases.

In our analogy between the mass-spring assembly and the panel absorber, the panel represents the mass and the air behind the panel acts as the spring (cushion). A smaller depth of air behind the panel represents a stiffer spring. Conversely, a greater cavity depth implies a more supple spring. This analogy provides an approximate relationship for calculating the resonant frequency of a panel as:

$$f_{res} = \frac{170}{\sqrt{m\,d}}$$

where, m = mass of panel in lb/ft$^2$ and d = air space behind the panel in inches. Thus, for a $^1/_2$ in. thick gypsum board panel weighing 4 lb/ft$^2$ with a 1 in. air space, the resonant frequency of the panel is:

$$f_{res} = \frac{170}{\sqrt{(4)\,1}} = 85\ Hz$$

Similarly, the resonant frequency of a 28 gauge steel panel weighing 0.75 lb/ft$^2$ with $^1/_2$ in. air space is 279 Hz. The resonant frequency of a practical panel lies somewhere between 50 to 400 Hz. Typical panel absorbers in building interiors include gypsum board partitions, wood paneling, glass windows and suspended ceilings.

The absorption coefficient of a panel absorber even at the resonant frequency rarely exceeds 0.4 because of the vibrations of the panel which makes it act as a sound radiator. However, if the panel's material lacks stiffness, i.e., if it is made of a limp material such as a thin lead sheet or a built-up roofing felt, the value of $\alpha$ at resonant frequency is nearly 1.0, because of the large damping present in the material.

The absorption coefficient of a panel absorber increases if a porous absorber is placed in the cavity space between the panel and the back-up, Figure 9.22. The inclusion of a porous material in the cavity introduces damping in the system which increases its absorption. In our analogy of the panel absorber with the mass-spring assembly, the introduction of porous material behind the panel is like increasing the viscosity of the medium in which the mass spring assembly oscillates. The change in the absorption coefficient of the panel is quite marked in the low frequency region near the resonant frequency. At high frequencies, the change is negligible

The most commonly used porous material in the cavity space is fiberglass. It is immaterial where in the cavity space the porous material is placed, although attaching the porous material to the panel's back is a convenient place to put it.

**FIGURE 9.22** Approximate frequency-α relationship of $^1/_2$ in. thick plywood panel backed by 1 in. air space — with and without a porous absorber in the cavity.

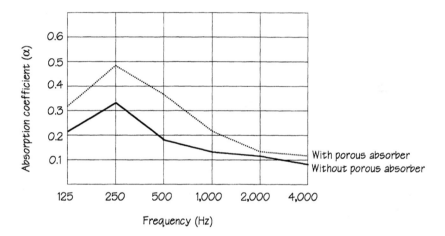

### 9.9.3 Volume Absorbers

The third and last class of absorbers is called a volume absorber or a cavity absorber, which is also referred to as the *Helmholtz resonator*. This type of absorber consists of a volume of air connected to the general atmosphere through a small volume of air called the neck. A Helmholtz resonator is similar to an "open bottle" where the volume of air in the bottle is connected to the outside atmosphere through the air in the bottle's neck, Figure 9.23.

When a sound wave impinges on an open bottle, the mass of air in the neck oscillates back and forth, similar to the mass-spring assembly. The air in the neck acts as the mass and the air in the body of the bottle as the spring. As the air in the neck oscillates, it loses energy by friction against the walls of the neck. The oscillation of the neck peaks at the resonant frequency of the bottle, which implies that the sound absorption provided by the bottle is maximum at the resonant frequency.

That an open bottle has a resonant frequency can be demonstrated by blowing across its neck. The bottle will always produce the same pitch of sound regardless of who blows it and how it is blown. Usually, the resonant frequency of a bottle lies in the low frequency region.

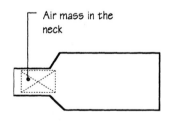

**FIGURE 9.23** An open bottle as a volume absorber.

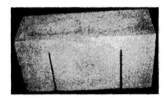

**Figure 9.24** The top of a sound block.

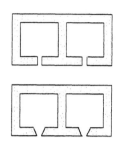

**Figure 9.25** Two commonly used profiles of slots in a sound block.

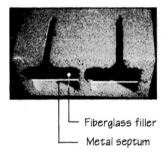

— Fiberglass filler

— Metal septum

**Figure 9.26** Sound block with fibrous filler and metal septum.

**Figure 9.27** Sound blocks used in Test Facility, General Motors, Detroit. Courtesy of: Proudfoot Company Inc., Monroe, Connecticut.

The most commonly used volume absorber is a slotted concrete masonry unit, more commonly referred to as the *sound block*. The sound block consists of a concrete masonry unit with a long narrow slot in each cell. Thus, in a two-cell unit, there are two slots. The slot functions as the neck and the cell space as the interior of the bottle. For a cell to function as a bottle, the cell cavity must be closed. Therefore, unlike a normal concrete block in which the cells are open on both sides, the cells in a sound block are closed on one side. The units are laid in the wall with their closed sides facing up, Figure 9.24.

The resonant frequency of the unit can be varied by an octave or so by changing the slot's width, height and profile. Two profiles are commonly used — a rectangular profile or a funnel shaped profile, Figure 9.25. In fact, several different types of sound blocks are available to suit different applications.

The sound absorption property of sound blocks can be improved by adding a fibrous filler laminated to a metal septum in each cell space, Figure 9.26. However, where noise control in high humidity spaces is required such as in indoor swimming pools and where manufacturing processes utilizing a great deal of water take place, fibrous pads are not used.

Sound blocks are used extensively for noise control in manufacturing spaces, school gymnasiums, air conditioning rooms, swimming pools, skating rinks, test facilities, etc., Figure 9.27. Their popularity lies in the fact that the units provide sound absorption as an integral part of a fire-rated structural wall, unlike the porous and panel absorbers which are mere addendums to a structural wall or ceiling. Sound blocks are also used in auditoriums and music rooms, particularly in the rear walls of auditoriums, Figure 9.28.

The sound block of Figure 9.29 is particularly suitable for loadbearing

**Figure 9.28** Sound blocks used in the rear wall of A-1 Classy Theater, University of Texas at Arlington.

**Figure 9.29** Sound block with additional cells for reinforcing and grouting.

wall applications since it consists of two twin cells. The two cells in the front are slotted to provide sound absorption. The two cells at the back are open at the top and bottom, like the normal units, so that they can be grouted and reinforced if required.

As stated previously, the maximum sound absorption of a sound block lies in the low frequency region — in 125 or 250 octaves. Approximate frequency-$\alpha$ relationships of an 8 in. thick unit with and without fibrous fillers are shown in Figure 9.30.

**FIGURE 9.30** Approximate frequency-$\alpha$ relationships of an 8 in. thick sound block — with and without a fibrous filler.

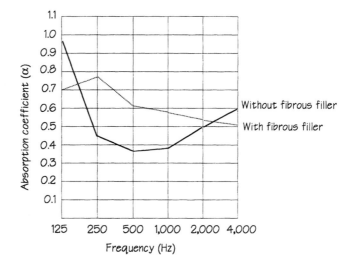

### 9.9.4 Acoustic Ceiling Tiles

An acoustical tile ceiling has become a standard feature of most commercial, educational and institutional interiors, Figure 9.31. An acoustical tile is a

**FIGURE 9.31** A typical acoustical tile ceiling. Courtesy of: The Celotex Corporation, Tampa, Florida.

prefabricated fiberglass or mineral wool rigid board available in modular sizes, usually in 2 ft x 2 ft or 2 ft x 4 ft units. Their thickness normally ranges from $1/_2$ in. to $1^1/_2$ in. and they are simply laid-in on an aluminum supporting framework suspended from the floor or roof.

Being made of a fibrous material, the absorption characteristics of ceiling tiles correspond with that of a porous absorber. However, since there is usually a large air space above the ceiling, the tiles also behave as panel absorbers. In other words, the sound absorption characteristics of a prefabricated tile ceiling combines the characteristics of a porous as well as a panel absorber. Manufacturers of these systems provide the values of $\alpha$ as a function of frequency in addition to the NRC data.

Ceiling tiles are usually prepainted. However, to improve their absorption, the fibers are exposed by piercing, fissuring or scoring the surface of tiles. A few of the commonly used surface textures of tiles are shown in Figure 9.32. Note that in-service painting of ceiling tiles will alter their absorption characteristics. Therefore, if the tiles must be repainted, it should be done according to the manufacturer's recommendations.

**FIGURE 9.32** Commonly used surface textures of ceiling tiles. Courtesy of: The Celotex Corporation, Tampa, Florida.

## 9.10 SCREENS OVER POROUS ABSORBERS

A porous absorber such as fiberglass or mineral wool should preferably be wrapped in an impervious membrane to prevent the accumulation of dust in its voids and to prevent loose fibers from mixing with the interior air. The membrane must be very thin and lightweight to respond to pressure fluctuations created by sound. Thus, it is not necessary for the air to penetrate the porous absorber. As long as the membrane is sufficiently lightweight to yield to pressure fluctuations, it will be able to pump air back and forth in the porous absorber and thus activate its absorption mechanism. Usually, a very thin plastic membrane (not exceeding 1 mil thick) is used. The membrane has virtually no effect on low frequency absorption, but may slightly reduce high frequency absorption.

In addition to being wrapped, a porous absorber must also be protected by a screen to prevent its physical damage and abuse. The screen modifies the absorption properties of a porous absorber. The modification depends on the acoustical transparency of the screen (see Section 9.7.2), the thickness of screen, and the depth of air space between the screen and the absorber. The more commonly used screens include perforated metal panels, perforated plywood or hardboard panels, natural or synthetic fabric, and screens made of wood slats.

### 9.10.1 Perforated Panels

The most commonly used perforated panels consist of aluminum, or galvanized/painted steel pans. The pans hold the porous absorber and are commonly used in ceiling installations in which the pans are simply laid in on a two-way network of supporting metal frame, similar to a standard acoustical tile ceiling. Fiberglass or mineral wool pads are placed over the pans before their installation, so that only the pans and the supporting frame are exposed to the interior. The pads are usually 1 to 2 in. thick mineral wool or fiberglass and may be wrapped in a lightweight plastic membrane.

Perforated metal pan ceiling systems are manufactured by several manufacturers, with only minor differences in their products. The system is particularly suitable in noisy spaces where the cleaning of ceiling panels may be required. The incombustibility of pans and their longer life is an additional advantage. In spaces where high humidity is present such as in food processing and dishwashing areas, aluminum pans and an aluminum support system are preferable over those of steel.

Pans with various perforation sizes and open areas (various visual transparencies) are available. Generally, the provision of perforated pans reduces the high frequency absorption of a porous absorber but improves its low frequency absorption. High frequency absorption is reduced because the solid areas between perforations reflect sound at high frequencies.

Pans improve the low frequency absorption of the porous absorber by functioning as membrane absorbers. In addition, each individual perforation functions as a cavity resonator wherein the perforation acts as the neck of the bottle and the space at the back of the panel as the bottle's cavity, further improving the low frequency absorption.

The frequency-$\alpha$ relationship of a perforated metal pan system depends on various factors, such as the size and spacing of perforations, thickness of pans, thickness of fibrous absorber, etc. Manufacturers of metal pan systems will provide data about this relationship.

### 9.10.2 Wood Slat Screens

Closely spaced horizontal or vertical wood slats are other commonly used screens over fiberglass or mineral wool. Their popularity lies in the attractiveness of wood and the reticulation provided by thin linear members, Figure 9.33. The fiberglass is covered with a chicken wire mesh or a grille cloth for additional protection before installing the wood screen.

**FIGURE 9.33** Wood slat covered rear wall of Keller High School Auditorium, Keller, Texas. Slats by Ventwood, Howard Manufacturing Company, Kent Washington. Architect: VLK Associates, Arlington, Texas. Acoustical consultant: Jim Johnson, Dallas, Texas.

### 9.10.3 Fabric Coverings

Woven fabrics are another means of covering fiberglass or mineral wool absorbers. A woven fabric is acoustically transparent (even at high frequencies), which implies that the absorption properties of the porous absorber are not modified by the covering. Since various colors and textures are possible in a fabric, fabric facing is an extremely convenient method of protecting a porous absorber.

Various prefabricated panels are commercially available in which the core of the panel consists of high density fiberglass or mineral wool and the facing consists of a decorative fabric. Fabric covered panels are commonly used as wall panels in which the panels can be attached to a wall, Figure 9.34. Fabric covered panels are also used in low height partitions in open plan offices where sound absorption is necessary to provide a measure of speech privacy between work stations.

Panels ————

**FIGURE 9.34** Fabric covered sound absorbing panels in the foyer of Keller High School, Keller, Texas.

Fabric covered porous absorbers may also be used in ceilings. They are usually suspended from the floor or roof, either in the form of rectangular panels or in hollow three-dimensional shapes, Figure 9.35. Suspended absorbers are particularly useful in situations where the ceilings are high, or where a conventional tile ceiling is impractical.

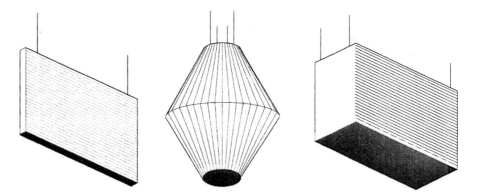

**FIGURE 9.35** A few shapes of suspended space absorbers.

**9.11 REDUCING NOISE BY USING SOUND ABSORBING MATERIALS**

The primary purpose of using sound absorbing materials is to reduce interior noise. Note that the use of sound absorbing materials reduces only the reflected sound. The direct sound from the source is not reduced. The reflected sound is the main contributor of noise at an interior location which is far away from the sound source. At a location near the source, it is the direct sound that dominates. Therefore, sound absorbing materials help to reduce noise levels due to distant sources; the reduction in noise levels from nearby sources is relatively small.

The amount of noise reduction by the addition of sound absorbing materials in an enclosure is given by the following formula:

$$\text{Noise reduction in dB} = 10 \log \frac{A_a}{A_b} \qquad (9.3)$$

where $A_a$ = sound absorption in the room after the addition of sound absorbing materials; $A_b$ = sound absorption in the room before the addition of sound absorbing materials.

### Example 9.2

An airport lounge 80 ft x 50 ft x 12 ft has reflective walls, floor and ceiling. The sound absorption coefficients of various surfaces of the lounge are: $\alpha_{ceil}$ = 0.02, $\alpha_{wall}$ = 0.02, $\alpha_{floor}$ = 0.1. Calculate the amount of reduction in noise level that will be achieved by providing acoustical tile ceiling, if $\alpha_{tile}$ = 0.8.

*Solution:* The area of four walls = 4(80x12) = 3,840 ft². From Equation (9.2), the amount of absorption provided by walls = 3,840 x 0.02 = 76.8 sabins. Similarly, the amount of absorption provided by acoustical tile ceiling = 4,000 x 0.02 = 80 sabins, and that by the floor = 4,000 x 0.1 = 400 sabins. Hence, $A_b$ = 76.8 + 80 + 400 = 556.8 sabins.
   $A_a$ = 76.8 + 400 + (4,000 x 0.8) = 3,676.8 sabins.
   $(A_a/A_b)$ = (3,676.8/556.8) = 6.6
   Hence, noise reduction = 10 log (6.6) = 8 dB. From Table 9.2, a noise reduction of 8 dB is a significant reduction.

### Example 9.3

If an absorption of 3,000 sabins in the form of sound absorptive wall panels is added to the lounge of Example 9.2 (which already has an acoustical tile ceiling), determine the additional noise reduction available.

*Solution:* From Example 9.2, $A_b$ = 3,676.8 sabins. $A_a$ = 3,676.8 + 3,000 = 6,676.8 sabins. Hence $(A_a/A_b)$ = (6,676.8/3,676.8) = 1.86. Therefore, noise reduction = 10 log (1.82) = 3 dB, which from Table 9.2, is only just perceptible.

From the above examples, we see that although the additional sound absorption in Example 9.3 is approximately the same as that in Example 9.2, its effect on noise reduction is considerably smaller. This is an important result which in general means that if an enclosure has little sound absorption, the additional sound absorption will significantly reduce noise levels. On the other hand, if the enclosure has a considerable absorption already, the additional absorption will not reduce noise levels significantly.

**9.12 SOUND INSULATION**

Another important acoustical property of concern to designers and builders is the sound insulation provided by building components — walls, floors, roofs, doors and windows. The greater the sound insulation of a component, the less sound will transmit through it.

In discussing the transmission of sound through a component, we distinguish between two types of sound: *airborne sound* and *structureborne sound*. Airborne sound transmission occurs when the sound from the source reaches the building component through air. Thus, the transmission of speech noise from the corridor of a hotel to an adjacent guest room (through the corridor wall) is airborne sound transmission. Similarly, the sound of music from a speaker system travels to an adjoining apartment, through the separating wall or the floor, as airborne sound.

Structureborne sound originates as vibration in the structure produced by direct impact. For example, the foot noise produced by people walking on a floor is transmitted to the lower floor as structureborne noise. The vibrations caused by a machine in a plant room are transferred to other parts of building as structureborne sound. The vibrations of the loudspeaker cabinet resting on a floor create structureborne sound, while the loudspeaker itself creates airborne sound.

The airborne sound transmission through a component is directly related to the transmission coefficient ($\tau$) of the component. Thus, the greater the value of $\tau$, the greater the transmitted sound. However, in practice we are more interested in the sound insulation of the component, which is inversely related to $\tau$. The sound insulation of a component is measured by its transmission loss (TL) which is related to $\tau$ as follows:

$$TL = 10 \log(1/\tau)$$

The unit of TL is the decibel. The greater the TL of a component, the more sound insulation it provides. A component with a TL of 50 dB is more insulating than one whose TL is 30 dB. A component with a TL of zero has perfect acoustical transparency.

Mass is the most important factor that determines the TL of a component. The greater the unit mass (lb/ft$^2$) of the component, the greater its TL. Thus, heavyweight components have a high TL value, and lightweight components, a low TL. In addition to the mass, the stiffness of the component affects its TL. The stiffer the component, the smaller the TL. Thus, limp materials such as lead and plastics provide a high TL.

Separating a component into two layers and reducing the mechanical connection between them increases the TL of the component. Thus, a component with two layers separated by a cavity space provides a higher TL than one without a cavity space, although the unit weight of both components may be the same. Thus, a brick cavity wall consisting of two wythes of 4 in.

thick brick with an intervening cavity provides a greater TL than one wythe of 8 in. thick brick wall.

### 9.13.1 Sound Transmission Class

Like all other acoustical properties, the TL of a component is also a function of frequency. Therefore, a single number index is required to compare the TL of one component with another, e.g., of one partition with another. This index is called the *sound transmission class* (STC). STC is measured in decibels. The greater the STC value, the more insulating the construction.

The STC of a component is determined from its frequency-TL relationship in such a way that the STC gives the overall performance of a component within six octaves ranging from 125 Hz to 4 kHz. Note that STC is not the average of TL values in the above octaves. Therefore in designating the STC of an assembly, the unit "decibel" is omitted. We refer to the STC of an assembly as 40, not 40 dB.

Building codes require a minimum STC value of 50 for the party wall between two individual apartments[9.2], However, for a good construction an STC of 60 or greater is desirable. The STC values of a few commonly used construction assemblies are given in Figure 9.36. For additional information, refer to Reference 9.3.

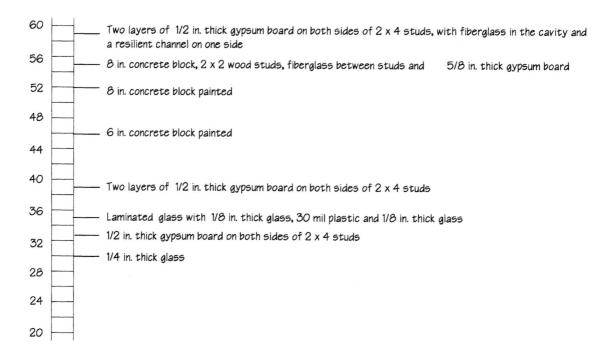

**FIGURE 9.36** Sound transmission class (STC) values of a few commonly used wall assemblies.
The data for this figure have been obtained, with permission, from tables given in Reference 9.3. For STC values of other assemblies, see the referenced tables.

### 9.13.2 Impact Isolation Class

The single number index that is a measure of the performance of an assembly (generally the floor-ceiling assembly) with respect to structureborne sound is called the *impact isolation class* (IIC). IIC is similar to STC and provides information of the insulating property of a floor-ceiling assembly against impact noise. The greater the IIC value, the greater the insulation provided. Building codes require a minimum IIC value of 50 between the floors of two apartment units.

**REVIEW QUESTIONS**

9.1  What is the relationship between frequency, wavelength and speed of sound? Does this relationship apply only to sound?
9.2  What is an octave band? List the octave bands used in architectural acoustics.
9.3  What is the wavelength of sound at 250 Hz, 1 kHz and 10 kHz?
9.4  How much sound absorption is provided by a wall panel with an area of 100 ft$^2$ and an absorption coefficient of 0.5?
9.5  How does a porous absorber such as fiberglass absorb sound? Explain.
9.6  Sketch an approximate relationship between frequency and absorption coefficient for a porous absorber.
9.7  Explain the mechanism of sound absorption of a panel absorber.
9.8  Sketch a sound block and explain how it absorbs sound.
9.9  With reference to Sweet's Catalog sketch some of the commonly used space absorbers.

**REFERENCES**

9.1  Schultz, Theodore: *Acoustical Uses for Perforated Panels*, Industrial Perforators Association, Milwaukee, Wisconsin, 1986.
9.2  International Conference of Building Officials, Whittier, California: *Uniform Building Code*, 1994, Vol. 1, Appendix Chapter 12, p. 425.
9.3  Harris, Cyril: *Noise Control in Buildings*, McGraw Hill Inc., 1994, pp. 5.33 - 5.77.

# 10 MOVEMENT CONTROL

## 10.1 INTRODUCTION

The dimensions of building components are constantly changing, not only with respect to their original dimensions but also relative to each other. For example, a window glass expands and contracts in response to environmental temperature changes. The changes in glass dimensions are usually different from the corresponding changes in the frame in which the glass is held. Therefore, the joint between the glass and the window frame must have adequate space to accommodate the differential movement between the glass and the frame.

Joints are a necessary part of a building. Although they may sometimes be provided for aesthetic reasons only, the joints are usually provided to accommodate the movements between components. In other words, a joint provides the space within which the components meeting at the joint can expand or contract. If a joint does not provide an adequate movement space and restrains the movements of components, the stresses caused in the components can create undesirable effects, which vary from material to material. Ductile materials such as metals and wood will buckle (bow or warp), while brittle materials such as concrete and masonry will crack or even break under the stress.

Joints must be provided at the junction of disparate materials/components because disparate materials/components will usually expand or contract at different rates. However, joints may also be necessary to subdivide a component into smaller sizes in order to reduce stresses in it, which may become excessive if it is not subdivided. It is for this reason that a concrete slab-on-grade is subdivided into smaller areas with a gridwork of joints, and a concrete or masonry wall is subdivided into smaller lengths with intervening joints (see Section 6.7.6).

In this chapter, we shall examine various factors that produce movements in buildings and the types of joints needed to accommodate these movements. Since a movement joint must be sealed against air, water and noise transmission (particularly the joints that occur in the external envelope of a building), we shall also examine the commonly used sealants and joint fillers.

**10.2 IMPORTANCE OF MOVEMENT JOINTS**

The importance of providing an adequate space for the movement of components may be appreciated by considering the expansion of a linear member such as a beam. Assume that the original length of a beam is L and it expands linearly by an amount $\delta$. If the expansion of the beam is restrained at its ends, the beam will be subjected to axial compression. Consequently, it will tend to buckle (bend upward or downward) as shown in Figure 10.1. If the deflection of the beam is denoted by h, we find that h is several times larger than the linear expansion of the beam ($\delta$). This fact is shown in Figure 10.2 which gives a graphical relationship between the quantity ($h/\delta$) on the vertical axis and ($\delta/L$) on the horizontal axis.

**FIGURE 10.1**   The relationship between the deflection and linear expansion of a member, restrained from expanding.

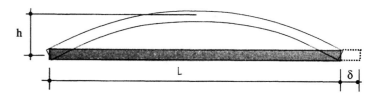

For instance, consider a 20 ft long beam which expands linearly by $\frac{1}{8}$ in. so that $\delta/L$ is (0.125/240), i.e., 0.0005. From Figure 10.2, we find that if the beam is completely restrained from expanding, the quantity ($h/\delta$) is nearly 29, so that h is approximately equal to 3.6 in. (obtained by multiplying 0.125 by 29). This is an extremely large deformation.

Apart from the fact that such a large deformation is visually unacceptable in buildings, it also creates structural problems. A beam made of a ductile material such as steel will bend as shown in Figure 10.1. On the other hand, a beam made of a brittle material such as concrete or masonry will simply break under such a large deformation because, being weak in tension, brittle materials cannot resist the tensile stress created by excessive bending.

The above example highlights the importance of providing movement joints, since an extremely small linear expansion of the beam resulted in an excessive bending. A similar situation would occur if the beam were to contract instead of expanding. Contraction would create axial tension in the beam, and most brittle materials will fail under large tensile stresses.

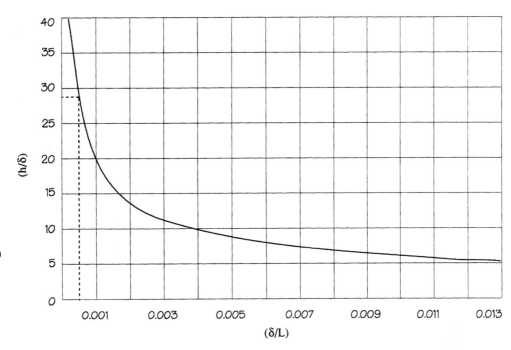

**FIGURE 10.2** Relationship between (δ/L) and (h/δ).

The stress created in a restrained member can be obtained from Equation (3.3) by multiplying the strain in the component by the modulus of elasticity of the material. Thus, in the above steel beam, the stress is equal to $0.0005(29 \times 10^6) = 14,500$ psi. A stress of 14,500 psi is an extremely large stress, considering that the allowable stress in A 36 steel (the most commonly used steel in buildings) is nearly 24,000 psi. (Note that the modulus of elasticity of steel is $29 \times 10^6$ psi, see Table 3.1).

Although the relationship of Figure 10.2 has been obtained from geometric considerations[1], it can also be visualized through a demonstration model. In this model, an approximately 4 ft long sheet made of a flexible material, such as acrylic, has been cut to fit snugly in the slot provided in a wooden base, Figure 10.3(a). The ends of the slot restrain the expansion of the sheet. If the length of the slot is slightly shortened (say by nearly $^1/_8$ in. by placing a 25 cent coin at each end), we find that the sheet curves up substantially, Figure 10.3(b).

**10.3 TYPES OF MOVEMENTS AND JOINT WIDTH**

The movement in a building component may be caused by some or all of the following factors:

- Thermal movement
- Moisture movement
- Elastic deformation and creep
- Other factors

---

[1] The relationship of Figure 10.2 has been obtained by considering that the member buckles as an arc of a circle. If (h/L) is denoted by z, from geometric considerations:

$$\frac{\delta}{L} = (1 + 4z^2)\left[\frac{\tan^{-1} 2z}{2z}\right] - 1$$

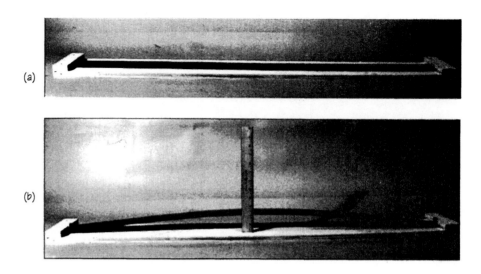

**FIGURE 10.3** (a) Acrylic sheet in an undeformed state. (b) Deformation of the same sheet (nearly 4 ft long), shortened by placing a 25 cent coin at each end.

While thermal movement and elastic deformation occur in all materials, the same is not true of creep and moisture movement. Steel does not creep and its dimensions are not affected by moisture variations. Thermal movement is reversible if the component is unrestrained. Moisture movement, on the other hand, may or may not be reversible depending on the material, as shown in Table 10.1. Creep deformation is always irreversible.

### 10.3.1 Thermal Movement

Thermal movement is by far the most important type of movement since it occurs in all materials, particularly those that are exposed to the external climate such as the external walls, cladding elements, roofing materials, flashings, slabs and paving.

### Table 10.1 Types of Movement in Structural Materials

| Building material | Thermal | Reversible moisture | Irreversible moisture | Elastic deformation | Creep |
|---|---|---|---|---|---|
| Steel | X | - | - | X | - |
| Concrete | X | X | - | X | X |
| Concrete masonry | X | X | - | X | X |
| Brick masonry | X | - | X | X | X |
| Wood | X | X | - | X | X |

X indicates the presence of and - indicates the absence of movement in the material.
Source: Reference 10.1, with permission.

The magnitude of thermal movement ($\delta_t$) of an unrestrained component is directly proportional to: (i) the length of the component (L), (ii) the temperature change ($t_{max} - t_{min}$), and (iii) the *coefficient of thermal expansion* ($\alpha$), so that:

$$\delta_t = \alpha L (t_{max} - t_{min})$$

(10.1)

$\alpha$ is a property of the material. The greater the value of $\alpha$, the greater the thermal movement. Plastics have the highest values of $\alpha$, followed by metals, and ceramic materials such as concrete, masonry and glass. Values of $\alpha$ for selected materials are given in Table 10.2.

Equation (10.1) can be used to determine the minimum width of joint required to prevent thermal stresses. From this equation, we note that the unit of $\alpha$ is $^\circ F^{-1}$, or $^\circ C^{-1}$.

The value of ($t_{max} - t_{min}$) is the difference between the maximum and minimum temperatures to which the component is subjected. This difference is usually not the same as the difference between the annual maximum and minimum outdoor temperatures at the location. The outdoor temperature is air temperature recorded under shade, while the value of ($t_{max} - t_{min}$) is the difference between the annual maximum and minimum temperatures of the component.

If the component is exposed to the sun, its maximum (surface) temperature is much higher than the maximum air temperature at the location. The difference between the maximum temperature of the component and the maximum air temperature may be as high as 60 $^\circ F$ (33 $^\circ C$), depending on the degree of exposure of the component to direct sun, its material, color, amount of insulation in the component, and wind speed[10.2].

## Table 10.2  Coefficient of Thermal Expansion of Materials

| Material | $\alpha$ (x $10^{-6}$) | | Material | $\alpha$ (x $10^{-6}$) | |
|---|---|---|---|---|---|
| | ($^\circ F^{-1}$) | ($^\circ C^{-1}$) | | ($^\circ F^{-1}$) | ($^\circ C^{-1}$) |
| Steel | 6.5 | 11.7 | Nylon | 60.0 | 108.0 |
| Cast iron | 6.0 | 10.8 | Acrylics | 40.0 | 72.0 |
| Aluminum | 13.0 | 23.4 | Polyethlene | 80.0 | 144.0 |
| Copper | 9.5 | 17.1 | Epoxy resins | 40.0 | 72.0 |
| Glass | 5.0 | 9.0 | Softwoods: | | |
| Clay brick | 3.5 | 6.3 | Across the grain | 30.0 | 54.0 |
| Concrete | 6.0 | 10.8 | Along the grain | 3.0 | 5.4 |
| Limestone | 2.0 to 7.0 | 3.6 to 12.6 | Hardwoods: | | |
| Sandstone | 4.5 to 7.0 | 8.1 to 12.6 | Across the grain | 25.0 | 45.0 |
| Marble | 4.0 to 12.0 | 7.2 to 21.6 | Along the grain | 3.0 | 5.4 |

Because of its greater solar absorptivity, a dark colored component gets hotter than a light colored component. Metals become hotter than nonmetals. If the component is insulated, its surface temperature is higher than an uninsulated component since an uninsulated component loses heat to the interior.

The minimum temperature of the component is also lower than the minimum air temperature at the location, as shown in Figure 10.4. This is due to the cooling of the component by the (cold) night sky — referred to as *nocturnal cooling*. This minimum surface temperature usually occurs in the early hours of the morning when the air temperature is minimum.

Thus we observe that the value of $(t_{max} - t_{min})$ depends on various factors. As a rough guide, nearly 50 °F (28 °C) may be added to the difference between the annual maximum and minimum air temperatures at the location to obtain the value of $(t_{max} - t_{min})$ for a horizontal surface such as a roof. Thus, if the annual maximum and minimum air temperatures at a location are 100 °F and 10 °F respectively, so that the difference between the annual maximum and minimum air temperatures is 90 °F, the value of $(t_{max} - t_{min})$ should be taken as 140 °F for a horizontal component. For a vertical component at the same location, a smaller value may be used since a vertical component receives a smaller amount of solar radiation, and its nocturnal cooling is not as pronounced as that of a horizontal component.

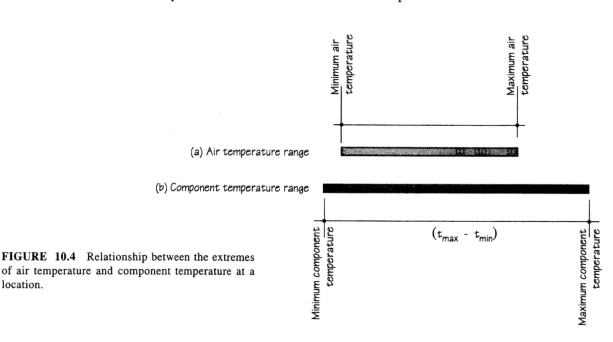

**FIGURE 10.4** Relationship between the extremes of air temperature and component temperature at a location.

**Example 10.1**

Determine the total elongation of a 50 ft long steel beam which is subjected to a temperature rise of 1,100 °F in a fire test.

*Solution*: L = 50 x 12 = 600 in., $\alpha = 6.5 \times 10^{-6}$, Table 10.2. From Equation (10.1), elongation = $6.5 \times 10^{-6} (600) \, 1,100 = 4.3$ in.

**Example 10.2**

A residential neighborhood which abuts a busy road is to be provided with a brick masonry fence wall along the road. It has been decided to use 50 ft long segments of the wall with intervening joints. Determine the minimum width of each joint considering the wall's thermal expansion. Maximum and minimum air temperatures at the location are 90 °F and -5 °F respectively.

*Solution:* L = 50 ft = 600 in. $(t_{max} - t_{min}) = [90 - (-5)] + 50 = 145$ °F, $\alpha = 3.5$ x $10^{-6}$. Hence, the elongation $= 3.5$ x $10^{-6}$ (600)145 = 0.30 in.

Thus, the required minimum joint width between each wall segment is 0.30 in. However, this does not include the provision for moisture expansion, construction and material tolerances which, as we shall see in the following section, must also be included in determining the total joint width for a wall.

### 10.3.2 Moisture Movement

Materials with a porous or cellular structure, such as brick, concrete, concrete masonry and wood, are influenced dimensionally by changes in their moisture contents. Unfortunately, the magnitude of moisture movement cannot be predicted with the same degree of accuracy as thermal movement. However, approximate coefficients of moisture expansion/shrinkage for brick, concrete and wood are available to estimate the width of movement joints.

When the moisture coefficient ($\mu$) is multiplied by the length of the component (L), the resulting quantity is the total moisture expansion/shrinkage of the component ($\delta_m$). Thus:

$$\delta_m = (\mu)L \qquad\qquad (10.2)$$

With the exception of clay brick masonry, materials expand with increasing moisture content and contract when the moisture content decreases — a reversible phenomenon. Clay bricks expand on exposure to water or moisture in the air, and their expansion is irreversible. In fact, a brick unit is smallest in size when it comes out of the kiln, after which it grows in size. The moisture expansion of clay brick depends primarily on its firing temperature. Bricks fired at lower temperatures expand more than those fired at higher temperatures. The moisture coefficient[10.1] of clay masonry varies from 0.0002 to 0.0009 but an average value of 0.0005 may be used.

**Example 10.3**

Determine the required width of each joint in the wall of Example 10.1, considering both temperature and moisture expansion.

*Solution:* From Example 10.2, the joint width required for thermal expansion = 0.30 in.

From Equation (10.2), the joint width required for moisture expansion = 0.0005(600) = 0.30 in.

Thus, the joint width = 0.30 + 0.30 = 0.60 in.

For construction and material tolerances, see Example 10.5.

Portland cement based materials such as concrete, concrete masonry and stucco shrink due to moisture loss and carbonation[2] during the setting process. For concrete, the total shrinkage depends on the type of aggregate, amount of portland cement and the curing of concrete. Concrete masonry units experience a similar phenomenon. The shrinkage coefficient of concrete or concrete masonry varies from 0.0004 to 0.0009[10.3]. An average value of 0.0006 may be used for most purposes.

## Example 10.4

If shrinkage (control joints) are provided in a concrete slab at 12 ft intervals, determine the required width of each joint.

*Solution:* $\mu = 0.0006$. L = 12 x 12 = 144 in. From Equation (10.2), width of each joint = 0.0006 x 144 = 0.09 in, i.e., $^1/_{10}$ in.

As shown in Figure 10.5(a), the microstructure of wood consists of hollow cellular tubes bundled together. In a living tree, both cell cavities and cell walls are saturated with water. When a piece of wood is cut from a tree and left exposed to air, it begins to lose water. The water contained in cell cavities evaporates first. After all the water from cell cavities has evaporated, the water contained in cell walls begins to evaporate next.

The shrinkage of wood begins only when the water from cell walls starts to evaporate. No shrinkage occurs during the evaporation of water from cell cavities. The weight of water contained in a piece of wood divided by the weight of (oven dry) wood is called the *moisture content* of wood.

The moisture content of wood at the point when shrinkage begins is approximately 30 percent in most species of wood. However, the wood used in buildings has much lower moisture content than 30 percent (usually between 8 to 15 percent), and varies with atmospheric relative humidity and temperature. As these two atmospheric parameters change, so does the wood's moisture content, and consequently the wood's dimensions. This explains

---

[2] Carbonation refers to the chemical reaction between free lime (in portland cement) with atmospheric carbon dioxide.

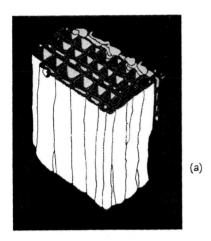

(a)

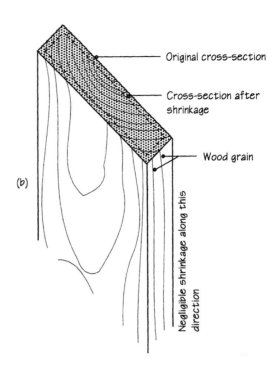

Original cross-section

Cross-section after shrinkage

Wood grain

Negligible shrinkage along this direction

(b)

**FIGURE 10.5** (a) Microstructure of wood. (b) Shrinkage of a wood member.

why wood swells and shrinks, and why a wood drawer moves in and out freely during dry weather but with some difficulty during wet weather.

The dimensional changes in a piece of wood occur mainly in its cross-section. We refer to it as "across-the-grain" shrinkage. The shrinkage of a wood member along its length ("along-the-grain") is almost negligible, Figure 10.5(b). Therefore in wood buildings, it is across-the-grain shrinkage that is taken into account. However, a piece of plywood shrinks and swells in both directions since wood grain is oriented in opposite directions in alternate veneers of plywood.

The wood industry has established empirical rules for providing movement joints in wood components. For instance, a 4 ft x 8 ft plywood sheet must be provided with $1/_8$ in. (3 mm) wide joints at ends and edges when used as roof sheathing. For additional details on dimensional control in wood, refer to a book on wood construction, such as Reference 10.4.

### 10.3.3 Elastic Deformation and Creep

Elastic deformation refers to the deformation of building components under loads. The term "elastic" implies that the deformation is reversible and varies with changing loads, i.e., deformation increases as the load increases, and decreases as the load decreases. Creep deformation (or simply creep), on the other hand, is inelastic deformation of components under loads, and is irreversible.

Another difference between elastic deformation and creep is that elastic deformation occurs instantaneously while creep takes place gradually over time. For instance, it takes nearly two years for creep deformation to reach its maximum value in concrete structures. Thus, creep is caused by sustained loads such as the dead loads on the structure. Short-term loads such as live loads, wind and earthquake loads do not cause creep.

The material in which creep is a significant factor is concrete. In concrete structures, creep deformation is nearly twice the elastic deformation. Although wood creeps, the creep in wood structures is usually not significant since the creep deformation in wood is only half the elastic deformation. Additionally, the dead loads on a wood structure are much smaller than the dead loads on a concrete structure. Since it is the dead load that is the primary contributor to creep, wood structures do not creep significantly.

Elastic and creep deformations can be determined with a great deal of accuracy from structural design procedures, and are done so routinely. The most important elastic and/or creep deformation occur in spandrel beams. Since spandrel beams have external walls anchored to them, it is necessary to provide flexibility in the anchorage of external walls so that the deflection of spandrel beams does not cause additional stresses in external walls.

If a nonloadbearing wall is placed directly under a beam, an adequate space between the underside of the beam and the top of the wall should be provided to allow the beam to deflect up and down with changing live loads. If an adequate movement space is not provided, the deflection of the beam may cause the beam to bear on the wall. That is why, the top of a metal stud wall is provided with a double track, as shown in Figure 10.6. The upper (top) track is anchored to the underside of the beam while the lower (top) track simply nests into the upper track. The space between the two tracks must be adequate to accommodate the live load deflection of the beam.

Similarly, an adequate clear space must be provided between the underside of a beam and a nonloadbearing masonry wall. This space should be filled with an elastomeric sealant (not masonry mortar). Lateral load resistance in the wall is provided by welding (nearly 6 in. long) steel angles at nearly 4 ft intervals to the underside of the beam, Figure 10.7.

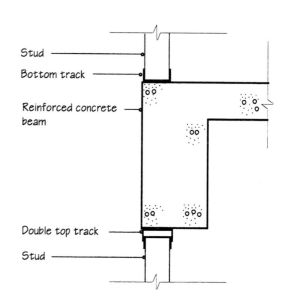

**FIGURE 10.6** Section through a metal stud wall framing showing double top track.

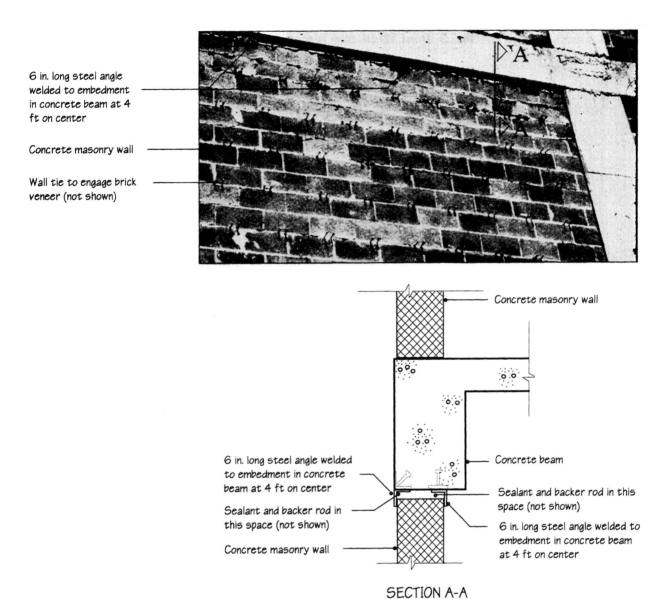

6 in. long steel angle welded to embedment in concrete beam at 4 ft on center

Concrete masonry wall

Wall tie to engage brick veneer (not shown)

Concrete masonry wall

6 in. long steel angle welded to embedment in concrete beam at 4 ft on center

Sealant and backer rod in this space (not shown)

Concrete masonry wall

Concrete beam

Sealant and backer rod in this space (not shown)

6 in. long steel angle welded to embedment in concrete beam at 4 ft on center

SECTION A-A

**FIGURE 10.7**  Joint between a beam and a nonloadbearing masonry wall.

### 10.3.4  Other Factors

In addition to the factors discussed above, there are several other factors that cause movement in some buildings, and should be addressed. These include foundation settlements and drift (side-sway) of structural frame due to wind or earthquake loads.

Some chemical processes may also cause movement. Steel expands as it corrodes. Excessive corrosion of steel can cause cracking and sometime spalling of concrete. Since water expands on freezing, the freezing of water causes similar effects in materials that absorb water such as brick, concrete, concrete masonry and wood.

### 10.3.5 Joint Width and Dimensional Tolerances

In addition to the joint width as calculated from various considerations described earlier, a certain amount should be added to the calculated joint width for material and construction tolerances. This fact is to recognize that building components will vary from their specified dimensions. For example, it is not uncommon to see brick or concrete masonry units as being undersized or oversized. Prefabricated concrete curtain wall panels can have noticeable differences in dimensions from those stated on the drawings. Although metal curtain wall panels are fabricated under stringent quality control, some tolerance should be expected in them as well.

In addition to material or component tolerances, construction tolerances should also be taken into account. For example, a joint in a masonry wall may be shown as a vertical joint on the drawings, but may not be absolutely vertical when constructed. Construction tolerances are a function of quality control during construction. Good construction supervision needs smaller tolerances, while poor supervision will require larger tolerances.

It is difficult to provide even rough guidelines for construction and material tolerances. All one can say is that the architect should use sound judgment in estimating the contribution of these tolerances to joint width.

---

### Example 10.5

Determine the total joint width for the wall of Example 10.3 including construction and material tolerances.

*Solution*: From Example 10.3, the joint width for thermal and moisture effects = 0.60 in. Add 0.20 in. for construction and material tolerances. Thus, the total joint width required = 0.60 + 0.20 = 0.8 in.

---

## 10.4 TYPES OF JOINTS AND JOINT DETAILING

The type of joint and its detailing depends on the type of movement it seeks to accommodate. The joints in buildings may, therefore, be grouped under the following four categories:
- Building separation joint
- Seismic joint
- Component expansion or control joint
- Construction joint

### 10.4.1 Building Separation Joint

A building separation joint (also referred to as *building expansion joint*) divides a large and geometrically complex building into smaller individual buildings which can move independent of each other. This joint, typically $1\frac{1}{2}$ to 2 in. (35 to 50 mm) wide, accommodates the cumulative effect of various types of movements that occur in a building as a whole, as distinct from the movements that occur in individual components of the building. Thus, a building expansion joint prevents the stresses created in one part of the building from affecting the integrity of the other part.

A building separation joint is needed in long buildings. As a rough guide, it should be provided every 200 ft (60 m) intervals, Figure 10.8. In addition, good practice requires the provision of building separation joints at the following discontinuities: (a) where a low building mass meets a tall mass, (b) where the building changes direction, such as in an L-shape or T-shape building, and (c) where the building's structural material changes, e.g., where a steel frame building meets a concrete frame.

Since a building separation joint divides a building into separate buildings, it runs continuously throughout the entire building, separating a floor from a floor, a roof from a roof, and foundation from foundation. Thus at a building

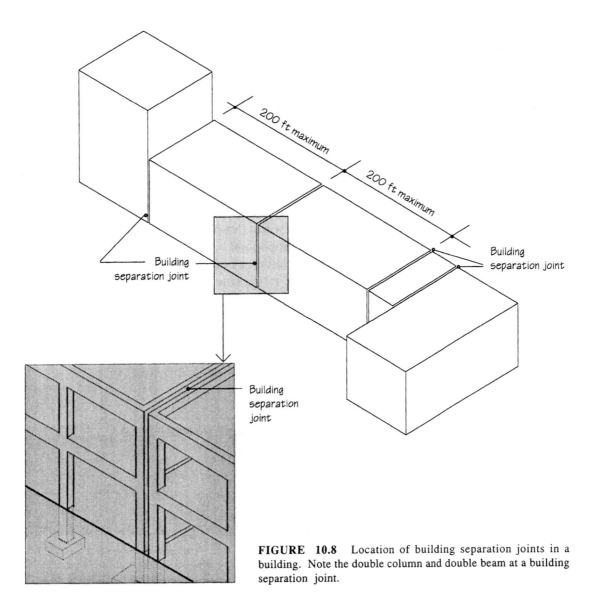

**FIGURE 10.8** Location of building separation joints in a building. Note the double column and double beam at a building separation joint.

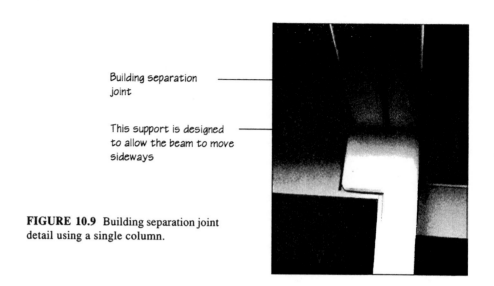

Building separation
joint

This support is designed
to allow the beam to move
sideways

**FIGURE 10.9** Building separation joint
detail using a single column.

separation joint, two columns and two beams are necessary, Figure 10.8. The
duplication of columns at the joint may be avoided as shown in Figure 10.9
in which one beam rests directly on the column and is cast monolithically
with the column, and the other beam is supported on column bracket. This
beam is not monolithic with column bracket, and is detailed to move
horizontally on column bracket.

Various proprietary products are available to cover separation joints at
floors, roofs and walls. A simple floor joint cover would consist of a metal
plate fixed to one side of the joint with an overlapping slip joint on the other
side, Figure 10.10. Alternatively, it may consist of a metal plate fixed to
each side of the floor with a flexible connection between the two plates, Figure
10.11. A roof separation joint cover is similar, but a little more complex. It
is important to ensure that a building separation joint is firestopped at each
floor to meet the fire rating requirements of the floor.

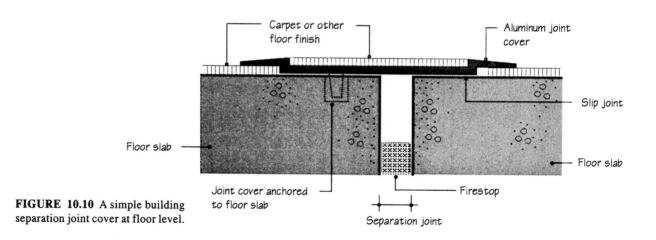

Carpet or other
floor finish

Aluminum joint
cover

Slip joint

Floor slab

Floor slab

Joint cover anchored
to floor slab

Firestop

Separation joint

**FIGURE 10.10** A simple building
separation joint cover at floor level.

**FIGURE 10.11** Typical proprietary building separation joint floor covers. Courtesy of: Balco Metalines, Oklahoma City, Oklahoma.

### 10.4.2 Seismic Joint

A seismic joint is similar to, but wider than a building separation joint (several inches wide depending on the expected horizontal displacement of floors). It is provided to separate a large building into smaller buildings to accommodate the seismic motion of buildings. Usually, the manufacturers of building separation joint covers also manufacture seismic joint covers.

### 10.4.3 Component Expansion Joint and Control Joint

A component expansion joint is provided between two components that tend to move due to thermal and/or moisture effects. A control joint, on the other hand, is a contraction (shrinkage) joint.

The distinction between these two joints must be recognized. If an expansion joint must be filled to control water penetration and air leakage, the joint filler must be compressible in order to accommodate the expansion of components. On the other hand, a control joint filler need not be compressible.

Since brick masonry expands, a brick masonry wall or a brick veneer wall requires an expansion joint, Figure 10.12(a). A concrete masonry wall, on the other hand, requires a control joint. Figure 10.12(b) shows a typical control joint in concrete masonry. The joint is filled with masonry mortar to provide shear key between the two parts of the wall. To ensure that the mortar will not adhere on both sides of the joint, thereby restraining the shrinkage of the wall, the joint between the mortar and concrete masonry is broken by providing an asphalt-saturated felt on one side of the joint.

Control joints are also required in a concrete slab-on-grade to accommodate the shrinkage of concrete. A typical control joint in a concrete slab consists of a $1/8$ in. (3 mm) wide groove. The depth of groove is generally $3/4$ in. to 1 in., (19 mm to 25 mm) not to exceed one-quarter the depth of slab. The groove is usually obtained by sawing the slab after the concrete has hardened sufficiently, but not fully cured.

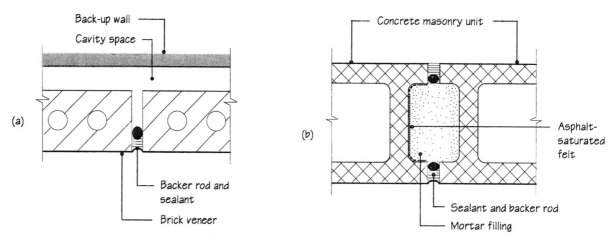

**FIGURE 10.12** (a) Expansion joint detail in a brick veneer wall. (b) Control joint detail in a concrete masonry wall.

If the control joints are not provided, shrinkage cracks will occur in a random and haphazard pattern in a concrete slab. Control joints are, therefore, lines of weakened slab sections provided at specified locations so that the slab will crack at these lines. As a rough guide, control joints are provided 10 to 15 ft ( 3 to 4.5 m) on centers in a concrete slab. Control joints in pavement slabs are usually given 6 ft (2 m) on centers and are not sawn but provided by tooling the joint while the concrete is still wet.

Control joints are only necessary on a slab-on-grade which does not have adequate reinforcement for temperature and shrinkage control of concrete. If adequate reinforcement has been provided in a slab-on-grade, control joints may be omitted. Control joints may also be omitted in a slab-on-grade if it is to be covered with a floor finish.

Since a suspended floor slab (a second and upper floor slab) is always provided with temperature and shrinkage reinforcement, control joints are unnecessary in a suspended concrete slab. In fact, the control joints should not be provided in a suspended concrete slab since they reduce the strength of the slab.

In addition to control joints, a concrete slab-on-grade also needs isolation joints. An isolation joint separates the slab into sections so that each section may move independent of the other. An isolation joint is required where a slab meets a column or a wall (with its own footing) since the movement of column or wall will not be the same as that of the slab. Unlike a control joint, an isolation joint runs through the entire thickness of slab. Once again, an isolation joint is only required in a slab-on-grade.

An isolation joint is formed by installing a slip surface in the joint such as $1/8$ in. thick asphalt-impregnated fiber sheet. Figure 10.13 shows the layout of control joints and isolation joints in a concrete in a slab-on-grade.

### 10.4.4 Construction Joint

A construction joint (also referred to as a cold joint) is simply a joint that is

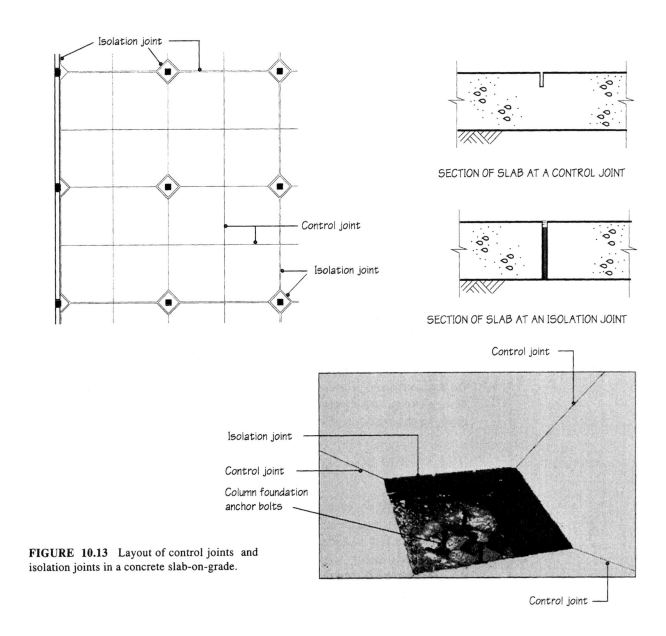

**FIGURE 10.13** Layout of control joints and isolation joints in a concrete slab-on-grade.

SECTION OF SLAB AT A CONTROL JOINT

SECTION OF SLAB AT AN ISOLATION JOINT

required in a large concrete slab because it is not possible to place the entire concrete in one operation. The provision of construction joints allows the concrete to be placed in two or more operations without sacrificing the appearance or performance of the slab. A construction joint may double as a control joint or an isolation joint.

**10.5 COMPONENTS OF A SEALED JOINT**

The primary purpose of sealing a joint is to prevent water penetration through the joint. However, control of air leakage, dust penetration and noise transmission are some additional benefits of sealing a joint. Although joint sealant is the most important component of a sealed joint, the following other components must be carefully selected:

- Substrate
- Primer
- Sealant back-up
- Bond breaker

### 10.5.1 Substrate

For a sealed joint to function effectively, it is important that the sealant should fully adhere to the surfaces of components meeting at the joint (the substrate). A nonadhering sealant will obviously give a leaky joint.

The adhesion of the sealant to substrate depends on the chemical compatibility of the sealant with the substrate material. Since all sealants are not compatible (or equally compatible) with all substrate materials, it is important to obtain compatibility information from sealant manufacturers. This is particularly important since some substrate materials such as concrete and masonry are sometimes treated with water-repellent treatments, and metals with paints and other protective coatings. These treatments may inhibit sealant adhesion.

Some substrate materials may require special joint preparation such as the application of primers to make the substrate compatible with the sealant. In any event, some preparation will be required on all substrates such as cleaning the surfaces of loose particles, contaminants, frost, ice, etc.

### 10.5.2 Primer

The purpose of a primer is to improve the adhesion of sealant to substrate. Some sealants require primers on all types of surfaces, while others require primers on a few surfaces. Most sealant manufacturers require primers for concrete and masonry substrates. On concrete and masonry, a primer stabilizes the substrate by filling the pores and strengthening weak areas.

Some sealants require different primers for different substrates. This poses problems when the joint is between disparate materials and should be considered in the selection of a sealant. Another consideration is the length of time that must pass between the application of primer and the sealant. Obviously, a sealant which can be applied almost immediately after the application of the primer is preferable.

### 10.5.3 Sealant Back-up

A sealant back-up is a compressible and resilient material such as a plastic foam or sponge. It is usually circular in cross-section, hence called a *backer rod*, although rectangular profiles are also used. The width of back-up is larger than the width of the joint so that the sealant back-up is forced into the joint, in which it is held by virtue of being under compression. The back-up performs the following functions:

(i) It controls the depth and shape of sealant.

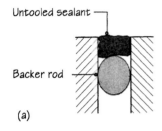

Untooled sealant

Backer rod

(a)

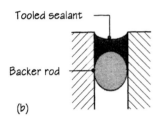

Tooled sealant

Backer rod

(b)

**FIGURE 10.14**  (a) Untooled joint and (b) tooled joint.

(ii) It allows the tooling of the sealant which provides adhesion between the sealant and substrate. In an untooled joint, the sealant will not fully adhere to the substrate, giving a leaky joint. A properly tooled joint, on the other hand, will have full contact with the substrate, Figure 10.14. For the joint to be tooled, it is necessary that the sealant back-up should be under sufficient compression so that it will not slide under the pressure of tooling.

(iii) It acts as a temporary joint seal until the sealant is applied. Some sealant back-ups can also act as secondary seals in the event of sealant deterioration due to weathering and aging. Such a sealant back-up must be of a closed-cell structure so that it does not absorb water. Open-cell sponge type materials cannot function as secondary seals. However, an open-cell sealant back-up has an advantage over a closed-cell back-up since it allows the sealant to cure from both sides.

In any case, for the sealant back-up to function as a secondary seal, it must remain elastic throughout its life and not develop significant compression set. A sealant back-up must be compatible with the sealant. Therefore, a sealant back-up that is approved by the sealant manufacturer should be used.

### 10.5.4 Bond Breaker

For the sealant to function effectively, it should be bonded to only two opposite surfaces of the substrate so that it comes under axial tension or axial compression when the joint moves. If the sealant is bonded to the third side of the joint (bottom surface), as shown in Figure 10.15(b), resistance to movement provided by the bond at the third surface creates stress concentration, leading to sealant detachment.

A bond breaker is required only if the third surface is hard and unyielding such as concrete, metal, masonry or any other inflexible back-up. A bond breaker is not required with a flexible back-up which will not significantly restrict the freedom of sealant movement. Thus, a bond breaker is not required in a conventional joint with a foam backer rod.

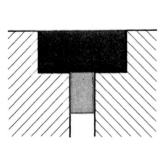

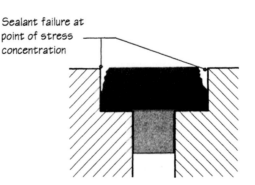

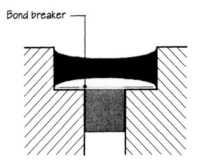

Sealant failure at point of stress concentration

Bond breaker

(a) Sealed joint in an unstressed (original) situation.

(b) Failure of a sealed joint under tension with no bond breaker between the sealant and the third surface.

(c) The sealant is correctly stressed when there is a bond breaker between the sealant and the third surface.

**FIGURE  10.15**  The effect of a bond breaker in a sealed joint.

**10.6 SEALING COMPOUNDS**

Joint sealing compounds may be divided in three categories: preformed tapes, caulks, and elastomeric sealants. Preformed tapes are available in rolls. They function as seals only if they are under pressure and are commonly used in window glazing, door jambs, and gypsum drywall.

Caulks are dough-like materials, and are the earliest sealing compounds. Glazing putty is an example of the earliest caulks used in buildings. It consists of nearly 12 percent linseed oil and 88% chalk (calcium carbonate). Its disadvantage is that it hardens as it cures (oil evaporation), leading to cracking, loss of elasticity, and hence loss of its sealing ability.

Elastomeric sealants are synthetic materials and are the ones most commonly used in contemporary construction. The following sections give some of the important properties of synthetic sealants.

### 10.6.1 Movement Capability

The most important property of a sealant is to withstand cyclic joint movements, defined as the movement a sealant can withstand before failure. Since a sealant is subjected to extension and shortening, this property is given as plus-minus movement ability of the sealant, as measured according to the ASTM C-719 test[10.5]. The plus value denotes the maximum stretch the sealant can withstand and the minus value, the maximum shortening. In fact, sealants are generally classified based on this property. Thus, a sealant with a movement capability of plus-minus 25% of joint width is called a *class 25 sealant*. Similarly, a sealant with a movement capability of plus-minus 12.5% of joint width is called a *class 12.5 sealant*.

Currently available sealants are classified into three categories: low-range sealants, medium-range sealants and high-range sealants. A low-range sealant has limited movement ability, of the order plus-minus 5% or less. These include: (a) the oil-based caulks (b) oil-and-resin-based caulks, and (c) polybutene-based sealants.

Low-range sealants should be used only in a nonmoving joint, or where the labor involved in recaulking is not an important consideration such as in a do-it-yourself project. Their principal advantage lies in their low cost.

Medium-range sealants have a movement range of up to plus-minus 12.5%, and high-range sealants have a movement range larger than plus-minus 12.5%. Silicones normally have the highest movement capability, around plus-minus 50%.

### 10.6.2 Strength and Modulus

A sealant must be able to withstand movement stresses. Most joint failures occur due to excessive tensile stress, measured in pounds per square inch. Tensile failure may occur either at the substrate-sealant interface (failure due to inadequate adhesion), or at the sealant (failure due to inadequate cohesion).

Modulus refers to the modulus of elasticity of sealant. Since modulus of elasticity is a measure of the stiffness of a material, a high modulus sealant is stiffer than a low modulus sealant. A high modulus sealant is desirable where joint movement is small and a greater stiffness of adhesive is required such as in structural glazing. A low modulus sealant, on the other hand, is desirable where joint movement is large and the sealant is required for purely sealing purposes.

### 10.6.3 Tooling Time, Cure Time and Temperature Range

Tooling time refers to the time (usually measured in minutes) that must be allowed to elapse before the sealant changes from liquid state to semi-solid state so that it can be tooled. Cure time refers to the time when sealant has hardened to its final elastomeric state.

Application temperature range refers to the ambient air temperature range within which the sealant can be applied. Performance temperature range is the range over which the sealant will maintain its properties after it has cured.

### 10.6.4 Life Expectancy

Life expectancy is the time (in years) after which the sealant may have to be reapplied. Most high grade sealants, such as the structural silicones, are quoted by their manufacturers to have a life expectancy of 20+ years.

## 10.7 CALCULATING JOINT WIDTH OF A SEALED JOINT

Since a sealant has a limited movement capability, it is obvious that a joint containing sealant must be wider than an unsealed joint. If we know the movement capability of the sealant (x), the width of the unsealed joint obtained by considering thermal effect, moisture effect, construction tolerances, etc., (W), then the width of the sealed joint (J) can be calculated from the following expression:

$$J = (100/x)(W) \qquad\qquad (10.3)$$

### Example 10.6

Calculate the width of a joint which is to be sealed by a class 25 sealant. The width of unsealed joint has been determined to be 0.5 in.

*Solution*: From Equation (10.3),
$J = (100/25)0.5 = 2.0$ in.

**REVIEW QUESTIONS**   **10.1**   List various types of movements to which a building is subjected.

**10.2**   A steel clad curtain wall has 10 ft long components which interlock at the joints. Determine the space that must be allowed in each joint for the panels to expand or contract given that the maximum and minimum air temperatures at the location are 110 °F and 15 °F respectively.

**10.3**   A concrete masonry wall is to be provided with $3/_8$ in. thick control joints. The joints are to be filled with an elastomeric sealant which has movement capability of plus-minus 50%. Determine the spacing of control joints in the wall.

**10.4**   Explain the difference between an expansion joint and a control joint. Which kind of joint will you provide in a brick masonry wall?

**10.5**   Concrete masonry walls are to be provided as infill walls in a high-rise building with a reinforced concrete frame structure. Sketch the joint between a spandrel beam and the wall.

**10.6**   Sketch the detail of Question 10.5 if the building is a steel frame building.

**10.7**   With the help of sketches and notes, explain where a bond breaker may be needed in a joint.

**10.8**   Write short notes on: (i) sealant back-up, (ii) primer, and (iii) elastomeric sealant.

**REFERENCES**   **10.1**   Brick Institute of America, Reston, Virginia: "Volume Changes and Effect of Movement", Part I, Technical Note 18, January 1991.

**10.2**   Panek, J., and Cook, J: *Construction Sealants and Adhesives*, John Wiley & Sons, New York, 1984, p. 35.

**10.3**   Portland Cement Association, Skokie, Illinois: *Building Movements and Joints*, 1982, p. 2.

**10.4**   U.S. Forest Products: *Wood Engineering Handbook*, Prentice Hall, New York, 1982.

**10.5**   American Society of Testing and Materials, Philadelphia, Pennsylvania: "Test Method for Adhesion and Cohesion of Elastomeric Sealants Under Cyclic Movement", C 719-93.

# APPENDIX I
## Units, Measurements and Dimensions

**I.1 THE SI SYSTEM OF UNITS**

The system of measurement (or units) currently used in the building industry in the United States is the foot-pound-second (FPS) system. In this system, the length is measured in the foot, or its multiples — the yard and the mile, or its submultiple — the inch. Weight is measured in pounds, ounces or grains. Time is measured in seconds. Although the United States was the first country to establish the decimal currency in 1785, it is one of the few countries where the nondecimal FPS system is still used. Therefore, the FPS system, earlier known as the Imperial System of units, is now commonly known as the *U.S. System of Units*.

The system of units used by most countries is the SI system. It is this system to which the United States has committed to change through the 1975 Metric Conversion Act, as amended by the Omnibus Trade and Competitiveness Act of 1988. These two acts establish the SI system as the preferred system of measurement in the United States and require that, to the extent feasible, the SI system shall be used in all federally funded projects and business related activities after September 30, 1992.

The SI system, popularly known as the International System, is in fact an acronym for Le Systeme International d'Unites, a name given by the 36 nations' meeting at the 11th General Conference on Weights and Measures (CGPM, an acronym for Conference Generale des Poids et Mesures) in 1960 in Paris. The SI system is a rationalized meter-kilogram-second system (MKS) system, and has been modified several times after the 1960 CGPM meeting.

The advantage of using the SI system is well known and lies primarily in that the multiples and submultiples of each unit (the secondary units) have decimal relationship with each other which makes computations easier and less susceptible to errors. For instance, the secondary units of length, the centimeter and the kilometer, are related to the base unit, the meter, by $10^{-2}$ and $10^3$ respectively. By contrast, the length unit in the U.S. system, the foot, does not bear a fixed relationship with its secondary units, the inch, yard and the mile.

Twelve prefixes have been standardized for use with the base unit to make the secondary units. These prefixes along with their symbols are given in Table I.1 The SI system uses seven base quantities, viz. length, mass, time, temperature, electric current, luminous intensity and the amount of substance. The units corresponding to the base quantities are listed in Table I.2. Of these, only the first four quantities are of concern to architects and builders, viz., length, mass, time and temperature.

Quantities other than the base quantities such as force, stress, pressure,

**Table I.1 Prefixes in the SI System**

| Factor | Prefix | Symbol |
|--------|--------|--------|
| $10^{12}$ | tera | T |
| $10^9$ | giga | G |
| $10^6$ | mega | M |
| $10^3$ | kilo | k |
| $10^2$ | hecto | h |
| 10 | deka | da |
| $10^{-1}$ | deci | d |
| $10^{-2}$ | centi | c |
| $10^{-3}$ | milli | m |
| $10^{-6}$ | micro | μ |
| $10^{-9}$ | nano | n |
| $10^{-12}$ | pico | p |

**Table I.2  Base Quantities and Their Symbols in the SI System**

| Quantity | Unit name | Symbol |
|---|---|---|
| Length | meter | m |
| Mass | kilogram | kg |
| Time | second | s |
| Temperature | Kelvin | K |
| Electric current | Ampere | A |
| Luminous intensity | candela | cd |
| Amount of substance | mole | mol |

velocity, acceleration, energy, etc., and their units are derived from a combination of two or more base quantities. For example, acceleration is the rate of change of velocity, which, in turn, is the rate of change of distance. Consequently, the units for acceleration are meters per second square ($m/s^2$).

Another advantage of SI system is that there is one and only one unit for each quantity — the meter for length, kilogram for mass, second for time, and so on. This is not so in the U.S. system where multiple units are often used. For instance, power is measured in Btu per hour, and horsepower.

### I.1.1  Rules of Grammar in the SI System

The symbols of units in the SI system are always used in lowercase unless the unit is after the name of a person, such as Newton, Pascal or Kelvin, in which case, the first letter of the symbol is in uppercase, and the second letter in the lowercase, as in Pa. The exception is, however, made in the case of the litre which, although not after the name of a person, is given the symbol in uppercase letter "L".

Multiples of base unit must be given with a single prefix. Double prefixes are not allowed. Thus, megakilometer (Mkm) is incorrect; instead, we use gigameter (Gm). Use prefixes as given in Table I.1 in which the prefixes are in uppercase for magnitudes $10^6$ and greater, and in lowercase for magnitudes $10^3$ and lower. No space should be left between a prefix and symbol. Thus, use km, and not k m.

The product of two or more units in symbolic form is given by using a dot between individual symbols (example N·m). Mixing symbols and names of units is incorrect (example N·meter).

Plurals are not used in symbols. For instance, we use 1 m and 50 m. Periods are not used after symbols except at the end of a sentence.

A space must be left between the numerical value and the unit symbol. Thus, use 300 m, not 300m. No space, however, is left between degree and Celsius.

In architectural drawings, dimensions should preferably be given in millimeters, and when that is done, avoid the use of mm. For instance, the measurements of a floor tile are given as 300 x 300, and not as 300 mm x 300 mm. Larger dimensions may be given in meters, if considered necessary. For instance, a building may be dimensioned as 30.800 m x 50.600 m in plan, but it is preferable to dimension it as 30,800 x 50,600.

## I.2 DEFINITIONS OF UNITS AND CONVERSION FACTORS

### I.2.1 Length, Thickness, Area and Volume

In the U.S. system, the standard unit of length is the foot: 1 ft = 12 in. Long distances are measured in miles. In the SI system, the standard unit of length is the meter. Most dimensions in the SI system are given in millimeters (mm), where 1 mm = $10^{-3}$ m. Long distances are given in kilometers (km).

1 ft = 0.3048 m;  1 m = 3.281 ft = 39.37 in;  1 in. = 25.4 mm.
1 mile = 1.609 km.

### I.2.2 Fluid Capacity

Fluid capacity is usually given in gallons in the U.S. system, and in litres (L) in the SI system. The imperial gallon is slightly larger than the U.S. gallon, but the imperial gallon is no longer used as a unit.

1 U.S. gallon = 4 quarts = 3.7854 L.
1 L = 0.001 $m^3$ (by definition) = 0.264 gallons.

### I.2.3 Mass, Force and Weight

In the U.S. system, the unit of mass is the pound (lb); the corresponding unit in the SI system is the kilogram (kg).

1 lb = 16 ounces (oz) = 7,000 grains (gr) = 0.4536 kg.
1 kg = 2.205 lb.

Force is defined as mass times acceleration. Since the unit of acceleration in the U.S. system is ft/second$^2$ (ft/s$^2$), the unit of force is (lb·ft/s$^2$). This unit is called pound-force, but usually referred to as the pound. In the SI system, the unit of force is (kg·m)/s$^2$. This complex unit is called the Newton (N), after the famous physicist Isaac Newton (1642-1727).

Since the weight of an object is the force exerted on it by the gravitational pull of the earth, the weight of an object is equal to mass x acceleration due to gravity. The acceleration due to gravity on earth's surface is 9.8 m/s$^2$. Therefore, the weight of an object whose mass is 1 kg is 9.8 (kg·m)/s$^2$, or 9.8 N.

We see that in the SI system, there is a clear distinction between the units of mass and the weight of an object. The distinction between the mass and the weight in the U.S. system is rather obscure since the pound is used as the unit for both the mass and the weight of an object.

1 kilogram-force = 9.8 N; 1 lb = 4.448 N;  1 N = 0.2248 lb
1 kilopound (kip) = 1,000 lb = 4.448 kN;  1kN = 0.2248 kip.

### I.2.3 Pressure and Stress

Since pressure or stress is defined as force per unit area, the unit for pressure or stress in the U.S. system is lb/ft$^2$ (psf). Other units commonly used are pounds per square inch (psi) and kilopounds per square inch (ksi). In the SI system, the unit of pressure or stress is N/m$^2$. This unit is called the Pascal (Pa), after the physicist Blaise Pascal (1623-62). Thus, 1 N/m$^2$ = 1 Pa.

   1 psf = 47.880 Pa;   1Pa = 0.208 85 psf.
   1 psi = 6.895 kPa;   1 kPa = 0.1450 psi.

In weather-related topics, the unit of pressure is the atmosphere (atm);  1 atm is the standard atmospheric pressure at sea level.

   1 atm = 760 mm of mercury (Hg) = 29.92 in. of Hg = 14.69 psi = 2,115.4 psf = 101.3 kPa. For all practical purposes, the atmospheric pressure may be taken as 2,100 psf or 101 kPa.

### I.2.4  Unit Weight of Materials

Density is defined as the mass per unit volume. Its units are lb/ft$^3$ in the U.S. system, and kg/m$^3$ in the SI system.

   1 lb/ft$^3$ = 16.018 kg/m$^3$;  1 kg/m$^3$ = 0.064 243 lb/ft$^3$.

In building construction, however, we are more interested in weight density of materials instead of the mass density. Weight density (or simply the unit weight) is defined as the weight per unit volume, and its units are lb/ft$^3$ and N/m$^3$ in the U.S system and SI system respectively.

   1 lb/ft$^3$ = 157.1 N/m$^3$.

The density of sheet materials such as plywood, gypsum board, floor tiles etc. is given in terms of their weight per unit area.  This (surface density) is also referred to as the unit weight.  Its units are lb/ft$^2$ (psf) in the U.S. system and N/m$^2$ or Pa in the SI system.  Whenever the unit weight is given in psf or Pa, the thickness of the sheet must be stated.

### I.2.5  Temperature and Energy

In the U.S. system, temperature is measured in degrees Fahrenheit (°F).  This scale was introduced during the early eighteenth century.  Zero on the Fahrenheit scale was established based on the lowest obtainable temperature at the time, and 100 °F, on the basis of human body temperature as it was then considered to be.

   On the Celsius scale (°C), earlier known as the Centigrade scale, the zero refers to the freezing point of water, and 100 °C to the boiling point of water.

   The unit of temperature in the SI system is the Kelvin (K). The preference for Kelvin over Celsius is due to the fact that on the Kelvin scale, the temperature is always positive. This is not so on the Celsius or the Fahrenheit scale on which the temperature may be positive or negative.  In other words, zero Kelvin (as we know it now) is the lowest obtainable temperature. 0 K is therefore called the *absolute zero temperature*.  The relationship between Kelvin and Celsius temperatures is:

T °C = (T + 273.15) K.  In other words, 20 °C = 293.15 K.  Other relationships are:

T °F = [(1.8) T + 32] °C;  T °C = [(0.555...)(T - 32)] °F.

The intervals in both the Kelvin and the Celsius scales are equal. Therefore, the Celsius and Kelvin scales start at different points but their subdivisions are equal.   Note that the prefix "degree" is not used on the Kelvin scale. Although Kelvin is the appropriate scale to use in the SI system, °C is also used because of the smaller numbers associated with the Celsius scale.

For energy units, refer to Section 4.2.

A comprehensive list of conversion factors to convert from the U.S. system to the SI system is given in Table I.3.

## I.3 BUILDING PRODUCTS' SIZE CONVERSION

The conversion of a physical quantity such as the length, weight or stress from the U.S. system to the SI system simply involves using the appropriate conversion factor.  However, when it comes to converting building products' sizes from the U.S. system to the SI system, three types of conversion are possible.

- Exact Conversion: This conversion is made simply by multiplying a value given in the U.S. system by the appropriate conversion factor to obtain the corresponding value in the SI system. For example, 12 in. is exactly equal to 304.8 mm.
- Soft Conversion: In this conversion, a product will not be converted in its size but only in its description. For example, a manufacturer may decide to continue making 12 in. x 12 in. floor tiles but market them as 305 mm x 305 mm tile. During the initial period of change-over to the SI system, most product sizes will be soft converted.
- Hard Conversion: In hard conversion, the physical size of the product will be changed to a new metric equivalent. For example, 12 in. x 12 in. floor tiles will most probably be changed to 300 mm x 300 mm. Hard conversion of a product requires a change in the manufacturing equipment, and a great deal of coordination among various related products, but has the advantage that the product sizes are rationalized.

## I.4 ACTUAL AND NOMINAL DIMENSIONS

In the U.S. system of units, some building products, such as the solid lumber and masonry units, are described by their "nominal dimensions". The nominal dimensions of a product differ from its actual dimensions. For example, a solid lumber piece whose actual cross-sectional dimensions are $1\frac{1}{2}$ in. x $3\frac{1}{2}$ in. is referred to by its nominal dimensions: 2 x 4. Similarly, the actual dimensions of a 4 x 10 lumber piece are $3\frac{1}{2}$ in. x $9\frac{1}{4}$ in.

The difference between the nominal dimensions and the actual dimensions of a solid lumber piece is the amount of lumber lost in sawing, planing and drying shrinkage.  Thus, the nominal dimensions of a lumber piece give us an idea of the size of lumber as it existed in the tree before its sawing, planing and shrinkage. Note that the inch marks are omitted in referring to the nominal

**Table I.3  Unit Conversion Factors**

| Quantity | To convert from | To | Multiply by |
|---|---|---|---|
| Length | mile | km | 1.609 344* |
| | yard | m | 0.9144* |
| | foot | m | 0.304 8* |
| | foot | mm | 304.8* |
| | inch | mm | 25.4* |
| Area | square mile | $km^2$ | 2.590 00* |
| | acre | $m^2$ | 4 046.87 |
| | acre | ha** | 0.404 687 |
| | sq ft | $m^2$ | 0.092 903 04* |
| | sq in. | $mm^2$ | 645.16* |
| Volume | cu yard | $m^3$ | 0.764 555 |
| | cu ft | $m^3$ | 0.028 3168 |
| | 100 board feet | m3 | 0.235 974 |
| | gal | L | 3.785 41 |
| | cu in. | $cm^3$ | 16.387 064 |
| | cu in. | $mm^3$ | 16 387.064 |
| Velocity | ft/s | m/s | 0.3048 |
| Rate of fluid flow, infiltration | $ft^3/s$ | $m^3/s$ | 0.028 3168 |
| | gal/h | mL/s | 1.051 50 |
| Acceleration | $ft/s^2$ | $m/s^2$ | 0.3048 |
| Mass | lb | kg | 0.453 59 |
| Mass per unit area | psf | $kg/m^2$ | 4.882 43 |
| Mass density | pcf | $kg/m^3$ | 16.018 5 |
| Force | lb | N | 4.448 22 |
| Force per unit length | plf | N/m | 14.593 9 |
| Pressure, stress | psf | Pa | 47.880 26 |
| | psi | kPa | 6.894 76 |
| | in. of mercury (in.Hg) | kPa | 3.386 38 |
| | in. of Hg (in.Hg) | psf | 70.72 |
| | atmosphere*** | kPa | 101.325 |
| Temperature | °F | °C | 5/[9(°F - 32)] |
| | °F | K | (°F + 459.7)/1.8 |
| Quantity of heat | Btu | J | 1055.056 |
| Power | ton (refrigeration) | kW | 3.517 |
| | Btu/h | W | 0.293 07 |
| | hp | W | 745.7 |
| | $Btu/(h·ft^2)$ | $W/m^2$ | 3.154 59 |
| Thermal conductivity | $Btu·in./(ft^2·h·°F)$ | $W/(m·°C)$ | 0.144 2 |
| Thermal conductance, or thermal transmittance, U | $Btu/(ft^2·h·°F)$ | $W/(m^2·°C)$ | 5.678 263 |
| Thermal resistance | $(ft^2·hr·°F)/Btu$ | $(m^2·°C)/W$ | 0.176 110 |
| Thermal capacity | $Btu/(ft^2·°F)$ | $kJ/(m^2·°C)$ | 20.44 |
| Specific heat | $Btu/(lb·°F)$ | $J/(kg·°C)$ | 4.186 8 |
| Vapor permeability | perm·in. | ng/(Pa·m·s) | 1.459 29 |
| Vapor permeance | perm | $ng/(Pa·m^2·s)$ | 57.213 5 |
| Angle | degree | radian | 0.017 453 |

\*    Denotes exact conversion.

\*\*    1 hectare (ha) = 100 m x 100 m.

\*\*\*  1 atmosphere = 29.92 in. of mercury.

**Table I.4 Actual and Nominal Dimensions of Solid Lumber**

| Dimensions | |
|---|---|
| Nominal | Actual (in.) |
| 2 | 1.5 |
| 4 | 3.5 |
| 6 | 5.5 |
| 8 | 7.25 |
| 10 | 9.25 |
| 12 | 11.25 |
| 14 | 13.25 |

dimensions of solid lumber. In other words, a 2 x 4 piece is not called 2" x 4". The relationship between nominal and actual dimensions of solid lumber is given in Table I.4.

In the case of masonry units, such as bricks and concrete blocks, the nominal dimension refers to the unit dimension plus one mortar joint thickness. The mortar joint thickness in masonry walls is usually $3/8$ in. Therefore, the actual unit dimension = nominal dimension - $3/8$ in. Thus, if the nominal dimensions of a concrete block are 8 in. x 16 in. x 8 in., its actual dimensions are $7^5/8$ in. x $15^5/8$ in. x $7^5/8$ in.

## I.5 THE GAGE NUMBER

The thickness of thin sheets is sometimes given in mil in the U.S. system of units. 1 mil = $1/1000$ in. Thus, a 6 mil thick sheet is $6/1000$ in. Another method of designating the thickness of sheets is the gauge (or gage) number. The gage number system is commonly used in specifying the thickness of metal sheets and wires.

In the gage number system, the thickness of the sheet or wire decreases as the gage number increases. Thus, a No. 10 gage sheet is thicker than a No. 12 gage sheet. However, the system itself is totally arbitrary. Therefore, a table which gives the relationship between the gage number and the actual thickness in inches or millimeters is always required.

Various different gage numbering systems are currently in use in the United States. For instance, the United States Steel Wire Gage (also called the Washburn and Moen Wire Gage) is commonly used to specify the thickness of steel wires by U.S. producers. The thickness of sheet steel is specified by the Manufacturers' Standard Gage for Sheet Steel. Table I.5 lists the gage number and its equivalents in inches and millimeters for galvanized sheet steel.

Another system, called the Brown and Sharpe Wire Gage (also called the U.S. Standard Wire Gage) is used in specifying the wall thickness of thin brass and copper tubes. In view of the multiplicity of gage numbers, it is preferable to use the actual thickness or diameter instead of (or along with) the gage number.

**Table I.5 Galvanized Sheet Steel Gage Number and Its Thickness**

| Gage number | in. | mm |
|---|---|---|
| 8 | 0.1681 | 4.27 |
| 10 | 0.1382 | 3.51 |
| 12 | 0.1084 | 2.75 |
| 14 | 0.0785 | 1.99 |
| 16 | 0.0635 | 1.61 |
| 18 | 0.0516 | 1.31 |
| 20 | 0.0396 | 1.00 |
| 22 | 0.0336 | 0.85 |
| 24 | 0.0276 | 0.70 |
| 26 | 0.0217 | 0.55 |
| 28 | 0.0187 | 0.47 |

# APPENDIX II
## Graphic Symbols for Plans and Sections

| EARTHWORK, CONCRETE, MORTAR AND GYPSUM | | Compacted earth | Cast-in-place or precast concrete | |
| --- | --- | --- | --- | --- |
| | | Gravel fill | Lightweight concrete | |
| | | Rock | Sand fill/ mortar/ plaster/ gypsum board | |
| MASONRY AND METALS | | Concrete block masonry | Steel or iron | |
| | | Brick masonry | Aluminum | |
| | | Adobe or rammed earth | Brass/ bronze | |
| INSULATION AND WOOD | | Rigid insulation | Rough unsurfaced wood | |
| | | Batt, blanket or loosefill insulation | Intermittent blocking | |
| | | Spray-on insulation | Finished wood | |
| FINISHES | | Acoustical tile | Glass | |
| | | Ceramic tile | Plywood | |
| | | Carpet and pad | Terrazzo flooring | |

# APPENDIX III
## Model Code Adoptions by State

| State | Building code | Amendments Yes | No |
|-------|---------------|----------------|----|
| Alabama | Standard[1] | x | |
| Alaska | Uniform[2] | x | |
| Arizona | None | | |
| Arkansas | Standard | x | |
| California | Uniform | x | |
| Colorado | Uniform | | x |
| Connecticut | National | x | |
| Delaware | None | | |
| Florida | Standard | x | |
| Georgia | Standard | | x |
| Hawaii | None | | |
| Idaho | Uniform[3] | | x |
| Illinois | None | | |
| Indiana | Uniform[4] | x | |
| Iowa | Uniform[5] | x | |
| Kansas | Uniform[6] | | x |
| Kentucky | National[7] | x | |
| Louisiana | Standard[8] | | x |
| Maine | None | | |
| Maryland | National[5] | | x |
| Massachusetts | National | x | |
| Michigan | National | x | |
| Minnesota | Uniform | x | |
| Mississippi | Standard[5] | | x |
| Missouri | National[5] | | x |
| Montana | Uniform[9] | x | |

| State | Building code | Amendments Yes | No |
|-------|---------------|----------------|----|
| Nebraska | Uniform[10] | | x |
| Nevada | Uniform | x | |
| New Hampshire | National[11] | | x |
| New Jersey | National | | x |
| New Mexico | Uniform | x | |
| New York | State-written | | |
| North Carolina | Standard | x | |
| North Dakota | Uniform[6] | | x |
| Ohio | National[2] | x | |
| Oklahoma | National[5] | | x |
| Oregon | Uniform | x | |
| Pennsylvania | None | | |
| Rhode Island | National | x | |
| South Carolina | Standard[5] | | x |
| South Dakota | Uniform[12] | x | |
| Tennessee | Standard[13] | | x |
| Texas | None | | |
| Utah | Uniform | x | |
| Vermont | National[14] | x | |
| Virginia | National | x | |
| Washington | Uniform | x | |
| West Virginia | National | | x |
| Wisconsin | State-written[15] | | |
| Wyoming | Uniform[8] | | x |
| District of Columbia | National | x | |

1 Does not apply to all buildings.
2 All buildings except one, two or three family dwellings.
3 State owned.
4 All buildings except one and two family and agricultural.
5 State buildings.
6 State buildings and schools.
7 All except agricultural.
8 All except one and two family dwelling.
9 All except four or less residential, agricultural, garages or mine buildings.

10 High-rise buildings.
11 All except single family.
12 Schools, day care, multiple family over 6 units, hotels, motels and state buildings.
13 All except one and two family dwellings, and health care facilities.
14 Public buildings, condos, multiple family and hazardous uses.
15 Public buildings and place of employment.

# APPENDIX IV
## Unit Weights of Materials

**Table IV. 1  Volume Density of Materials**

| Material | Weight lb/ft$^3$ | Material | Weight lb/ft$^3$ |
|---|---|---|---|
| Bituminous Products | | Wood | |
| Asphalt | 81 | Ash | 41 |
| Tar | 75 | Oak | 47 |
| Metals | | Douglas fir | 34 |
| Brass | 526 | Hem fir | 28 |
| Bronze | 552 | Southern pine | 37 |
| Cast iron | 450 | Wood Products | |
| Copper | 556 | Plywood | 36 |
| Lead | 710 | Particle board | 45 |
| Steel | 490 | Gypsum Products | |
| Zinc | 450 | Gypsum wallboard | 50 |
| Cement and Concrete | | Lath and plaster | 55 |
| Concrete (normal weight) | 145 | Insulating Materials | |
| Reinforced concrete (normal weight) | 150 | Fiberglass | 1.0 - 2.5 |
| Structural lightweight concrete | 70 - 105 | Rockwool | 1.0 - 2.5 |
| Perlite/vermiculite concrete | 25 - 50 | Extruded or expanded polystyrene | 2.0 |
| Portland cement | 94 | Polyisocyanurate | 2.0 |
| Lime | 45 | Glass (flat glass) | 160 |
| Masonry | | Earth | |
| Clay brick | 110 - 130 | Clay, silt or sand (dry packed) | 100 |
| Concrete block (light weight) | 105 - 125 | Gravel | 110 |
| Concrete block (normal weight) | 135 | Crushed stone | 100 - 120 |
| Masonry mortar or grout | 130 | Water | 63 |
| Stone | | Ice | 57 |
| Granite | 165 | Air | 0.075 |
| Limestone | 165 | | |
| Marble | 170 | | |

## Table IV.2  Surface Density of Materials

| Component | Weight lb/ft$^2$ | Component | Weight lb/ft$^2$ |
|---|---|---|---|
| **Roof and Wall Coverings** | | **Roof Decks** | |
| Asphalt shingles | 2 | Metal deck, 20 gage | 2.5 |
| Clay tiles | 12 - 18 | 2 in. wood deck | 5 |
| Cement tile | 10 - 16 | 3 in. wood deck | 8 |
| Wood shingles | 3 | Wood sheathing ($^1/_2$ in. thick) | 1.5 |
| 5-ply gravel covered built-up roof | 6 | Fiberboard ($^1/_2$ in. thick) | 1 |
| **Insulation (per 1 in. thickness)** | | **Ceilings** | |
| Cellular glass | 0.7 | Gypsum board (per $^1/_8$ in. thickness) | 0.55 |
| Fiberglass | 0.1 - 0.2 | Plaster on wood lath | 8 |
| Extruded/expanded polystyrene | 0.2 | Suspended steel channel system | 2 |
| Polyurethane/polyisocyanurate | 0.2 | Acoustic fiber tile | 1 |
| Perlite/vermiculite | 2.0 | Mechanical duct allowance | 4 |
| **Floors and Floor Finishes** | | **Clay Masonry Walls** | |
| Hardwood flooring, $^7/_8$ in. thick | 4 | 4 in. thick | 39 |
| Plywood (per $^1/_8$ in. thickness) | 0.4 | 8 in. thick | 79 |
| Hardboard (per $^1/_8$ in. thickness) | 0.4 | **Hollow Concrete Block Walls** | |
| Sturdifloor (per $^1/_8$ in. thickness) | 0.4 | 4 in thick, 70% solid, lightweight units | 22 |
| Linoleum, vinyl or asphalt tile ($^1/_4$ in. thick) | 1 | 4 in. thick, 70% solid, normal weight | 29 |
| Marble or slate (per 1 in. thick) | 15 | 6 in. thick, 55% solid, lightweight units | 27 |
| Terrazzo ($1^1/_2$ in. thick) | 19 | 6 in. thick, 55% solid, normal weight units | 35 |
| **Frame Partitions and Walls** | | 8 in. thick, 52% solid, lightweight units | 35 |
| Wood/steel studs + $^1/_2$ in. gyp bd both sides | 8 | 8 in. thick, 52% solid, normal weight units | 45 |
| Wood/steel studs + $^5/_8$ in. gypsum board both sides + insulation + siding | 11 | **Floor Fill** | |
| | | Sand (per inch) | 8 |
| Wood/steel studs + $^5/_8$ in. gypsum board both sides + insulation + brick veneer | 48 | Cinder concrete (per inch) | 9 |

# APPENDIX V
# Heating Degree Day and Thermal Properties

**HEATING DEGREE DAY CONCEPT**

Crucial to the understanding of the heating degree day (HDD) concept is the *balance point temperature* of a building. The balance point temperature is defined as the external air temperature at which the heat gain of the building from the sun and internal sources (such as lighting, cooking, humans, etc.) equals the heat loss through the building envelope. Thus, if the external air temperature equals the balance point temperature, no mechanical heating of the building is required.

We see from its definition that the balance point temperature is a function of several factors. If the building is well insulated, and leaks very little air through its envelope, its balance point temperature will be lower than that of a building which is not so well insulated.

Balance point temperature of a building usually varies with time. If the sun is up, or if the heat gain from internal sources is high, the balance point temperature of the building is lower. Late at night, the balance point temperature is usually minimum because there is no solar heat gain and there is usually very little heat gain from internal sources and activities such as lights, cooking, etc. Finally, the balance point temperature is also a function of the required internal air temperature. If the thermostat is set at a lower temperature, the balance point temperature will also be lower.

The balance point temperature for an average building during winters in the United States is usually taken as 65 °F. This implies that when the external air temperature falls below 65 °F, an average building in the United States will require to be heated. The amount of heating required is obviously a function of two factors: (i) the difference between the external air temperature and 65 °F, i.e. (65 °F - $T_o$), where $T_o$ is the external air temperature, and (ii) the length of time during which the temperature remains below 65 °F. The greater the temperature difference, or the longer the duration of this temperature difference, the greater the amount of heating required.

If we now define the outdoor air temperature, $T_o$, as the average daily temperature, then it may be said that on the day when the average daily temperature is lower than 65 °F, heating of the building will be required. We define the sum of the product of these two factors as the annual heating degree days, HDD. In other words,

$$\text{HDD} = \Sigma(65 \text{ °F} - T_o)(\text{number of days in the year when } T_o < 65 \text{ °F})$$

Thus, if on a particular day, the average outdoor air temperature at a location is 35 °F, then that day will contribute (65 - 35) = 30 heating degree days to the annual HDD of the location. On the following day at that location, if the outdoor air temperature is 30 °F, then an additional 35 heating degree days will be added to the annual HDD of the location.

Thus, the annual HDD is a measure of the severity of winters of a place. The greater the value of HDD, the more severe the winter. In addition to describing the severity of winters of a location, the HDD value has been found to be directly related to the amount of energy consumed by buildings. HDD values for various locations in the U.S. and Canada are given in Table V.1.

**Table V.1 Annual Heating Degree Days for Cities in the United States and Canada**

| Location | HDD | Location | HDD | Location | HDD |
|---|---|---|---|---|---|
| Alabama | | Connecticut | | South Bend | 6,439 |
| Birmingham | 2,551 | Bridgeport | 5,617 | Iowa | |
| Huntsville | 3,070 | Hartford | 6,235 | Burlington | 6,114 |
| Mobile | 1,560 | New Haven | 5,897 | Des Moines | 6,588 |
| Montgomery | 2,291 | Delaware | | Dubuque | 7,376 |
| Alaska | | Wilmington | 4,930 | Sioux City | 6,951 |
| Anchorage | 10,864 | D.C. | | Waterloo | 7,320 |
| Fairbanks | 14,279 | Washington | 4,224 | Kansas | |
| Juneau | 9,075 | Florida | | Concordia | 5,479 |
| Nome | 14,171 | Daytona Beach | 879 | Dodge City | 4,986 |
| Arizona | | Fort Myers | 442 | Topeka | 5,182 |
| Flagstaff | 7,152 | Jacksonville | 1,239 | Wichita | 4,620 |
| Phoenix | 1,765 | Lakeland | 661 | Kentucky | |
| Tuscon | 1,800 | Miami | 214 | Covington | 5,265 |
| Winslow | 4,782 | Orlando | 766 | Lexington | 4,683 |
| Yuma | 974 | Tallahassee | 1,485 | Louisville | 4,660 |
| Arkansas | | Tampa | 683 | Louisiana | |
| Fort Smith | 3,292 | West Palm Beach | 253 | Alexandria | 1,921 |
| Little Rock | 3,219 | Georgia | | Baton Rouge | 1,560 |
| Texarkana | 2,533 | Atlanta | 2,929 | Lake Charles | 1,459 |
| California | | Augusta | 2,397 | New Orleans | 1,254 |
| Bakersfield | 2,122 | Columbus | 2,383 | Shreveport | 2,184 |
| Bishop | 4,275 | Macon | 2,136 | Maine | |
| Blue Canyon | 5,596 | Savannah | 1,819 | Caribou | 9,767 |
| Burbank | 1,646 | Thomasville | 1,529 | Portland | 7,511 |
| Eureka | 4,643 | Hawaii (all cities) | 0 | Maryland | |
| Fresno | 2,611 | Idaho | | Baltimore | 4,111 |
| Long Beach | 1,803 | Boise | 5,809 | Frederick | 5,087 |
| Los Angeles | 2,061 | Lewiston | 5,542 | Massachussetts | |
| Mt. Shasta | 5,722 | Pocatello | 7,033 | Boston | 5,634 |
| Oakland | 2,870 | Illinois | | Nantucket | 5,891 |
| Sacramento | 2,419 | Chicago (O'Hare) | 6,639 | Pittsfield | 7,578 |
| San Diego | 1,458 | Chicago City | 5,882 | Worcester | 6,969 |
| San Francisco | 3,001 | Moline | 6,408 | Michigan | |
| Santa Maria | 2,967 | Peoria | 6,025 | Alpena | 8,506 |
| Colorado | | Springfield | 5,429 | Detroit | 6,232 |
| Alamosa | 8,529 | Indiana | | Escanaba | 8,481 |
| Colorado Springs | 6,423 | Evansville | 4,432 | Flint | 7,377 |
| Denver | 6,283 | Fort Wayne | 6,205 | Lansing | 6,909 |
| Pueblo | 5,462 | Indianapolis | 5,699 | Marquette | 8,393 |

| Location | HDD | Location | HDD | Location | HDD |
|---|---|---|---|---|---|
| Sault Ste. Marie | 9,048 | Ohio | | Seattle | 4,424 |
| Minnesota | | Cincinnati | 4,410 | Spokane | 6,655 |
| Duluth | 10,000 | Cleveland | 6,351 | West Virginia | |
| Minneapolis | 8,382 | Columbus | 5,660 | Charleston | 4,476 |
| Rochester | 8,295 | Dayton | 5,622 | Huntington | 4,446 |
| Mississipi | | Toledo | 6,494 | Parkersburg | 4,754 |
| Jackson | 2,239 | Oklahoma | | Wisconsin | |
| Meridian | 2,289 | Oklahoma City | 3,725 | Green Bay | 8,209 |
| Vicksburg | 2,041 | Tulsa | 3,860 | Madison | 7,863 |
| Missouri | | Oregon | | Milwaukee | 7,635 |
| Kansas City | 4,711 | Eugene | 4,726 | Wyoming | |
| St. Joseph | 5,484 | Meacham | 7,874 | Casper | 7,410 |
| St. Louis | 4,900 | Portland | 4,109 | Cheyenne | 7,381 |
| Springfield | 4,900 | Salem | 4,754 | Sheridan | 7,680 |
| Montana | | Pennsylvania | | | |
| Billings | 7,049 | Harrisburg | 5,251 | Alberta | |
| Glasgow | 8,996 | Philadelphia | 4,486 | Calgary | 9,703 |
| Great Falls | 7,750 | Pittsburgh | 5,053 | Edmonton | 10,268 |
| Havre | 8,182 | Williamsport | 5,934 | Lethbridge | 8,644 |
| Nebraska | | Rhode Island | | British Columbia | |
| Lincoln | 5,864 | Providence | 5,954 | Prince George | 9,755 |
| Norfolk | 6,979 | South Carolina | | Vancouver | 5,515 |
| Omaha | 6,612 | Charleston | 2,033 | Victoria | 5,699 |
| Nevada | | Columbia | 2,484 | Manitoba | |
| Elko | 7,433 | Florence | 2,387 | Churchill | 16,728 |
| Ely | 7,733 | South Dakota | | Winnipeg | 10,679 |
| Las Vegas | 2,709 | Rapid City | 7,345 | New Brunswick | |
| Reno | 6,332 | Sioux Falls | 7,839 | Fredricton | 8,671 |
| New Hampshire | | Tennessee | | Moncton | 8,727 |
| Concord | 7,383 | Chattanooga | 3,254 | St. John | 8,219 |
| New Jersey | | Knoxville | 3,494 | Newfoundland | |
| Atlantic City | 4,812 | Memphis | 3,232 | Argentina | 8,440 |
| Newark | 4,589 | Nashville | 3,578 | Corner Brook | 8,978 |
| Trenton | 4,980 | Oak Ridge | 3,817 | St. John's | 8,991 |
| New Mexico | | Texas | | Northwest Territories | |
| Albuquerque | 4,348 | Amarillo | 3,985 | Fort Norman | 16,109 |
| Clayton | 5,158 | Austin | 1,711 | Resolution Island | 16,021 |
| Raton | 6,228 | Dallas-Fort Worth | 2,363 | Nova Scotia | |
| Silver City | 3,705 | Houston | 1,278 | Halifax | 7,361 |
| New York | | Corpus Christi | 914 | Yarmouth | 7,340 |
| Albany | 6,201 | Lubbock | 3,578 | Ontario | |
| Buffalo | 7,062 | San Antonio | 1,546 | Ottawa | 8,735 |
| New York City | 4,871 | Utah | | Toronto | 6,827 |
| Rochester | 6,748 | Milford | 6,497 | Prince Edward Island | |
| Syracuse | 6,756 | Salt Lake City | 6,052 | Charlottetown | 8,164 |
| North Carolina | | Vermont | | Quebec | |
| Asheville | 4,042 | Burlington | 8,269 | Montreal | 8,203 |
| Charlotte | 3,191 | Virginia | | Quebec | 9,372 |
| Raleigh | 3,805 | Cape Henry | 3,279 | Saskatchewan | |
| Wilmington | 2,347 | Norfolk | 3,421 | Prince Albert | 11,630 |
| North Dakota | | Richmond | 3,865 | Saskatoon | 10,870 |
| Bismarck | 8,851 | Roanoke | 4,150 | Yukon Territory | |
| Fargo | 9,226 | Washington | | Dawson | 15,067 |
| Williston | 9,243 | Olympia | 5,236 | Mayo Landing | 14,454 |

Source: American Society of Heating, Refrigerating and Air-conditioning Engineers, Inc., Atlanta, Georgia: "Energy Efficient Design of New Low Rise Residential Buildings", ASHRAE Standard 90.2, 1993, reprinted with permission.

**Table V.2  Maximum U-values for Floors Over Crawl Space, and Basement Walls**

| Floor over crawl space | | Basement wall | |
|---|---|---|---|
| HDD | Maximum U-value | HDD | Maximum U-value |
| 0 - 1,000 | 0.08 | 0 - 1,499 | None required |
| 1,001 - 2,500 | 0.07 | 1,500 - 4,500 | $0.205 - HDD (233 \times 10^{-7})$ |
| 2,501 - 15,500 | 0.05 | 4501 - 8500 | $0.11125 - HDD (25 \times 10^{-7})$ |
| > 16,500 | 0.04 | 8,501 - 9,000 | $0.6 - HDD (600 \times 10^{-7})$ |
| | | > 9,000 | 0.06 |

Reproduced from the 1993 edition of the *CABO Model Energy Code*™, copyright © 1993, with the permission of the publisher, the International Code Council.

**Table V.3  Minimum R-values of Perimeter Insulation Under Concrete Slabs-on-Grade**

| | Heating degree days | R-value |
|---|---|---|
| Heated slab | 0 - 499 | None required |
| | 500 - 4,500 | R 6 |
| | 4,500 - 19,000 | $2.5862 + HDD (75.9 \times 10^{-5})$ |
| | > 19,000 | R 17 |
| Unheated slab | 0 - 2,499 | None required |
| | 2,500 - 4,500 | R 4 |
| | 4,501 - 19,500 | $1.0 + HDD (60 \times 10^{-5})$ |
| | > 19,500 | R 14 |

Reproduced from the 1993 edition of the *CABO Model Energy Code*™, copyright © 1993, with the permission of the publisher, the International Code Council.

**Table V.4  Specific Heat of Materials**

| Material | Specific heat $Btu/(lb \cdot °F)$ | Material | Specific heat $Btu/(lb \cdot °F)$ |
|---|---|---|---|
| Metals | | Organic materials | |
|   Steel | 0.12 |   Wood (average value) | 0.50 |
|   Aluminum | 0.21 |   Wood charcoal | 0.20 |
| Ceramic materials | | Insulating materials | |
|   Clay bricks | 0.19 |   Vermiculite or perlite (loose fill) | 0.21 |
|   Concrete (normal weight) | 0.16 |   Lightweight insulating concrete | 0.18 |
|   Limestone | 0.20 |   Fiberglass (blanket or batt) | 0.17 |
|   Marble | 0.21 |   Expanded polystyrene | 0.18 |
|   Sandstone | 0.20 |   Extruded polystyrene | 0.18 |
|   Glass | 0.18 |   Polyisocyanurate | 0.18 |
|   Portland cement plaster | 0.20 | Air | 0.25 |
|   Gypsum wallboard | 0.26 | Water | 1.0 |

# APPENDIX VI
## Temperature Gradient and Dew Point

**TEMPERATURE GRADIENT ACROSS AN ASSEMBLY**

If the envelope contains several layers of different materials, it can be shown that the temperature drop across any layer is a function of the resistance of that layer, the total resistance of the envelope, and the temperature difference between the inside and the outside air, as given by the following equation:

$$\text{Temperature drop across layer} = \frac{\text{Resistance of layer}}{\text{Total resistance of assembly}} \left[ \begin{array}{c} \text{Temperature difference between inside and outside air} \end{array} \right]$$

The above equation can be used to determine the temperatures at various points in an assembly, from which the temperature gradient can be drawn. The following example illustrates the procedure.

**Example VI.1**

By determining the temperatures at various points within the wall assemblies of Figures VI.1(a) and VI.1(b), compare their temperature gradients. The two wall assemblies are otherwise similar except that the wall of Figure VI.1(a) is uninsulated and that of Figure VI.1(b) is insulated with 3.5 in. thick (th.) fiberglass insulation. Assume that the inside and outside air temperatures for both wall assemblies are 70 °F and - 10 °F respectively.

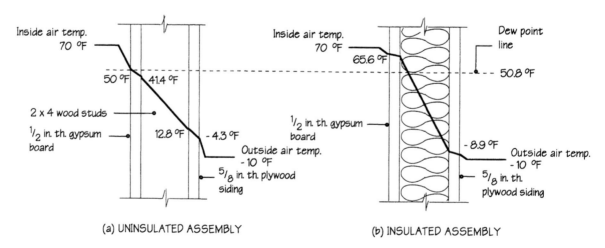

(a) UNINSULATED ASSEMBLY        (b) INSULATED ASSEMBLY

**FIGURE VI.1**   Temperature gradients in (a) uninsulated wall and (b) insulated wall of Example VI.1

*Solution*: Uninsulated Wall Assembly of Figure VI.1(a).

R-values of various layers of the wall are shown in column 2 of the following table[1]. The total R-value of this assembly = 0.7 + 0.3 +1.0 + 0.6 + 0.2 = 2.8.

| Layer | R-value of layer | Temp. drop across layer, °F | Temperature on either side of layer, °F |
|---|---|---|---|
| | | | ... 70.0 |
| Inside surface resistance | 0.7 (Table 4.5) | 20.0 | |
| | | | ... 50.0 |
| Gypsum board (¹/₂ in. th.) | 0.3 (Table 4.4) | 8.6 | |
| | | | ... 41.4 |
| Cavity space | 1.0 (Table 4.7) | 28.6 | |
| | | | ... 12.8 |
| Plywood siding (⁵/₈ in. th.) | 0.6 (Table 4.4) | 17.1 | |
| | | | ... - 4.3 |
| Outside surface resistance | 0.2 (Table 4.5) | 5.7 | |
| | | | ... - 10.0 |
| Total R-value | 2.8 | | |

The temperature difference between the inside and the outside air = 70 - (- 10) = 80 °F. The temperature drop across each layer, calculated by using the above equation, is shown in column 3. The temperatures of both sides of each layer are shown in column 4 of the above table.

Insulated Wall Assembly of Figure VI.1(b).

Calculations for this wall are similar to those of the wall of Figure VI.1(a). The total R-value of this assembly = 0.7 + 0.3 + 11.0 + 0.6 + 0.2 = 12.8. The temperature drops across each layer are shown in the following table:

| Layer | R-value of layer | Temp. drop across layer, °F | Temperature on either side of layer, °F |
|---|---|---|---|
| | | | ... 70.0 |
| Inside surface resistance | 0.7 (Table 4.5) | 4.4 | |
| | | | ... 65.6 |
| Gypsum board (¹/₂ in. th.) | 0.3 (Table 4.4) | 1.9 | |
| | | | ... 63.7 |
| Insulation (3¹/₂ in. th.) | 11.0 (Table 4.7) | 68.8 | |
| | | | ... - 5.1 |
| Plywood siding (⁵/₈ in. th.) | 0.6 (Table 4.4) | 3.8 | |
| | | | ... - 8.9 |
| Outside surface resistance | 0.2 (Table 4.5) | 1.2 | |
| | | | ... - 10.0 |
| Total R-value | 12.8 | | |

1 Note that in Figure VI.1, vapor retarders or air retarder have not been shown, since their R-values are negligible. Hence they do not affect the temperature gradient.

The temperature gradients for both wall assemblies can now be drawn from the values given in column 4 of the above tables. These are shown by heavy lines in Figures VI.1(a) and (b).

By comparing the two temperature gradients, we observe that the insulation makes the warm side of the wall warmer, reducing the possibility of surface condensation on the inside of the building. Insulation also makes the cold side of the assembly colder, which increases the potential of condensation within the insulation.

## DEW POINT DETERMINATION

The following example illustrates the calculation of the dew point of air.

### Example VI.2

Determine the dew point of inside air of Example VI.1 (temperature = 70 °F and relative humidity = 50%).

*Solution*: The problem can be solved by using either Equation (5.1) or (5.2), see Chapter 5. Here, Equation (5.1) has been used.

From Table 5.2, the water vapor content corresponding to 70 °F and 50% RH = 55.2 gr. Since the air is saturated at dew point, the problem reduces to determining the temperature of air at which it will be saturated with a water vapor content of 55.2 gr. From Table 5.2, it may be seen that the dew point of this air mass lies between 50 °F and 60 °F. The actual value is obtained by linearly interpolating between 50 °F and 60 °F values as shown below.

|  | Temperature | Saturation vapor content |
|---|---|---|
|  | 60 °F | 77.3 gr |
|  | 50 °F | 53.4 gr |
| Difference | 10 °F | 23.9 gr |

Thus, the saturation vapor pressure changes at the rate of 2.39 gr for every 1 °F change in temperature between 50 °F and 60 °F. The temperature at which the saturation vapor content of air is 55.2 gr, is:

$$50 + \frac{55.2 - 53.4}{2.39} = 50.8$$

Thus, the dew point of this mass of air is 50.8 °F.

The dew point is shown by the dashed line in Figures VI.1(a) and (b). Notice that in the case of the uninsulated assembly, the condensation occurs at the inside wall finish, and in the case of the insulated assembly, the condensation occurs within the insulation.

# INDEX